T0212974

Communications
in Computer and Information Science

630

Commenced Publication in 2007
Founding and Former Series Editors:
Alfredo Cuzzocrea, Dominik Ślęzak, and Xiaokang Yang

Editorial Board

More information about this series at http://www.springer.com/series/7899

Hamid Jahankhani · Alex Carlile
David Emm · Amin Hosseinian-Far
Guy Brown · Graham Sexton
Arshad Jamal (Eds.)

Global Security, Safety and Sustainability

The Security Challenges of the Connected World

11th International Conference, ICGS3 2017
London, UK, January 18–20, 2017
Proceedings

 Springer

Editors
Hamid Jahankhani
GSM London Meridian House
London
UK

Guy Brown
Northumbria University
London
UK

Alex Carlile
SC Strategy Limited
London
UK

Graham Sexton
Northumbria University
Newcastle upon Tyne
UK

David Emm
Kaspersky Lab
London
UK

Arshad Jamal
QAHE with Northumbria University
London
UK

Amin Hosseinian-Far
Leeds Beckett University
Leeds
UK

ISSN 1865-0929   ISSN 1865-0937   (electronic)
Communications in Computer and Information Science
ISBN 978-3-319-51063-7   ISBN 978-3-319-51064-4   (eBook)
DOI 10.1007/978-3-319-51064-4

Library of Congress Control Number: 2016960564

Printed on acid-free paper

This Springer imprint is published by Springer Nature
The registered company is Springer International Publishing AG
The registered company address is: Gewerbestrasse 11, 6330 Cham, Switzerland

Preface

The Security Challenges of the Connected World

Welcome to the proceedings of the 11th International Conference on Global Security, Safety, and Sustainability. Northumbria University London Campus was delighted to host this year's conference with the highly topical theme of "The Security Challenges of the Connected World."

Northumbria University has a long established background in providing world-class research, teaching, and consultancy in the field of computer and information sciences. Key research groups from our Computer and Information Sciences Department include: Computer and Electronic Security Systems (CESS); Computer Vision and Artificial Intelligence Group (CVAI); Computer Games and Visual Effect; Digital Consumers, Behaviors, and Literacy; Digital Libraries, Archives, and Records; and Digital Socio-technical Design.

The papers presented at this year's conference reflect the security challenges we read and hear about on a daily basis in news, whether this be smart cities, smart health, smart metering, and smart homes and the subsequent implications on privacy and potential for cyber attacks.

The launch of the new National Cyber Security Centre set to bring UK expertise together is an exciting prospect for the industry. With a growing threat of cyber attacks from nation states, serious crime gangs, hacking groups, as well as terrorists, the conference provides a forum for discussion of how the National Cyber Security Centre can best foster collaboration from academic and practitioner experts.

We will also consider the political and economic priorities placed on cyber security. As an example, the Horizon 2020 work program – Secure Societies: Protecting Freedom and Security of Europe and Its Citizens – is about protecting our citizens, society, and economy as well as our assets, infrastructures, and services, our prosperity, political stability, and well-being. Any malfunction or disruption, intentional or accidental, can have detrimental impact with high associated economic or societal costs. This indicates security is an issue that can only be tackled effectively if all stakeholders cooperate. As key stakeholders, the question we ask is, "What are the implications and how can we be fully engaged?"

This preface can only offer a hint of the insights that emerged from the conference. With themes including systems security, safety and sustainability, cyber infrastructure protection, the future of digital forensics, information systems security management, cyber law and cyber arbitration, cyber intelligence and operation, remote system intelligence and counter-measures, we hope you find the papers in these proceedings intellectually engaging, relevant, stimulating, and enjoyable.

November 2016

Guy Brown
Graham Sexton

Organization

General Chair

Hamid Jahankhani   GSM London, UK

Steering Committee

Babak Akhgar   Sheffield Hallam University, UK
Bobby L. Tait   University of South Africa, South Africa
Amie Taal   Deutsche Bank, NY, USA
Ali Hessami   Vega Systems, UK
Christos Kalloniatis   University of the Aegean, Greece
Stefanos Gritzalis   University of the Aegean, Greece
Sérgio Tenreiro   Catholic University of Portugal, Braga, Portugal
    de Magalhães
Mathews Z. Nkhoma   RMIT International University Vietnam, Ho Chi Minh
     City, Vietnam
Mamoun Alazab   Macquarie University, Sydney, Australia
Amin Hosseinian-Far   Leeds Beckett University, UK
Paul Dwight-Moore   Westwood Associates, UK
Gianluigi Me   LUISS University, Italy
Vitor Sa   University of Minho, Braga, Portugal
Yasmine Arafa   Greenwich University, UK
Antonio Mauro   Octo Telematics S.p.A., Italy
William Kapuku-Bwabwa   Metropolitan Police, Special Operations, Counter
     Terrorism Command, UK
Petra Saskia Bayerl   Rotterdam School of Management (RSM), Erasmus
     University Rotterdam, The Netherlands
Ameer Al-Nemrat   University of East London, UK
Omar S. Arabiat   Balqa Applied University, Jordan
Chafika Benzaid   CERIST, University of Sciences and Technology
     Houari Boumediene, Algeria

Program Chairs

Systems Security, Safety and Sustainability, Cyber Infrastructure Protection

Ali Hessami   Vega Systems, UK
Shahin Gheitanchi   Intel Corporation, UK

The Future of Digital Forensics

Amie Taal   Deutsche Bank, NY, USA
Carlisle George   Middlesex University, UK

Information Systems Security Management

Gianluigi Me   University of Rome LUISS Guido Carli, Italy
Antonio Mauro   Octo Telematics S.p.A., Italy

Cyber Intelligence and Operation

Babak Akhgar   University of Sheffield Hallam, UK
Petra Saskia Bayerl   Rotterdam School of Management (RSM), Erasmus
                          University Rotterdam, The Netherlands

Cyber Law and Cyber Arbitration

Mohammad   Durham Law School, UK
   Hedayati-Kakhki

Secure Software Engineering

Christos Kalloniatis   University of the Aegean, Greece
Stefanos Gritzalis   University of the Aegean, Greece

Remote System Intelligence and Counter-Measures

Bobby Tait   University of South Africa, South Africa
Paul Dwight-Moore   Westwood Associates, UK

Cyber Security Education, Training and Awareness Development

Yasmine Arafa   Greenwich University, UK

Program Committee

Talal Al-Kharobi   Kings Fahad University of Petroleum and Minerals,
                          Saudi Arabia
Samir Al-Khayatt   Sheffield Hallam University, UK
Muhammad Ali Babar   IT University of Copenhagen, Denmark
Ali Chehab   American University of Beirut, Lebanon
Xiaochun Cheng   Middlesex University, UK
Mohammad Dastbaz   Leeds Beckett University, UK
Ken Dick   Nebraska University Center for Information Assurance,
                          USA

Contents

Information Systems Security Management

Systems Security, Safety and Sustainability Cyber Infrastructure Protection

The Future of Digital Forensics

Deconstruct *and* Preserve (DaP): A Method for the Preservation of Digital Evidence on Solid State Drives (SSD)

I. Mitchell[(✉)], T. Anandaraja, S. Hara, G. Hadzhinenov, and D. Neilson

Middlesex University, London, UK
i.mitchell@mdx.ac.uk

Abstract. Imaging SSDs is problematic due to TRIM commands and garbage collectors that make the SSD behave inconsistently over time. It is this inconsistency that can cause a difference between images taken of the SSD. These differences result in unmatched hash number generation and would normally be attributed to contamination or spoliation of digital evidence. DaP is a proposed method that ensures all images taken of the SSD are consistent and removes the volatility normally associated with these devices. DaP is not focused with the recoverability of deleted data, however DaP does stabilise the device to prevent unintentional contamination due to garbage collection. Experiments show that the DaP method works on a range of devices and consistently produces the hash-identical images. The conclusions are to consider DaP as a new Standard Operating Procedure (SOP) when imaging SSDs.

1 Introduction

A principle throughout all stages of any forensic investigation is the preservation of evidence. Digital Forensics is not exempt from this principle and has been identified at an embryonic stage in McKemmish [6], in digital forensic guidelines [1,11,14] and digital forensic frameworks [2,4]. Beebe and Clarke [2] state that digital evidence preservation is a fundamental principle and should be considered in all phases of a digital forensic investigation and continue to suggest that spoliation of digital evidence should be kept minimal and extensive contemporaneous notes are to be taken in such cases. These are cases where in order to extract the evidence it is necessary for the competent investigator to alter that evidence, this is not the case with SSDs. It has been demonstrated in [5] that with the investigator following SOPs and imaging the SSD, the digital evidence on the SSD changes. These changes are due to garbage collection and are independent of write-blockers, meaning that an SSD can change over time. Such "covert" changes yield inconsistencies between third party images. It is becoming common knowledge among practitioners that the practicality of producing two or more exact byte-for-byte images (hash-identical) from SSDs for all parties is becoming problematic [3]. Generally, the probability of producing hash-identical images is diminished as the time between seizure and data acquisition stage is increased.

© Springer International Publishing AG 2016
H. Jahankhani et al. (Eds.): ICGS3 2017, CCIS 630, pp. 3–11, 2016.
DOI: 10.1007/978-3-319-51064-4_1

Nisbet *et al.* [8] showed that for some TRIM enabled file systems deleted data is unrecoverable after 1 h. This includes time between different data acquisitions and is due to the volatility of SSDs, TRIM enabled file systems and the variance of aggressiveness of the manufacturer's garbage-collector. Furthermore there has been an increase in manufacturing of SSDs [13] that indicate SSDs will become ever more present in Digital Forensic Investigations. The problem is that there is a preconceived idea that these are storage media and therefore treated as traditional HDD. This treatment of digital evidence could jeopardise the evidential integrity and therefore raise questions about its admissibility in court. In addition TRIM enabled file systems can wipe clean SSDs in less than a minute. This is ideal for a quick sanitisation and permanent removal of all data without the prospect of recovery. The unrecoverability is attractive to criminals, who would rather loose their data then have it seized, examined and analysed for prosecution or as a result of e-Discovery requests.

McKemmish [6] states, "meaning of the data accessed by such change has not been unduly compromised". As long as the change can be accounted for, completed with competence and contemporaneous notes taken results in the potential digital evidence not being unduly compromised then change to digital evidence can be allowed in a court of law. In Carrier and Spafford's DFF [4] digital Crime Scene Preservation and Documentation sub-phase it states, ".... preserve the state of as many digital objects as possible by reducing the number of additional events that may occur...". The proposed DaP procedure does exactly this by prohibiting the activation of the garbage collector and the non-execution of TRIM commands on the SSD.

The need for a systematic way of producing hash-identical images for SSDs would be advantageous to all parties and may include: reduction in time spent on questioning the evidential integrity of digital evidence obtained from SSDs; and reduce administrative and cognitive burden on Digital Forensic Analyst to ensure that minimal steps taken to reduce the risk of contaminating the data on SSDs. The proposed Standard Operating Procedure (SOP), Deconstruct and Preserve (DaP), is explained in Sect. 3, experiments on DaP are described in Sect. 3, results of experiments are described in Sect. 4 and finally conclusions are in Sect. 5.

2   Background

2.1   Solid State Drives, SSD

SSDs cannot over-write like HDDs. This, along with wear-levelling [3], means that the equivalent of sectors have to be reset to zeroes, before being written to. This creates all kinds of problems that is the responsibility of the controller. One of the most notorious challenges to computer forensics is the garbage collector. To increase the efficiency of the reset/write process on SSDs the garbage collector will identify deleted files, and their associated blocks and reset them. This means that if the garbage collector is scheduled then any deleted data on the SSD will be lost. A write-blocker will not prevent the loss of data since the garbage collector is located in the controller.

To help this process further file systems have developed TRIM. When TRIM is enabled it allows the Controller to identify deleted/unallocated space on the SSD and start the reset process. TRIM has a scheduled time and initiates the garbage collector. Why is this an issue for Digital Forensics? There are two reasons: (i) data loss; and (ii) evidential integrity.

Data Loss. Wipe commands are more effective on SSDs. This allows devices to be wiped quicker, essentially this is the responsibility of the garbage collector and manufacturers have established aggressive ways of resetting gates to zero. Whereas to wipe a HDD may take two takes and many hours, SSDs can do this in one take and minutes. It will not be long before suspects can initiate a wipe of the SSD remotely. Once the SSD has been wiped then recovery of data is impossible; this data-loss is a threat to digital forensics and would change the SOP of seizure and collection of digital evidence.

Evidential Integrity. Evidence integrity forms the basis of certainty that evidence under investigation has not been changed upon seizure or when volunteered. All best practice guidelines [1] stipulate that evidence in the first instance should not be changed, or when change is necessary this process must be documented and be repeatable by third parties using the same steps.

Typically a digital forensic investigation of a device can be described in [6] and by the following notation in Fig. 1. This shows the Acquisition stage and importantly the verification that the images, $I_i, \forall i > 0$, are byte for byte copies of the device, I_0. The verification of evidential integrity is described in the acquisition stage by ensuring that the hashes match. When hashes do not match during an acquisition stage the evidential integrity has been compromised.

Whilst other technology that is susceptible to change (such as GPS, mobile, network seeking technology) can be managed by investigators by using methods to physically secure those types of devices to prevent access, change to data and deliberate deletion, SSDs have no such measure.

SOP on mobile devices have adopted to best perfect techniques that can recover data from volatile devices, non-standard operating systems, hybrid devices, encrypted and locked devices. Peer acceptance from investigators together with pseudo-standardised processes offered by forensic vendors have led to a community practice where in mobile phone investigations it is an accepted practice that at times agents [7] may need to be installed on Android devices to extract data from devices and removed post extraction.

The proposed DaP SOP wants to create a peer accepted methodology for SSD technology regardless of manufacturer differences. This development would provide assurance to practicing investigators that evidence has not been altered and provides confidence that steps are repeatable by third parties. By ensuring evidential integrity suspects and defence teams cannot argue that crucial evidence has been lost that would aide in their defence.

Seizure: $S(I_0)$
Management: $M(I_0)$
Acquisition: $D(I_0) = I_1$
     — $D(I_0) = I_i$
       where $D(I_0)$ is the duplication process
     — $H_k(I_0) = H_k(I_i) \ \forall i$,
       where
       $i = 1, 2, 3, ..., n$;
       H_k is a hashing algorithm, e.g. SHA1 then H_{SHA1}; and
       n is the number of images of the device, I_0, required.
Analysis: $A(I_1)$
Report: $R(I_1)$

Fig. 1. Nomenclature to describe five stages of Digital Investigation as indicated in [6]. This notation indicates the device as I_0 and any resulting image of that device as I_n, where $n > 0$. For example, the Acquisition stage yields I_1 and subsequent stages use I_1, an image, and not I_0, the original device.

3   Method

The set of experiments show how evidence can be deliberately deconstructed in order to preserve evidence. The experiment demonstrates how this would work on traditional devices without loss or effect to content. This paper then continues the experiment on SSD and provides a procedure for preserving evidence via deconstruction. Table 1 outlines the stages in DaP, this is further described in the list below and would be encapsulated in standard operating procedures for seizure, transportation, storage, analysis, reporting and presentation of digital evidence.

1. **Pre-verification:** Non-essential, but strongly recommended and required to prove preservation of potential digital evidence and no contamination has occurred. Also benefits Digital Forensic Investigators to confirm and verify the data acquisition stages, see stages 5–6. Using a hashing algorithm, hash the SSD to yield H_{I_0}.
2. **Deconstruction:** Completed by competent practitioner trained in DaP. Deconstructs the SSD/partition and identifies the component responsible for management, e.g. MBR or VBR. Once identified the start and end of the offset address of the component are recorded, it is then extracted from I_0 and stored as I_1 in a secure location by the custodians.
3. **Preservation:** Completed by competent practitioner trained in DaP. Preserving the SSD partition requires inserting, $\oplus$, the component identified in the deconstruction stage with zeroes, Z_{y-x}. The size of Z is determined by $y - x$ and the start location is at offset x. This stage preserves the SSD by putting it in a stable state and therefore prevent any risk of contamination. It is recommended to Hash the device that can be matched in stage 4 and thus ensure that the acquisition stage is completed correctly.

Table 1. Stages for Deconstruct and Preserve, DaP. Explanation of stages as follows: 1. H - hashing function e.g. SHA256, to uniquely identify device; 2. E_x^y - deconstructs and extracts VBR between offset x, y; 3. Z_{y-x} - zeroes of length $y - x$; $\oplus_x^y$ - inserts the first operand, Z_{y-x}, into the second operand, I_0. 4. $D(I_0)$ - data acquisition producing an exact byte-for-byte copy, I_j. 5. $\oplus$ inserts the output from deconstruction into the image, I_j between offset x, y. 6. H - complete hashing on reconstructed image, the result equals the original device for all images.

Stage	Input Visual	Process	Output	Output Visual
1. Pre-verification		$H_k(I_0)$	H_{I_0}	0e43 75 43 8ad801 960c4bb 1767 78b02 33 21 4f0f d0 78 54 8b 62 fa 98 be 40 2d7 96c3b 32 77 7a 27 31 f41 6904 fa 4abc 251 9a1 30 43 49 b0 fb 347 9ea20 ed713 7a46 3xc1a90
2. Deconstruction		$E_x^y(I_0)$	I_1	
3. Preservation		$Z_{y-x} \oplus_x^y I_0$	I_0	
4. Acquisition		$D(I_0)$	I_j	
5. Reconstruction		$I_1 \oplus_x^y I_j, j \geq 2$	I_j	
6. Verification		$H_k(I_j), j \geq 2$	H_{I_j}	$H_{I_0} = H_j, \forall_{j \geq 2}$

4. **Acquisition:** Using write-blockers and NIST approved software duplicate the original device, I_0. This stage can be repeated many times to yield I_j, where $j \geq 2$.
5. **Reconstruction:** Request I_0 from the custodians along with the start and end offset addresses, x, y. Insert, $\oplus$, the original component, I_0, into the image of the preserved SSD, I_j, to yield a new image that can be read and analysed.
6. **Verification:** Non-essential but strongly recommended. Using a hashing algorithm, hash the image, $H_k(I_j)$, and test for match with H_{I_0}.

All stages are fully automated using code as described in experiment. DaP is formally described as in Fig. 2.

$$
\begin{aligned}
\textbf{Pre} - \textbf{Verification} &: & H_k(I_0) &\rightarrow H_{I_0} \\
\textbf{Deconstruction} &: & E_x^y(I_0) &\rightarrow I_1 \\
\textbf{Preservation} &: & Z_{y-x} \oplus_x^y I_0 &\rightarrow I_0 \\
\textbf{Acquisition} &: & D(I_0) &\rightarrow I_j, \; j \geq 2 \\
\textbf{Reconstruction} &: & I_1 \oplus_x^y I_j &\rightarrow I_j, \; j \geq 2 \\
\textbf{Verification} &: & H_k(I_j) &= H_{I_0}, \; \forall j \geq 2
\end{aligned}
$$

Fig. 2. Description of DaP as a generalised formal process. The operation $Q \oplus_x^y P$ indicates insert Q in P between the offset address x, y

4 Results and Evaluation

4.1 Control Experiment

The following list explains the process of the experiment, that is not too different from [3]. The minor differences are: (i) Python code, instead of batch code; (ii) the replacement of 'EVIDENCE' with '12345678'; and (iii) the size of the files. The major difference is the **Deconstruct and Preserve** stage that backs up data from the VBR (FAT file system was used here), thus rendering the file system useless and disabling the ability of any file system dependent information being altered. Then by reconstruction of the device as an image so that software can be used to analyse and produce reports.

The control experiment was completed on a USB using FAT16. The size of the USB was small at ≈256 Mbytes. This experiment demonstrates an implementation of DaP and its principles, albeit on a small scale. The experiment was repeated 5 times and results shown in Table 2. The hashing algorithm used was SHA with 512 Byte option, reducing hash collision [10] to an insignificant probability. These set of results had 100% matches and therefore the practical supports the theory with non-volatile media. In the next sub-section the aim is to apply this to SSDs.

Table 2. Control experiment and yields identical SHA512 hashes for Device and Repatriation. Results were conducted on a ≈256 MByte USB, a non-volatile data storage medium.

Test	Device SHA512	Repatriation SHA512	Recovery percent
1	Match	Match	100
2	Match	Match	100
3	Match	Match	100
4	Match	Match	100
5	Match	Match	100

4.2 SSD Without DaP

Section 4.1 shows that DaP works on traditional media. To see if DaP works on SSDs (file system: EXT4, OS: Linux, Ubuntu 14.04 LTS) an experimental framework was set up to test the hypothesis: does the introduction of DaP preserve evidence? To test this two experiments are required: (i) to prove without DaP evidence is destroyed; and (ii) to prove with DaP evidence is preserved. The following steps were repeated 5 times on various partitions, all code written in python and available on request from first author. The following steps outline the experiment:

Format: Create a ≈15 Gbyte TRIM enabled partition. External Partition connected SATA to eSATA, since TRIM commands can be executed through SATA [12].

Generation: Generate a template/file with string '12345678'

Populate: Fill (98%) the partition with the file.

Deletion: Delete Files

Hash: Hash the partition, H_1

TRIM: Issue TRIM command, `fstrim -v /media/user/sdb1`. This is similar to pseudo-activation of `cron`, or likewise in other operating systems, to instantiate and identify deleted files.

Hash: Hash the partition, H_2

Table 3. SSD without DaP. All hashes before and after TRIM do not match.

Test	Device	TRIM enabled	$H_1 = H_2$
1	SanDisk	Yes	False
2	OCA-Agility	Yes	False
3	Micron M510	Yes	False
4	Kingston V Series	No	n/a
5	SK Hynix SC210	Yes	False

This experiment demonstrates without DaP the evidence on the SSD is changed and thus the two images before and after differ (Table 3).

4.3 SSD with DaP

The above results in Sect. 4.2 show that after issuing the TRIM command the evidence changes. In this section the experimental framework introduces DaP, all other conditions remain, e.g. OS. The experiment is described in the list below:

Format: Create a ≈15 Gbyte TRIM enabled partition. External Partition connected SATA to eSATA, since TRIM commands can be executed through SATA [12].

Generation: Generate a template/file with string '12345678'

Populate: Fill (98%) the partition with the file.

Deletion: Delete Files

Hash: Hash the partition, H_1

DaP: Complete stages 1–2 of DaP.

TRIM: Issue TRIM command, `fstrim -v /media/user/sdb1`

DaP: Complete stages 3–4 of DaP.

Hash: Hash the image partition, H_2

Table 4. SSD with DaP. All hashes before and after TRIM command match.

Test	Device	TRIM enabled	$H_1 = H_2$
1	SanDisk	Yes	True
2	OCA-Agility	Yes	True
3	Micron M510	Yes	True
4	Kingston V Series	No	True
5	SK Hynix SC210	Yes	True

The results show that the partitions before and after TRIM are preserved and therefore future images of this partition can match. The content can be retrieved once the image is reconstructed. In all cases this produced a match with the original content and thus preserves digital evidence (DaP also worked on TRIM disabled SSD) (Table 4).

The hypothesis is accepted, DaP preserves digital evidence on: TRIM enabled SSDs; TRIM disabled SSDs; and traditional non-volatile storage media.

5   Conclusion

DaP is a proposal to effectively resolve issues related to digital evidence preservation on SSDs and ensures the stability and consistency of current and future images taken from the SSD. To emphasise DaP is not going to increase the ability to recover data from SSD. Market share of SSD is increasing, along with that is knowledge by defendants that there are methods to wipe the information with 0% chance of no data recovery. Research [3,5,8] has backed this fact up and shows under certain circumstances how this can be achieved. Under e-Discovery requests, such violations are covered by the wilful destruction of evidence under the guise of a preservation order [9], however a preservation order does not exist at crime scenes. The defendant can exercise the deletion of data remotely, once the TRIM and deletion command is issued the garbage collector destroys any chance of recovering the data. This all happens whilst in the Digital Forensic Lab. DaP is able to preserve the data on the SSD and keep the data consistent between different images taken of the SSD. With the above experiments this has been shown to be stable and valid; each experiment was duplicated a few times to ensure the reproducibility and each time each image gave the same result, identical hash number. DaP would work on HDD as well and add a further layer of protection along with traditional hardware, such as write-blockers. With this in mind the introduction could change several SOPs for first response teams. Finally, there are some recommendations for the use of DaP.

5.1   Recommendations

DaP has been presented as a SOP to handle the data acquisition stage of an SSD. The recommendations are as follows:

- Follow SWDGE, NIJ or other national [11,14] guidelines for Digital Evidence Sequestration for First Response Teams (FRT).
- complete the extraction stage as early as possible, and even consider this as part of the FRT's procedures.
- use a custodian database to store the extraction of H_1. This is future work and would involve chain of custody updates for other requests to image the device.

References

1. Association of Chief Police Officers (ACPO): Good practice guide for digital evidence (ver. 5), March 2012. https://www.7safe.com/research-and-insight/acpo-guidelines
2. Beebe, N.L., Clark, J.G.: A hierarchical, objectives-based framework for the digital investigations process. Digit. Invest. **2**(2), 147–167 (2005)
3. Bell, G.B., Boddington, R.: Solid state drives: the beginning of the end for current practice in digital forensic recovery? J. Digit. Forensics Secur. Law **5**(3), 1–20 (2010)
4. Carrier, B., Spafford, E.H.: An event-based digital forensic investigation framework. In: Digital Forensic Research Workshop, pp. 11–13 (2004)
5. King, C., Vidas, T.: Empirical analysis of solid state disk data retention when used with contemporary operating systems. J. Digit. Invest. **8**, S111–S117 (2011)
6. McKemmish, R.: What is Forensic Computing? Trends and Issues in Crime and Criminal Justice, no. 118 (1999)
7. MSAB: XRY – Android basics: debugging and extractions (2015). XRY Certification Course
8. Nisbet, A., Lawrence, S., Ruff, M.: A forensic analysis and comparison of solid state drive data retention with trim enabled file systems. In: Australian Digital Forensics Conference, pp. 103–111 (2013)
9. Redgrave, J.M.: The Sedona Principles: Best Practices, Recommendations & Principles for Addressing Electronic Document Production. Pike & Fischer-A BNA Company (2007)
10. Rogaway, P., Shrimpton, T.: Cryptographic hash-function basics: definitions, implications, and separations for preimage resistance, second-preimage resistance, and collision resistance. In: Roy, B., Meier, W. (eds.) FSE 2004. LNCS, vol. 3017, pp. 371–388. Springer, Heidelberg (2004). doi:10.1007/978-3-540-25937-4_24
11. Scientific Working Group on Digital Evidence (SWDGE): Model standard operation procedures for computer forensics (ver. 3). https://www.swgde.org/
12. Shu, F., Obr, N.: Data set management commands proposal for ATA8-ACS2. Management **2**, 1 (2007)
13. Statista.com: Global shipments of HDDs and SSDs in PCs from 2012 to 2017, June 2016. http://www.statista.com/statistics/285474/hdds-and-ssds-in-pcs-global-shipments-2012-2017/
14. U.S. Department of Justice: Electronic Crime Scene Investigation: An On-the-Scene Reference for First Responders. National Institute of Justice, November 2009

Bitcoin Forensics: A Tutorial

David Neilson$^{(\boxtimes)}$, Sukhvinder Hara, and Ian Mitchell

Middlesex University, London, UK
{d.neilson, s.hara, i.mitchell}@mdx.ac.uk

Abstract. Over the past eighteen months, the digital cryptocurrency Bitcoin has experienced significant growth in terms of usage and adoption. It has also been predicted that if this growth continues then it will become an increasingly useful tool for various illegal activities. Against this background, it seems safe to assume that students and professionals of digital forensics will require an understanding of the subject. New technologies are often a major challenge to the field of digital forensics due to the technical and legal challenges they introduce. This paper provides a set of tutorials for Bitcoin that allows for learners from both backgrounds to be taught how it operates, and how it may impact on their working practice. Earlier this year they were delivered to a cohort of third year undergraduates. To the author's knowledge, this represents the first integration of the topic into a digital forensics programme by a higher education provider.

Keywords: Bitcoin · Blockchain · Curriculum design · Digital forensics

1 Introduction

Bitcoin [1] is a decentralized cryptocurrency and payment network that allows for transactions to be conducted peer-to-peer amongst its users. Introduced in 2009, it has rapidly gained traction and currently has a market capitalization of almost ten billion dollars. A huge industry has grown to support these developments and the currency is now accepted as a method of payment by a number of large retailers. It has spawned a wide number of imitations and there are currently over two hundred cryptocurrencies which are referred to as alt-coins. There is now little doubt as to whether these technologies are here to stay and are likely to grow even further over the coming years. Bitcoin introduces a number of challenges to digital investigations mainly due to the elements of anonymity it provides a user, and the decentralized network which it operates within. These features have made it an attractive means of exchange for those engaged in criminal activities online. It has the potential to be used for money laundering and tax avoidance [2], and has been used extensively to purchase illicit goods and services through online marketplaces such as Silk Road [3]. It is also used as the method of payment for ransomware attacks which have witnessed huge growth during this time [4]. Currently there exists little in the literature to suggest that practitioners have the requisite knowledge of this technology to investigate crimes with Bitcoin.

© Springer International Publishing AG 2016
H. Jahankhani et al. (Eds.): ICGS3 2017, CCIS 630, pp. 12–26, 2016.
DOI: 10.1007/978-3-319-51064-4_2

This situation is likely to change in the coming years and serves as the main motivation for the development of a training course in the form of seven tutorials.

Any learner, whether from Public/Private/Financial Sector, Security Agencies, Law Enforcement Agencies or Education, will rely on certain Learning Styles [5] with varying levels. In addition to learning styles, the framework also has to accommodate effective formative and summative feedback, to ascertain if learners have achieved learning objectives.

Often there is a reliance on experience when developing and designing something new, this applies to most areas, e.g. software engineering. Is it possible to prepare and design a curriculum without reliance and dependence on experience? LEAF [6] has been chosen partly to answer this question and support curriculum development and learners' learning styles, and allow the integration of effective formative and summative feedback. The disadvantage of the framework is that it shifts the burden from the learner to the facilitator to provide good preparation that is shown from the study to be positively correlated with good results. Briefly, LEAF has two phases: (i) design; and (ii) implementation. In design phase, there are three stages: Lecture; Exercise; Apply and there are four stages in the implementation phase: Lecture; Exercise; Apply; and Feedback and hence the acronym. LEAF was chosen since previous results show that on average 60% achieve over 70% in assessment, this is important in the delivery of material to professionals, which often require a higher pass grade than Higher Education Providers, typically 40%, for accreditation or membership.

The approach suggested in this paper allows for the following tutorials to be applied by learners from both academic institutions in teaching of undergraduates, and also professionals already employed in the industry.

2   Background

Bitcoin is a distributed payment network that is built on the foundation of a number of key technologies; public key cryptography, p2p networks, and cryptographic hash algorithms. These combine to produce a payment system that requires no central authority to validate transactions conducted amongst its peers. Fundamental to this system is a data structure called the blockchain, which is essentially a database containing every transaction that has ever taken place in this payment network. There are two main features of this dataset that makes it extremely secure as a store of data and therefore of use to digital investigators. Firstly, the data written to it is immutable, which is achieved through its use of a proof-of-work algorithm [7]. Once written to, it is practically impossible to modify the data contained within it. Secondly, a copy of it is maintained by every node within the Bitcoin network, meaning there is no single point of failure. These features make it an extremely useful source of evidence for the digital forensics practitioner.

However, the data contained within it is quite limited and the design of the system makes establishing the identity of its users extremely difficult providing a level of anonymity. There is no concept of accounts, and transactions are conducted between addresses that the user holds in what is called a wallet. Transactions are broadcast as messages to the network and propagated peer-to-peer, containing no IP address data that would indicate where the transaction originated from. In counter to this, every transaction and its associated addresses are permanently recorded in the blockchain and viewable to anyone who has a copy. Each and every transaction is chained together, allowing for the path that funds take to be traced back to the first transaction. For these reasons Bitcoin is said to be pseudonymous rather than anonymous. Its current lack of acceptance as a major means of exchange means that at some point there will be conversion to Fiat currencies, and this provides investigators a means to reveal suspects identities, due to the regulatory requirements placed on money transmitters.

The lack of an established framework, and peer accepted methodologies to process bitcoin related evidence, may leave investigators without the required skills to conduct an investigation. For technically capable professionals, the learning of the subject should not pose too many problems. However an understanding of the general operating environment is also required, and in the event of an investigation this may be time that could be damaging to the pursuit of a suspect.

3 Course Design

3.1 Lecture, Exercise, Apply

The course is split into seven tutorials which are composed of both a lecture and an associated lab session. The lectures provide description and explanation of the key concepts and components, supporting theoretical and activist learning styles. This knowledge will then be applied through a number of exercises using Bitcoin, supporting pragmatic and reflectivist learning styles. The knowledge gained from each of the tutorials is directly relevant to parts of the assessment at the end and represents the apply stage of the LEAF model. The elements related to forensics were gradually introduced over the series of tutorials. This is so that learners can concentrate initially on understanding how the network and operating environment work, without any distraction from investigatory issues.

The lectures are designed to break down the main components of Bitcoin into easily digestible sections, which reflect the main topics of interest. The exercises were designed to follow on from the lecture and allows for learners to gradually familiarize themselves with the tools and software. The learners conduct a number of different transactions between their desktop wallets, and also a web based wallet they create in the lab. An important component of the exercises is that the learners are provided with a log sheet, which they use to record the pertinent details of every transaction they carry out. This forms an extremely important part of the curriculum design as they promote good practice of maintaining contemporaneous notes, which are then used by the learners to trace their own activity throughout the individual lessons. When the learners reach the later labs and start to analyze the blockchain, they will use these log sheets to verify the transactions they have carried out.

The apply stage comes at the end of the lecture and lab sessions, and is designed to test their understanding of the concepts and skills they have learnt. A crime scenario involving bitcoin transactions has been created that allow learners to explore a number of pieces of evidence, which enables them to conduct an investigation. For the students we have taught at undergraduate level, they are asked to produce a report in the style of a digital investigation. This forces the learner to consider the investigation in the same manner as they would with a traditional one. Due to time considerations this method for assessment would probably not be appropriate for professionals, but could be replaced with a presentation of their findings and results.

3.2   Lab Setup

Good planning is essential to the successful delivery of the course and there are a number of things to organize and prepare. The first consideration should be given to which piece of wallet software should be used on the lab workstations, from where the learners will carry out most of their transactions. The ideal choice here would be to use a complete client such as Bitcoin Core. This is known as a full node and allows for all functions within the network to be carried out; transactions, mining, verification and propagation. To carry out these functions requires it to maintain a full copy of the blockchain which at the time of writing stands at 75 Gigabytes, and this creates maintenance issues. To keep the blockchain up to date the workstations must be left on throughout the teaching period, or they must be switched on periodically to let them catch up before the delivery of the next tutorial. The second option is to use a wallet that is called a Simplified Payment Verification (SPV) client, which does not keep a copy of the blockchain. While these types of client are slightly weaker from a security perspective [8], this will have no impact upon their use for the tutorials purposes.

A number of other pieces of software are also required to follow this tutorial plan. Numisight is a blockchain transaction explorer that generates a graph of transaction inputs and outputs, and is used in Tutorial 6. It is essential in helping learners to learn blockchain analysis techniques and also to identify the nature of a transaction structure. Due to the complexity of the data used, a visual representation of these connections can improve both the quality and speed at which this analysis can take place. Learners will also require access to an internet browser throughout all of the tutorials for two main purposes; to let learners create and use web based wallets to carry out transactions, and also to make use of online block explorers which learners will use to verify their transactions. The workstations should also have Python installed, so that they can utilize the script which simulates the process of mining used in Tutorial 4 The final requirement is that there needs to be access to the parts of the blockchain that contain the transactions they have carried out. If the Bitcoin Core client has been employed, then every workstation with the software will have a full copy of the blockchain. For those using SPV clients however it will be necessary to keep a record of which blocks are mined during the tutorials. This is used for the lab exercises where the leaners manually parse transactions on the blockchain with use of a hex editor in Tutorial 5.

Learners must have enough bitcoins to be able to carry out transactions and pay the associated transaction fees, which represents the only direct financial cost for the delivery of the tutorials. Each cohort of twenty learners would require approximately 0.025 BTC which is worth just over fifteen US Dollars at the time of writing, and of which 0.005 would be reclaimed at the conclusion of the course. The final consideration is to have digital copies of the log sheet that is to accompany the lab exercises. While most practitioners still maintain handwritten contemporaneous notes, the extensive use of long cryptographic keys makes this approach impractical for this type of investigation.

3.3 Assessment

A crime scenario has been developed though the creation of a number of web based resources, and a series of Bitcoin transactions. This allows leaners to explore all of the topics that have been looked at during the tutorials and apply them through a hypothetical investigation. It involved the creation of a number of accounts and leaving traces of activity so that the learners could build a case around the information they find. The assessment is designed to test the learners understanding of the Bitcoin environment and to display the techniques they have learnt over the period of the course. Learners are expected to analyze the transactions with use of the appropriate methods to trace and verify their findings, determine the leads generated by the evidence and to suggest what further steps could be taken to locate the suspect, and assess how much evidential weight they give to their discoveries and the limitations of them. The relevant information is not difficult to locate, as it was important to ensure that less capable learners are not disenfranchised from completing the assessment effectively.

The learners are informed that law enforcement arrived at the suspects home with a warrant to search her premises. Upon arrival they find that the suspect appears to have fled and there are no relevant possessions to be found in the home. They find one piece of evidence in her dustbin; a piece of paper that has three items handwritten on it; a Bitcoin address, the term 'Coingenie', and the address of a Tor hidden service indicated with the suffix '.onion'.

Bitcoin Address. The bitcoin address provided, is the address that is used to purchase the fake documents from the Tor website in the scenario. This places it at the center of a distinct chain and this allows the learners to try and establish the source and destinations of the bitcoins transferred. The transactions were designed so that it would be easy to pick up the trail, and make sense of the relevant chains to the case. Here the learners are able to detect some the transaction types and patterns that they have learnt. Critical to this, are the amounts that the transactions represent, as these can be linked to the values of some of the forged documents available for sale on the Tor website. Complicating this is the fact that when these funds are sent, transactions for almost exactly the same amount are moved from the receiving address to another, the monetary difference due to the transaction fee. This tests the student's ability to organize the correct transaction. The transactions are designed so that the issue of address reuse is apparent and the implications that can be taken from this activity. Depending on which blockchain explorer is employed to assist their investigation they may manage to discover that the funds are transferred to a leading cryptocurrency exchange, and allows the learners to suggest that this may be in order to launder the bitcoins, a topic that is covered in Tutorial 7.

Coingenie. An account was setup on the popular bitcoin forum bitcointalk.org. Here the user had left a series of posts in two threads they had created, that were designed to reveal some information about Jean herself and some possible leads. The first thread was entitled 'newbie needs a new wallet'. In this she states that she is looking for a wallet that is web based and in the next post indicates that she may use Circle, a well-known provider. This would allow learners to suggest that a request could be made to the service provider, to try and reveal the identity of the user. They learn in

Tutorial 2 that Circle requires identity to sign up and buy and sell bitcoins, complying with anti-money laundering regulations. The other important thing that they could suggest is that the nature of her posts reveals that she has limited understanding of bitcoin and so is unlikely to adopt techniques such as changing addresses and not reusing. The second account created was at localbitcoins.com. This is a well-known method that allows users to meet and exchange bitcoins for cash, and is a means by which a user can mask their identity. An advert was setup to sell bitcoin from a location in England, the same country for where the transactions indicated the fake documents had been purchased for. An unexpected benefit of this term is that it produces a number of search engine results that were not created by the authors, allowing for the use of their logic to establish that they were not relevant.

Tor Hidden Service. This was used to setup a website and is designed to draw on what they had been taught through the case study of Silk Road in Tutorial 7. When accessed using Tor, learners are taken to a webpage that advertises the selling of fake documents. There are a few important pieces of information that the student may glean from here, the most critical being the values of the documents that are on sale. Passports, ID cards and Drivers licenses are available for a number of different European countries and importantly, different values are given for each of them. This enables the learners to find a link between these and some of the transactions that linked to the bitcoin address they are provided with. The suggestion made by the transaction data suggests that two UK documents have been purchased. This also allows a link to be made with the localbitcoins.com account which was also based in the UK. The website's FAQ also contains a subtle clue, which helps to suggest without any doubt which transactions were responsible for purchasing the documents. The transaction chain has an almost identical transaction value right after the documents have been purchased, the difference being the transaction fee. The FAQ states that customers should "not ask for discounts" and this suggests that learners should look very closely to determine the correct transactions.

4   Tutorials

4.1   Tutorial 1

Lecture. The first lecture provides an overview of the entire system so that learners can appreciate what it is, and how it works at a simple level. This provides the foundation for the later lectures, where the significant components are dealt with in more detail. The lecture begins by starting with a short history about what money is. This is important as it allows the student to appreciate that there have been a variety of methods used as a means of exchange, allowing them to appreciate the similarities and difference with cryptocurrencies. Next the main technologies that Bitcoin utilizes are described; public key cryptography, peer-to peer networks, and cryptographic hash functions. It is essential that a student has at least a basic understanding of these before trying to look at the topics in greater detail, so they can appreciate the design aspects that make Bitcoin a secure system. Each of the main components are explained, and the overriding objective is to get learners to understand that transactions are conducted peer-to-peer without the need for a central authority to verify them. The session concludes by showing the example of a transaction and all of the main steps that are involved in processing one.

Exercise. The first lab is mostly concerned with setting up all of the relevant accounts and wallets that the learners will use to carry out transactions in the subsequent labs. They are also given a copy of the log sheet and record details of their accounts into these. The learners all send a copy of a receive address to the teacher so that they can distribute the bitcoins that they will be using for all of the tutorials exercise. The main objectives for the exercise session are for the student to become familiar with the wallet software that will be used, and to conduct their first transactions.

Apply. Due to the simple level with which the material is dealt with at this point, there is not too much here that helps to inform the student greater about their coursework. One part that is perhaps most important here is that the units and notation of bitcoin is introduced. This can have implications for their work in the labs, and also on the correct presentation of their work for their assessment.

4.2   Tutorial 2

Lecture. The two main topics for the second tutorial are the storage and acquisition of bitcoins. The most important concept for the learners to understand here is that wallets do not store bitcoins, they store addresses. The first part of the lecture describes the process for creating addresses and this necessitates a need to explain how public key cryptography works. This is done at a relatively high level, as it is not necessary to have a deep understanding of the ECRSA algorithm used by Bitcoin. They are then shown how the bitcoin address is converted from its public key form through hashing and finally encoded as a Base58 string. The next part of the lecture concentrates on how a user is able to purchase or acquire bitcoins. The main methods are discussed and allows for a comparison between their relative merits and disadvantages. Of most importance here are the levels of anonymity and the possibility for a criminal to prevent tracing. The potential to use the system for money laundering is introduced, and the point is made that the weakest point in the system is the point of exchange with the current financial system. Finally, the lecture looks at wallets and the various different methods of storage users have at their disposal.

Exercise. During Tutorial 1's lab session, the transactions the learners make, use the default addresses provided by the wallets they create. In the first exercise for Tutorial 2, the learners conduct transactions by creating and making use of new addresses in both their desktop client and also their web based wallets. They also specify new change addresses for these transactions to reinforce the concept of avoiding reuse of them. The second exercise requires the leaners to work in small groups and asks them to sign up for some other online wallet providers, allowing them to compare the different security requirements for signup, and also the security features they provide to the user. The final exercise involves the learners creating backups of their desktop wallets, and also the creation of paper wallets to securely store a very small amount of bitcoins from their allocation.

Apply. One transaction within the crime scenario shows quite explicitly that an address has been reused, and allows the student to conclude that the purchaser of the first fake document was the same person who purchased the second document. The learners are also given information in a bitcoin forum that the suspect is considering using an online service provider. This allows the student to put in their report what actions would be helpful given this information. They should be able to say that they would contact the service provider who may provide either an IP address, or the name and address details linked to a payment card.

4.3   Tutorial 3

Lecture. Tutorial 3 looks at transactions in detail and the learners are first given a quick overview of addresses as they are the main components of the transaction. They are shown how each transaction is broadcast as a message to the network, which is then propagated to each and every node for validation. The main part of the lecture focuses on the construction of these messages, and how transactions consist of a number of input and output addresses [9]. These all form a chain of transactions that is important in terms of tracing the source and destination of funds. The most common transaction forms and types are described showing how it is possible to have multiple inputs and outputs for any given transaction, and how in most cases the need for a change address will mean that every transaction will usually have at least two outputs. A byte descriptor table is introduced (Table 1 below) showing the specific details of the data structure, and help explain the interaction between private and public keys, through the use of locking and unlocking scripts.

Table 1. Byte offset descriptions of transaction structure.

Field	Size	Description
4 bytes	Version	Specifies which rules this transaction follows
1–9 bytes (VarInt)	Input counter	How many inputs are included
Variable	Inputs	One or more transaction inputs
1–9 bytes (VarInt)	Output counter	How many outputs are included
Variable	Outputs	One or more transaction outputs
4 bytes	Locktime	A Unix timestamp or block number

Exercise. The exercises for Tutorial 3 consist of carrying out a number of transactions between their desktop and web based wallets. They also explore the transaction functionality of the wallets such as the ability to define the size of transaction fee and the use of labelling. These are done with specific amounts so that different types of transaction are simulated, which will then be analyzed when the leaners revisit them in Tutorial 7's lab session. A transaction is carried out with the same change address as the input address so that when the student analyses them later this action of reuse will be very apparent to them. For the second part of this lab the leaners are placed into groups to research and make a comparison of different web based block explorers. Using some of their previous transactions they are asked to determine which one provides the most useful features and then discuss with the rest of the cohort.

Apply. The assessment requires that the student understand a number of concepts and resources that they will use in their investigation. The chaining of transactions and how they can be traced with block explorers, provide the first introduction to blockchain analysis. Understanding how transaction fees are calculated as implied as part of the transaction and not included as an output, can be critical to the learners correctly identifying which transactions were used to purchase the fake documents in the assessment scenario. The issue of address reuse is also covered again here.

4.4   Tutorial 4

Lecture. Tutorial 4 looks at the peer-to-peer network, and the components that allow it to achieve consensus in the absence of a central authority. The Bitcoin protocol and the main types of nodes are explained, and how all these parts are required to achieve a shared view of the networks state. During the course of the lecture the learners are introduced to what Antonopoulos refers to as the 'four pillars of consensus' [10]; verification of every transaction by each node in the network during propagation, collection of transactions into blocks and processed through use of a proof-of-work algorithm, verification of newly created blocks by each network node and added to the blockchain, each nodes selection of the longest chain of blocks. The process of mining is explained and how through their use of a proof-of-work algorithm, they secure the network against subversion and attack. The process of new coin generation is descri-bed, and how this provides incentive for the miners to commit their hashing power. The overall aim for the lecture is to allow leaners to appreciate the system as a whole.

Exercise. Now that the learners have seen all of the components work they should be able to understand how they all work together. However due to the systems complexity this may not be the case, and it is vital that all the learners understand this before progressing to forensic analysis. This led to the design of an exercise whereby the learners become components of the network, to carry out a physical simulation of a transaction being processed from broadcast to its commitment to the blockchain. Essential to this is that two learners act as miners competing to find a hash below a certain value so that they can claim the coinbase reward for doing so. The following Python Script has been developed for this purpose;

```
import hashlib
text = ("Miner 1 this is another example of the hash of a
block header")
for nonce in range(10000):
    input = text+str(nonce)
    hash = hashlib.sha256(input.encode()).hexdigest()
    print (input, hash)
    if hash.startswith("00"):
        print ("Found Hash")
        break
```

The value found within the *if* statement of the code (representing the nonce) can be modified to search for more zeroes which will let the program run for longer before finding a match. This enables the concepts of hashing power and hash difficulty to be demonstrated very clearly. For the second miner involved in the demonstration, modifying the variable text to "Miner 2" will result in different hashes being generated for each miner.

Apply. While there are no distinct parts to this tutorial that are directly related to their assessment it does represent one of the most fundamental parts to the course. An understanding of this tutorial is essential for the learners to make sense of the investigation as a whole.

4.5   Tutorial 5

Lecture. Up to this point the blockchain has not been looked at in any detail and has simply been treated as a database that keeps a record of every transaction, and therefore can validate whether a transaction can be processed. In this tutorial the data structure is looked at in detail and is broken down with use of the byte tables describing the various fields. The learners are shown how the hash of the previous block header field, is the essential piece of data in maintaining the chain of blocks, and prevents modification of the data within the blockchain. The two methods for identifying a block are described; the block hash (a hash of the block header) and the block height, with the latter of these not being a unique identifier due to the possibility of forks being generated in the blockchain. The potential for two copies of the blockchain to temporarily coexist is explained, as is the way in which these forks are resolved. The lecture concludes by describing the various types of chain, and their relationship with the 'longest chain', which all nodes accept as being the correct version of the blockchain.

Exercise. The learners are provided with a block.dat blockchain file and are taken through an example by the teacher with each step clearly explained. Each field is located with a hex editor and a description of the various fields shown in Tables 2 and 3 below. These are then converted to determine the values and compare them with the results of an online block explorer. The learners are then asked to do the same for the first transaction they have carried out in Tutorial 1's lab session. The relevant block will need to be provided, and due to the fact that they were all created at the same time, all of the cohort's first transactions should be within the same blockchain file. Due to the presence of variable length fields, this task can be fairly demanding on the learner and the teacher may need to repeat their example again.

Table 2. Byte offset descriptions of the block.

Field	Size	Description
Block size	4 bytes	Size of block in bytes
Block header	80 bytes	For details view block header (Table 3) below
Transaction counter	1–9 bytes (VarInt)	How many transactions in block
Transactions	Variable	The transactions (see transaction byte table)

Table 3. Byte offset descriptions of the block header.

Field	Size	Description
Version	4 bytes	Version No. to track protocol upgrades
Previous block hash	32 bytes	Reference to hash of parent block
Merkle root	32 bytes	Hash of the root of the Merkle tree for this block
Timestamp	4 bytes	Approximate block creation time (Unix Time)
Difficulty target	4 bytes	Difficulty of POW algorithm for this block
Nonce	4 bytes	Counter used to generate POW algorithm

Apply. As part of the assessment learners are expected to verify the transactions. This can be carried out with use of online block explorers, but this data should also be verified manually. The learners are provided with the block.dat files from the blockchain that allow for manual parsing. This is quite a difficult task as the only way in which they are able to locate the relevant transaction is by making use of the Bitcoin API function *addresstohash*. This allows for the address used to be located and represents the first step in finding the data in the blockchain. The other parts of this transaction can then be verified through use of the field descriptions shown in Table 3.

4.6   Tutorial 6

Lecture. The main topic for Tutorial 6 is crime that involves the use of bitcoins. Before this however the potential for the network to be compromised is considered, beginning with a detailed look at how forks within the network develop and how they are resolved. The learners are reintroduced to the concept of a 51% attack, and presented with a hypothetical case showing how it could be carried out. Other attacks such as denial of service are also considered as is the ability to detect the IP address of the user who makes a transaction [11], although it is made clear the limitations of these methods. The second half of the lecture looks at the types of crime that have been carried out using bitcoin and the methods they employ to remain undetected. This begins with a reminder of what makes it attractive to criminals, looking in particular at the huge rise in ransomware attacks. The collapse of former bitcoin exchange Mt Gox is also examined, and for both of these cases, the ability to trace the proceeds of crime through the blockchain. The infamous case of the Silk Road marketplace accessed through Tor is described, and how the funds could be linked to the suspect due to his laptop containing a wallet associated with the relevant addresses. The final part of the lecture looks at the methods that can be employed to prevent tracing such as coinjoin transactions and bitcoin mixing services.

Exercise. In this lab session the learners conduct their final transactions for the course, all of which are analyzed in the final lab session. They are asked to send all of their remaining bitcoins to an address setup by the teacher on a different wallet to the one they use to distribute the learner's bitcoins in Tutorial 1. The teacher then sends to funds to bitmixer.io, a bitcoin mixing service that takes incoming bitcoins and breaks the link with. This allows for the transaction to be analyzed in the final tutorials exercises. While it would be advantageous for learners to do this by themselves the min transfer amount of 0.01 BTC places pressure on the cost of the courses delivery. Due to their own chains being linked to this the learners can still look at this data when they start to analyze their own history in Tutorial 7. The class is also introduced to Tor, and they are asked to explore the environment to understand the scale and variety of criminal behaviour that is occurring. The learners then share their experience and findings with the rest of the cohort provoking discussion around the implications.

Apply. The tutorial has provided details of the types of crime involved and this provides some hints as to what may have happened in the crime scenario they have been studying provides them with the knowledge... The coin mixing exercise has particular relevance to the assessment. The crime scenario's chain of transactions eventually leads to an address that suggests the intention is to lauder the proceeds of the crime. The use of Tor will also form part of their assessment, and this part of the tutorial provides them with knowledge of how it works, and the limitations this also places on an investigation.

4.7 Tutorial 7

Lecture. The final lecture deals with blockchain analysis and how to make sense of transaction history and chaining. The learners are reminded of the benefits that the blockchain provides investigators, in particular the transparency and auditability it provides. The design of the system means that transactions effectively form a directed acyclic graph, and learners are exposed to some of the academic work that has been carried out in this area [12, 13]. The need for visualization is stressed and also the benefits this can bring in terms of making the evidence easier for a jury to understand. The lecture integrates a discussion with the learners as to what data should be displayed, and also the most effective way in which to do so. The learners are then introduced to Numisight, a blockchain explorer which as shown in Fig. 1 displays the transactions as a graph, and enables manipulation of different display variables. This style is then used to describe the most common patterns of transaction that are found, and the types of behavior these may represent.

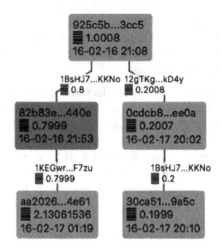

Fig. 1. Numisight blockchain explorer used to produce graphs of transactions.

Exercise. Having conducted a number of transactions of different types throughout all of the lab sessions the learners have created their own chain of address and transaction use. In this final lab session, the learners make use of this to perform the types of analysis they learnt about in the proceeding lecture, using their own transaction history. This is an important element of the courses design, and has the benefit of making it easier for the learners to identify with and understand the transactions, which is helpful considering the relative difficulty of recognizing long strings of random characters used in a lot of Bitcoins data structures.

Apply. This final tutorial provides the awareness and skills needed to effectively describe the transactions that take place within the assessment. The transaction types they have learnt about are much easier to detect visually and some of the ones described in this tutorial are very apparent in the crime scenario, such as relay and self-spending. It also makes the learners aware of the different ways in which it can be displayed allowing for the leaner to develop their own methods for presenting the evidence.

5 Delivery

The main aim and motivation of this research is to develop a clear and concise curriculum on Bitcoin that can be delivered to students and professionals alike. Typical delivery in a Higher Education Institute/Provider to a student base typically is over 6 weeks, composing of 1 h lecture, 2 h lab/tutorial and a further 3–4 h independent study with suggested reading. An optional further two weeks can be added for summative and formative feedback. Such a delivery would require that pre-requisite learning outcomes have been achieved elsewhere on the course, e.g. Encryption, and if not would extend the delivery by a further week. With this in mind it is possible to see that by the time you allow for effective formative feedback (assuming an in-course assessment is set) then this could easily extend to 12 weeks, or a term. Typical delivery to professionals is over 3 days; with a lecture and tutorial in morning (9:30–13:00) and afternoon sessions (14:00–16:30).

Reflective and Activist learning styles are important to the understanding of a subject, but often require total understanding of the fundamentals in technology-based fields, e.g. a basic understanding of Bitcoin security is required before it can be challenged. Generally, there may be exceptions, LEAF covers learning styles as follows:

- Lecture – Theoretic and Activist
- Exercise – Pragmatic and Theoretic
- Apply – Pragmatic and Theoretic
- Feedback – Activist and Reflective

In the design above some prudent managers may expect the tutorial to be squeezed into 2 days, however, this would not allow questions and answers sessions that have been designed to extend and test learners understanding at the end of each tutorial. This promotes feedback to the learner and accommodates reflective and activist learning styles.

The assessment scenario that has been developed allows for leaners to be tested in a number of formats. For undergraduates this ideally should be the production of a forensic report, which they should have had some experience of during their degree studies. The amount of material that can be developed lends itself very well to students working in teams of three or four students. However for professionals who may well been covering the material within an intensive short period this is not appropriate, and can easily be adapted to working in teams and then providing a presentation of their findings. Their existing skillset means this is likely to be achievable.

6 Conclusion

The main contribution of this paper is to satisfy the aim of a developing a clear and concise curriculum, using LEAF, for a Bitcoin tutorial. Many tutorials are difficult to get right the first time of delivery and experience is relied on during the design phase or a lack of preparation shifts the burden onto the learner and yields the statement, "the easiest way to teach leads to the hardest way to learn". Here the LEAF framework has helped get this balance correct. However, LEAF goes on to show that good preparation are related to good results, and therefore the shift of burden yields the converse of the previous statement, which is, "Easiest way to learn is the hardest way to teach".

The other major contribution this paper makes is in proposing a unique method of assessment that is strongly linked to professional practice. While hypothetical in nature it provides an environment in which learners can make use and develop their skills for a new area that is still to be defined. While the paper is not trying to develop a framework for Bitcoin investigations, it does suggest a number of approaches that may be applicable to future investigations. It also helps learners to think beyond the restrictions of what they have been taught, and this type of adaptability maybe useful if other new technologies arrive which may also bring challenges to the field of digital forensics.

At the time of writing the results for the first students to have participated in the course have just been received. Of the thirty-six students who took part, only 3 of them failed to achieve a pass grade of 40%. This represents a success rate exceeding 90% of the students and endorses the use of LEAF to help in the first delivery of a new topic for digital forensics.

References

1. Nakamoto, S.: Bitcoin: a peer-to-peer electronic cash system (2008). https://bitcoin.org/bitcoin.pdf. Accessed 25 June 2016
2. Möser, M., Böhme, R., Breuker, D.: An inquiry into money laundering tools in the Bitcoin ecosystem. In: eCrime Researchers Summit (eCRS), pp. 1–14. IEEE (2013)
3. Ron, D., Shamir, A.: Quantitative analysis of the full Bitcoin transaction graph. In: Sadeghi, A.-R. (ed.) FC 2013. LNCS, vol. 7859, pp. 6–24. Springer, Heidelberg (2013). doi:10.1007/978-3-642-39884-1_2
4. Kharraz, A., Robertson, W., Balzarotti, D., Bilge, L., Kirda, E.: Cutting the gordian knot: a look under the hood of ransomware attacks. In: Almgren, M., Gulisano, V., Maggi, F. (eds.) DIMVA 2015. LNCS, vol. 9148, pp. 3–24. Springer, Heidelberg (2015). doi:10.1007/978-3-319-20550-2_1
5. Honey, P., Mumford, A.: The Manual of Learning Styles. Peter Honey Publications, Maidenhead (1992)
6. Mitchell, I., Sheriff, M.: Lecture, exercise, apply and feedback: turning a new leaf in curriculum design. In: 18th International Conference on Software Process Improvement, Research and Education, INSPIRE 2013. The British Computer Society (2013)
7. Back, A.: Hashcash-a denial of service counter-measure (2002). http://www.hashcash.org/papers/hashcash.pdf. Accessed 25 June 2016
8. Biryukov, A., Pustogarov, I.: Bitcoin over Tor isn't a good idea. In: 2015 IEEE Symposium on Security and Privacy, pp. 122–134. IEEE (2015)
9. Androulaki, E., Karame, G.O., Roeschlin, M., Scherer, T., Capkun, S.: Evaluating user privacy in Bitcoin. In: Sadeghi, A.-R. (ed.) FC 2013. LNCS, vol. 7859, pp. 34–51. Springer, Heidelberg (2013). doi:10.1007/978-3-642-39884-1_4
10. Antonopoulos, A.M.: Mastering Bitcoin: Unlocking Digital Cryptocurrencies. O'Reilly Media Inc., Sebastopol (2014)
11. Koshy, P., Koshy, D., McDaniel, P.: An analysis of anonymity in Bitcoin using P2P network traffic. In: Christin, N., Safavi-Naini, R. (eds.) FC 2014. LNCS, vol. 8437, pp. 469–485. Springer, Heidelberg (2014). doi:10.1007/978-3-662-45472-5_30
12. Meiklejohn, S., Pomarole, M., Jordan, G., Levchenko, K., McCoy, D., Voelker, G.M., Savage, S.: A fistful of Bitcoins: characterizing payments among men with no names. In: Proceedings of the 2013 Conference on Internet Measurement Conference, pp. 127–140. ACM (2013)
13. Reid, F., Harrigan, M.: An analysis of anonymity in the Bitcoin system. In: Altshuler, Y., Elovici, Y., Cremers, A.B., Aharony, N., Pentland, A. (eds.) Security and Privacy in Social Networks, pp. 197–223. Springer, New York (2013)

Forensic Analysis of Secure Ephemeral Messaging Applications on Android Platforms

M.A. Hannan Bin Azhar$^{(\boxtimes)}$ and Thomas Edward Allen Barton

Computing, Digital Forensics and Cybersecurity,
Canterbury Christ Church University, Canterbury, UK
{hannan.azhar,tbl150}@canterbury.ac.uk

Abstract. Secure messaging applications have been used for the purposes of major crime, creating the need for forensic research into the area. This paper forensically analyses two secure messaging applications, Wickr and Telegram, to recover artefacts from and then to compare them to reveal the differences between the applications. The artefacts were created on Android platforms by using the secure features of the applications, such as ephemeral messaging, the channel function and encrypted conversations. The results of the experiments documented in this paper give insight into the organisation of the data structures by both Wickr and Telegram, as well as the exploration of mobile digital forensics techniques to recover artefacts removed by the ephemeral functions.

Keywords: Wickr · Telegram · Ephemeral data · Secure messaging application · Android · Forensic analysis · Mobile forensics

1 Introduction

Wickr and Telegram are Secure Messaging Applications (SMAs), with an estimated 1–5 and 100–500 million installs on Android Platforms respectively [1]. The popularity of SMAs, while a great tool for change and communication for many, have also seen them used for major crimes. In 2015, there was a huge spike in acts of terrorism in both European countries and around the world [2, 3]. While terror attacks are not new, some recent events have seen a new trend: the usage of social media and networking by terrorist groups, for the proliferation of their causes [4–6]. Whether used for co-ordinations, communications or recruitments, the need for forensic analysis and a greater understanding of the SMAs has never been more urgent.

The capitalization of mobile applications by markets such as Google Play [1] and the iTunes App Store [7] has driven the advent of new functionality for all applications, including SMAs. In this age of information, the demand for secure methods of communication has increased. SMAs ensure privacy of communications, which regardless of the implications, present a challenge to the digital forensic investigators because of the intentional obfuscation and removal of artefacts, which hampers investigations, often by increasing the amount of time and money invested, eventually reducing the likelihood of a successful completion [8].

This paper will forensically analyse two secure messaging applications, Wickr [9] and Telegram [10]. These applications were chosen with their features in mind.

H. Jahankhani et al. (Eds.): ICGS3 2017, CCIS 630, pp. 27–41, 2016.
DOI: 10.1007/978-3-319-51064-4_3

Both apps have an ephemeral messaging function. Ephemeral messaging is a relatively novel and popular way of social networking. Ephemeral messaging applications (EMA) use transient data, data that are permitted to exist for a limited amount of time before they become inaccessible, by obfuscation or deletion. An example of an EMA that rose to huge popularity among the eighteen to thirty-four year old age range (which happens to be statistically the largest demographic for smartphone ownership in the United States [11]) was SnapChat [12], an application that allowed users to send photos and images that would be deleted after opening. SnapChat brought EMAs into general knowledge and since then, many other applications have adopted the ephemeral feature, including SMAs.

The remainder of the paper is organised as follows: Sect. 2 describes related work, similar forensic research into various types of secure and non-secure social media applications. Section 3 covers the experimental setup used, including acquisition types, forensic tools and methods used, and the chosen Android test platforms. Sections 4 and 5 reports the experimental results, and finally Sect. 6 concludes the paper.

2   Related Work

Messaging applications on mobile platforms arose from the low-cost of mobile internet compared to individual Short Message Service (SMS) messages [13]. Internet messaging also allows for the easy transmission of multimedia messages. Adoption of security measures such as encryption and ephemeral functions came from security concerns due to hacking attacks and privacy issues [14, 15]. Mutawa et al. [16] conducted research into three popular social networking applications: Facebook, Twitter and MySpace on iOS, Android and Blackberry platforms. The applications were installed on the test platforms and scenarios were created by logging in and using their features, inputting a list of keywords that would later be used in searching for artefacts. The acquisition of data was performed by rooting the device, which was necessary as without rooting, areas of the device where some artifacts are stored cannot be accessed [16]. Wu et al. [17] investigated two ephemeral messaging applications: SnapChat and Burner on iOS and Android platforms. Physical acquisition of the platforms and subsequent analysis revealed that the transient data from SnapChat, once expired, was not securely removed, and in some cases only the filename had been changed, which lead to recovery of artefacts. Since the release of SnapChat, ephemeral messaging applications have adopted a focus on security. The latest includes applications such as Wickr and Telegram, which function as a normal messaging application, but offer a heightened focus on security.

Walnycky et al. [18] conducted investigations into a wide range of mobile messaging applications. Using the recovery and analysis of the database file for each respective app, a group of applications were analysed, including Wickr, which was identified as having no vulnerabilities, as in no artefacts were recovered due to encryption. Another investigation into Wickr carried out by Mehrotra and Mehtre [19] using a pre-analysis scenario creation method found no artefacts related to Wickr. The investigation employed a backup of the Android platform and used string searches to analyse the acquired data. The lack of results was caused by Wickr's extensive use of encryption in its data storage techniques.

Satrya et al. [20] analysed Telegram on Android devices, finding that the application uses a database to store messages, as well as other storage locations for sent and received files. The methodology used in [20] highlighted three areas of interest, including the Telegram ".apk" installer package, the internal storage directory, and the "cache4.db" database. The "cache4.db" database was SQLite formatted, and was logically acquired using a backup program before being analysed with SQLite Database Browser.

3   Experimental Setup

The investigation reported in this paper focussed on the ephemeral messaging functions on both Wickr and Telegram and also the channel feature of Telegram. As well as expanding on the research carried out by Satyra et al. [20] by incorporating Telegram's Channel, the experiments were conducted using physical data acquisition and analysis, which has not been previously carried out in the context of both applications. A variety of different forensic analysis methods were used to recover artefacts from both Wickr and Telegram. Due to the differences in the security measures taken by the applications, such as encryption, the methods and artefacts for each vary. The flow of experimental work started with the initial step of scenario creation, followed by logical analysis of data. If data examined were encrypted, then the methodology focussed on the analysis of the application itself and its ephemeral data. If plaintext data were recovered, analysis of the artefacts and ephemeral data followed. In any case, Random Access Memory (RAM) acquisition and analysis were completed to recover artefacts.

3.1   Data Acquisition

The acquisition methods used in this paper can be divided into two categories, logical and physical. Logical data acquisition in this context refers to the use of the device's filesystem to recover files. In this case, the chosen method of logical acquisition was ADB pull, a command from the Android Debug Bridge [21], a set of tools used for development and testing of Android applications.

The physical acquisition method used in this context was to create a bit-for-bit copy of the target platforms' "user" partition, which on Android stores all files related to user activity, including both application information and personal files. To create the copy, the tool Data Dump (dd) [22] was used. Other Android partitions, including the cache and the system partition were also acquired and analysed using a string search, however in this case no related artefacts were recovered, so these partitions were not included in the scope of the investigation.

In addition to the recovery of data from the Android platform's secondary storage, the Random Access Memory (RAM) of the device was also acquired. An application for android called Memory Dump [23] was used for this purpose. Memory Dump allows the user to choose an application running on the platform and acquire the memory associated with that application. This is useful in cases of encryption, as encrypted data may be stored in plaintext format in RAM when in use, for ease of access by the application.

3.2   Wickr

Wickr is a highly secure messaging application. Offering "privacy by design" [9], its simple easy to use interface hides an array of anti-forensics techniques, such as encryption of local data and network traffic [18], as well as ephemeral messaging features. In the face of such features, forensics techniques such as pre-analysis scenario creation and string searching acquired data fall down [18, 19]. Instead of recovering artefacts, the application and its effect on the Android platform, were analysed for a greater understanding in a forensic context.

The Wickr application itself is stored on the Android platform in the form of an ".apk" installer package. Inside this package is a file called "classes.dex", which is a file containing all the definitions for the functions of the application. To extract the "classes.dex" file, the ".apk" was opened using the archive extraction utility in Windows, and the file was extracted. To analyse the file, it was converted to a Java archive. A specialised tool exists for this purpose, called "dex2jar" [24]. The output from this tool is a Java archive that was analysed using another tool, Java Decompiler [25]. When analysed, the file revealed all the class definitions for Wickr, which gives an insight into how it operates.

To analyse the files associated with Wickr, the application's data directory ("/data/data/com.mywickr.wickr2") was logically acquired. To find out how the ephemeral data function works in Wickr, the data directory was acquired multiple times at different stages of the test scenario. These were: before messages were received, after messages had been received, after messages had been removed by the ephemeral function and after the "secure shredder" had been run. The "secure shredder" offers the shredding of deleted data. The various acquired versions of the directories were analysed and compared to look for any changes in files as well as the size of Wickr's database "wickr_db".

The physically acquired image was analysed in Autopsy 3.0.8 [26]. Autopsy is the graphical frontend for a set of Linux forensics tools called the Sleuthkit. This contains tools that allow for the recovery of deleted data. Autopsy also allows for the processing of unallocated space, which is an important part of the analysis as ephemeral messaging functions rely on the deletion of data. Artefacts such as files sent as attachments to messages that had been deleted via the ephemeral messaging function were recovered using Autopsy.

3.3   Telegram

Telegram is a feature-rich messaging application that also incorporates security into its operation, by adding end-to-end encryption as well as ephemeral messaging. Telegram offers a unique way of communication called the channel feature. Introduced in 2015 with the version 3.2.1 [27], this feature allows any user to start a channel which can either be public or private. Any other Telegram user can locate public channels using the search function, whereas private channel rely on an invite-only URL based system. Once the channel is established, owners and admins broadcast material to all subscribers. Telegram's channel feature was used by an active terrorist organisation to disseminate propaganda [28], which highlights the potential for the features use in major crime, and creates the need for forensic analysis.

The work carried out by Satrya et al. [20] established methods of recovering messages sent via Telegram, recovering artefacts by logically acquiring the "cache4.db" database file from the platform, which was analysed using SQLite Database Browser [29]. In our work, the channel feature was analysed using this methodology to reveal additional artefacts related to channels. In addition to this, artefacts related to the ephemeral messaging function were recovered by analysing the physically acquired image using Autopsy, as mentioned in Sect. 3.2.

To locate where remnant channel messages may be stored on the test platform, the filesystem clusters of the "cache4.db" database had to be identified. As Android uses a UNIX-like filesystem, EXT4, this information is stored in a meta-structure known as an "inode". After identifying the "inode" of the "cache4.db" database by mounting the physically acquired image and using the "ls" command, the tool "istat" from the Sleuthkit [26] was used to identify filesystem clusters. The tool "istat" was used to print out the "inode" statistics from the physically acquired image for examination of data. The output of "istat" can be seen in Fig. 1 - under "Direct Blocks", importantly, the clusters on which the file was stored can be seen.

```
inode: 593
Allocated
Group: 0
Generation Id: 4090733212
uid / gid: 10177 / 10177
mode: rrw-------
Flags: No A-Time, Extents,
size: 1191936
num of links: 1

Inode Times:
Accessed:       2016-07-06 16:15:12.522272844 (BST)
File Modified:  2016-07-10 16:46:41.755999914 (BST)
Inode Modified: 2016-07-10 16:46:41.755999914 (BST)
File Created:   2016-07-06 16:15:12.522272844 (BST)

Direct Blocks:
79465 79466 79467 619627 80752 80753 617905 617908
617911 617914 617917 617920 617923 80757 80758 619632
67024 67025 67026 67027 67028 67029 67030 67031
67032 67033 67034 67035 67036 67037 67038 67039
67872 67873 67874 67875 67876 67877 67878 67879
```

Fig. 1. Output of the "istat" command for Telegram's "cache4.db" database.

To examine the clusters, the physically acquired image was opened in the hex editor WinHex [30]. To locate the data from the list of clusters, a simple calculation [31] was made to find the byte offset of the clusters:

$$B = C * SpC * S \tag{1}$$

Where B is the byte offset in bytes, C is the cluster number, SpC is the sectors per cluster and S is the sector size in bytes. In the case of the test platform, the SpC was 8 and S was 512, so the calculation was performed as per the chosen cluster. A specific add-on for Telegram, offered by Oxygen Forensic Suite 2014 [32], was used to recover encrypted messages. Oxygen Forensic Suite 2014 also provides a file browser for viewing and recovering files stored as attachments, however, Oxygen Forensic Suite 2014 is limited to active files, i.e. files that have not been deleted [33]. Later versions (2015 onwards) do support recovery of deleted files [32]; however, in this case, Autopsy 3.0.8 was used.

3.4 Linux Utilities

When examining data on a Linux forensic workstation, basic file utilities, such as "ls", "cat", "strings" and "grep" were used to examine directory structures and files. The tool "strings" extracts all string format data from a file. A bash script was created to perform string searches on the output of the strings utility. The script is shown in Fig. 2. The first part of the script's command, cat, sends the saved "strings" output to the second part, grep, which searches for matches to a keyword dictionary, and saves the results to a new file. This technique was used to search the physically acquired images for keywords relating to the respective application, as well as the live memory acquisition files.

```
#!/bin/bash

for ITEM in $(cat item_list.txt)
do

cat /media/xubuntu/7AEF-B34E/MEMDUMP/memdump_strings.txt | grep $ITEM > ~/searchresults/memdump_strings_$ITEM.txt

done
```

Fig. 2. String search bash script.

3.5 Platforms

A Samsung Galaxy S4 Mini [34] was the primary platform used for the experimental setup. An AllWinner A13 Android tablet [35] was used as an alternate platform in order to ensure the repeatability of all experiments performed, as well as sending and receiving messages to and from the test platform. The choice of test platform in this case, a phone from Samsung's flagship galaxy range, reflects the current state of the worldwide smartphone market, which is dominated by Android [36], the market for which is in turn dominated by Samsung [36]. Another reason for choosing Android was its large online developer community, which stems from its open source status.

The applications were both installed on the platform using Android's built-in app store, Google Play [1]. The test platforms and the application versions used are listed in Table 1.

Table 1. Android platforms and application versions.

Name	Specifications				
	Model number	Android version	Kernel version	Wickr version	Telegram version
Samsung Galaxy S4 Mini [34]	GT-I9195I	4.4.4 (KitKat)	3.10.28-5334500	2.6.4.1	3.10.1
AllWinner A13 [35]	Q8	4.4.2 (KitKat)	3.4.39	2.6.4.1	N/A

Once the applications were installed on the test platform, scenarios were created by creating accounts on the respective applications and using the features, to simulate a suspect's device. As the apps differ in their features somewhat, the artefacts creation procedure also slightly differed. To test both the regular and ephemeral messaging functions, messages were sent with identifiable text, as well as attachments, to the test platform. For Wickr, these messages simulated a conversation which included an attachment, a picture (.jpg) file, as well as some key words.

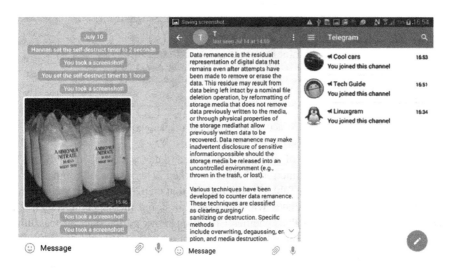

Fig. 3. Established scenario on Telegram.

For Telegram, the scenario creation involved both the creation of, and subscription to channels. In addition to creating custom channels, a number of public channels were subscribed to also, which meant that the messages received via these channels were included in the list of potential artefacts. Unlike Wickr, in Telegram's scenario more messages were required to utilise the channel function. For this purpose, bulk text was copied from the internet, as seen in Fig. 3. The range of artefacts recovered from both standard conversations and channels included message text, files (images and documents) and usernames. Due to the inclusion of channel function in Telegram, the number of artefacts incorporated in the analysis was more than Wickr's.

4 Results for Wickr

Analysis of the installer package for Wickr revealed the techniques it uses to store data. When applications store data in databases, they sometimes use a programming object called a "Database Helper". In Wickr's case, the class of functions called "WickrDBAdapter.class" reveals the use of "SqlCipher", a database encryption library for SQLite. The use of such a library explains why any messages received by Wickr were not stored in plain text. An extract from the "WickrDBAdapter.class" is shown in Fig. 4.

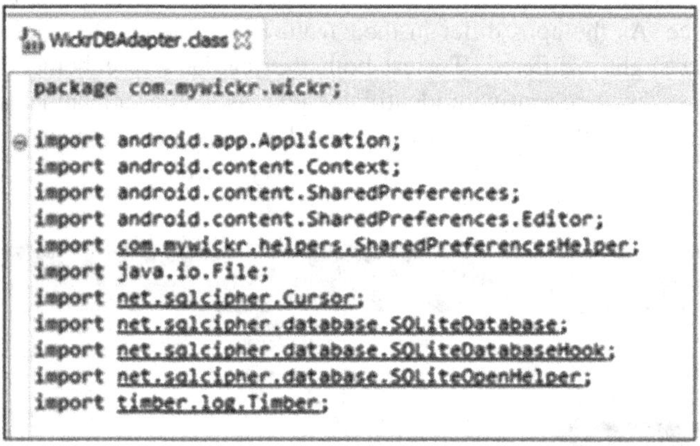

```
WickrDBAdapter.class

package com.mywickr.wickr;

import android.app.Application;
import android.content.Context;
import android.content.SharedPreferences;
import android.content.SharedPreferences.Editor;
import com.mywickr.helpers.SharedPreferencesHelper;
import java.io.File;
import net.sqlcipher.Cursor;
import net.sqlcipher.database.SQLiteDatabase;
import net.sqlcipher.database.SQLiteDatabaseHook;
import net.sqlcipher.database.SQLiteOpenHelper;
import timber.log.Timber;
```

Fig. 4. Extract from "WickrDBAdapter.class".

Acquisition and analysis of Wickr's associated data as described in Sect. 3.2 revealed how the ephemeral function of Wickr worked. The results of comparison of the acquired data are shown in Table 2, which show that on a logical level, the presence of encrypted ".wic" files correlates with the status of stored messages in Wickr. The results in Table 2 reveal that the ephemeral function removed the data, at least logically. The process of the ephemeral function caused the start of file decay: firstly the files were logically deleted.

The proposed operation of Wickr's file decay is shown in Table 3, which demonstrates the varying levels of file storage and deletion in Wickr at the stages listed in Table 2. As the results of Table 2 rely on logical acquisition, analysis of the physically acquired images of the Android platform was required to further investigate the deletion process and recover deleted artefacts. Navigating to the Wickr data directory on the physically acquired image using Autopsy revealed filesystem references to previously present ".wic" files. A screenshot of this is shown in Fig. 5.

Table 2. Wickr data analysis results.

Stage of file removal (arbitrary)	Secure shredder status	Copy taken	Files directory and further observations
1	Before	Before images were received	Only two ".wic" files, "pcc.wic" and "pcd. wic" were present in the files directory
2	Before	After images were received	Two ".wic" files, each with 64 character string file names, were present in the files directory. Their sizes were 47488 and 54136 bytes respectively
3	Before	After images were removed	Two ".wic" files were not present
4	After	After images were removed	Two ".wic" files were not present

Table 3. Model of Wickr's file decay.

Stage of file removal (arbitrary)	1	2	3	4
Status of received file	N/A	File present, encrypted, stored in.wic file	File present, encrypted, filesystem header removed	File overwritten with random or null data
Process required to recover file	N/A	Logical level acquisition, for example copy	Low level acquisition, such as device data dump or chip-off analysis	File unrecoverable

Finally, analysis of the RAM dump acquired using the method described in Sect. 3.1 revealed that, much like the other areas of storage, Wickr does not expose much data and analysis found very few artefacts. Using the string search method described in Sect. 3.4, the dumped RAM data was analysed. The results are

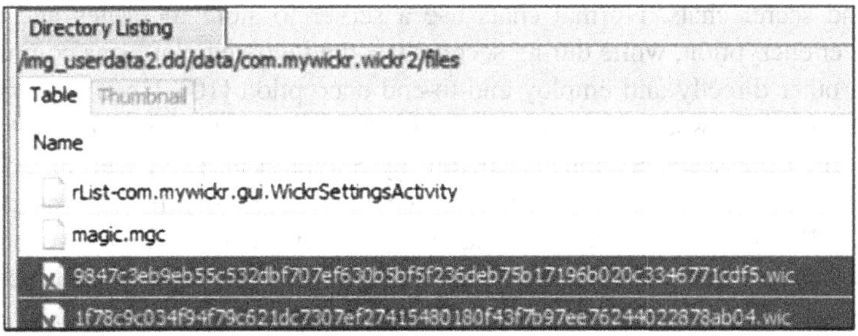

Fig. 5. Files subdirectory of Wickr's data directory in Autopsy.

shown in Table 4. Any field within the "< ... >" parenthesis represents information which was omitted for privacy purposes.

Table 4. Results of Wickr's RAM dump string search.

Search expression	Reason	Results
Wickr	Name of the App	Returned paths of files in the data directory of Wickr, as well as extracts from various core Wickr libraries
\<Hidden\>	Password used to register Wickr account	No matches
cccumobilef	Username used to register Wickr account	Matching String found in *dumped__7428b000-7428e000_rw-p* dump file
Ocelotorus	Username of account used in scenario	No matches
an.jpg	Filename of picture uploaded – file extension added because "an" too ambiguous	No matches
Invicta	See above	No matches
Goods	Excerpts from messages sent in pre-analysis scenario creation	No pertinent matches
Yes	See above	No pertinent matches
Meet	See above	No pertinent matches

The results in Table 4 show that Wickr does not store information such as received messages in plaintext in RAM. However, a single artefact, the name of the account used to sign up to Wickr, was found. The account name could be used in co-operation with Wickr and telecom services to locate the user that signed up using the captured device. This artefact was not reported in the work carried out previously by Walnycky et al. [18] and Mehrotra and Mehtre [19], which used searching of Wickr's stored data.

5   Results for Telegram

The standard messaging capabilities of Telegram are divided into two separate features: normal and secret chats. Normal chats use a server to store messages and employ client-server encryption, while during secret chats the involved platforms communicate with each other directly and employ end-to-end encryption [10]. Upon analysis using SQLite Database Browser, the messages received via channels were stored in the same way as normal messages, established before by Satyra et al. [20], with an additional artefact, the link to join a private channel. In the database, these artefacts was identified using the UID column, which was unique to the conversation. Figure 6 shows the suspect channel, "test channel (create)", identified in the chats table of the "cache4.db" database. The UID was captured from the selected entry as shown in Fig. 6. Records were retrieved from the messages table using this UID. The status of the out column in the messages table identifies the suspect's platform as being an owner or admin of the suspect channel, as the value of "1" in the out column shown in Fig. 6 denotes the messages were sent. Corresponding entries in the chat settings table revealed the private URL which was used to join the channel, as seen in Fig. 7.

Table:	chats		
	uid	name	data
	Filter	Filter	Filter
9	1051999595	gadget	BLOB
10	1052277223	test channel (create)	BLOB
11	1061775389	test channel (subscribe)	BLOB
12	1067317571	tech guide	BLOB

	mid	uid	read_state	send_state	date	data	out
	Filter	1052277223 ✕	Filter	Filter	Filter	Filter	Filter
1	4519496259110€	-1052277223	3	0	1468495449	BLOB	1
2	4519496259110€	-1052277223	2	0	1468495584	BLOB	1
3	4519496259110€	-1052277223	2	0	1468495648	BLOB	1
4	4519496259110€	-1052277223	2	0	1468495700	BLOB	1
5	4519496259110€	-1052277223	2	0	1468497935	BLOB	1

Fig. 6. Suspect channel in Chats Table of Telegram's "cache4.db" database.

In a real world scenario, it is possible that channels are un-followed or other anti-forensics measures are taken preceding the capture of the target platform. In order to examine messages left over from un-followed or deleted channels, the "cache4.db" file was examined on the imaged physical user partition. Using WinHex to examine the data at the byte with the technique mentioned in Sect. 3.3 revealed artefacts from the public Telegram channels subscribed to during the scenario creation. These messages remained in the "cache4.db" database even though the channel had been unfollowed

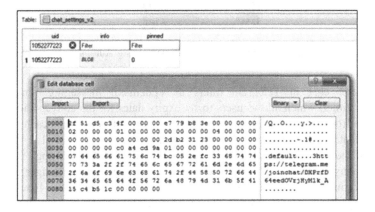

Fig. 7. Retrieval of channel join link in Telegram's "cache4.db" database.

telegram_final_image.dd

Offset	0	1	2	3	4	5	6	7	8	9	10	11	12	13	14	15	
0274431264	53	04	00	00	00	77	40	26	19	00	00	00	00	17	8C	01	S w@& Œ
0274431280	00	7E	A8	F9	DC	8A	4F	8D	F5	20	03	00	00	8F	01	00	~¨ùÜŠO õ
0274431296	00	3E	03	01	00	15	C4	B5	1C	01	00	00	00	38	25	D0	> Äµ 8%Ð
0274431312	6E	34	00	00	00	55	00	00	00	3C	0A	00	00	00	00	00	n4 U <
0274431328	00	85	14	9E	B8	8F	F5	80	80	80	82	71	07	00	04	04	… ž¸ õ€€€‚q
0274431344	01	8A	14	C3	1F	80	B0	57	65	93	DF	03	5F	E4	9B	C0	Š Ã €°We“ß _ä›À
0274431360	A0	46	00	00	71	02	00	00	32	E5	DD	BD	50	7F	E0	3C	F q 2åÝ½P à<
0274431376	DF	93	65	57	4C	48	6F	77	20	74	6F	20	44	6F	77	6E	ß“eWLHow to Down
0274431392	67	72	61	64	65	20	69	4F	53	20	31	30	20	42	65	74	grade iOS 10 Bet
0274431408	61	20	74	6F	20	69	4F	53	20	39	20	77	69	74	68	6F	a to iOS 9 witho

Fig. 8. Messages from unfollowed channel.

and was no longer accessible via the normal interface. Figure 8 shows a message viewed in WinHex at byte offset 274431264. Files received via channels were stored in the "Telegram" directory on the internal storage, which has the absolute path of "/data/media/0/Telegram/" [20]. Upon unfollowing of channels, the files received from these channels are still present, lacking signs of deletion.

Table | Thumbnail

Name	Size	Flags(Dir)	Flags(Meta)	Mode	UserID
222829946_118819.jpg	2227	Allocated	Allocated	rrw-rw-r--	1023
222833375_116547.jpg	1847	Allocated	Allocated	rrw-rw-r--	1023
1052861977929449485_1299364215.jpg	52608	Unallocated	Allocated	rrw-rw-r--	1023
425312815_1902.jpg	1792	Allocated	Allocated	rrw-rw-r--	1023
q_-2147483648_-210019.jpg	0	Unallocated		rrw-------	10177

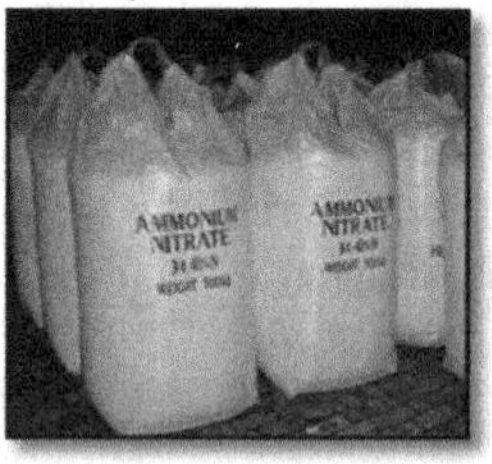

Fig. 9. Recovery of expired image using Autopsy.

The secret chat in Telegram offers an ephemeral messaging function, the self-destruct timer, which allows users to set expiry dates for the conversation. Before the message from the test scenario expired, examination of Telegram's cache directory located at "/data/media/0/Android/data/org.telegram.messenger/cache" [17] showed the presence of the file, stored as "1052861977929449485_1299364215.jpg", as well as few accompanying thumbnails. Upon expiry, the message was no longer accessible from the normal interface, and was no longer present in the cache. However, this expired image file was recovered in the cache directory on the physical image when Autopsy's file browser tool was used, as shown in Fig. 9. It was found that in this case, the file system entry was removed after the expiry; however, the file was still present in the device. These findings reveal that Telegram uses a logical deletion process to handle ephemeral message attachments, allowing for the recovery of expired multimedia messages using physical acquisition and examination of the captured device.

Table 5. Results of Telegram's RAM analysis.

Search expression	Reason	Results
<First name>	First name used to create Telegram account, potentially identifying artefact	Matching string found in dumped__78ea2000-78fd7000_rw-p and dumped__7a993000-7a99c000_rw-p dump files
<Second name>	Surname name used to create Telegram account, potentially identifying artefact	Matching string found in dumped__78ea2000-78fd7000_rw-p and dumped__7a993000-7a99c000_rw-p dump files
<Phone number>	Phone number used to sign up to Telegram account, potentially identifying artefact	No matches found
+44	National mobile telephony prefix	A number of matches related to Graphical User Interface (GUI), but no identifying artefacts
Magnetic	Excerpts from messages sent in pre-analysis scenario creation	A number of matching strings found in dumped__77cb0000-77cb9000_rw-p dump file, among others
Overwrite	See above	A number of matching strings found in dumped__77cb0000-77cb9000_rw-p dump file, among others

Table 5 reports the results of Telegram's RAM analysis which was acquired using the method described in Sect. 3.1 and analysed using the string search method described in Sect. 3.4. Results revealed the recovery of many plaintext artefacts. Fields within the "< ... >" parenthesis represents confidential information which was omitted due to privacy purposes.

6 Conclusions

The experiments in this paper provided understanding of the manner in which secure messaging applications like Wickr and Telegrams store their data. Results revealed that the Wickr stored it's received messages in encrypted ".wic" files in the data directory. While the messages did cause the production of ".wic" files, they did not affect the size of the application's database. Unlike Wickr, in the case of Telegram, the standard forensics tools had built-in modules to recover encrypted artefacts. Our analyses documented these artefacts in greater detail, including information relating to the joining of channels, and the recovery of messages after the channels had been unfollowed. The RAM dump technique for Wickr recovered a plaintext account username, which was valid only in the context of live analysis where the phone had not been turned off since being captured. Like Wickr, The RAM dump was also successful in recovering Telegram's plaintext artifacts, which shows the integrity of this method in analysing similar applications. The direction of future research will focus on the decryption techniques and also the application of proposed methods in analysing similar SMAs on other popular platforms such as iOS and Windows Phones.

References

1. Google Play. https://play.google.com/store?hl=en_GB. Accessed Sept 2016
2. Almasy, S., Meilhan P., Bittermann, J.: Paris massacre: at least 128 killed in gunfire and blasts, French officials say (2015). http://edition.cnn.com/2015/11/13/world/paris-shooting/. Accessed Sept 2016
3. Madi, M., Ryder, S., Macfarlane, J., Beach, A., Park, V.: As it happened: Charlie Hebdo attack (2016). http://www.bbc.co.uk/news/live/world-europe-30710777. Accessed Sept 2016
4. Roussinous, A.: The social media Accounts of British Jihadis in Syria just got a lot more distressing (2014). http://www.vice.com/en_uk/read/british-jihadis-beheading-prisoners-syria-isis-terrorism. Accessed Sept 2016
5. Torok, R.: (2015). http://theconversation.com/how-social-media-was-key-to-islamic-states-attacks-on-paris-50743. Accessed 20 July 2016
6. Vidino, L., Hughes, S.: ISIS in America: from retweets to Raqqa (2015). http://www.stratcomcoe.org/download/file/fid/2828. Accessed Sept 2016
7. Apple App Store. http://www.apple.com/uk/itunes/. Accessed Sept 2016
8. Perklin, M.: (2012). https://www.defcon.org/images/defcon-20/dc-20-presentations/Perklin/DEFCON-20-Perklin-AntiForensics.pdf
9. Wickr Official Website. https://www.wickr.com. Accessed Sept 2016
10. Telegram Official Website. https://telegram.org. Accessed Sept 2016
11. Anderson, M.: The demographics of device ownership (2015). http://www.pewinternet.org/2015/10/29/the-demographics-of-device-ownership/. Accessed Sept 2016
12. SnapChat (2014). http://mwpartners.com/snapchat-is-now-the-third-most-popular-social-network-among-millennials/. Accessed Sept 2016
13. Barot, T., Oren, E.: Guide to Chat Apps (2015). http://towcenter.org/research/guide-to-chat-apps/. Accessed Sept 2016
14. Amir, W.: Viber to Put Full End-to-End Encryption on Their Messaging App (2016). https://www.hackread.com/viber-end-to-end-encryption-on-messaging-app/. Accessed Sept 2016
15. Mathur, N.: Facebook Messenger joins WhatApp in end-to-end encryption (2016). http://www.livemint.com/Consumer/lllJ9Est0ZZIYfmvRSsTZP/Facebook-Messenger-joins-WhatsApp-in-endtoend-encryption.html. Accessed Sept 2016
16. Mutawa, N.A., Baggili, I., Marrington, A.: Forensic analysis of social networking applications on mobile devices. Digit. Invest. **9**, 24–33 (2012)
17. Wu, C., Vance, C., Boggs, R., Fenger, T.: Forensic Analysis of Data Transience Applications in iOS and Android (2013). http://www.marshall.edu/forensics/files/Wu-Poster.pdf. Accessed Sept 2016

18. Walnycky, D., Baggili, I., Marrington, A., Moore, J., Breitinger, F.: Network and device forensic analysis of Android social-messaging applications. Digit. Invest. **14**, 77–84 (2015)
19. Mehrotra, T., Mehtre, B.M.: Forensic analysis of Wickr application on android devices. IEEE International Conference on Computing Intelligence and Computing Research, pp. 1–6 (2013)
20. Satrya, G.B., Daely, P.T., Nugroho, M.A.: Digital forensic analysis of Telegram Messenger on Android devices. In: 10th International Conference on Information and Communication Technology and System, Indonesia (2016)
21. ADB tool. https://developer.android.com/studio/command-line/adb.html. Accessed Sept 2016
22. Linux Man Page. http://linux.die.net/man/1/dd. Accessed Sept 2016
23. Memory Dump. https://play.google.com/store/apps/details?id=com.cert.memdump&hl=en. Accessed Sept 2016
24. Dex2Jar tool. https://github.com/pxb1988/dex2jar. Accessed Sept 2016
25. Java Decompiler tool. http://jd.benow.ca. Accessed Sept 2016
26. SleuthKit tool. http://www.sleuthkit.org. Accessed Sept 2016
27. Telegram Channel (2015). https://telegram.org/blog/channels. Accessed Sept 2016
28. Cuthbertson, A.: (2015). http://www.ibtimes.co.uk/isis-telegram-channel-doubles-followers-9000-less-1-week-1523665. Accessed Sept 2016
29. DB Browser for SQLite Official Website. http://sqlitebroswer.org. Accessed Sept 2016
30. X-Ways Forensics: WinHex. https://www.x-ways.net/winhex/index-m.html. Accessed Sept 2016
31. Sedory, D.B.: Drive Offset and Sector Conversions (2012). http://thestarman.pcministry.com/asm/mbr/DriveOffsets.htm. Accessed Sept 2016
32. Oxygen Forensics Official Website. http://www.oxygen-forensic.com. Accessed Sept 2016
33. Shortall, A., Azhar, M.A.H.B.: Forensic acquisitions of WhatsApp data on popular mobile platforms. In: Sixth International Conference on Emerging Security Technologies (EST), pp. 13–17. IEEE Press, Technische Universitaet Braunschweig, Germany (2015)
34. Samsung Galaxy Mini Official Web Page. http://www.samsung.com/uk/consumer/mobile-devices/smartphones/galaxy-s/GT-I9195ZKABTU. Accessed Sept 2016
35. Allwinner A13 User Manual. http://linux-sunxi.org/A13. Accessed Sept 2016
36. Woods, V., Meulen, R.V.D.: Gartner Says Worldwide Smartphone Sales Grew 3.9 Percent in First Quarter of 2016 (2016). http://www.gartner.com/newsroom/id/3323017. Accessed Sept 2016

Digital Evidence: Disclosure and Admissibility in the United Kingdom Jurisdiction

Reza Montasari[✉]

Department of Computing and Mathematics, University of Derby, Derby, UK
r.montasari@derby.ac.uk

Abstract. Digital forensics, originally known as computer forensics, first presented itself in the 1970s. During the first investigations, financial fraud proved to be the most common cause on suspects' computers. Since then, digital forensics has grown in importance in situations where digital devices are used in the commission of a crime. The original focus of digital forensic investigations was on crimes committed through computers. However, over the past few years, the field has extended to include various other digital devices in which digitally stored information can be processed and used for different types of crimes. This paper explores how the admissibility of digital evidence is governed within the United Kingdom jurisdictions.

Keywords: Digital forensics · Digital evidence · Admissibility · Disclosure · Digital investigation · U.K. jurisdiction

1 Introduction

Digital forensics, originally known as computer forensics, first presented itself in the 1970s [1]. During the first investigations, financial fraud proved to be the most common cause on suspects' computers [2]. Since then, digital forensics has grown in importance in situations where digital devices are used in the commission of a crime [3]. The original focus of digital forensic investigations was on crimes committed through computers [4]. However, over the past few years, the field has extended to include various other digital devices in which digitally stored information can be processed and used for different types of crimes [5]. Palmer defines digital forensics as,

> *The use of scientifically derived and proven methods towards the preservation, collection, validation, identification, analysis, interpretation, documentation and presentation of digital evidence derived from digital sources for the purpose of facilitating or furthering the reconstruction of events found to be criminal, or helping to anticipate unauthorised actions shown to be disruptive to planned operations [6].*

This definition is widely accepted within the digital forensic community [2, 4, 7, 8] and is therefore adopted within this paper. A digital forensic investigation (DFI) is the process of linking extracted information and digital evidence in order to establish factual information for review by the judiciary [4, 9]. Cohen [10] highlights the need to establish factual information as the outcome of such an investigation. A DFI is carried out as an investigation after the occurrence of an incident [11, 12]. It is therefore a

© Springer International Publishing AG 2016
H. Jahankhani et al. (Eds.): ICGS3 2017, CCIS 630, pp. 42–52, 2016.
DOI: 10.1007/978-3-319-51064-4_4

distinct type of investigation "where the scientific procedures and techniques used will allow the results, in other words digital evidence, to be admissible in a court of law" [13]. Due to the fact that digital evidence is contained in a digital device and cannot be observed by the naked eye, forensic tools such as Encase [14] and FTK [15] are used to extract and examine data representing potential digital evidence. The extent of the value of the digital evidence is based not only on the extent to which a tool is trusted [16, 17], but also on the competence and experience of the investigator carrying out the digital investigation [18, 19].

There are four basic principles of DFIs which must be considered. These are auditability, repeatability, reproducibility and justifiability. Auditability refers to the need for an independent investigator to be able to evaluate the activities performed by other investigators to determine whether or not a suitable scientific method was followed [20]. Repeatability requires one investigator to be able to arrive at the same conclusion as another under similar conditions [8, 21]. Reproducibility is established when the same test results are produced using the same method, but with different instruments and under different conditions, and can be reproduced at any time after the original test [18]. Justifiability refers to an investigator being able to justify all the actions and methods they used during the course of a digital investigation [18]. A DFI is often initiated in order to ascertain certain facts after an incident has occurred. It must be conducted in such a methodical manner that it can withstand scrutiny by the court and defence team [4]. There exist various types of DFIs, including live forensics, static forensics, proactive forensics and cloud forensics [22, 23]. The fundamental point of any DFI is to answer 'what', 'why', 'how', 'who', 'where' and 'when' type questions in relation to the data analysis and evidence in order to confirm or refute allegations of suspicious activity [9, 24]. 'What' refers to the data attributes or metadata, 'why,' the motivation [25], 'how,' the manner in which the incident was initiated or the way in which the necessary evidence was isolated [23], 'who,' the people involved [26], 'where,' the location of the potential digital evidence [4] and 'when,' the time of occurrence [27].

The remainder of this paper focuses only on the question of "how", which must be addressed by the steps of the investigative process undertaken to acquire digital evidence in a forensically sound manner.

2 Background to Digital Evidence

Nowadays, almost all transactions from the commercial world, government and private individuals exist only in digital form [4, 28, 29]. In such cases it is only through digital evidence that one can demonstrate that something did or did not happen [22, 30]. Digital footprints of individuals' activities are left in the digital world, from which their actions and intentions can be deduced [29]. Digital evidence is the product of the digital forensics process [10, 30, 31] and can be extracted from various sources, including digital devices (such as desktop and laptop computers, thumb drives, mobile devices, digital cameras and tablets), network servers (such as supporting applications including Web sites, e-mail and social networks) and network hardware (such as routers) [4, 32, 33]. "Forensics" refers to the application of scientific evidence in courts of law, where judges play a vital role as gatekeepers in deciding what evidence is and is not admissible [10, 30, 31, 34, 35]. Authors in [4, 6] argue that while the actual mechanics of digital forensics are different from the better-known physical and medical forensics, the processes of all forensic sciences are fundamentally the same. Each phase in the process must be performed in such a way that the integrity of the evidence is preserved and its admissibility assured. Digital evidence can be employed in many types of criminal investigations, such as homicide, sex offences, missing persons, child abuse, drugs, fraud and theft of personal information [4]. Digital evidence can show how a crime was perpetrated, provide investigative leads, prove or refute witness statements and identify potential suspects. Various similar definitions of digital evidence have been proposed in the literature [12, 36, 37]. However, for the purposes of this paper, the following definition given by Casey [4], which is widely accepted within the digital forensic community, is used:

> any data stored or transmitted using a computer that support or refute a theory of how an offense occurred or that address critical elements of the offense such as intent or alibi.

The term "computer" in the above definition can be replaced with 'digital device' to cover various types of devices, such as computers, laptop computers, tablets and smart mobile devices. Data in Casey's [4] definition of digital evidence essentially refers to numbers that represent information of various types such as text, images, audio and video. A simple computer file can contain incriminating information and have corresponding properties that are useful in an investigation. For instance, details such as when a file was created, who may have created it, or that it was created on another computer, can all be essential. Notwithstanding its pervasiveness, few people are well-acquainted with the evidential, technical and legal issues associated with digital evidence. Consequently, digital evidence is often disregarded, acquired incorrectly or examined and analysed ineffectively. Digital evidence is often challenged in court because of the ease with which it can be altered, which is due to poor handling. The manner in which searches of digital evidence are authorised and carried out, the way in which it is handled, received and rejected, and the various legal issues associated with digital evidence, all differ from one jurisdiction to another. The topic of digital evidence explored in this paper focuses on the United Kingdom jurisdiction, occasionally incorporating the United States jurisdiction for the purposes of comparison.

3 Background to Digital Evidence

Digital evidence is increasing in both size and significance in criminal and civil trials [4, 10, 30–32, 38–40]. It is latent in the same way as a fingerprint or DNA sample [19]. However, digital evidence is more complex and volatile as it can be accidently or improperly modified, damaged or destroyed during the investigative process [41–45]. Due to its fragility, courts pay close attention to the process in which the digital evidence was acquired and stored [30]. Investigators' methods in carrying out digital investigations are often scrutinised by the courts [7, 46]. Therefore, to be admissible in court, digital evidence must have all the characteristics of other types of scientific and technical evidence and fulfil the standards associated with them [4, 30]. However, electronic-based evidence presents far greater challenges, both for the courts and in relation to the procedures [29, 30]. The manner in which it is extracted plays a significant role in weighing the probative and prejudicial value of the evidence when presented in court [10, 31, 35, 47]. To withstand the stringent admissibility requirements, the evidence produced by law enforcement agencies must be robust. Evidence presented in court can be "real", "documentary", "technical", "expert" and "derived" and must satisfy two criteria of "admissibility" and "weight" [29]. To be admissible, it must fulfil legal acceptability tests. This is a function of jurisdiction which derives from English common law rather than European civil codes. The following three sections discuss the practices carried out by courts in relation to the admissibility of digital evidence. Emphasis is placed on the U.K. courts, but comparisons are also made with the U.S. jurisdiction.

3.1 Challenges Facing Judiciary

Judges play a vital role in protecting the legal system from the impacts of flawed evidence [10]. Just as judges need to remove "junk science" from the courtroom, so they need to keep out poor-quality digital evidence [10, 31]. They play the role of gatekeeper, determining what evidence is and is not admissible in their courtrooms [10, 30, 31, 34, 35]. Judges weigh the evidentiary value against the prejudicial effect of any evidence produced [10, 31]. However, their role has various subtleties and complications. One of the greatest challenges facing both judges and juries (lay audiences) is their lack of proper understanding of digital technology. Kessler [30] states that for a judge to be able to fairly assess the merits of digital evidence, they need to have some understanding of basic ICTs and the applications from which digital evidence is extracted [30]. Other researchers have raised this issue, arguing that a lack of familiarity with digital technology and the subsequent detrimental effect on court cases might indicate the necessity for "new laws of evidence" or "specialist judges" [5, 48].

As there has been no such initiative to date, such a lack of appreciation could prevent judges from critically assessing the evidence submitted to them [49]. There is currently no study in the literature in relation to judges' perceived knowledge of digital evidence within the U.K. jurisdiction [30, 49–51]. This must be considered an imperative subject area for future research. Technical terms have also proved challenging for judges and juries. For instance, the forensic copy of an evidentiary medium was previously called a "mirror image" [52]. Whilst researchers in the field of computer science understand this terminology, it has been misinterpreted by "lay audiences" to denote a reverse copy, as mirrors reflect an opposite image [30, 32]. To remove such confusion, the process is now called a bit-by-bit forensic copy [4].

3.2 United States Jurisdiction

As with any evidence, the proponent of digital evidence has to lay an appropriate foundation in relation to its reliability [53]. Various practices are carried out across different jurisdictions in terms of laying such a proper foundation. In the United States, the admission in a federal court of scientific evidence (including digital evidence) is governed by the Federal Rules of Evidence (FRE) [29, 54]. These rules require the trial judge to act as a gatekeeper, determining, prior to its admission, whether the evidence is scientifically valid and relevant to the case [30]. Across the U.S. federal courts, judges employ the Daubert Test [55] in order to determine the admissibility of the scientific or technical evidence. The Daubert Test includes the following five assessments [55]:

(1) whether the theory or technique in question can be and has been tested;
(2) whether it has been subjected to peer review and publication;
(3) its known or potential error rate;
(4) the existence and maintenance of standards controlling its operation; and
(5) whether it has attracted widespread acceptance within a relevant scientific community.

Using the Daubert Test, a judge can objectively determine the reliability of any digital evidence presented in the courts. The Kumho Tire v. Carmichael [56] decision extended the Daubert guidelines to any form of technical evidence. In addition, FRE Rule 702 provides guidelines for qualifying expert witnesses and minimizing adversarial bias in expert testimony [54]. The Rule 702 requirement for reliability may work against its design to balance "the imperatives of maintaining an adversarial system and mitigating bias" [30]. In particular, Rule 702 can be employed to prevent the admission of an expert's assumptions, which a judge might otherwise find useful, as assumptions cannot be considered to be reliable [57]. In conclusion, the Daubert Test and Rule 702 are employed in the U.S. courts to determine the admissibility of digital evidence as well as any other types of scientific and technical evidence [30, 58–60].

3.3   United States Jurisdiction

In the United Kingdom, judges can exercise their discretion within the boundaries of U.K. law (discussed in this section) to dismiss evidence that has been acquired unfairly. In many cases, digital evidence is ruled inadmissible in the U.K. courts if it has not met certain conditions (also discussed in this section). The concept of admissibility requires courts to establish whether evidence is "safe" to place before a jury and whether it will provide a solid foundation for arriving at a decision in the case. In practice, admissibility amounts to a set of legal tests performed by a judge to evaluate an item of evidence [4]. This evaluation process can be complex, especially when evidence has not been handled properly or has characteristics that make it less reliable or more prejudicial. In the U.K. legal system, "admissibility" refers to legal rules that are applied to an item of potential evidence prior to a court considering the value of the fact that it claims to offer [29]. There exist various laws and rules that govern the admissibility of digital evidence in U.K. courts.

The most important laws associated with the admissibility of digital evidence are the Criminal Justice Act 2003 [61], the Regulation of Investigatory Powers Act 2000 [62], the Computer Misuse Act 1990 [63] and the Police and Criminal Evidence Act 1984 [64]. For instance, section 117 of the Criminal Justice Act 2003 [61] regulates the admissibility of communication data that has been obtained under warrant. Under section 17 of the Regulation of Investigatory Powers Act 2000 [62] content is not admissible. However, it will become admissible if it has been acquired from a foreign law enforcement agency within its own jurisdiction and is available to an investigator to be presented in the U.K. court [29]. Another example is section 78 of the Police and Criminal Evidence Act 1984 [64], according to which intercepted data content can only be used for intelligence purposes; it cannot be admitted as evidence. Also relevant to the issue of the admissibility of digital evidence is whether the material is a "business record," as outlined under section 117 of the Criminal Justice Act 2003 [61], an "expert report," defined under section 118(8) and 127 of that Act, or "real evidence". Importantly, under section 78 of the Police and Criminal Evidence Act 1984 [64], courts can reject any evidence deemed to have been acquired unfairly.

Compared with the U.K. legal system, admissibility rules in other European counties are much more relaxed and, although admissibility rules in the United States follow the English common law model, they have evolved differently. For instance, authorisations to seize evidence in the U.S. must be drawn up with far greater precision than in the U.K. [29] and any material acquired outside the warrant is likely to be considered inadmissible. Another deviation relates to the way in which technical evidence is handled. Within the U.K. courts, the jury is simply provided with opposing expert witnesses, while in the United States, technical evidence is an admissibility issue with the judge acting as a gatekeeper to protect the jury from scientific evidence which has not been established as "generally accepted" [55].

U.K. judges often consider three issues before deciding whether or not to admit digital evidence. These can be classified as issues relating to search warrants, reliability and best evidence.

(1) **Search Warrants**

Acquiring digital evidence under "proper authorisation" is vital for its admission in the U.K. legal system. Investigators must obtain a search warrant or subpoena before they can search, seize or examine digital devices. Subpoenas are employed to seize a company's business records, while search warrants are needed to access more detailed information such as customer-owned files [4]. For instance, in circumstances involving an Internet Service Provider (ISP), a subpoena might be required to identify the name of an individual owning a specific e-mail account and a search warrant used to extract the contents of e-mail or user profiles [35]. As already stated, digital evidence acquired without authorisation will not be admitted in courts. In order to acquire the necessary warrant, investigators must demonstrate to a judge that a crime has been committed, evidence of the crime exists and the evidence is likely to exist at the place to be searched. Search warrants in the United Kingdom can be more loosely defined than in the United States. In the U.K. legal system, there are several types of warrants such as a "specific premises warrants", all-premises warrants" and "multiple entry warrants" [4]. Even when investigators have obtained authorisation to search a computer, they must focus only on the crime under investigation. If they identify evidence of other crimes during their investigation, that evidence will not be admissible as it is outside the scope of the warrant. In such circumstances, investigators would have to obtain a second warrant before being able to use evidence to charge the offender [4, 29].

Furthermore, investigators may need to acquire two separate warrants for a seized computer: one for the computer itself and one for the files contained in it. Seized computers usually constitute 'real' evidence for admissibility purposes, with individual files having to be admitted separately in accordance with section 117 of Criminal Justice Act 2003 [61]. This is of particular importance where more than one individual has had access to a computer. In such situations, in order to adhere to Computer Misuse Act 1990 [63], investigators must prove that they are authorised to access the computers.

(2) **Best Evidence**

The "best evidence" rule refers to a legal principle that an original copy of a document is superior evidence. In the past, based upon this rule, secondary evidence such as a copy or "facsimile" would not be admissible if an original document was in existence and could be acquired [68]. The original purpose of the rule was to ensure that decisions reached in courts were based on the best available information [4]. However, with the arrival of photocopiers, scanners, computers and other technology that can produce effectively identical replicas, duplicates became acceptable instead of the original. According to Blackstone's Criminal Practice [68], the best evidence rule in England and Wales is now all but defunct. Therefore, evidence that is not an original will be admitted provided it meets other admissibility requirements. If a question is raised in relation to the authenticity of the original or the accuracy of the copy, or if the circumstances dictate that it would be unfair to admit the copy in place of the original, the best evidence rule will still apply. As most forms of digital evidence can be duplicated exactly, this issue does not often arise and copies are usually admitted in the U.K. courts. In fact, producing a duplicate of digital evidence is often preferred as it removes the possibility of the original being accidently modified.

According to the "Hearsay Rule", digital evidence would not be admissible if the witness (the digital forensic analyst) was not present in court to verify its truthfulness. Under section 114(1) of the Criminal Justice Act 2003 [61], "hearsay" in criminal proceedings is "a statement not made in oral evidence in the proceedings that is evidence of any matter stated." There are exceptions for evidence that describes events accurately and is simpler to authenticate, but the discussion of these is outside the scope of this research.

4   Concluding Remarks

Digital evidence has been presented in a growing number of criminal and civil court cases over the last decade. In order to be admissible in courts of law, digital evidence needs to meet the standards of other scientific and technical evidence. The lay audience (judges and jury) decide cases based on their understanding of evidence that is presented at trial. Knowledge of ICTs because of everyday use of computers, smart mobile devices, and other digital devices and network services might be understood by the lay audience as interpreting how digital evidence is extracted from digital sources. A knowledge of how digital evidence is acquired determines the way in which judges and jury weigh the probative and prejudicial value of this evidence when presented in court. In order to assess the value of digital evidence fairly and impartially, judges and jury will need to have some understanding of the fundamental ICTs and applications from which digital evidence is extracted such as computers, the Internet and e-mail. However, there is no study in the literature revealing the judges' perceived knowledge of digital evidence. Thus, investigating judges' perceived knowledge of digital evidence within the U.K. jurisdiction must be considered an imperative subject area for future research.

References

1. Pollitt, M.: A history of digital forensics. In: Chow, K.-P., Shenoi, S. (eds.) DigitalForensics 2010. IAICT, vol. 337, pp. 3–15. Springer, Heidelberg (2010). doi:10.1007/978-3-642-15506-2_1

2. Kohn, M., Eloff, M., Eloff, J.: Integrated digital forensic process model. Comput. Secur. **38**, 103–115 (2013)

3. Garfinkel, S.: Digital forensics research: the next 10 years. Digit. Invest. **7**, 64–73 (2010)

4. Casey, E.: Digital Evidence and Computer Crime: Forensic Science, Computers and the Internet, 3rd edn. Elsevier Academic Press, New York (2011)

5. Nance, K., Hay, B., Bishop, M.: Digital forensics: defining a research agenda. In: 42nd Hawaii International Conference on System Sciences, pp. 1–6 (2009)

6. Palmer, G.: A road map for digital forensic research. In: 1st Digital Forensic Research Workshop (DFRWS), pp. 27–30 (2001)

7. Montasari, R., Peltola, P., Evans, D.: Integrated computer forensics investigation process model (ICFIPM) for computer crime investigations. In: Jahankhani, H., Carlile, A., Akhgar, B., Taal, A., Hessami, A.G., Hosseinian-Far, A. (eds.) ICGS3 2015. CCIS, vol. 534, pp. 83–95. Springer, Heidelberg (2015). doi:10.1007/978-3-319-23276-8_8

8. Valjarevic, A., Venter, H.: A comprehensive and harmonized digital forensic investigation process model. J. Forensic Sci. **60**(6), 1467–1483 (2015)

9. Ieong, R.: FORZA - digital forensics investigation framework that incorporate legal issues. Digit. Invest. **3**, 29–36 (2006)

10. Cohen, F.: Toward a science of digital forensic evidence examination. In: Chow, K.-P., Shenoi, S. (eds.) DigitalForensics 2010. IAICT, vol. 337, pp. 17–35. Springer, Heidelberg (2010). doi:10.1007/978-3-642-15506-2_2

11. Freiling, C., Schwittay, B.: A common process model for incident response and computer forensics. In: 3rd International Conference on IT-Incident Management and IT-Forensics, pp. 19–40 (2007)

12. Rowlingson, R.: A ten step process for forensic readiness. Int. J. Digit. Evid. **2**(3), 1–28 (2004)

13. Agarwal, A., Gupta, M., Gupta, S., Gupta, C.: Systematic digital forensic investigation model. Int. J. Comput. Sci. Secur. **5**(1), 118–130 (2011)

14. Guidance Software: EnCase Forensics (2016). https://www.guidancesoftware.com/encase-forensic. Accessed 11 June 2016

15. AccessData: Forensic Toolkit (FTK) (2016). http://accessdata.com/products/computer-forensics/ftk. Accessed 09 June 2016

16. Wojcik, M., Venter, H., Eloff, J., Olivier, M.: Applying machine trust models to forensic investigations. In: Olivier, M.S., Shenoi, S. (eds.) Digital Forensics 2006. IAIC, vol. 222, pp. 55–65. Springer, Heidelberg (2006). doi:10.1007/0-387-36891-4_5

17. Ciardhuáin, O.: An extended model of cybercrime investigations. Int. J. Digit. Evid. **3**(1), 1–22 (2004)

18. SO/IEC: ISO/IEC 27037: Guidelines for Identification, Collection, Acquisition, and Preservation of Digital Evidence. British Standards Institution, London (2012)

19. ACPO: ACPO Good Practice Guide for Digital Evidence. U.K. Association of Chief Police Officers (2012)

20. ISO/IEC: ISO/IEC 27043: Incident Investigation Principles and Processes. British Standards Institution, London (2015)

21. Solms, S., Louwrens, C., Reekie, C., Grobler, T.: A control framework for digital forensics. In: Olivier, M., Shenoi, S. (eds.) DigitalForensics 2006. IAIC, vol. 222, pp. 343–355. Springer, Heidelberg (2006). doi:10.1007/0-387-36891-4_27

22. Rogers, M., Goldman, J., Mislan, R., Wedge, T., Debrota, S.: Computer forensics field triage process model. In: Conference on Digital Forensics, Security and Law, pp. 27–40 (2006)

23. Beebe, N., Clark, J.: A hierarchical, objectives-based framework for the digital investigations process. Digit. Invest. **2**(2), 147–167 (2005)

24. Kruse, W., Heiser, J.: Computer Forensics: Incident Response Essentials. Addison-Wesley, Boston (2001)

25. Grobler, C.P., Louwrens, C.P., Solms, S.H.: A multi-component view of digital forensics. In: ARES 2010 International Conference on Availability, Reliability and Security, pp. 647–652 (2010)

26. Carrier, B., Spafford, E.: Getting physical with the digital investigation process. Int. J. Digit. Evid. **2**(2), 1–20 (2003)

27. Mandia, K., Prosise, C., Pepe, M.: Incident Response and Computer Forensics, 2nd edn. McGraw-Hill/Osborne, Emeryville (2003)

28. Cohen, F.: Update on the state of the science of digital evidence examination. In: Proceedings of the Conference on Digital Forensics, Security, and Law, pp. 7–18 (2012)

29. Sommer, P.: Directors' and corporate advisors' guide to digital investigations and evidence. U.K. Information Assurance Advisory Council (2008). https://www.ucisa.ac.uk/~/media/Files/members/activities/ist/DigitalInvestigationsGuide.ashx. Accessed 17 June 2016

30. Kessler, C.: Judges' awareness, understanding, and application of digital evidence. Ph.D. thesis, Nova Southeastern University (2010)

31. Cohen, F.: Digital Forensic Evidence Examination, 2nd edn. Fred Cohen & Associates, Livermore (2009)

32. Brown, C.: Computer Evidence: Collection and Preservation, 2nd edn. Course Technology, Boston (2009)

33. Gonzales, A., Schofield, R., Hagy, D.: Digital evidence in the courtroom: a guide for law enforcement and prosecutors. U.S. Department of Justice (2007). https://www.ncjrs.gov/pdffiles1/nij/211314.pdf. Accessed 17 June 2016

34. Jones, A.: Computer science and the reference manual for scientific evidence: defining the judge's role as a firewall. Intellect. Prop. Law Bull. **14**(1), 23–40 (2009)

35. Kerr, O.: Computer Crime Law, 2nd edn. Thomson/West, St. Paul (2009)

36. Mason, S.: Electronic Evidence: Disclosure, Discovery and Admissibility. LexisNexis Butterworths, London (2007)

37. Whitcomb, C.: An historical perspective of digital evidence: a forensic scientist's view. Int. J. Digit. Evid. **1**(1), 1–9 (2002)

38. Kerr, O.S.: Fourth amendment seizures of computer data. Yale Law J. **119**(4), 700–724 (2010)

39. Ball, C.: What judges should know about computer forensics. National Workshop for District Judges II, pp. 1–19 (2008)
40. Manes, G., Downing, E., Watson, L., Thrutchley, C.: New federal rules and digital evidence. In: Conference on Digital Forensics, Security and Law, pp. 31–40 (2007)
41. Giova, G.: Improving chain of custody in forensic investigation of electronic digital systems. Int. J. Comput. Sci. Netw. Secur. 11(1), 1–9 (2011)
42. Holder, E., Robinson, L., Rose, K.: Electronic crime scene investigation: an on-the-scene reference for first responders. U.S. Department of Justice (2009). https://www.ncjrs.gov/pdffiles1/nij/227050.pdf. Accessed: 11 June 2016
43. Mukasey, M., Sedgwick, J., Hagy, D.: Electronic crime scene investigation: a guide for first responders. U.S. Department of Justice (2008). https://www.ncjrs.gov/pdffiles1/nij/219941.pdf. Accessed 10 June 2016
44. Bem, D., Feld, F., Huebner, E., Bem, O.: Computer forensics - past, present and future. J. Inf. Sci. Technol. 5(3), 43–59 (2008)
45. Ashcroft, J., Daniels, D., Hart, S.: Forensic examination of digital evidence: a guide for law enforcement. U.S. Department of Justice (2004). https://www.ncjrs.gov/pdffiles1/nij/199408.pdf. Accessed 10 June 2016
46. Rogers, M.: DCSA: A Practical Approach to Digital Crime Scene Analysis, vol. 3, 5th edn. Purdue University, West Lafayette (2004)
47. Frowen, A.: Computer forensics in the courtroom: is an IT literate judge and jury necessary for a fair trial? (2009). http://realestatearticles4u.com/computer-forensics-in-the-courtroom-is-an-it-literate-judge-and-jury-necessary-for-a-fair-trial/. Accessed: 17 June 2016
48. Shaw, B.: Judging juries: evaluating renewed proposals for specialized juries from a public choice perspective. UCLA J. Law Technol. 10(2), 3–4 (2006)
49. Losavio, M., Wilson, D., Elmaghraby, A.: Prevalence, use, and evidentiary issues of digital evidence of cellular telephone consumer and small-scale digital devices. J. Digit. Forensic Pract. 1(4), 291–296 (2006)
50. Scarborough, E., Rogers, M., Frakes, K., San Martin, C.: Digital evidence. In: Crimes of the Internet, pp. 477–488 (2009)
51. Rogers, M., Scarborough, K., Frakes, K., San Martin, C.: Survey of law enforcement perceptions regarding digital evidence. In: Craiger, P., Shenoi, S. (eds.) DigitalForensics 2007. ITIFIP, vol. 242, pp. 41–52. Springer, Heidelberg (2007). doi:10.1007/978-0-387-73742-3_3
52. Garber, L.: Computer forensics: high-tech law enforcement. IEEE Comput. Mag. 34(1), 22–27 (2001)
53. Ryan, D., Shpantzer, G.: Legal aspects of digital forensics. In: Proceedings of Forensics Workshop, pp. 1–7 (2002)
54. U.S. Courts: Federal rules of evidence. Administrative Office of the U.S. Courts (2015). http://federalevidence.com/rules-of-evidence. Accessed 21 June 2016
55. Daubert v. Merrell Dow Pharmaceuticals, Inc. (92-102), 509 U.S. 579 (1993)
56. Kumho Tire v. Carmichael (97-1709), 526 U.S. 137, 131 F.3d 1433 reversed (1999)
57. Bernstein, D.: Expert witnesses, adversarial bias, and the (partial) failure of the Daubert revolution. George Mason Univ. Law Econ. Res. Pap. 93(451), 100–137 (2008)
58. Rothstein, B., Hedges, R., Wiggins, E.: Managing discovery of electronic information: a pocket guide for judges (2007). https://bulk.resource.org/courts.gov/fjc/eldscpkt.pdf. Accessed 21 June 2016
59. Meyers, M., Rogers, M.: Digital forensics: meeting the challenges of scientific evidence. In: Pollitt, M., Shenoi, S. (eds.) DigitalForensics 2005. ITIFIP, vol. 194, pp. 43–50. Springer, Heidelberg (2006). doi:10.1007/0-387-31163-7_4

60. Noblett, M., Pollitt, M., Presley, L.: Recovering and examining computer forensic evidence. Forensic Sci. Commun. **2**(4), 1–13 (2000)
61. Criminal Justice Act 2003. Chapter 44. The Stationary Office, London
62. Regulation of Investigatory Powers Act 2003. Chapter 23. The Stationary Office, London
63. Computer Misuse Act 1990. Chapter 18. The Stationary Office, London
64. Police and Criminal Evidence Act 1984. Chapter 60. The Stationary Office, London
65. Adams, R.: The advanced data acquisition model (ADAM): a process model for digital forensic practice. Ph.D. thesis, Murdoch University (2012)
66. Steel, C.: Windows Forensics: The Field Guide For Conducting Corporate Computer Investigations. Wiley Publishing, Indianapolis (2006)
67. Buskirk, E., Liu, V.: Digital evidence: challenging the presumption of reliability. J. Digit. Forensic Pract. **1**(1), 19–26 (2006)
68. Ormerod, D., Perry, D.: Blackstone's Criminal Practice, 26th edn. Oxford University Press, Oxford (2015)

Combating Cyber Dependent Crimes: The Legal Framework in the UK

Oriola Sallavaci[✉]

Anglia Ruskin University, Chelmsford CM1 1SQ, UK
Oriola.Sallavaci@anglia.ac.uk

Abstract. Computer crimes and digital investigations comprise a substantial part of criminal policy, law and practice as information becomes the cornerstone of global economy. Innovative ways of attacking, exploiting and interfering with computer and communication technologies are regularly emerging, posing increasing threats to the society, economy and security. It is essential that in tackling cybercrime the right legal framework of offences is in place and that there is clarity in how the powers that are used to investigate cybercrime interact with the offences designed to catch cyber criminals. This paper reviews the current legal framework to cyber dependent crimes in the UK, including its recent amendments, and highlights areas that remain problematic and in need of attention from policymakers.

Keywords: Cybercrime · Computer misuse · Computer security · Hacking

1 Introduction

The internet and digital technologies are transforming the world we live in by driving economic growth and providing new ways for people to connect, communicate and co-operate with one another. Cyberspace is transforming business, making it more efficient and effective by opening up markets, allowing commerce to take place at lower cost and enabling people to do business on the move. Yet, as the internet and digital technologies are becoming increasingly central to nations' economy and society, the growing role of cyberspace has also opened up new threats as well as new opportunities.

Cybercrime has increased correspondingly with the increased amount of computers and internet access. In 2015, in the UK, 22.5 million households (86%) had internet access (up from 56% in 2006) and 39.3 million adults (78%) accessed the internet every day [1]. The new and fast developing technologies provide for new opportunities to commit crime and, as technological developments become more widely available, an ever increasing number of criminals are taking advantage. The Internet Security Threat Report 2016 by Symantec shows an overall increase in cybercrime during 2015 with a 25% increase in breaches since 2013, and over 429 million global identities exposed via cyber-attacks, up 23% since 2014 [2]. Hacking continues to be the primary cause of data breaches in 2015, with the data stolen across breaches more valuable and the impact to the business greater than in previous years [2].

Whilst cyberattacks against businesses and nations hit the headlines with an overwhelming regularity, the cyber threat has been assigned a 'Tier One' threat status

© Springer International Publishing AG 2016
H. Jahankhani et al. (Eds.): ICGS3 2017, CCIS 630, pp. 53–66, 2016.
DOI: 10.1007/978-3-319-51041-4_5

in the UK's national security strategy which indicates one of the highest priorities for action [3]. To assist in tackling the cyber threat, £860 million of public funding was set aside as part of a five-year National Cyber Security Programme. The national cyber security strategy set out the key objectives that the Government intended to achieve by 2015 in relation to cyber security and cyber-crime, to both tackle the threats and reap the benefits of cyberspace [4]. Among other measures in fighting cybercrime, having in place a national legal framework fit for purpose, has been one of the main strategic priorities of the government [4].

Cybercrime is an umbrella term used to describe two distinct, but closely related criminal activities: *cyber-dependent* and *cyber-enabled* crimes [5].[1] *Cyber-dependent crimes*, also known as computer related crimes, are offences that can only be committed by using a computer, computer networks, or other forms of information and communications technology (ICT). These acts include the spread of viruses and other malicious software, hacking, distributed denial of service (DDoS) attacks etc. Cyber-dependent crimes are primarily acts directed against computers or network resources, although there may be secondary outcomes from the attacks, such as fraud. *Cyber-enabled crimes* are traditional crimes that are increased in their scale or reach by the use of computers, computer networks or other ICT. Unlike cyber-dependent crimes, they can still be committed without the use of ICT [5].

In the UK, specific offences most commonly associated with cyber-dependent crimes, such as hacking and the creation or distribution of malware, are defined in the Computer Misuse Act 1990 (CMA) which remains the main legal instrument in combating these types of crime. CMA was drafted almost three decades ago, with no possible foresight concerning technology's evolution and its impact into creating new forms of offending [7, 8]. During the past decade CMA has undergone several amendments: initially by the Police and Justice Act 2006 (PJA) and more recently by the Serious Crime Act 2015 (SCA) in a bid to bring the legislation up to date with the outstanding developments of the digital world.

This paper provides an overview of the current legal framework on tackling cyber dependent crime with the aim of identifying the remaining problems that need be addressed to ensure an effective and robust response to cybercrime. It is hoped that this will help to drive forward policy decisions in this area which is vital in the context of emerging forms of cybercrime and technological developments.

2 Computer Misuse Act 1990: The Unauthorised Access Offences

Computer Misuse Act 1990 was introduced to deal with computer related offences and, to this day, remains the main legislative measure in force to combat cyber dependant crime. The aim of the Act is to secure computer material against unauthorised access or modification; and for connected purposes. In its initial form it established three main

---

[1] Other classifications include computer integrity offences, computer related offences and content related offences [6].

offences namely: unauthorised access to computer material (s1), unauthorised access with intent to commit further offences (s2) and unauthorised acts with intent or with recklessness to impairing the operation of the computer (s3). s3 which was replaced by PJA 2006 will receive attention further below alongside other important amendments to CMA.

2.1   Section 1 – The Offence of Unauthorised Access

Section 1 of the Computer Misuse Act 1990 is the main provision on hacking. It was introduced to cover all forms of unauthorised access to computer material regardless of a hacker's motives and intended to act as a deterrent to all forms of hacking, including by the so called 'innocent hackers' who break through security systems as a hobby [9]. Section 1 CMA states:

> 'A person will be guilty of unauthorised access to computer material if he causes a computer to perform any function with intent to secure access to any program or data held in any computer, or to enable any such access to be secured; if the access he intends to secure, or to enable to be secured, is unauthorised; and if he knows at the time when he causes the computer to perform the function that this is the case.'

Section 1 carries a maximum penalty of two years imprisonment on conviction on indictment or an unlimited fine, or both.

Computer Misuse Act 1990 does not provide a definition of 'computer' due to considerations that any such definition would soon become outdated given the rapid and continuous development in technology [6, 10].[2] This approach is appropriate, especially considering that we have entered the age of 'Internet of Things' where even domestic appliances, cars and any object that incorporates computer technology can become target for attack [6]. On application, courts in the UK have adopted the contemporary meaning of the word 'computer' which is defined by the Oxford Dictionary as 'an electronic device which is capable of receiving information (data) in a particular form and of performing a sequence of operations in accordance with a predetermined but variable set of procedural instructions (program) to produce a result in the form of information or signals'. According to s17(6) CMA programs and data in this sense refer to any removable storage held in the computer. For definition purposes, courts have focused on the features of a computer rather than its physical nature. In *DPP v Jones* [1997] 2 CR App R 155 a computer was defined as a device for storing, processing and retrieving information.[3]

The offence itself focuses on the functions used to gain access to any program or data held in the computer. As such, reading confidential information displayed on a screen or using forms of electronic 'computer eavesdropping', for example using embedded laptop microphone as a listening device, do not constitute offences under this section [11]. According to s17(2) *functions* can include outputting; using; copying; deleting and modifying a program or data. Most actions by computer users will fall

---

[2] Note that both the Convention on Cybercrime Art 1(a) and Directive 13/40/EU Art 2 (a) provide definitions which are similar to one another.

[3] At p.163 (Lord Hoffman).

under the classification 'to perform any function' including switching on/off a computer or using a non-open computer which has been left accidentally logged on by authorised users, as established in *Ellis v DPP* (No1) [2001] EWHC Admin 362 whereby the offence was deemed as sufficiently wide to cover the use of logged in terminals without permission.[4]

The *mens rea* of the offence covers two aspects. First, the defendant must know that his intended access was unauthorised and, second, the defendant must have intended to secure access to any program or data held in the computer. Intention is extended to include enabling someone else to secure unauthorised access to a computer or to enable the defendant themselves unauthorised access to a computer at a later time - s1(1)(a) CMA. Mens rea does not however extend to recklessness as s1 only deals with 'deliberate activities' whereby the offender must have knowledge that the access is unauthorised [12]. According to Section 1(2) the intent to secure access does not need to be directed at any particular program or data, a program or data of any particular kind or a program or data held in a particular computer. This is important in making the legislation enforceable, as in practice it would be very difficult for the prosecution to prove otherwise.

Access is considered unauthorised if a person is not entitled to control access to the program or data, or if no consent has been given from someone who is so entitled – s 17(5) CMA. As discussed below, the issue of authorisation has been problematic; the application of the section has been easier for external offenders but less straightforward in cases of inside hackers such as an employee [13]. In the latter situations, it is the duty of the organisation in question to clearly specify the persons with authority to access the computer or system in issue. Contracts of employment and any surrounding information such as oral advice and office practices will be looked at to determine whether an employee has exceeded the limits of the authorisation [11, 14].

Good intent will not affect the applicability of s1 CMA. The case of *R v Cuthbert* [2005] (Unreported, Horseferry Road Magistrates Court, 6 October 2006) demonstrated that ethical hackers could be found guilty of unauthorised access to computer material. Cuthbert, a computer security consultant, performed penetration tests on the Disasters Emergency Committee website as he was suspicious that the website was not authentic. It was held 'with some considerable regret' that he had committed an offence under s1 by knowingly performing unauthorised access against DEC's systems. Uninvited security testing was considered a form of vigilantism which clearly breaches the computer Misuse Act 1990 [15].

2.2   Section 2 CMA– The Ulterior Intent Offence

Section 2 CMA deals with those cases where more serious offences are intended to be committed after the gaining of unauthorised access to computer material. These ulterior offences need not be completed, merely intended by the offender. Offences such as fraud, theft and blackmail could all be ulterior offences under Section 2. If the ulterior

---

[4] Para 16 (Lord Wolf).

offence has actually been committed, then *that* will be the one charged. For instance, most on-line frauds (such as on-line/internet banking fraud, i.e. fraudulent withdrawals from internet bank accounts using stolen identities) are prosecuted under the Fraud Act 2006, while CMA offences are used for "pure" hacking or denial-of-service prosecutions. As discussed further below, while this could provide an explanation on the low prosecution rates under CMA, the effectiveness of CMA as a legal instrument still warrants criticism [16].

According to s2 CMA 'a person will be guilty of an offence if he commits the Section 1 offence of unauthorised access with intent to commit a further offence, or facilitate the commission of such offence'. It is not necessary for the ulterior offence to involve the use of a computer even though it usually will [9]. This section was introduced as the existing law relating to criminal attempts was deemed inadequate to address cases of hacking with intent to commit ulterior offences. The Criminal Attempts Act 1981s 1(1) requires that the offender must have done an act which is more than merely preparatory to the commission of an offence. To go beyond a purely preparatory act means 'to embark on the crime proper', that is to commence the actual commission of the offence – *R v Gullefer* [1990] 1 WLR 1063, 1065. A hacker who accesses a bank's computer system with intention to transfer funds but is unable to get past further security systems would not be guilty of an attempt of theft as the hacker's conduct at that point would be considered merely preparatory [11]. Section 2 ulterior offence makes it possible for a hacker in this situation to be found guilty under CMA.

R v Delamare (Ian) [2003] EWCA Crim 424 demonstrates the severity with which courts view the Section 2 offence as compared to the Section 1. D, a bank employee obtained and disclosed bank details to an acquaintance, who then impersonated one of the account holders to obtain £10000 from the bank. D was convicted to two charges under s2 for facilitating the commission of a further offence, in this case fraud. It did not matter that the ulterior offence took place on a different occasion to the unauthorised access under s2(3), nor did it matter that the further offence was committed by another person under s2(1)(b) [17].

2.3   Interpretative Challenges on Unauthorised Access Offences

While Computer Misuse Act 1990 achieved the criminalisation of hacking behaviour which previous legal instruments had struggled to do, there have been several key areas of complexity and uncertainty surrounding the existing law. Courts have faced considerable challenges in interpreting and applying the legislation particularly with regard to the issue of *authorisation*. There has been much inconsistency in the application of these offences and it can be argued that one of the main reasons is a lack of understanding and expertise in new and emerging areas of criminal activity [6].

Judicial interpretation emerged as one of the main difficulties in the application of unauthorised access offences especially in the early period of the Act's establishment. Such difficulties were seen in *R v Cropp* (Snaresbrook Crown Court, 4 July 1991) which was the first prosecution under the Act. The interpretation made by the judge in the case to the then Section 1(1)(a) as requiring a second computer to be involved for the offence to be committed, if upheld, would have seriously limited the scope of CMA especially since the majority of instances of hacking are those carried out within organisations [6]. *AG-s reference* (No1 of 1991) [1992] 3WLR 432 rejected the Crown Court's interpretation and clarified that the wording of the provision 'any computer' literally meant that; there were no grounds for importing the word 'other' between 'any' and 'computer' (at para 437).

The application of unauthorised access offences to inside offenders has often been inconsistent. An offence is *not* committed under s.1 by a person who is authorised to access particular computer data, but does so for unauthorised purposes – as per *DPP v Bignell* [1998] 1 Cr. App. R. 1 whereby police officers authorised to obtain car registration details from the Police National Computer for police work purposes, accessed - via an operator - details of cars from Police National Computer for their own private/personal purposes. The defendants appealed successfully that using authorised access for unauthorised purposes was not unlawful. The court distinguished the activity of 'breaking into computers' from the 'misuse of data'. Bignells' actions would have constituted an offence under s.55 Data Protection Act 1998 but this was not charged.

Bignell has received considerable criticism. As a commentator puts it: 'authorisation relates to the giving of permission, which concerns not only the area of conduct, but the conduct itself within it' [16]. The House of Lords had an opportunity to review the *Bignell* decision in *R. v Bow Street Metropolitan Stipendiary Magistrate Ex p. Allison v United States* (No. 2) [2000] 2 A.C. 216 an extradition case involving an authorised employee of a credit card company who gained an unauthorised access to credit card details in order to create forged cards. The facts of the case were similar to *Bignell* in the sense that defendants used authorised access to gain access to unauthorised material. However unlike *Bignell*, the defendant was found guilty. The court held that, the authority to access *a particular piece of data* was not authorisation to access *similar data* in the absence of permission to do so. The ambiguity regarding the definition of "unauthorized" was resolved; the term relates to the specific data accessed rather than the same kind of data suggested in *Bignell*.

However it must be noted that, while some of the Divisional Court's reasoning in relation to s.17(5) was disapproved, the House of Lords concluded that the result in *Bignell* was 'probably right'. Authorisation was secured as the police officers 'merely requested' information from the computer operators who are authorised to access the Police National Computer. Critics of the decision note that this is problematic; due to the application of the doctrine of innocent agency, operators should not have been viewed as participants in the alleged offences [16].

In some cases such as *Ex p. Allison above and Bonnett* (November 3, 1995, Newcastle under Lyme Magistrates' Court), courts supported convictions of police officers who had themselves accessed the PNC for unauthorised purposes. However, at the same time courts denied support to convictions in cases where, like the Bignells, defendants had asked others to access the data in question for them, such as in *Farquarson* (Croydon Magistrates Court, 9 December 1993). As a commentator puts it, 'the confusion and lack of clarity in the application of the crucial concept of "authority" has somewhat undermined the Act' [16].

3   The Police and Justice Act 2006 Amendments: Impairing the Operation of a Computer and Misuse of Devices

Since the enactment of the Computer Misuse Act 1990 new forms of offending have emerged alongside the technological advancements which were not envisaged at the Act's creation. In order to deal with new types of cyber dependent offences, amendments were introduced by the Police and Justice Act 2006 which created two new offences. The previous Section 3 offence regarding unauthorised modification of computer material was replaced with a new, wider offence concerning unauthorised acts with intent to impair the operation of a computer – s36 PJA. In addition, s3A was introduced in order to criminalise the misuse of devices; namely the making, supplying or obtaining of articles for use in computer misuse offences – s37 PJA. These amendments tried to address the lack of effectiveness of CMA in coping with computer dependent crime. However it is questionable whether the broadening of the scope of the offences established by the CMA has achieved this ambition.

3.1   Section 3 Offence

The old Section 3 offence dealing with the modification of the contents of a computer was replaced by PJA 2006 due to the uncertainty as to whether the existing offence captured all types of denial of service (DoS) attacks. Many DoS attacks were not being investigated because 'no crime could be framed' [10]. With direct attacks, the nature of the communications sent to the target machine will often fall within a class of transmission which the target machine was designed to receive. As such, while there may be the necessary intention to cause modification and impairment, the modification itself may not be considered unauthorised. *DPP v Lennon* [2006] EWHC 1201 (Admin); (2006) 170 J.P. 532, clarified on its facts that there is no deemed authority/consent to send emails to a person's email address where the purpose of sending the emails is to disrupt the operation of the computer. Even though the Divisional Court was considering the original s.17(8)(b) prior to the 2006 amendment, its analysis and reasoning are still helpful.

The new s3 offence is much wider in scope so as to encompass all DoS attacks. It captures a wider range of offending conduct which will be deemed unauthorised if the person doing or causing an act to be done is not responsible for the computer, or entitled to commit an act, or if no consent has been given by any such person - s17(8) CMA. An unauthorised act for these purposes can include a series of acts - s.3(5)(b) - which is essential in making DoS attacks unlawful in cases where an attacker floods a system with multiple messages. The sending of viruses and other malware constitutes unauthorised acts under this section, just as they did under the former Section 3 offence. Interference with websites constitutes an unauthorised act, as depicted by *R v Lindesay* [2002] 1 Cr App R (S) 86 whereby the defendant was sentenced to nine months imprisonment for deleting data off of his former employer's client websites.

The main issue with the amended provision is that it hinges on *impairment* rather than *modification* [18]. CMA does not include a technical definition for 'impairment'. The term is given its ordinary meaning, defined by the Oxford dictionary as 'the state of being diminished, weakened or damaged'. This causes interpretive problems as the offence revolves around a subjective concept rather than an objective one. Under the former modification offence, either a change was to computer data or it was not, making the modification offence relatively straightforward to establish [18]. However impairment can amount to different things due to the many characteristics of a computer [19]. CMA does not provide a way to differentiate between different types of impairment caused. The threshold to which a decline in system performance for instance, crosses the boundary into impairment, is unclear and problematic especially considering that the impairment can be temporary - s.3(5)(c) CMA [20]. Equally, evidential difficulties may arise as, once a system has been rectified, proving the requisite amount of impairment had occurred at the appropriate time and linking it to an unauthorised act could be problematic [16].

Another major change was the introduction of *recklessness* to the *mens rea* of the s3 offence. For the impairment offence to occur, merely for data to be impaired is not enough; this should be done with intent or must be foreseen by the offender. If it was foreseeable that the unauthorised act would cause impairment, prevention or hindrance to any computer, program or data, and the person involved foresaw that risk but took it anyway, s/he would be found guilty of the s 3 offence committed through recklessness. It must be noted that no other offence in CMA includes recklessness as a form of mens rea, nor was it proposed by the All Party Internet Group (APIG) in its recommendations for this offence [10]. Its inclusion was clearly made as an attempt to improve the enforceability of CMA and raise the prosecution rates, as in practice it is easier to prove the foreseeability of a risk rather than the intention to behave in a certain way to achieve particular results. However the expansion of the scope has been criticised in terms of it potentially triggering questionable attempts to prosecute and creating further interpretative difficulties [16].

3.2   Section 3A – Making, Supplying or Obtaining Articles for Use in Offences

One of the main reasons as to why computer related offences have become so common is because relevant tools and articles are freely available on the internet. Many of these tools do not require any special skill to be used. In order to deter the accessibility and subsequent use of hacking tools, Police and Justice Act 2006 added Section 3A. This was done so as to ensure compliance with Article 6 of Cybercrime Convention which requires that:

> 'Each party shall adopt such legislation and other measures as they may be necessary to establish as criminal offences under its domestic law, when committed intentionally and without right: the production, sale, procurement for use, import, distribution or otherwise making available of a device ...computer password ... or similar data by which the whole or any part of a computer system is capable of being accessed with intent that it be used for the purpose of committing any of the offences established'.

S3A establishes three offences. The first prohibits making, adapting, supplying, or offering to supply any article intending it to be used to commit, or to assist in the commission of any of ss1-3 offences. The second prohibits supplying or offering to supply any article believing that it is likely to be used to commit, or to assist in the commission of an offence. The third offence prohibits obtaining any article with a view to it being supplied for use to commit or to assist in the commission of a ss1-3 offence.

The application of s3A has not been without controversy. The main problem concerns the legitimate use of developing and supplying tools for computer security. Many hacking tools are dual-use and are indistinguishable from utilities that are essential for the maintenance and security of computers and networks. These tools can be used for lawful and unlawful purposes. Originally the APIG advised Parliament not to legislate the criminalisation of hacking tools as it would only cause unnecessary confusion and anxiety to the legitimate users of these programs [10]. Researchers in information security, penetration testers and other professionals in the field may develop and make available such tools in the course of their study or business [6]. If these tools are then used, security researchers may fear that they can be found guilty under Section 3A(2) [21].

The criminalisation of possession, fabrication and distribution of hacking tools seems to have a broad remit, leading to problematic definitions and situations when attempting to establish one's (malicious) intent [22]. The provision allows wide powers to the law enforcement in deciding who is or not an offender. In order to establish whether s3A(2) can be applied, the *likelihood* of the article being used to commit an offence need be considered. However, how the 'likelihood' is to be determined is not clarified in the provisions themselves, which creates interpretive difficulties. As a commentator puts it 'criminal law requires clarity, not generalised ambitions; a court - a judge or a jury - needs to know what tests to apply; investigators need to know what evidence to assemble' [21].

In determining the likelihood of an article being used (or misused) to commit a criminal offence, the Crown Prosecution Service (CPS) has provided the following list of factors to be taken into consideration when prosecuting:

- Has the article been developed primarily, deliberately and for the sole purpose of committing a CMA offence (i.e. unauthorised access to computer material)?
- Is the article available on a wide scale commercial basis and sold through legitimate channels?
- Is the article widely used for legitimate purposes?
- Does it have a substantial installation base?
- What was the context in which the article was used to commit the offence compared with its original intended purpose? [14].

Prosecutors are required to look at the functionality of the article and at what, if any, thought the suspect gave to who would use it; whether for example the article was circulated to a closed and vetted list of IT security professionals or was posted openly [14]. The first factor in the guidance is helpful and could have been included in the provision itself. However the remaining factors are somewhat problematic. The second factor misses the legitimate freeware tools while answers to the third factor would not add significant insight to proving one's intent, as there are dual use tools, such as nmap, and more offensive tools, such as nessus, which are widely used for both benevolent and malicious purposes. The last question is a complex one which requires professional expertise contribution on a case by case basis, whilst the introduction of 'context' could cause problems with respect to the dual use of the hacking tool [22].

Section 3A does not provide that legitimate users of such hacker tools will avoid liability and, as a result, security testers may stop using dual use tools until proper precedent has been made. This could cause a decrease in computer security which is the opposite of what s3A intends to achieve [22]. It is regrettable that s3A does not adopt the wording of Article 6(2) of the Cybercrime Convention (Budapest Treaty) which is as follows:

> 'an article shall not be interpreted as imposing criminal liability where the production, sale, procurement for use, import, distribution or otherwise making available or possession...of this article is not for the purpose of committing an offence established in accordance with Articles 2 through 5 of this Convention, such as for the authorised testing or protection of a computer system.'

If the wording of s3A reflected Article 6 (2) of the Cybercrime Convention then legitimate users of dual usage tools would feel less cautious about using them. Until the legitimate usages of hacking tools have been identified or s3A has been amended, the latter will continue to be 'a black hole in cyberspace rather than an efficient battleship' [23]. However it is important to note that the aim of restricting the availability of hacking tools cannot be achieved solely by finding an appropriate form of words. Informed prosecutorial policy decisions will have to be taken, balancing the need to make more difficult the casual attack on information systems against the need for tools to protect legitimate users [21].

4 Amendments to CMA Introduced by the Serious Crime Act 2015

Serious Crime Act 2015 amended Section 3A CMA so as to comply with the EU Council Directive 2013/40 EU on attacks against information systems. The aim of the Directive is to establish a set of minimum rules within the European Union on offences and sanctions relating to attacks against information systems. It also aims to improve the cooperation between competent authorities in EU Member States. The existing UK legislation was deemed compliant with the Directive save in two respects: tools used for committing offences (Article 7) and jurisdiction (Article 12). The amendments in the Serious Crime Act 2015 addressed these gaps.
According to Article 7:

> 'Member states shall take the necessary measures to ensure that the intentional production, sale, procurement for use, import, distribution or otherwise making available of ... a computer programme or password... without right and with intention to commit any offence is punishable as a criminal offence, at least for cases which are not minor' [24].

The existing Section 3A met the requirements of Article 7 except in one respect: 'procurement for use' of tools to commit an offence [25, 26]. A loophole had been created by Section 3A(3) whereby it was an offence to obtain an article with a view to supplying it to another for the commission of an offence but it was not an offence to obtain it for personal use with intention of committing an offence. In other words, the offence required the involvement (or intended involvement) of a third party. Section 42 of the Serious Crime Act extended Section 3A of the 1990 Act to include an offence of obtaining a tool for use to commit a Section 1, 3 or 3ZA offence *regardless of an intention to supply that tool* – thus removing the requirement of the involvement, or intended involvement, of a third party and ensuring that the offence covers individuals acting alone.

This amendment makes Section 3A more effective in principle, as it allows the police to intervene and interrupt an attack before it has taken place i.e. at the time the offender obtains a tool or article for usage. Before the amendment, individuals could obtain tools such as malware having the knowledge that they had a good chance not to be prosecuted unless it could be proved that they obtained the tool with the view to supply it to commit a computer misuse offence. The amendment creates a deterrent effect on such individuals as it will be easier for the prosecution to prove that they procured such tools with the intention of committing an offence due to the very nature of the tools involved.

The second amendment arising from the Directive widens the territorial scope of the Act by amending the two sections (ss.4 and 5) dealing with jurisdiction. Article 12 of the EU Directive covers jurisdiction and requires Member States to establish their jurisdiction with regards to a cyber offence being committed by one of their nationals. Before the amendment, CMA provisions concerning the arrangements for the extra territorial application of the offences (that is, the ability for the UK courts to try cases in respect of conduct committed outside their jurisdiction) required the prosecution to show a significant link to the UK – that being that either the individual or the affected/intended affected computer needed to be present in the UK at the time of the offence.

The amendments made by SCA 2015 extended the categories of "significant link to the jurisdiction" in s.5 of the Act to include "nationality". This provides a basis for the UK to prosecute a UK national who commits any s.1 to 3A offence whilst outside the UK and where the offence has no link to the UK other than the defendant's nationality, provided that the offence was also an offence in the country where it took place - Pt 2 s.43 SCA.

One of the most significant aspects of the reform is that SCA 2015 introduced a new Section 3ZA, creating an offence which covers 'unauthorised acts causing or creating risk of serious damage' – s41 SCA. This is essentially an aggravated form of the 'impairment offence' found on Section 3 but with the added *actus reus* of causing or creating risk of serious damage of a material kind [25]. Damage to material kind covers damage to human welfare, the environment, the economy or national security. If the damage is in respect of threat of life, loss of life or damage to national security, the maximum penalty is life imprisonment [25]. Considering the detrimental effects of hacking on the economy, security, environment and general wellbeing it is understandable that the high sentencing tariffs introduced in Section 3 are necessary and potentially could have a greater deterrent effect. It was deemed that the maximum sentence of 10 years' imprisonment which s3 offence carried did not sufficiently reflect the level of personal and economic harm that a major cyberattack on critical systems could cause [26].

With regard to sentencing, it is difficult to assess whether or not the increased sentencing powers under CMA, initially through PJA 2006 and then with SCA 2015, have or will result in higher sentences. Despite the 10 year maximum sentence available for s.3 offences since 2006 for example, these offences still appear to receive relatively low sentences often measured in months rather than years [27]. One reason for this may be that, as mentioned above, many of the more serious on-line attacks resulting in significant financial loss are prosecuted and sentenced under the Fraud Act 2006 and so do not readily lend themselves to direct comparison with offences prosecuted as computer misuse. In addition, a significant proportion of modern day computer misuse offences are committed by young people under 18 who are subject to a different sentencing regime from adults, which results in lower sentences than one might otherwise have expected considering the apparent seriousness of the offences [27].

While SCA was introduced as a reform measure to ensure that the legal framework in the UK is fit for purpose, the problems with the application of CMA discussed above still remain and must receive consideration. Following the previous trends, the wording of the new sections is not sufficiently precise and could cause interpretive difficulties. Offences that would be more suited to fall under the lesser offence could be unduly classified as aggravated. Most importantly, prosecution rates have been significantly low [16] both before and after the amendments introduced by the Serious Crime Act 2015, which begs for a different approach to be taken.

5   Conclusion

The rapid development of digital information technology and its widespread use have created opportunities for new forms of criminal activity. In the UK, it was essential that the CMA 1990 was implemented in order to criminalise computer related offences. The other offences under the existing criminal law in England and Wales were not designed to encompass cyber dependent crime. However, during the past 26 years courts have faced recurring challenges in the interpretation of the law which has led in inconsistent applications. This is partly due to the drafting of the legislation as well as insufficient understanding of the complex technical concepts involved.

CMA has been trying to catch up with technology ever since its enactment. Emerging hacking techniques and the increasing threat to economy and security prompted the government to enact amendments in 2006 and 2015. By widening the scope of the Act to incorporate the new offences involving denial of service attacks and hacking tools, interpretive issues have arisen particularly surrounding the definition of impairment and dual use articles. The reform implemented by way of Serious Crime Act 2015 does not resolve any of the existing issues. It focuses in closing the legal loophole whereby an offender could obtain a tool for his own use and adds a new aggravated Section 3 offence following the previous trend of insufficiently precise terminology that could cause interpretive issues.

It is questionable whether CMA has provided an effective measure to combating cyber dependant crime considering the low prosecution rates under the Act [7, 16].[5]

---

[5] During 1990–2006 when amendments were introduced by PJA 2006, only 214 defendants were brought to the magistrates' courts and 161 were found guilty. In comparison with the high occurrence of computer hacking these numbers are significantly low [7, 16].

While theoretically the chances of prosecuting hackers should have been improved following the amendments made by the Police and Justice Act 2006, in practice they have not produced the desired results. Prosecutions under both offences have been rare with very few cases being reported. Section 3A only had two prosecutions in England and Wales since 2011 [28].

This state of affairs has been partly due to a reluctance to report and/or bring proceedings under CMA. Many organisations are unwilling to prosecute their employees, preferring instead to adopt internal disciplinary procedures. Arguably, if there were prospects for restitutionary damages or compensation for loss then organisations would be more willing to prosecute [7, 16]. Most importantly, organisations fear the adverse publicity that the reporting of attacks would cause as well as publicising weaknesses that could attract further attacks [2].[6]

At the same time the enforcement of legislation is beset with difficulties of a procedural and evidentiary nature. Apprehending a remote hacker can be extremely difficult due to the anonymity that the use of internet provides and the opportunity to hide the true location of the offender. If prosecutions rates are to be improved, more expertise need be provided to the police. While the legal framework on cyber dependent crime can without a doubt contribute to the control of the misuse of information technology, it cannot successfully and effectively do so in isolation.

References

1. Office for National Statistics: Internet Access – Households and Individuals 2015 (Statistical Bulletin). https://www.ons.gov.uk/peoplepopulationandcommunity/householdcharacteristics/homeinternetandsocialmediausage/bulletins/internetaccesshouseholdsandindividuals/2015-08-06#main-points
2. Symantec: Internet Security Threat Report, April 2016. https://www.symantec.com/en/uk/security-center/threat-report
3. HMSO: A Strong Britain in an Age of Uncertainty: The National Security Strategy. HMSO, London (2010)
4. Cabinet Office: The UK Cyber Security Strategy: Protecting and Promoting the UK in a Digital World. Cabinet Office, London (2011)
5. Home Office: Cybercrime: a review of the evidence research report 75 (2013)
6. Walden, I.: Computer Crimes and Digital Investigations. Oxford University Press, Oxford (2016)
7. Fafinski, S.: The UK legislative position on cybercrime: a 20-year retrospective. J. Internet Law **13**, 3–13 (2009)
8. Fafinski, S.: Cyber crime. New Law J. **157** (2007)
9. Dumpbill, E.: Computer misuse act 1990 – part 1. NLJ **140**, 1117 (1990)
10. All Party Internet Group: Revision of the Computer Misuse Act: Report of an inquiry by the All Party Internet Group, June 2004. https://www.cl.cam.ac.uk/~rnc1/APIG-report-cma.pdf

---

[6] Symantec reports that in 2015, more and more companies chose not to reveal the full extent of the breaches they experienced. Companies choosing not to report the number of records lost increased by 85 percent [2].

11. Law Commission: 'Computer Misuse' Law Com No 186 Cm 819, HMSO (1989)
12. Explanatory Notes to the Police and Justice Act 2006
13. Wasik, M.: The emergence of computer law. In: Jewkes, Y., Yar, M. (eds.) Handbook of Internet Crime, p. 395. Routledge, Abingdon (2011)
14. CPS: Computer Misuse Act 1990 Legal Guidance. http://www.cps.gov.uk/legal/a_to_c/computer_misuse_act_1990/
15. Walton, R.: The Computer Misuse Act. 11 Information Security. Technical report 39 (2006)
16. MacEwan, N.: The Computer Misuse Act 1990: lessons from its past and predictions for its future. Crim. Law Rev. 12, 955 (2008)
17. Fafinski, S.: Access denied: computer misuse in an era of technologic change. JCL 70, 424 (2006)
18. Fafinski, S.: Computer misuse: the implications of the Police and Justice Act 2006. J. Crim. Law 72(1), 53 (2008)
19. Worthy, J., Fanning, M.: Denial of service: plugging the legal loopholes? CLSR 23, 194 (2007)
20. Fafinski, S.: Hacked off. Solicit. J. 150, 560 (2006)
21. Sommer, P.: Criminalizing hacking tools. Digit. Invest. 3, 68–72 (2006)
22. Katos, V., Furnell, S.: The security and privacy impact of criminalising the distribution of hacking tools. Comput. Fraud Secur. 2008, 9–16 (2008)
23. Rahman, R.: The legal measure against DoS attacks adopted by the UK legislature: should Malaysia follow suit? Int. J. Law Inf. Technol. 20, 85–101 (2012)
24. Council Directive (EC) 2013/40/EU of 12 August on attacks against information systems, replacing Council Framework Decision 2005/222/JHA [2013] OJ L218/8
25. Explanatory notes to the Serious Crime Act 2015. http://www.legislation.gov.uk/ukpga/2015/9/notes/contents
26. Home Office: Serious Crime Act 2015 - Fact sheet: Part 2: Computer misuse. https://www.gov.uk/government/publications/serious-crime-bill-computer-misuse. Accessed 04 Aug 2016
27. Zoest, J.: Computer Misuse Offences. Sweet & Maxwell, Insight, 5 May 2015
28. Home Office: Serious Crime Bill: Amendments to Computer Misuse Act 1990 Impact assessment (2014). https://www.gov.uk/government/uploads/system/uploads/attachment_data/file/317527/2014-06-03_signed_IA_CMA_EU_Directive.pdf

Cyber Intelligence and Operation

Aspects of Voice Communications Fraud

Alexandre Helenport and Bobby L. Tait[✉]

School of Computing, University of South Africa, Pretoria, South Africa
57634440@mylife.unisa.ac.za, taitbl@unisa.ac.za

Abstract. Voice communications fraud is prevalent in our society and yet often overlooked. Most approaches to securing voice communications focus on one or two main areas but fail to address the risks holistically. This paper outlines all areas that need to be considered when looking to address voice communications security inclusive of social engineering protection and proposes additional research to build an effective framework aimed at securing the enterprise against all types of voice communications fraud.

Keywords: Voice security · Toll-fraud · Telephony fraud · Phreaking · Session border controllers · Telephony denial of service · Social engineering

1 Introduction

From the moment they are born, humans communicate with each other. That communication uses different means (written, verbal, gesture, etc.) depending on a variety of factors such as age and development of the subjects, familiarity, location, environmental factors, emotional state, the existence of a common language and many others.

When possible, the use of an oral communication channel considerably enhances the effectiveness of the communication over the written channel [1, 2]. This makes verbal communication a prime mean of interaction between humans.

The evolution of technology over the years has brought verbal (and indeed visual) communications to a whole new level. Such communications no longer require physical presence and two persons can have a meaningful conversation even when separated by thousands of miles. Technology can even allow for near real-time translation and closed captioning when desired.

Telephony is a technology, or rather a collection of technologies, that has proven to be a game changer for our society. We rely on our phones and supporting infrastructure at home and at work, in business and in education, in private and in public. The telephone (both landline and mobile) has already made our world smaller by bringing people together across great distances whilst at the same creating many new possibilities and, alongside other communication technologies, even driving significant changes in our society [3, 4].

In a way, the telephone has brought increased security in our lives. It provides a way to ask for help quickly and efficiently. Even cars are now being fitted with built-in telephones to be able to provide immediate assistance in the event of an accident [5].

Conversely, the telephone became a target for fraudsters looking for financial and non-financial gains soon after it became widespread. The 1950s saw the beginning of

© Springer International Publishing AG 2016
H. Jahankhani et al. (Eds.): ICGS3 2017, CCIS 630, pp. 69–81, 2016.
DOI: 10.1007/978-3-319-51064-4_6

phreaking (this term is used to describe the act of illegally leveraging a telephone system to make free long-distance phone calls) [6]. This practice continues today, although in different ways given the changes in underlying technology. The recent telephony evolution to Voice over Internet Protocol (IP) has created new exploit vectors [7]. Beyond those new exploit vectors, Voice over IP (VoIP) has also greatly increased the number of phone systems that are exposed, directly or indirectly, to private and public data networks and brought the scale of phone systems to new levels which can make fraud both more lucrative (by providing the ability to conduct a larger exploit) and more transparent (by hiding the fraud amongst large volumes of calls).

2   Voice Communications Fraud

2.1   The Direct Cost of Voice Communications Fraud

The Centre for Strategic and International Studies estimates that cybercrime has an annual cost of the global economy of somewhere between $375 billion and $575 billion [8]. Fraud related to voice communications represents a very significant portion of that cost. Surveys have shown that over the last ten years, global fraud loss in voice communications ranges between $40 billion and $60 billion [9–12] therefore representing 10–15% of the total cost of cybercrime.

By its own definition, communications requires interconnectivity between platforms and between multiple parties. To provide the wide range of services typically offered, service providers and corporations build large infrastructures composed of a variety of platforms and including a number of interconnection points to external parties. As fraud can be both external and internal, each platform and each interconnection point should include adequate protection. Such complexity is clearly shown in the results of the Communications Fraud Control Association (CFCA) surveys [9–12] which outline the spread of fraud losses across many services as well as the fact that many vectors of attack are leveraged by the fraudsters.

Looking at CFCA survey results over the years we see a significant increase in global service provider revenue. In parallel, carriers have taken significant steps to combat fraud. This results in a relative decline in fraud but the numbers clearly show that it remains prevalent in the industry accounting for 1.7% to 5.1% of total revenue. Table 1 below shows the evolution of both telecom revenues and fraud losses over the last 10 years as recorded by the CFCA surveys conducted every two to three years.

Table 1. Fraud loss vs telecom revenue (source CFCA [11, 12])

	2005	2008	2011	2013	2015
Estimated global revenues	$1.2 tn	$1.7 tn	$2.1 tn	$2.2 tn	$2.25 tn
Estimated global fraud loss	$61.3 bn	$60.1 bn	$40.1 bn	$46.3 bn	$38.1 bn
% Loss	5.11%	3.54%	1.88%	2.09%	1.69%

To put voice communications fraud into context, the global fraud losses on credit cards in 2014 was $16.3 billion which represents only 0.057% of the $28.8 trillion in credit card transactions over the same period [13].

There are two main types of fraudsters targeting voice communications:

- Casual fraudsters who are typically looking to either challenge themselves, or make a little bit of many. Steve Wozniak and Steve Jobs for example are known to have tried their hand at phreaking [6]. There is a large number of online resources available to such fraudsters to guide them through their fraud attempts [14]
- Large criminal organisations with vast resources generating multi-million dollar revenues from their activities [14, 15]

Even more worrying is the fact that a portion of these voice communications fraud revenues is used as a means to fund terrorism [14, 15]. In fact, two of the FBI most wanted cybercriminals are fraudsters [16].

2.2   Voice Communications Fraud with Indirect Cost

We mentioned earlier that global fraud loss ranges between $40 billion and $60 billion annually and represents 10–15% of the total cost of cybercrime. These numbers exclusively represent the cost to service providers and their customers related to voice communications fraud and do not consider the costs related to loss of information directly resulting from a compromise in voice communications which would significantly increase the part that voice fraud plays in the overall cybercrime cost.

Compromising the privacy of voice (or visual) communications can result in a fraudster gaining access to confidential data, inclusive of intellectual property or personal information. Although this doesn't generate a direct voice communication cost to service providers or their customers, the compromise of that data is a portion of the cost of cybercrime. The loss of 800 million personal information records in 2013 is estimated to represent a $160 billion annual cost [8].

This number also does not show the loss of revenue from enterprises related to Denial of Service (DoS) attacks on their telephony or Contact Centre platforms. Such attacks can result in unavailability of a critical business offering or customer service. In addition to direct loss of revenue, depending on the scale of the attack, the associated outage and the press around it, the image of the company can be seriously tarnished resulting in sometimes very significant drop of sales (or drop of margin to attempt to continue attracting the customers by offering unbeatable prices). As an example, the Credit Card breach experienced by Target had a direct impact on its revenue and profit due to loss of customer confidence [17].

Last but not least: social engineering. According to Wikipedia, "Social engineering, in the context of information security, refers to psychological manipulation of people into performing actions or divulging confidential information" [18]. To put it into simple terms, the attacker is simply trying to get useful information through a direct contact with their target or a related party. Telephone conversations are a prime medium for social engineering attacks. Contrary to written exchanges, the attacker can adapt their approach in the middle of the interaction based on their assessment of the cooperation, or lack thereof, and assessed mind-set of their target.

Whilst gathering a little bit of information at a time through social engineering can seem cumbersome and not really worthwhile, it is the doors that those pieces of information open that are the real benefit to the fraudsters. According to security expert Aamir Lakhani, 100% of penetration testing is successful when using social engineering as part of the effort [19, 20]. The use of social engineering provides information allowing attackers to go past the technical defences in place to protect access to information [19, 21, 22] and in some cases secure immediate financial gain [23, 24].

With 48% of companies having already suffered a social engineering attack, with 75% success rate on calls to businesses [25, 26] and with governmental agencies with high security awareness falling into the traps [19, 20], everyone is a target and everyone is at risk.

2.3   Main Categories of Voice Communications Fraud

Voice communications fraud can be split into four main categories:

1. Toll-Fraud
2. Breach of confidentiality
3. Identity theft
4. Denial of service

The first category, toll-fraud, is where infrastructure is used without the permission (and sometimes knowledge) of the responsible entities and at a cost to them. As mentioned earlier, toll-fraud has an annual cost of $40 billion to $60 billion.

Breach of confidentiality, consists in unauthorised eavesdropping on communications or disclosure of protected information to third-parties by unsuspecting employees or contractors. Social engineering fits into this category although it is not alone: the ability to intercept a conversation that is meant to be private is also breach of confidentiality.

Identity theft, where one or multiple third-parties present themselves as a specific individual or as a representative of a company with ill intensions. Social Engineering attacks leverage in most cases identity theft techniques to achieve their goal. Caller ID spoofing is an example of identity theft, but it could go much beyond that through the compromise of a phone system.

Telephony Denial of service (TDoS) occurs when one or multiple third-parties overload a phone system resulting in its inability to provide the service for which it was built. TDoS can take multiple forms, sometimes with the inclusion of a social networking aspect to it by effectively using social networking sites to convince normal users to participate in a TDoS attack by calling a specific phone number at a specific time as retaliation against a company (either willingly or inadvertently [27]).

Note that some exploits may fit into more than one of the above categories. This categorisation has been used by others in the past (in some cases with minimum differences in the categories) [28] and there are others categorisations that are equally valid [29, 30]. The intention here is not to compare them but simply to show the breadth of voice communications fraud.

3 Security Landscape for Voice Communications

3.1 Transport Layer Security

Legacy non IP platforms operated on dedicated circuit switched networks segregated from the packet switched data networks. That simple separation meant that as a first step to a compromise of a voice infrastructure, the attacker needed to gain access to the underlying transport which typically required physical access. Once the attacker had gained that access and wanted to use it to compromise the voice platform, they were limited to a set of clearly defined voice commands for their attacks since that is all that the voice platforms would understand. Even PBX management consoles were typically isolated systems with a direct console connection to the PBX that required physical access to make any change. Physical security would guarantee the protection of the system.

The move to IP transport has significantly changed the voice environment. Voice traffic is now co-existent with data traffic on both private and public networks. Computers and voice platforms co-exist on the same network and can interact with each other. The generalisation of softphones and unified communications clients even furthers this co-existence by transforming the computer into a telephone. Although there are many benefits to this transport convergence, it also comes with risks. One of the most obvious risks is the fact that vulnerabilities at the IP transport layer now have a direct impact on the security of voice communications [31]. As a result, voice communications have a direct reliance on data network security to provide it with adequate protection.

The basics of network security need to be applied to environments hosting VoIP platforms. Security zones play a very important part in setting up a network [32] and the zoning principle needs to be applied to the networks hosting the voice platforms. Voice platforms should be installed in the appropriate network security zone (note that the appropriate zone might be different from system to system depending on its criticality and the nature of the calls it facilitates). Best practices in network security dictate security zones to be segregated through the use of firewalls and intrusion detection and prevention systems (IDPS) [33].

Zoning in itself is not sufficient. To provide adequate protection, the network infrastructure itself needs to ensure that the segregation is maintained at all times, that attackers can't get a copy of the traffic, that they can't insert themselves in the path, and more. Well known exploits such as VLAN hopping, Man-in-the-Middle attack, and others need to be prevented [34].

There is extensive research and documentation available detailing how to adequately protect the network infrastructure. Implementing those protections is a mandatory first step to securing voice communications. As an example, [35] provides a general view of processes and technologies that allow securing the infrastructure (both network and platform). This also needs to include adequate on-going processes to manage and enforce security policies on those platforms [36].

3.2   Voice Layer Security

Voice platforms can be proprietary appliances running on custom operating systems or simply leverage hardened or out-of-the-box operating systems widely available. Those platforms may be physical platforms or virtual machines. Over the last few years, the market has evolved greatly towards virtual machines and even when the hardware is mandated and sold by the voice platform manufacturer, it generally runs a custom hypervisor with the voice platform itself running on virtual machines. There is a common saying that "Security is as Strong as its Weakest Link" (believed to be attributable in its original form to Reid [37]) and voice communications are no exception. The underlying physical platforms, the virtual machine hypervisor, the operating system and the voice application itself all need to be adequately secured to ensure the desired level of protection for voice communications.

Once the desired security of the underlying transport and platform has been attained, we must move our focus to the application layer itself, in our case the voice layer. Mostly due to its real-time nature and uniqueness of payload compared to typical applications, Voice over IP does not utilise proven protocols that existed at its inception such as File Transfer Protocol (FTP) or Simple Mail Transfer Protocol (SMTP). Instead, new protocols were developed to make VoIP possible. The most common protocols used by VoIP are:

- RTP and RTCP (RFC 1889 superseded by RFC 3550) [38, 39]
- SRTP and SRTCP (RFC 3711) [40]
- H.323 (ITU-T recommendation H.323 11/96 superseded by H.323 12/09) [41, 42]
- SIP (RFC 2543 superseded by RFC 3261 and numerous extensions) [43, 44].

Those protocols have inherent differences that make some of them more appropriate to a secure deployment. At this time, the industry is moving towards SIP signalling. This is also visible in the selection of SIP as the base protocol for the IP Multimedia Subsystem (IMS) framework adopted by the cellular network industry [45]. Enterprises choosing to deploy encrypted communications are leveraging the capabilities built within the SIP protocol to secure voice communications [46] along with SRTP to secure the media.

The actual protocol implementation within the application is key to ensuring that the security built into the protocol is maintained [47]. In addition to this, it is good practice to do protocol analysis at the border, comparable to the analysis that firewalls perform for other protocols and applications. In the case of voice protocols, this function is performed by a Session Border Controller (SBC). SBCs are platforms dedicated to voice over IP security. They have a thorough understanding of voice protocols, much beyond that of a typical firewall, and can identify exploit attempts within the voice protocols [48]. Security conscious organisations deploy those SBCs as border elements between their voice infrastructure and external parties for all voice and video traffic (aside from the different codec used to encode the media and the associated payload, there is little to no difference in the protocols used for voice over IP and video over IP).

Beyond ensuring that there are no exploits leveraged at the protocol layer, most Session Border Controllers also provide some level of protection against Denial of

Service attacks (through Call Admission Control), ensure topology hiding and validate call routing (for example allowing only inbound calls destined to the organisation and blocking exploit routes through the organisation) [48].

The main purpose of the voice infrastructure is to carry phone calls. One of the key capabilities it provides is the ability to connect with outside parties. Similar to what we see with email communications, one of the challenges is that outside parties are not authenticated but yet have a legitimate need to connect through the voice platform. This opens the door to attempted abuse of the voice platform through what needs to remain an open access. As an example, an audio conferencing platform offers the opportunity for external callers to dial in with a meeting identifier and/or code. Fraudsters might try a brute force attack on the audio conferencing platform by dialling through that channel repeatedly and attempting multiple meeting identifiers and/or codes. This further increases the complexity of voice security as each call taken individually is valid yet the multitude of them makes it fraud. Most voice platforms are built to handle each session independently, in particular given the fact that they are providing a critical real-time service requiring a near instant response, and ill-positioned to analyse trends.

There are two main approaches to identifying such fraud:

- Proactive through the use of a voice platform able to do dynamic analysis of call patterns as they happen
- Reactive through the use of a Call Details Record (CDR) analyser platform

Such fraud is located at the voice layer itself and is therefore independent of the underlying transport. It works on both legacy infrastructure and voice over IP networks and has existed pretty much since telephony was invented. Unfortunately, this is an area where voice security is particularly lacking. The theoretical capabilities to create such fraud prevention systems exist [49, 50], and there are some product offerings on the market (SecureLogix, TollShield, TransNexus and others) but the largest telephony platforms manufacturers (with the notable exception of NEC and their Toll Guard product) do not offer that capability natively in their portfolio (Avaya, Cisco, Microsoft, Mitel). This creates a gap in most enterprises who typically rely on a small number of key partners for all their telephony services and apply best practices as communicated by those vendors. Such best practices are incomplete and put a significant portion of the protection requirements onto the service providers. This is clearly visible in the multitude of successful toll-fraud attacks targeting enterprises [14, 15, 51].

Another important aspect of voice security is endpoint registration, authentication and authorisation. Once registered, an endpoint has a set of permissions associated to it depending on the endpoint profile created on the voice platform. To avoid fraud, the registration process must include sufficient protection to ensure that only legitimate endpoints connect to the voice infrastructure and prevent registration hijacking [7]. This is partially achieved by limiting registration origination to only trusted source networks but also requires a secure registration and authentication process for both initial and subsequent registrations. Most phone systems offer that capability natively, relying on well-known authentication mechanisms (unique identifiers, certificates, key exchange, etc.).

In addition to this, the permissions associated to each endpoint must be limited to only that which is justified by the business requirements (and updated as needed over time). This ensures that any fraud related to this specific endpoint is contained by those permissions therefore limiting the extent of the damage. As voice platforms have native support for permissions management, the configuration and on-going management of those permissions is where the complexity lies. Configuration management is an often overlooked aspect of voice security [52].

3.3   Information Security Culture, Social Engineering and Voice Communications

Employees are the most cited source of security incidents and as a result 53% of Businesses invest in employee training and awareness programs [53]. It is a well-known fact that training and awareness programs play a key part in information security.

In most enterprises, such training tends to focus on sharing the internal information security policies and well recognised best practices such as "do not share your password". Very few, if any, organisations implement thorough controls that allow near real-time detection of targeted social engineering attacks over all possible vectors. Enterprises use a number of automated tools to prevent social engineering attacks leveraging email and web browsing medium. SPAM and phishing filters are used to prevent such attacks along with email tagging techniques (for example prepending the subject of all external emails with the word EXTERNAL) [54]. Proxy servers and website filtering lists are used to prevent access to websites deemed risky or compromised. Data Loss Prevention (DLP) technology can also be used to prevent sharing of company confidential information with external parties [55].

Unfortunately, very little of the training and awareness programs, and very little technology focus on voice communications fraud. At a high level, the only difference between email and voice is the medium. Both of them facilitate communication of information between parties. Email security is now mature with multiple technologies allowing for the validation of each and every email looking at source, path, content, historical profiles and other attributes of emails.

Although the same technological principles could be applied to voice communications (performing call validation through analysis of the origin of the call, its path, the actual content of the conversation, historical call profiles and more), there are not many solutions on the market that perform such analysis. All fraud protection solutions available today are focused solely on the historical call profile analysis (see above discussion on fraud detection based on CDR analysis and dynamic real-time analysis of call patterns) and there are no available products offering fraud detection through analysis of call origination, call path and content of conversation at any given time. Limitations in existing voice communications technology may prevent the immediate creation of such products or limit their effectiveness, but we believe that research in this space is required and would enable improved fraud detection similar to the benefits that technologies such as Domain Name Resolution Real-time Black hole List System (DNSRBL) brought for fraudulent email detection [56]. Hoffstadt et al. actually proposed a framework to extend RBL to voice communications [57].

South African scholars have proposed a Social Engineering Attack Detection Model (SEADM) to allow for near real-time detection of social engineering attacks [58, 59]. Such a model can be implemented via policy, or indeed by routing password reset and other requests through an automated interactive voice response (IVR) system designed to determine the legitimacy of a request.

Social engineering attackers have mastered techniques of persuasion [60] and combine those techniques with the leverage of known weaknesses of the voice communications infrastructure to achieve their goals (misrepresenting calling source, etc.) [61]. This, along with the fact that our society favours face-to-face and voice interactions over written exchanges [1, 2], clearly outlines the importance of including social engineering detection as part of a holistic approach to voice communications security.

4 Identified Gaps and Upcoming Research

Voice communications represent a very attractive target for fraudsters looking for either immediate financial gain or information (either valuable information such as personal data, intellectual property, company secrets, etc.... or even what could seem very basic and innocent such as a high-level view on current projects or name of co-workers).

Although awareness around security and risk is continuously increasing and most enterprises have cybersecurity organisations, policies and best practices in place, in most cases those overlook the risk associated with voice communications and put their focus on securing applications and IP transport along with user education and awareness program. This approach leaves a gap that can be exploited by fraudsters allowing them to leverage voice communications as a means to bypass the protections put in place by the enterprise.

Simple searches in Google Scholar also outline the difference in research focus between voice communications security and network security. Table 2 captures the number of search results on June 12th 2016 focusing on somewhat adjacent voice and data security terms.

Table 2. Count of Google Scholar search results

Voice term		Data term	
VoIP security	2,050	Network security	304,000
Session border controller	1,480	Firewall	152,000
SIP vulnerabilities	152	FTP vulnerabilities	20,300
SRTP	8,320	HTTPS	2,400,000
SPAM over IP telephony	205	Email spam	5,930
Toll-fraud	834	Credit-card fraud	18,600

Although the terms used in the search where fairly generic terms, the results show that Voice security remains a topic of limited interest outside voice communication security specialists.

This paper clearly shows that there are several gaps in existing research around Voice Communications Fraud and associated security. As outlined by Professor Keromytis in his extensive survey of research material around Voice over IP Security, there is a particular lack of holistic approach to voice over IP security [52]. Service abuse threats, configuration management, denial of service as well as voice communications payload are all areas that would particularly benefit from additional research. For example, we failed to identify any research that proposes to leverage automated real-time tools to detect and block social engineering attacks by looking at the characteristics of voice communications.

As cellular networks are also migrating to IP transport and SIP, it becomes increasingly critical to address those gaps. Although highly beneficial overall and a great technological progress, this migration opens up additional fraud opportunities in voice communications and it is of paramount importance to ensure adequate protection.

Although most enterprises have significant programs and organisations dedicated to ensuring an appropriate level of IT security, we believe that most of those Enterprises are not aware of the significance of the risk that toll-fraud and other voice communications frauds represent to their business, nor are adequately protected against it.

To complement existing research, we propose to conduct interviews of security and telecommunications technical leaders and executives in large enterprises, service providers and voice product manufacturers with a goal to assess perceived adequacy of large enterprises protection against voice communications fraud. The outcome of these interviews alongside survey results of employees within a large enterprise will then be used to propose a practical framework aimed at ensuring the security of voice communications in a large enterprise. This research can then be further enhanced by expanding the scope beyond large enterprises.

5   Conclusion

Voice communications fraud is prevalent in the industry resulting in billions of dollars of direct revenue losses. Data illegitimately acquired through voice communications breaches is also used as a means to facilitate cybercrime in other areas. In contrast, the research in this space is considerably more limited than other areas of cybercrime.

This paper identifies the various aspects of voice communications fraud along with the main risk areas and provides some guidance around protecting against those risks. It also outlines a number of gaps in available protection and proposes additional research to gather a more holistic view around risks associated with voice communications fraud and compile a framework to be used as the bases for protection against such fraud.

We hope that this paper will bring some much needed awareness around voice communications fraud whilst at the same time encouraging further collaboration on this topic. We would like to encourage anyone interested in such a collaboration to contact the authors of this paper directly.

References

1. Westmyer, S.A., DiCioccio, R.L., Rubin, R.B.: Appropriateness and effectiveness of communication channels in competent interpersonal communication. J. Commun. **48**, 27–48 (1998)
2. Perse, E.M., Courtright, J.A.: Normative images of communication media mass and interpersonal channels in the new media environment. Hum. Commun. Res. **19**, 485–503 (1993)
3. de Sola Pool, I.: Forecasting the Telephone: A Retrospective Technology Assessment. Ablex, New York (1983)
4. Overå, R.: Networks, distance, and trust: telecommunications development and changing trading practices in Ghana. World Dev. **34**, 1301–1315 (2006)
5. Opel news - opel OnStar to set new standards in vehicle safety and connectivity - opel ireland. http://www.opel.ie/experience-opel/opel-about/opel-news/2015/March/opel-onstar-to-set-new-standards-in-vehicle-safety-and-connectivity.html. Accessed 6 Oct 2016
6. Phreaking. Wikipedia (2016). https://en.wikipedia.org/wiki/Phreaking. Accessed 6 Oct 2016
7. Butcher, D., Li, X., Guo, J.: Security challenge and defense in VoIP infrastructures. IEEE Trans. Syst. Man and Cybern. Part C: Appl. Rev. **37**, 1152–1162 (2007)
8. Centre for Strategic & International Studies: Net losses: Estimating the global cost of cybercrime. (2014)
9. Communications Fraud Control Association: 2009 global fraud loss survey (2009)
10. Communications Fraud Control Association: 2011 global fraud loss survey (2012)
11. Communications Fraud Control Association: 2013 global fraud loss survey (2013)
12. Communications Fraud Control Association: 2015 global fraud loss survey. (2015)
13. HSN Consultants: The Nilson report - July 2015. 1068 (2015)
14. Markowitz, E.: The inside story of how Pakistan took down the FBI's most-wanted cybercriminal (2015). http://www.ibtimes.com/inside-story-how-pakistan-took-down-fbis-most-wanted-cybercriminal-1860808. Accessed 6 Nov 2016
15. Gallagher, S.: How filipino phreakers turned PBX systems into cash machines for terrorists. ars Technica (2011). http://arstechnica.com/tech-policy/2011/11/how-filipino-phreakers-turned-pbx-systems-into-cash-machines-for-terrorists/. Accessed 6 Nov 2016
16. FBI: FBI - cyber's most wanted. FBI. https://www.fbi.gov/wanted/cyber. Accessed 6 Nov 2016
17. McGrath, M.: Target profit falls 46% on credit card breach and the hits could keep on coming. Forbes (2014). http://www.forbes.com/sites/maggiemcgrath/2014/02/26/target-profit-falls-46-on-credit-card-breach-and-says-the-hits-could-keep-on-coming/#2c1a6eac5e8c. Accessed 6 Nov 2016
18. Social engineering. Wikipedia (2016). https://en.wikipedia.org/wiki/Social_engineering_(security). Accessed 6 Nov 2016
19. Constantin, L.: Fake social media ID duped security-aware IT guys. PC World (2013). http://www.pcworld.com/article/2059940/fake-social-media-id-duped-securityaware-it-guys.html. Accessed 6 Nov 2016
20. Blue, V.: Government agency compromised by fake facebook hottie. ZDNet (2013). http://www.zdnet.com/article/government-agency-compromised-by-fake-facebook-hottie/. Accessed 6 Nov 2016
21. Lambert, P.: Security's weakest link: technology no match for social engineering. TechRepublic (2013). http://www.techrepublic.com/blog/it-security/securitys-weakest-link-technology-no-match-for-social-engineering/. Accessed 6 Nov 2016

22. Hulme, G.V.: Social engineering attacks from the front lines. CSO (2015). http://www.csoonline.com/article/2876707/social-engineering/social-engineering-stories-from-the-front-lines.html. Accessed 6 Nov 2016

23. IRS: Scam phone calls continue; IRS identifies five easy ways to spot suspicious calls. IRS (2014). https://www.irs.gov/uac/newsroom/scam-phone-calls-continue-irs-identifies-five-easy-ways-to-spot-suspicious-calls. Accessed 6 Nov 2016

24. Cooper, C.: IRS calling? Nope. It's a scam. CNET (2014). http://www.cnet.com/news/scam-draft-internal-revenue-service-irs-phishing/. Accessed 6 Nov 2016

25. DuPaul, N.: Hacking the mind: how and why social engineering works. Veracode (2013). https://www.veracode.com/blog/2013/03/hacking-the-mind-how-why-social-engineering-works. Accessed 6 Nov 2016

26. Help Net Security: 48% of enterprises targeted by social engineering attacks. Help Net Security (2011). https://www.helpnetsecurity.com/2011/09/21/48-of-enterprises-targeted-by-social-engineering-attacks/. Accessed 6 Nov 2016

27. Fox News: Rapper the game may face charges tied to flash mob calls. Fox News (2011). http://www.foxnews.com/entertainment/2011/08/14/rapper-game-may-face-charges-tied-to-flash-mob-calls.html. Accessed 6 Nov 2016

28. Thermos, P., Takanen, A.: Securing VoIP Networks. Pearson Education, Upper Saddle River (2007)

29. Lazzez, A.: VoIP technology: Security issues analysis. IJETTCS **2**, 333–341 (2013)

30. Park, P.: Voice Over IP Security. Pearson Education, Upper Saddle River (2008)

31. Almeida, F., Cruz, J.: Mitigation of security concerns of VoIP in the corporate environment, pp. 257–269 (2013)

32. Malik, S.: Network Security Principles and Practices. Cisco Press, Indianapolis (2003)

33. Gontarczyk, A., McMillan, P., Pavlovski, C.: Cyber security zone modeling in practice (2015)

34. Kiravuo, T., Sarela, M., Manner, J.: A survey of ethernet lan security. IEEE Commun. Surv. Tutorials **15**, 1477–1491 (2013)

35. Vacca, J.R.: Network and System Security. Elsevier, New York (2013)

36. Macfarlane, R., Buchanan, W., Ekonomou, E., Uthmani, O., Fan, L., Lo, O.: Formal security policy implementations in network firewalls. Comput. Secur. **31**, 253–270 (2012)

37. Reid, T.: Essays on the Intellectual Powers of Man. Cambridge University Press, Cambridge (1855)

38. Schulzrinne, H., Casner, S., Frederick, R., Jacobson, V.: RTP: a transport protocol for real-time applications. RFC1889 (1996)

39. Schulzrinne, H., Casner, S., Frederick, R., Jacobson, V.: RTP: a transport protocol for real-time applications. RFC3550 (2003)

40. Baugher, M., McGrew, D., Naslund, M., Carrara, E., Norrman, K.: The secure real-time transport protocol (SRTP). RFC3711 (2004)

41. ITU-T Study Group 16: Packet-based multimedia communications systems. ITU-T H.323 (11/1996) (1996)

42. ITU-T Study Group 16: Packet-based multimedia communications systems. ITU-T H.323 v7 (12/2009) (2009)

43. Handley, M., Schulzrinne, H., Schooler, E., Rosenberg, J.: SIP: Session initiation protocol. RFC2543 (1999)

44. Rosenberg, J., Schulzrinne, H., Camarillo, G., Johnston, A., Peterson, J., Sparks, R., Handley, M., Schooler, E.: SIP: Session initiation protocol. RFC3261 (2003)

45. 3GPP: IP multimedia subsystem, stage 2.3GPP TS 23.228 (2016)

46. Basicevic, I., Popovic, M., Kukolj, D.: Comparison of SIP and H.323 protocols, pp. 162–167 (2008)

47. Gupta, P., Shmatikov, V.: Security analysis of voice-over-IP protocols, pp. 49–63 (2007)
48. Hardwick, J.: Session border controllers enabling the VoIP revolution. Metaswitch Networks, London (2005)
49. Hofbauer, S.: A privacy conserving approach for the development of SIP security services to prevent certain types of MITM and toll fraud attacks in VoIP systems (2014)
50. Kim, K., Kim, T., Cho, N., Kim, M.: Toll fraud detection of VoIP service networks in ubiquitous computing environments. Int. J. Distrib. Sens. Netw. **2015**, 5 (2015)
51. TransNexus: $166,000 telecom fraud case study - TransNexus. TransNexus (2014). http://transnexus.com/company/news-events/press-releases/2014-press-releases/166000-telecom-fraud-case-study/. Accessed 6 Dec 2016
52. Keromytis, A.D.: A comprehensive survey of voice over IP security research. IEEE Commun. Surv. Tutorials **14**, 514–537 (2012)
53. PwC: The global state of information security survey 2016 (2016)
54. Almomani, A., Gupta, B., Atawneh, S., Meulenberg, A., Almomani, E.: A survey of phishing email filtering techniques. IEEE Commun. Surv. Tutorials **15**, 2070–2090 (2013)
55. Tahboub, R., Saleh, Y.: Data leakage/loss prevention systems (DLP), pp. 1–6 (2014)
56. Popovici, Z.O., Brad, R.: DNS real-time black hole list system (2009)
57. Hoffstadt, D., Rathgeb, E., Liebig, M., Meister, R., Rebahi, Y., Thanh, T.Q.: A comprehensive framework for detecting and preventing VoIP fraud and misuse, pp. 807–813 (2014)
58. Bezuidenhout, M., Mouton, F., Venter, H.S.: Social engineering attack detection model: SEADM, pp. 1–8 (2010)
59. Mouton, F., Leenen, L., Venter H.: Social engineering attack detection model: SEADMv2., pp. 216–223 (2015)
60. Luo, X.R., Brody, R., Seazzu, A., Burd, S.: Social engineering: the neglected human factor for. IRMJ **24**, 1–8 (2011)
61. Gupta S., Gupta P., Ahamad M., Kumaraguru, P.: Abusing phone numbers and cross-application features for crafting targeted attacks (2015)

Scalable Frameworks for Application Security and Data Protection

Ilya Kabanov[(⊠)]

CDI Corporation, Cambridge, MA, USA
Ilya.Kabanov@sloan.mit.edu

Abstract. Nationwide organizations face the challenge of managing the cyber risk profile while delivering software solutions to meet growing and changing requirements of customers, regulators, and internal stakeholders. Companies operate in competing priorities having limited resources available. It is crucial to design and deploy scalable frameworks that help prioritizing actions in the "Identify. Protect. Detect. Respond. Recover." paradigm. Unsecure practices at developing, and deploying applications and dependency on improperly managed web and cloud-based services may lead to data compromise. In the article, the author introduces an approach to identify high-yield opportunities for building cybersecurity capabilities and proposes a framework for delivering application security and compliance on scale. Effective frameworks allow the transformation of costs into value for businesses and their customers through achieving compliance, measuring security risks, and keeping them under control.

Keywords: Framework · Application security · Data protection · Regulatory compliance

1 Introduction

The information technology landscape of global conglomerates is usually extremely complex. It comprises various components that interact at different levels internally compared to exposure to an external environment. These interactions can provoke unexpected phenomena. At the same time, organizations are obliged to achieve and maintain compliance with a variety of public and commercial regulatory requirements. Personal data privacy regulations provide an example, including The General Data Protection Regulation (GDPR) for organizations that process personal data of EU residents; another example includes the Health Insurance Portability and Accountability Act (HIPAA), which applies to health care clearinghouses and health care providers that use electronic transactions to transfer personal information in the United States. Further, the Payment Card Industry Data Security Standard (PCI DSS) required by various credit and debit card brands, increases cardholder data privacy requirements to improve fraud protection. The enterprises need to secure themselves against cyber-attacks by rigorously defending their networks, systems, and operations against a variety of internal and external threats. Because companies do not have unlimited resources, they need to act in a rational way to apply information security measures and controls to their systems.

© Springer International Publishing AG 2016
H. Jahankhani et al. (Eds.): ICGS3 2017, CCIS 630, pp. 82–95, 2016.
DOI: 10.1007/978-3-319-51064-4_7

The complexity of systems composed of many parts that interact with and adapt to each other cannot be understood easily and adequately by only studying their component parts. "This is because the behavior of such systems arises through the interactions among those parts" [1]. These complex systems may lead to an increase of the probability and potential severity of cyber risks because of technical vulnerabilities, human errors, or failures in organizational and operational processes. These phenomena occur in multiple time and space scales. Evaluating risk requires actors to consider various parameters at the same time. It is helpful to consider these parameters in the context of classic modeling forms, such as statistical models, probabilities, system dynamics, and mathematical models. Modeling makes the concept of systems easier to understand because it takes the complexity of interactions and system behavior into account. Given this context, the use of systems modeling can help companies prioritize cyber risk management activities through a better understanding of a dynamic behavior of systems.

There is no one-size-fits-all solution for cybersecurity and compliance, and neither regulatory bodies nor standard organizations can provide comprehensive, prescriptive guidelines for all entities across industries. These various options offer a variety of standards for improving cybersecurity, but most to do not address every critical area. These generic frameworks have many challenges related to implementation and general operation on a large scale. As these frameworks develop, state-mandated programs and voluntarily initiatives seem to focus on a bottom-up approach to enhancing private-sector cybersecurity. In addition, there have been many attempts to identify similarities and differences between a large variety of regulations, standards, and frameworks to harmonize cybersecurity best practices while also mapping controls to streamline compliance processes for businesses and empowering them by comprehensive cyber protection instruments.

There are several groups of objectives that global companies would typically like to achieve:

1. Compliance with numerous U.S. and foreign governmental and commercial regulatory requirements is vital to enable business in certain regions or specific industries. This increases the overall ability to work as a global business, which, in turn, allows the business to increase profits and sales. Compliance with PCI DSS is a prime example.
2. Certain industries also require advanced compliance. The healthcare industry is particularly relevant. HIPAA compliance focuses on protecting individuals' medical records and other personal health information and applies to health care providers that conduct certain health care transactions electronically. Another example is bidding on a Department of Defense (DoD) contracts, because vendors need to meet DFARS (Defense Federal Acquisition Regulation Supplement), subpart 204.73. Commercial business partners also have various contractual data security requirements as well.
3. Processing of personal data also requires compliance with regulatory requirements. The environment is emerging and very complex, and requirements vary. This creates a problem for global companies as they attempt to conduct business in several countries.

4. Compliance with insurance requirements regarding cybersecurity also creates another layer of complexity. Entities must deliver and constantly maintain compliance with requirements of cybersecurity insurance[1] carriers in order to maintain eligibility for the coverage of potential cyber-related risks. Requirements for insurance purposes may include the use of encryption, patching, regular vulnerability assessment, and many others.

5. Lastly, all of these compliance considerations must also align with cybersecurity best practices through compliance with internal policies, standards, and guidelines in the areas of information technology security, data protection, and information technology service delivery.

To support these statements, the author refers to the survey conducted by Dimensional Research in March 2016, which assesses adoption patterns for widely used security frameworks. The survey was completed by 338 IT and security professionals in the United States. It reveals that "84% of organizations surveyed already leverage some type of security framework." [2] Thus, adoption of security frameworks is considered common practice.

Use of a framework was attributed to three key motivations:

- aligning with cybersecurity best practices: 70%;
- business partner requirements: 29%; and
- federal contract requirements: 28%.

Nearly half of organizations surveyed reported that they use more than one framework in their security program. In fact, 15% of organizations are using three or more. The rates for adoption rates of individual frameworks vary significantly by size of the organization and the particular industry in which it works (Fig. 1).

The banking and finance sectors generally have at least one security framework. Information technology organizations are also more likely to have at least one security framework. Further, "banking and finance, information technology, government, and manufacturing all have security framework adoption rates above 80%. Education and healthcare follow slightly behind at 77% and 61% respectively" [2]. Perhaps the rationale for this difference among industries is, in part, due to the various levels of regulation imposed both internally and by the government or regulating authority. Banking and finance, for example, is one of the most heavily regulated industries in the United States, especially regarding security, so the fact that they adopt security frameworks at higher rates seems logical. In addition, the risks associated with a

---

[1] "Cybersecurity insurance is designed to mitigate losses from a variety of cyber incidents, including data breaches, business interruption, and network damage. A robust cybersecurity insurance market could help reduce the number of successful cyber attacks by: (1) promoting the adoption of preventative measures in return for more coverage; and (2) encouraging the implementation of best practices by basing premiums on an insured's level of self-protection. Many companies forego available policies, however, citing as rationales the perceived high cost of those policies, confusion about what they cover, and uncertainty that their organizations will suffer a cyber attack. In recent years, the Department of Homeland Security National Protection and Programs Directorate (NPPD) has engaged key stakeholders to address this emerging cyber risk area." The Department of Homeland Security, (June 30, 2016), https://www.dhs.gov/cybersecurity-insurance.

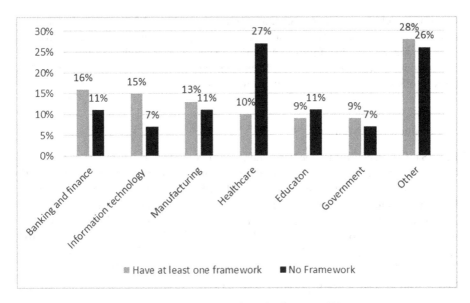

Fig. 1. Industry security adoption rates [2]

compromise of private financial information can lead to a host of other problems. In essence, the exposure to risk is higher, which means that the stakes of noncompliance are higher as well. In addition, the potential for negative consequences not only affects the individual, it also affects the financial institution as a whole.

Security teams struggle to balance the need for cybersecurity with their limited resources to find a framework that works for their industry or individual business. Although they have guidance, they are receiving suggestions and "best practices" from a variety of sources, many of which conflict one another. The struggle becomes even more difficult because entities do not have the funds available to test and implement a framework that works. Funding limitations lead to the need to prioritize certain cyber security concerns over others.

2   Frameworks Landscape Analysis

As the survey conducted by Dimensional Research in March 2016 points out, there is no single security framework that is being used by the majority of companies. "There are several security frameworks in common use including PCI (47%), ISO (35%), CIS (32%), and CSF (29%). The survey participants who took the time to write in "Other" answers added HIPAA, FFIEC, HITECH, CIP, and internally-developed guidelines to this list" [2]. Therefore, the author had to perform the frameworks landscape analysis to identify the most effective solution for the global company to comply with personal data privacy regulatory requirements and achieve a sustainable cyber risk profile, taking into account the objectives described above.

Unfortunately, organizations cannot rely on one standard framework. Relying on just one overarching framework would promote simplicity and efficiency, but there is no single framework that fulfills all of the needs of every industry and is able to accommodate a variety of objectives. Each framework has strengths in some areas, but falters in other areas and usually fails to meet competing requirements.

2.1 Frameworks Mapping

The NIST Cybersecurity Framework claims to be comprehensive in that it addresses the needs of objects of critical infrastructure (Table 1). The creation of the framework was ordered in Executive Order 13636, issued on February 19, 2013. The order states: "The Cybersecurity Framework shall provide a prioritized, flexible, repeatable, performance-based, and cost-effective approach, including information security measures and controls, to help owners and operators of critical infrastructure identify, assess, and manage cyber risk." [3] The final framework was released on February 12, 2014. In 2015, Gartner estimated that the framework is used by 30% of U.S. organizations, with projected use of 50% by 2020 [4].

Table 1. 16 sectors of critical infrastructure as defined by The US Presidential Policy Directive 21(Department of Homeland Security, Critical Infrastructure Sector)

Chemicals	Dams	Financial services	Information
Commercial	Emergency	Government facilities	technology
facilities	services	Critical manufacturing	Nuclear reactors,
Communications	Water &	Transportation systems	materials, & waste
Healthcare &	wastewater		Food & agriculture
public health	systems		
Energy	Defense		
	industrial base		

The author designed the framework at the largest leading global energy management provider and, in that process, the major assumption was that the NIST framework could be taken as the key framework that the global company should consider when applying essential mechanisms to elevate existing cybersecurity capabilities.

"The NIST framework has created a common language to facilitate the conversation about cybersecurity processes, policies, and technologies, both internally and with external entities, such as third-party service providers and partners" [5]. However, there are some factors that blocked the adoption of the framework on a solo basis.

First, the framework lacks personal data privacy regulatory requirements and standards. Experts from PWC argued that "NIST abandoned its proposed methodology to address privacy and civil liberties concerns due to a lack of consensus and support from industry participants" [6]. Many practitioners are also concerned that the approach proposed by NIST is not consistent with private-sector practices, which might inhibit adoption of the Framework.

Second, it does not address the need to implement processes tailored to a specific organization. A successful framework will work to identify and understand an organization's unique threats and capabilities. It should also specifically address the data these organizations use and gather. These obligations should be an integral part of a cyber security strategy. An effective cybersecurity program can only apply commensurate safeguards once it understands and identifies concern areas.

Third, lead time before deployment and use can be extensive. This will be a key challenge for many, as will be the lengthy timeframe necessary to adopt the framework fully. The initial identification of assets may take several years for large organizations, and this process may delay implementation of detection activities. Nonetheless, the organization cannot defer cybersecurity implementation.

These limitations were recognized and extensively considered. They also triggered the decision to consider the problem holistically to develop a proprietary framework that will address these limitations. Perhaps melding other frameworks together would produce the best overall approach. A broader look at all of the options is necessary. The author started his analysis for the global organization mentioned above from a broad review and categorization of the regulatory landscape, existing frameworks, and applicable standards (Table 2).

Table 2. Categorization of cybersecurity and compliance regulatory requirements, frameworks, and standards

Category III	"The critical security controls", The Center of Internet Security (CIS)
	"Cloud Control Matrix", The Cloud Security Alliance (CSA)
Category II	ISO 27001:2013 – Information security management
	ISO 27003:2010 – Information security management system implementation guidance
	ISO 27005:2011 – Information security risk management
	ISO 27018:2014 – Code of practice for protection of personally identifiable information (PII) in public clouds acting as PII processors
	ISO 27034:2011 – Application security
	ISO/IEC DIS 29134 – Privacy impact assessment (draft)
Category I	The EU General Data Protection Regulation (GDPR)
	National Personal Data Protection Regulations
	NIST Framework for Improving Critical Infrastructure Cybersecurity
	The Payment Card Industry Data Security Standard (PCI DSS)
	NIST Security and Privacy Controls for Federal Information Systems and Organizations SP 800-53
	NIST Assessing Security and Privacy Controls in Federal Information Systems and Organizations SP 800-53A

Cybersecurity, compliance regulatory requirements, frameworks, and standards were classified into three categories in order to apply a systematic approach to a future design of a proprietary framework, allows the framework to address needs of the organization taking into account specificities of the organization, strategic priorities, and natural limitations. The first category contains regulatory and contractually enforced requirements relevant for the organization; the second unites standards that were developed and published by The International Organization for Standardization (ISO); and industrial best practices and mappings were put into the third category.

The purpose of the analysis of first group of documents was to identify and understand the cybersecurity and compliance requirements and to design and deploy the framework for achieving the objectives of company. Understanding of the requirements had to be gained with respect to the global presence of the company and regardless of where in the acquisition life cycle the IT programs of the company are performed. The set of ISO standards was used as formal specifications that allowed the organization to have overall management and control in handling information security risks. These standards create requirements for establishment, implementation, review and oversight, maintenance, and improvement.

Although they do not mandate specific information security controls, these standards provide a comprehensive layer of organizational management system methods. The Critical Security Controls (CSC) [7] and the Cloud Security Alliance Cloud Control Matrix (CCM) [10] have no official standing or authority. Instead, they are designed to provide thorough mapping to major information security and regulatory compliance requirements and standards. Because of this role, these standards are the most helpful for organizations that want to use a practical approach to operationalize and industrialize cybersecurity regulatory compliance.

The Top 20 CSC includes recommendations for cyber defense. [8] The Controls were designed as a set of actionable methods to stop some of the most common and damaging cyber-attacks. They were developed by a volunteer group of hundreds of security experts from both the private and public sectors as standards for the use of large-scale entities. They were specifically designed to complement the NIST. [9] The Framework under CSC is not new; it combines several cybersecurity practices that are often considered the best practices in the field, including NIST and ISO. It is also not industry specific. It integrates common responses to pervasive threats and provides a way to combat vulnerabilities that large enterprises of any industry often face.

CCM focuses on security for cloud venders and provides these vendors with a way to assess their customers' potential risks. It includes 13 domains that help organizations recognize and implement the need for cybersecurity practices. [10] The key domains for our purposes include:

- Application & interface security;
- Data security and information lifecycle management;
- Encryption and key management;
- Governance and risk management;
- Security incident management; and
- Identity and access management

These domains allow CCM to provide a common working language for both internal and external communication with regard to cloud-based services. It works directly with standards and frameworks such as the ISO 27001/27002, ISO 27018, NIST, PCI DSS and others. It helps build strong, secure information control environments by placing special emphasis on business information security requirements and reducing security threats and vulnerabilities that are of special concern in the cloud. The Cloud Security Alliance also updates the framework regularly to assure compliance with new regulatory requirements.

2.2   Risk Assessment

Risk assessment was crucial for designing an effective certification framework for applications security and data protection. The framework needed to allow the organization to assess and identify relevant cyber- and compliance-related risks in the beginning of the project delivery lifecycle. The key challenge was to balance comprehensiveness of risk assessment and resources required to allocate prior to a project execution phase. Accurately assessing risk requires that you assess the value of the data processed and how it is stored. Conducting this analysis first will help actors understand the current system and identify vulnerabilities.

Five key frameworks and standards were considered, and their strengths and weaknesses, with emphasis on the objectives of the organization and ability to operationalize and scale the framework in a real-world setting were evaluated.

- Operationally Critical Threat, Asset and Vulnerability Evaluation (OCTAVE) is a suite of tools, techniques, and methods for risk-based information security strategic assessment and planning [11].
- Factor Analysis of Information Risk (FAIR) The Standard Value at Risk (VAR) Model for Information Security and Operational Risk is a practical framework to aid in understanding and measuring information risk to make better-informed decisions regarding risk management [12].
- The NIST Risk Management Framework (RMF) SP 800-37 is the unified information security framework for the entire federal government. It replaces the legacy Certification and Accreditation processes, which has been used in various federal departments and agencies, the Department of Defense, and the Intelligence Community as a whole.
- Threat Agent Risk Assessment (TARA), and Threat Assessment & Remediation Analysis (TARA) work to identify and assess cyber threats and use effective countermeasures to disengage those threats [13].
- ISO 27005:2011 – Information technology – Security techniques – Information security risk management provides guidelines for information security risk management. "It supports the general concepts specified in ISO/IEC 27001 and is designed to assist the satisfactory implementation of information security based on a risk management approach" [14].

Each framework provides a way to understand and address information security risks in an organization. Under FAIR, actors can also use monetary estimates for losses and probability values for threats and vulnerabilities. Although each framework is relatively compressive, there were still certain limitations identified.

For example, many of the frameworks required the use of specifically trained individuals to perform risk assessments. These individuals are necessary to put appropriate information into each of the models in order to base conclusions and findings on reliable information. Further, none of the systems is automatic. They require extensive monitoring and documentation, which makes the entire process time consuming and subject to human error. Further, some do not focus on the key priority areas that end up being the most egregious threats to cyber security.

In addition, experience of other companies was used to identify real life best practices. For example, the team learned that, following the announcement of new software-based solutions, one of the world's largest publicly traded international oil and gas company decided to focus on risk assessment with an attempt to calculate a potential exposure to cyber related risks. The company analyzed historical data to identify top drivers of potential impact and severity of cyber risks in the enterprise specific for the company's environment and developed a proprietary risk assessment methodology to perform risk assessments effectively and on scale without a need to conduct extensive trainings for all stakeholders (Table 3).

Table 3. Top drivers of potential impact and severity of cyber risks

Criteria I	Hosting environment
	Connectivity model
Criteria II	Data type and volume
	Regions of deployment
	Scale of deployment – number of users
Criteria III	New components introduction
	Compliance with company's technology standards

As a result of the analysis of existing methodologies and practices in risk assessment of cyber-related risks, it was decided to design and apply a proprietary risk assessment model in order to capture specific risks of the organization as well as to better capture the objectives of the company to address a variety of risks in cyber, compliance, and service delivery domains.

2.3   Framework Challenges

We determined that there were several primary challenges the organization needed to address. In particular, the organization generally needs to focus their resources and energies on high-yield risks to maximize inputs for outputs. Actually preforming a risk assessment first can help combat this problem, but many organizations had trouble implementing this first step. Scalability was also a problem for many organizations. Efforts to avoid control duplication were also a major challenge. Further, organizations struggled to implement frameworks into their already existing procedures and processes.

No framework provides a one-size-fits-all approach to managing cybersecurity and compliance risks. Organizations will continue to have unique risks, including varying threats, vulnerabilities, and risk tolerances. Accordingly, how an organization implements its own framework integrating regulatory requirements, standards, and best practices will vary. Organizations should determine which activities are important to critical service delivery, and then it can prioritize to maximize the impact of each dollar spent.

3   Framework Design and Deployment

The following framework design and deployment process was used at the largest leading global energy management and automation provider, implemented by the author. Prior to design and implementation of the framework, the priorities were set to focus on compliance with personal data privacy requirements, security of new applications, and data protection in applications. The company needed to deliver secure applications and protect confidential data in order to comply with emerging regulatory requirements in the European Union. This example provides a look at some of the key frameworks and provides an overview of both their strengths and weaknesses as applied in a real-world setting.

3.1   Starting from Compliance

The EU General Data Protection Regulation (GDPR) was published in the EU Official Journal on May 4, 2016, after four years in the making. It applies going forward beginning on May 25, 2018. This Regulation provides sweeping updates to various data protection rules that the world has not seen in over 20 years.

Every company that processes personal data of EU citizens will be subject to GDPR. It imposes stiff penalties for non-compliance, including fines upwards of €20 million, or approximately $23 million, and/or 4% of the company's global revenue. Although companies of all sizes will be challenged, GDPR most significantly affects global companies with a broad international presence. Challenges arise from companies having to expand the scope of already very complex IT landscapes and the cross-border transmission of personal data.

Usually, any compliance comes at a cost. Nonetheless, effective companies and their leaders successfully generate value for businesses and their customers by designing and deploying responsive data privacy and compliance programs. These programs can allow companies to expand customer satisfaction and build trusting relationships with customers. This, in turn, could trigger additional revenue growth. Implementing best practices could also eventually lead to lowering the overall cost of compliance in the future.

As an example, the organization proposed three major objectives for its worldwide personal data protection compliance initiative:

1. Reduce the risk of breaching Personal Data Protection Regulations by operating under regulations imposed by the EU and other countries where the company operates.
2. Enable and support the growth of rich customer experiences in the area of mobile options and Internet of Things solutions the company offers.
3. Achieve a reduction in the cost of compliance with personal data protection legislation by utilizing binding corporate rules through the application of different compliance methods, including self-certification, with respect to the risk profile of IT applications and systems involved in personal data processing.

In addition, the company believes its global responsibility goes beyond regulatory compliance. The company has solid principles of conducting business ethically, sustainably, and responsibly around the globe. Responsibility is the key objective at the heart of a company's corporate governance. This determines the commitment of the company to set and meet the highest standards in ethics and privacy, and enables it to shape the future of the industry by introducing tomorrow's best practices today. These ideals instill confidence in their customers around the world.

3.2 Framework Design

The project team designed the certification framework to ensure the security and compliance of software applications and systems, guaranteeing clients, customers, and employees the adequate protection of their personal and corporate data, entitlement to rights granted by legislations, and corporate and industrial standards and policies. The unprecedented scope of this framework covers the hundreds of software applications released annually that store billions of records of structured and unstructured data and is accessed by millions of people worldwide.

At an early stage of framework development, the team recognized that the compliance process should comprehensively cover the applications journey along the whole lifecycle from "Idea" to "Retire," and ensure the "privacy by design" concept and data protection at every stage. The team proposed a four-step process in the framework including Risk Assessment, Risk Mitigation, Certification, and post-certification Audit phases (Fig. 2).

Risk assessment was a starting point for every project that aims to deliver a new application or make significant changes on existing ones. The risk assessment report covers major risks relevant for the application and helps project-delivery teams to plan and execute risk mitigation activities along the project delivery journey. Comprehensive technical threat vulnerability assessments were recognized as very important measures to reduce risk profiles of applications and became a mandatory part for all applications delivered. Customer-focused applications and applications exposed to the Internet also go through comprehensive penetration tests and project-delivery teams are obliged to remediate detected vulnerabilities prior to putting applications into production. Certification is a step in which an independent team applies controls and checks confirming that all risk mitigation activities have been done properly and risk that had been identified was properly mitigated. The audit is a necessary step to maintain the security level of applications and especially to ensure a continuous compliance with personal data protection regulatory requirements in a run mode.

Fig. 2. Framework phases.

The team reported four main challenges it faced that inhibited framework design adoption.

1. The complexity of the external and internal regulatory environments was enormous. The framework had taken a significant number of laws, policies, standards, and guidelines into account, and then simplified them into applicable risk assessment procedures, recommendations, and controls.
2. The initial maturity of policies required intensive involvement of experts for assessing risks, guiding project delivery teams on implementation, and applying controls. This was a serious impediment for scaling the framework, and therefore, the team tackled the challenge by applying an experimentation approach. This enabled them to develop best practices and document them in the form of hands-on guidelines for project-delivery teams and application owners.
3. The complexity of an existing information technology landscape where the data is processed became an additional challenge. Because of this hurdle, the team put a lot of effort into learning about the existing architecture and mapping data.
4. The large scale of the program's implementation, diverse geography of deployment and the inconsistent level of awareness about data privacy among thousands of key stakeholders spread across all 24 time zones created a significant challenge for the rapid deployment of the framework.

The framework was the result of perfectly orchestrated and consolidated work of a numerous of employees from all continents representing key functional verticals. The team has worked tirelessly across cultures, languages, and time zones, all while staying focused on designing and deploying this framework.

3.3   Challenges

While there are different views on the processes that global organizations can adopt to establish and manage regulatory and compliance risks, the challenges that enterprises need to consider are actually very common.

1. The capacity and availability of experts — the lack of information security expertise and the scarcity of experts in the personal data protection field slow down and complicate the process of building compliance frameworks. Global companies fight for the limited number of experts who can lead complex applications security and data protection programs and often experience challenges in educating employees about risks and protection measures.
2. Complexity — the volume and increasing complexity of regulatory landscapes has gained momentum, particularly in the European Union, the United States, and some emerging countries. Global companies need to comply with a variety of regulatory legislations on national levels and ensure compliance across all business dimensions.
3. Agility and Consistency — laws and regulations change constantly, and the time it takes for new software-based products to reach the market is shrinking. Compliance with these changes must also reflect a condensed period to be effective. Companies must bring consistency to compliance structures, but it should also be implemented

in real-time and accurately reflect changes in rules and new regulations. Compliance with new regulations means making sure that multiple systems and multiple processes are compliant not only at implementation, but throughout the software delivery lifecycle.

Although companies face daunting challenges such as scale, geographic diversity, competing priorities, and communications, the outlook for these companies is not bleak. There are certain factors that will help forge a compliance framework with greater chance for success.

3.4 Factors of Success

Design and deployment of compliance programs will vary greatly. Each organization needs to ensure that compliance is properly embedded into current organizational processes. The more complex the organization, the more difficult it will be to ensure that privacy programs or initiatives are integrated into, or throughout, the organization.

The highest level of integration of a framework into existing project and program management processes guarantees the robustness and comprehensiveness of its free-of-redundancy controls. The framework needs to be aligned with processes that may have different names in organizations, such as an end-to-end project excellence and software development lifecycle governance. This will help ensure that applications processing data will follow the framework to safeguard security and compliance at every stage of the lifecycle, along with executing "privacy by design" and "security by design" principles.

Communication is a critical part of successful integration of the framework into a company's operations and projects-delivery routine. Communication at scale is a challenging exercise. To achieve success, teams need to collaborate with a variety of stakeholders, design and drive a multi-wave communication campaign as part of a change-management process, raising awareness about the framework, as well as educating project-delivery teams on key data privacy and security risks.

Applications security and data protection issues are not solely the purview of information technology and security departments. All facets of an organization must be committed to implementing any new rules and regulations and to integrate those new factors throughout every department and at every organizational echelon of the company.

Many challenges exist for companies to create a framework that works for their industry or individual company. Each framework will have to be adjusted to fit the particular company. However, companies can use the general certification framework as laid out above to evaluate and deal with cybersecurity threats and vulnerabilities as a starting point to move toward compliance and delivering more secure applications and strengthening data protection approaches.

4 Conclusion

When used correctly, a framework can be a vital component of global and cybersecurity compliance efforts. Every framework creation project should start with an in-depth analysis of the needs of a particular organization. This requires taking a hard look at vulnerabilities and areas of concern. Further, developing and using the right framework for a particular industry or organizational size can be challenge. It may require combining several standard frameworks to find one that is tailored to the unique risks and threat of an individual organization or business sector.

Most global companies are already looking to strengthen their compliance frameworks based on ISO standards, and are waiting for publication of ISO/IEC 29151:2015 — Code of practice for personally identifiable information protection and ISO/IEC DIS 29134:2016 — Privacy impact assessment. Beyond these ISO standards, frameworks with a properly established application security and data protection efforts will help ensure the company's ability to safely protect personal data well into the future.

References

1. The Emergence of Risks: Contributing Factors. Report of International Risk Governance Council, Geneva (2010)
2. Trends in security framework adoption. A survey of IT and security professionals. Dimensional Research, March 2016
3. Executive Order—Improving Critical Infrastructure Cybersecurity. The White House, Office of the Press Secretary, 12 February 2013. https://www.whitehouse.gov/the-press-office/2013/02/12/executive-order-improving-critical-infrastructure-cybersecurity
4. Cybersecurity: 'Rosetta Stone' Celebrates Two Years of Success. NIST, 18 February 2016. https://www.nist.gov/news-events/news/2016/02/cybersecurity-rosetta-stone-celebrates-two-years-success. Updated 23 July 2016
5. Framework for Improving Critical Infrastructure Cybersecurity Version 1.0. National Institute of Standards and Technology, U.S. Department of Commerce. http://www.nist.gov/cyberframework/upload/cybersecurity-framework-021214-final.pdf
6. Why you should adopt the NIST Cybersecurity Framework. PricewaterhouseCoopers, May 2014. https://www.pwc.com/us/en/increasing-it-effectiveness/publications/assets/adopt-the-nist.pdf
7. The CIS Controls for Effective Cyber Defense Version 6.0. The Center for Internet Security (CIS). https://www.cisecurity.org/critical-controls/
8. CIS: Critical Security Controls Poster, SANS. https://www.sans.org/media/critical-security-controls/critical-controls-poster-2016.pdf
9. NIST: CIS Security Frameworks See Mainstream Adoption. Infosecurity, 11 May 2016. http://www.infosecurity-magazine.com/news/nist-cis-security-frameworks-see/
10. Cloud Controls Matrix: CSA. https://cloudsecurityalliance.org/group/cloud-controls-matrix/
11. OCTAVE: CERT. http://www.cert.org/resilience/products-services/octave/
12. RiskLens' Purpose Built Platform: RiskLens. http://www.risklens.com/platform
13. Threat Assessment and Remediation Analysis (TARA): MITRE, October 2011. https://www.mitre.org/sites/default/files/pdf/11_4982.pdf
14. Cloud Controls Matrix v3.0.1: Cloud Security Alliance, June 2016. https://cloudsecurityalliance.org/download/cloud-controls-matrix-v3-0-1/ISO/IEC

Balancing Targeted Delivery of Content and Personal Freedom in the Digital On-line Video Marketing Landscape

Kenneth Revett[1(⊠)], Sérgio Tenreiro de Magalhães[2,3],
Maria Jose Magalhães[2], and H. Jahankhani[4]

[1] Anastamose, International, Boston, MA, USA
ken.revett@gmail.com
[2] Faculdade de Filosofia e Ciências Sociais,
Universidade Católica Portuguesa, Braga, Portugal
{stmagalhaes,mjmagalhaes}@braga.ucp.pt
[3] Department of Computer Science, University of Beira Interior,
Covilhã, Portugal
[4] Head of Doctoral Studies, Faculty of Social Sciences, Law and Technology,
Department of Digital Technology and Computing, GSM London, London, UK
hamid.jahankhani@gsmlondon.ac.uk

Abstract. With the maturation of the internet, many organizations have relied on the ubiquitous reach of the internet targeting. On average, every "consumer" is exposed to over 300 advertisements throughout a given 24 h period. What is disturbing is that we remember approximately 12 of these advertisements – a paltry 4%! A viable solution is to utilize a heuristic search for consumers, and this is where audience targeting becomes central to a successful marketing campaign. Audience targeting – tracking our activities, utilizing cookie data, and other strategies for acquiring information necessary for developing individualized consumer-centric models, has clearly engendered distrust amongst many internet consumers. In addition, bots, non-human traffic, and Malvertising all pose threats to our sense of security while on the internet. Somehow, the IT industry, working in conjunction with marketing standards boards must find a way to ensure digital marketing continues, without costing undue levels of distrust from the suer community.

Keywords: Cookie data · Digital marketing · DMP · Internet security · On-line video delivery · Malvertising · Real-time bidding

1 Introduction

The digital community (the internet) continues to expand at an unprecedented rate since its inception 25 years ago, with over 3.3 Billion users in 2015, just over 45% of the world's population [1]. This scale of human-machine (person/interface) interaction has never heretofore been dreamed possible. The ability to interact on a truly global scale, with a variety of rich media, at virtually millisecond time scales provides opportunities to transform lives through the dissemination of vast quantities of information.

© Springer International Publishing AG 2016
H. Jahankhani et al. (Eds.): ICGS3 2017, CCIS 630, pp. 96–105, 2016.
DOI: 10.1007/978-3-319-51064-4_8

The marketing world has clearly utilized this technological framework as a platform for distributing product and service information. Initially, the internet was viewed as a canvas for replicating standard advertising themes, such as banner ads serving as electronic equivalents of highway billboards. The addition of dynamic content has provided a more interactive approach, engaging the viewer into the process. Digital marketing, without exception, is a major mechanism for increasing sales and brand lift. The issue is that we are spoiled for choice. The ability to allocate billboards at the right location was critical – the assumption being: once seen, once bought. Now, we can reach almost half the planet, so reach is not the critical issue. The question is how do we allocate marketing resources appropriately, so that the ROI is maximal, without engendering a sense of personal encroachment that will cause consumers to reflexively recoil away?

I will focus on the on-line video marketing domain, where publishers generate, as part of their marketing spend, videos that are published on select websites. These videos are the equivalent of TV commercials, which are played within a browser (which, can of course be displayed on a SmartTV!) It is estimated that in Q4 2016/Q1 2017, browser based commercials will exceed TV based commercials for the first time, with an estimated annual spend of well over 70$ Billion in the U.S. alone. The process by which most of the digital video is being disseminated is quite complicated, typically relying on a real-time bidding base auction process, as depicted in Fig. 1.

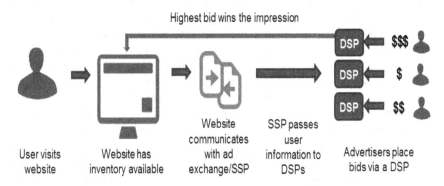

Fig. 1. A brief overview of the real-time bidding process for delivering a video ad in a bowser. (Source: [2], page 4)

In the "olden" days of advertising, a marketing person would generate a campaign for a product, and mass deliver product information in a variety of forms, such as billboard ads, print ads, and possibly TV commercials. With the advent of the internet (ca. 1989), marketing very gradually moved into the digital domain. They started by transplanting billboards into display ads, and with the advent of YouTube and social media generally, digital video was born. The idea was to utilize the www as a medium for disseminating product information en masse. After the excitement about the opportunities had worn off, marketers began the reality check – which was to determine the ROI for their video digital display campaigns. Sadly, the numbers were not what they expected. Market research yielded data that indicates a mere 4% of people actually remember any form of advertising they were exposed to. Digital video fared little better than a typical billboard we see in the subway wall on the way to work. The question the digital marketing domain asked is 'how can we improve our ROI?'

The IAB (Interactive Advertising Board) was established a framework for programmatic bidding of digital advertisement materials. The IAB established the Real-Time Bidding (RTB) Project, formerly known as the OpenRTB Consortium, assembled technology leaders from both the Supply and Demand sides in November 2010 to develop a new API specification for companies interested in an open protocol for the automated trading of digital media across a broader range of platforms, devices, and advertising solutions [2]. The OpenRTB service provided a mechanism for marketers to not only deliver their products in a well-established fashion, but they could also programmatically evaluate their effectiveness. Real-time bidding is fast becoming a significant player and the standard by which on-line advertisers are conducting their marketing business. As depicted in Fig. 1, the RTB process is an auction, where supply side and demand side processes are performed automatically, without human intervention. Data regarding the transaction is recorded, and can be utilized either in real time, or off-line, for ROI analysis.

The data generated from RTB based advertising provides quantitative data regarding how a marketing campaign is performing, at least with respect to their digital display venue. Note that most marketing strategies are mixtures of digital, print, and other modes of content delivery (evaluated using mixed marketing models). The results from RTB based approaches (which is expected to account for @30% of the digital advertising spend by 2017) is sobering: like traditional advertising approaches, most of the content is lost into the ether. There are two issues with digital advertising: (1) we have a choice as to whether we wish to view it, and (2) we only remember a small amount of what we do view! Note that many digital video ads are click-to-play, in that we have to click on the start button to activate the video (much like a YouTube video). Therefore, the transformation to a browser based approach to digital marketing is not necessarily a step in the right direction. The issue is, as always, is to match content to the right viewer. This aspect of marketing, has generated a burgeoning business enterprise in its own right. The principal business model for organizations such as Nielsen's Marketing Cloud, is to provide their clients with detailed level marketing data, analytics, within an RTB enabled data management platform (DMP). The essence of a DMP is to provide, in a real-time environment, access to audience targeting lists to their clients. Digital media publishers then tune their campaigns to specific audience targets, in hopes of gaining enhanced views, and subsequent enhanced brand lift and increased purchase intent. This is good news for publishers, but consumer awareness of audience targeting has many people installing ad blockers. It is clear that marketing is a necessary tool for business, without which, sales would move slowly, and prices would rise. There is a significant benefit to marketing campaigns, though their deployment through the internet may seem like an intrusion into our personal lives. How do we strike a balance between digital video marketing, and consumer protection?

1.1   Audience Targeting

Companies such as DataLogix claim they build precise targeting strategies using verified offline purchase and activity data on more than 110 million households [3]. Our 100% 1:1 deterministic matching guarantees advertisers the most accurate audiences available online. Exactly how do they accomplish this coverage? Well, it is all about data collection. For instance, Oracle's BlueKai, Oracle's data as a Service Blue book, contains a wealth of information about literally millions of people – potential consumers The information in the data service includes the following [4]:

Individual Demographics
    Occupation
    Education
    Gender
Household Demographics
    Marital status
    Presence of children
Head-of-household info Financial
    Income
    Net worth
Investors Real Property Data
    Home type
    Home value
    Length of residence Age
    Age
    Date of birth for individual and household members Buying Activity
    Categorized purchase history information
Interest
    Interests of members of the household
Vehicle
    Make
    Model
    Year data
    Brand propensity Technology
Types of devices
    Technology adoption model
Behavior
    Charities
    Media channel preference
    Green living
Life Event
    New parents
    New movers
    Empty nesters

Travel
    Destinations
    Cruise
    Casino propensity
Personic
    Household-level segmentation product

This information is generally very reliable (with an expected error rate on the order of <10%), and ubiquitous, in terms of coverage. How is the level of data acquired? Organizations collect publicly available information, surveys and information from other information providers. Their data products are used by companies, political organizations and non-profit organizations in their marketing, fundraising and customer service programs, and both offline and online. The level of detail is partly based on raw input data, and some is derived through sophisticated market modeling analysis. This is just one example of one organization's attempt at providing data to other businesses for use in their targeted marketing campaigns. Much of the information that has been acquired, if it is sourced digitally, is acquired through a personal computer based browser session. The market at the moment has been heavily biased towards desktop and possibly some tablet (i.e. iPad) utilization. The trend is to move towards mobile based targeting, getting people on the run, delivering targeted ads in situ. This trend is termed location-based audience targeting.

Location Data is typically acquired by mobile devices that indicate where a user is. The user location data generated by the device takes the form of latitude and longitude coordinate pairs, for example the 20.1234, −21.5678, indicating you are at some building which can be readily identified, say as a school. The quality of a given location-based audience profile is dependent on the quality and quantity of the underlying location data. The data needs to be precise to be most useful in developing audiences, and the more extensive the history, the more accurate and extensive the audience profile will be. The quality of user location data varies due to many factors: (1) Source Site/App (2) Handset & Technology (GPS) (3) whether your location was determined in presence of WiFi or OTA (4) Indoor vs. Outdoor location.

The great advantage of mobile technology is that it is ubiquitous, and ties a person to a specific target, which can serve as the basis for delivering an Advertisement. If it is determined that you are at a local supermarket, then they suppliers of ads will tailor the ad accordingly. If the local supermarket has a digital marketing campaign of their own, this information can be used to tailor digital display ads at the check-out counter, ads appearing throughout the store, etc. By synergistically displaying ads that display a common theme, their effectiveness will increase considerably. Mobile technology is the way forward with digital marketing, serving to reach us where ever we are. Note, millennials spend approximately 1 day per week (approximately 3.2 h/day) on their devices. They form a huge market, though their spending power is not as high as say the baby boomer generation.

In addition, marketing campaigns are cross-device, with ads appearing first, say on our desktop at work, will then follow you on your mobile on the way home, and then appear on you laptop at home! This multi-device approach can be very effective, and certainly makes us feel that we are being pursued by consumer oriented marketers.

I personally become annoyed when I see the same ad appearing multiple times within a day. Digital marketing now place caps no the number of times the same ad is displayed onto the same device, so this helps somewhat. But the overwhelming sense for many people is that they feel they are being pursued – almost coerced into watching an ad. Furthermore, the question is how did the ad find me in the first place? How much of my personal information has become inserted into an oracle database, only to be used to push ads I didn't request onto the middle of a page I am reading? The biggest concern is personal privacy. One solution that many people are deploying as ad blockers, which are browser extensions that can very effectively block most types of digital display advertisements. It has been estimated that almost half of US internet uses have installed some form of ad blocker [5]. What is the consequence of ad blockers – well, obviously, it is huge amounts of lost revenue for organizations. Adobe says that $21.8 billion in global ad revenue will be blocked this year. They are not alone. Ad blocking costs money to companies, which in turn, is passed onto the consumer. How can we have the best of both worlds? One solution is to provide ads that are meaningful to the potential viewer. We are caught in a Catch-22 scenario – how do we know what a person wants unless we know something about the person? Yet, by acquiring information about me, without my knowledge is an invasion of privacy. It is this dilemma that is plaguing the industry, costing literally trillions of dollars world-wide in lost revenue.

The most successful ad blocker (Adblock Plus, a German based company) provides a very effective means of ad blocking, which simply acts as a filter between the ad and the browser it is trying to load into. The people at AdBlock have been sued over its deployment, being accused of losing revenue for organizations via reductions in revenue attributable to advertising reduction opportunities. Adblock won their case, and argued that they serve as a sort police force for users, blocking out unwanted ads. This was especially true in the gaming industry, where adblockers first made their appearance. Another company, Shine, based out of Israel, has generated a solution that blocks ads before they reach your device! Their argument is that ads are typically large in size, and consume bandwidth, as they not only need to be downloaded to the device, but they continue to ping the tower for geo-location information. Their revenue model is from the mobile carriers, whom provide reduced rates to customers if they install the ad blocking software, as it reduces the need to beef up their towers and the network providers' hardware. In the end, ad blocking costs us money, and without the revenue generated by ads, may put a lot of internet based organizations out of business. Somehow, a compromise has to be reached that is suitable to everyone.

2   On the Need for International Standards in Digital Ad Display

The new L.E.A.N. Ads program — an acronym for *light, encrypted, ad choice supported, non-invasive* ads — devised by the IAB Tech Lab, is meant to quell the havoc that ad tech has wrought on digital advertising experiences and quell the ad-blocker-reliant rebellion against terrible user experiences. The L.E.A.N. program proposes an alternative set of standards to address the reasons consumers are turning to ad blockers:

"Among the many areas of concentration, we must also address frequency capping on retargeting in Ad Tech and make sure a user is targeted appropriately before, but never AFTER they make a purchase. If we are so good at reach and scale, we can be just as good, if not better, at moderation. Additionally, we must address volume of ads per page as well as continue on the path to viewability. The dependencies here are critical to an optimized user experience [6]."

What this statement is indicating is that we should not have ads following us around, seeing them multiple times in a short time span. Frequency capping places an upper bound on the number of times and ad is served to the same device. Re-targeting occurs when we repeatedly target a device with different but possibly related ads. This issue typically reflects a lack of creativity, in that advertisers do not have a robust view of their target audience, and hence they keep delivering very similar ads to them. Viewability is an issue of integrity. In order for advertisers to receive payment for the delivery of an ad, it must be completely viewable on the device. Companies are paid to deliver ads on behalf of customers that wish to advertise digitally. Ad delivery vendors are paid for impressions they can deliver, where an impression is an ad displayed on a device. Every time an ad is loaded on a device, they get paid. The people paying for the delivery of ads expect a return on their investment – brand lift, purchase intent, increased sales, etc. Many companies discovered they were paying for an enormous number of ads, but many were not actually being seen by the end user on their devices. The ad may appear on a browser, but not completely on the screen, and in some cases, may not be visible at all! The content delivery mechanism would be paid if the viewer clicks on the screen anywhere, regardless of the visibility of the ad. Thus, viewability is not becoming a requirement for payment. The IAB has stated that at least 50% of the ad must be visible for at least 2 s before you can charge for the ad. Viewability is one of the worst culprits in the industry. It cheats viewers and the advertisers, making the middle man rich!

The statement above from the IAB sets the tone for the industry – that there must be mutual respect between viewers and advertisers. Without such a compromise, the ad tech industry will not only continue to have to generate funding any way it can, which typically means at the viewers' expense, but it also compromises the philosophical foundations of the internet – which is predicated on freedom of expression.

People should be allowed to deploy ad blockers if they so choose. The onus is on publishers to ensure that the content they are delivering is relevant, and delivered in a non-intrusive fashion. Most importantly, content should be delivered without compromising an individual's digital security. This is where the IT industry needs to step in, and work with agencies like the IAB to ensure all needs are satisfied.

3 The Role of the IT Industry in Digital Marketing Security

Clearly, the internet is a wide open platform, designed to provide everyone connected to it with free and anonymous rights to retrieve information, share thoughts/ideas, communicate freely, perform business, etc. Digital advertising has become a marketing cornerstone, especially for startups. Given this backdrop, it is alarming to realize that according to the Association of National Advertisers, 4.5$ Million dollars are lost in the advertising domain every hour! That amounts to 6.3$ Billion US dollars annually! [6] Who/what is responsible for this fraud? For the most part, it is as simple as Bots. Nearly 25% of all videos/ads that are delivered for display are being placed on fraudulent websites, maintained by bots! Nearly 10% of ads are fraudulent themselves. Nearly two-thirds of all ad tech fraud comes from computers that have been hacked. Fraud within the ad Tech space covers the full gambit of internet based activities. I will focus on the deployment of bots and how HTML5 is opening up mobile ad tech, with significant security risks.

Bots are software based ventriloquist, designed to emulate human activities within a digital venue. They must inject into a host PC, and once there, like a virus, can act as long as they remain undetected. Ingenious methods have been devised to deliver bots, such as filling out an incentivized form, which will then install the bot into your browser. Theses bots can then interact on your behalf, clicking on ads, running videos silently in the background. These actions result in payment being made to some ad exchange, without any benefit to the actual producer of the ad/video. In addition, bots can also collect and over write cookie data, which are valuable to audience targeting firms, looking to scoop up as many viable cookies as possible for resale to marketing strategy firms. Needless to say, these activities cost advertisers billions of dollars in lost advertising, which we, as consumers, end up paying the price for. What is being done about this? Many websites have CAPTCHAs installed on their site (CAPTCHA is an acronym for 'Completely Automated Turing test to tell Computers and Humans Apart). – sorry Alan!' Bots are now sophisticated enough to be able to enter the CAPTCHA phrase programmatically.

CAPTCHA type of approaches to detecting non-human traffic (NHT) is simply not enough. Consider what happens when we move to the mobile world – security becomes a huge issue. HTML5 has provided the means to allow us to move across devices effortlessly. HTML5, replacing FLASH, is enticing advertisers to serve their ad on mobile devices. Note that FLASH is still quite a prevalent tool still in wide use [7].

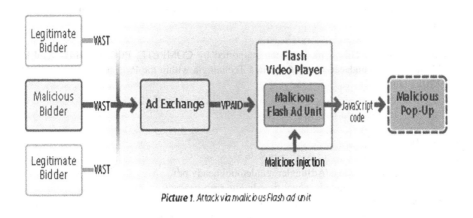

Picture 1. Attack via malicious Flash ad unit

www.geoedge.com · Ad Security & Verification · info@geoedge.com   2

Fig. 2. A typical Malvertising scenario utilizing Flash based delivery of video content (Source: [11], page 2)

What HTML5 has done is to bring to marketers' attention the role of mobile computing in advertising. One vulnerability engendered by mobile display of video is Malvertising. In the scenario depicted in Fig. 2, a legitimate video ad was delivered (with VAST/VPAID support) to a Flash video player. The video has the appropriate signatures, and passes any verification tests that might exist (which is minimal at best). Generally, these malvertising ads contain javascript, and when the video is played (via an actionscript method invocation), the javascript code snippet executes, installing pop-ups on the host device. In a typical scenario, the pop-up will ask the user to upgrade their browser to the latest version. Once the user consents, the malware has been installed on the host device, and now they have control over what happens - a new form of virus. This scenario is on the benign side of the realm of possibilities. Other attacks deliver malicious URLs, which direct you to sites via an Angler of the realm of possibilities. Other attacks deliver malicious URLs, which direct you to sites via an Angler exploit kit, which can automatically infect your device without any user intervention [8–10]. It is hoped that FLASH5, under the auspice of WHATWG will respond to the international community, putting in place enhanced security provisions to help reduce mobile based fraud.

Other attacks deliver malicious URLs, which direct you to sites via an Angler exploit kit, which can automatically infect your device without any user intervention. It is hoped that FLASH5, under the auspice of WHATWG will respond to the international community, putting in place enhanced security provisions to help reduce mobile based fraud.

There is a lot to do in the digital video domain with respect to enhancing security, reducing the burden on users, and maintaining the equity that businesses depend on. This introduction to the topic hopefully will remind people of what is happening on many devices, and it could easily happen to us if we are not careful. The IT industry must respond to these challenges, working directly and in conjunction with the marketing industry (most notably the ANA and IAB). There are startups that are providing solutions to particular problems, but there is a dire need for a more global solution to these problems.

Acknowledgements. This work has been supported by COMPETE: POCI-01-0145-FEDER-007043 and FCT – Fundação para a Ciência e Tecnologia within the Project Scope: UID/CEC/00319/2013 (author 2).

References

1. http://adjuggler.com/docs/AdJuggler_guidetoonlineadv.pdf
2. http://www.iab.com/guidelines/real-time-bidding-rtb-project/
3. http://www.datalogix.com/wp-content/uploads/2013/10/DLX_Audience_Guide_Mar2014.pdf
4. http://www.oracle.com/us/corporate/acquisitions/bluekai/general-presentation-2150582.pdf
5. http://www.mmaglobal.com/files/documents/guidance_report-_location_audience_targeting.pdf
6. http://www.iabeurope.eu/files/7514/2365/8232/IAB_Europe_Viewable_Impressions_White_Paper_Feb_2015.pdf

7. http://www.cjr.org/business_of_news/will_ad_blockers_kill_the_digital_media_industry.php
8. http://marketingland.com/the-iab-takes-on-ad-blocking-by-first-admitting-the-industry-screwed-up-147235
9. http://cdn2.hubspot.net/hubfs/418991/Digital_Ad_Fraud.pdf?t=1436331135031
10. White Ops Inc., The Bot Baseline: Fraud in Digital Advertising, December 2014
11. http://www.geoedge.com/downloads/documents/Security_Aspects_of_HTML5_in_Video_Ads.pdf?ge_campaign=html5_video

Towards an Enterprise Architecture Framework for Community Policing

Helen Gibson[✉] and Babak Akhgar

CENTRIC, Sheffield Hallam University, Sheffield, UK
h.gibson@shu.ac.uk

Abstract. The activities of policing and community policing may be considered fundamentally different from the processes that occur within business organisations; however, at a high-level both groups still require people, systems and processes in order to effectively carry out their functions and achieve their goals. Therefore, through the identification of community policing (CP) stakeholders, the activities, processes and information flows and the governance, training and management procedures all carried out under CP's remit we are able to understand the current state of play within CP, how we might wish CP to be in the future and the processes that need to be put in place to get there. Using an Enterprise Architecture approach we provide an initial formal description of CP, its interdependencies, relationships, principles and guidelines in order to lay the groundwork for a fully featured CP model in Europe.

1 Introduction

Community Policing (CP) is a concept which aims to develop a closer relationship between the police and the communities they serve in order to build better a better community environment for all. As opposed to normal policing methods, CP is inherently considered to be a more proactive approach compared to the reactive state of many policing activities, it requires citizen involvement and is decentralised [3]. Therefore, the tactics, tasks and strategies that are employed for CP must be with the aim of improving and working together with the community. In this paper, we present an Enterprise Architecture approach to modelling CP that can be used as a springboard to understand the current state of CP in Europe and provide a foundation to build towards a future vision of CP.

2 Unity

Unity is an EU Horizon 2020 funded project that aim to enhance the relationships and communication channels between the police and the communities they serve. To this end Unity aims to identify CP best practices, and use these practices to develop technological solutions to improve the communication between police and communities and as a foundation for the development of police training and awareness around CP.

© Springer International Publishing AG 2016
H. Jahankhani et al. (Eds.): ICGS3 2017, CCIS 630, pp. 106–112, 2016.
DOI: 10.1007/978-3-319-51064-4_9

Unity began the project with four high-level goals for CP: Trust, Information Sharing, Prevention and Accountability. Through further background research and a number of interviews with existing CP stakeholders these have evolved into four important CP concepts:

1. Working together, cooperation and collaboration between police and external groups
2. Building relationships of trust, confidence and understanding between police and external groups
3. Communication, interaction and sharing of information between police and external groups
4. Addressing local needs and issues, both proactively and reactively.

These concepts provide us with an initial framework and a set of high-level concepts from which the rest of the project is able to build out from.

3 Enterprise Architecture

Enterprise Architecture (EA) as defined as "The fundamental organization of a system, embodied in its components, their relationships to each other and the environment, and the principles governing its design and evolution" [1]. We can consider the fundamental organisation of a system to be CP and its structure. The components are the stakeholders involved in CP as well as the processes, procedures, tools and technologies required to carry it out, their corresponding relationships and those to their environment (such as the local communities and wider society). The principles that govern the design of CP include existing practices, laws, societal norms and expectations, and CP communication methods. Furthermore, it is not the aim when constructing an architecture framework to simply understand what is happening in CP now, an architecture framework also helps to facilitate the process of moving from where it is now towards the vision of how CP should be in the future. Thus, the EA constitutes a formal description of an organisation's components, functions, and structure, the interrelationships and, consequently, their dependencies upon one another.

Within Unity we are using the Open Group Architecture Framework (TOGAF) [4] in order to construct our models. TOGAF is built upon the idea that in order to understand the system we are observing we need to understand its business architecture, applications architecture, data architecture and the technical architecture. In order to gather the information that is required to build the architecture there are a certain amount of information about the existing system we need to understand. This information includes:

– Who are the stakeholders?
– What are the main tasks, processes and procedure?
– What are the information flows, and what information is exchanged?
– What are the communication channels?
– In which locations does the system arise?
– What are the governance structures and performance indicators?
– What is the functionality of existing technology and information systems?
– What is the extent of training in these areas?

Using existing research, research conducted within the Unity project with CP stakeholders across Europe and building on current EA models of policing we are able to begin answering these questions, identifying the areas in which these methods are deficient or require an update to incorporate modern technologies and methods into their processes and move towards a new and updated model of community policing.

4 Towards an Enterprise Architecture for Community Policing

The aim of defining an EA for CP is to provide a clear vision for Unity and, by extension, CP in Europe of how CP can move from its existing state (current operating model) towards a state which embodies the best and most effective practices within Europe for CP (target operating model).

4.1 Mapping of Core Tasks to Outcome Areas

As mentioned above, we began Unity with four high-level goals (Prevention, Information Sharing, Trust and Accountability). Our first task within the development of the current operating model was to realise where the core tasks as identified through interviews with police and communities within eight European Countries (UK, Belgium, Croatia, Estonia, Germany, Finland, Macedonia and Bulgaria) carried out in another component of the project, mapped to each of these outcome areas. In this initial sift, 57 possible core tasks within CP were identified. They are then mapped to one or more of the four outcome areas. The results of this mapping is then displayed in Fig. 1. This mapping provides us with an overview of key tasks within CP and also highlights how many of these tasks do not just map to a single outcome area but, in fact, impact upon multiple CP concepts.

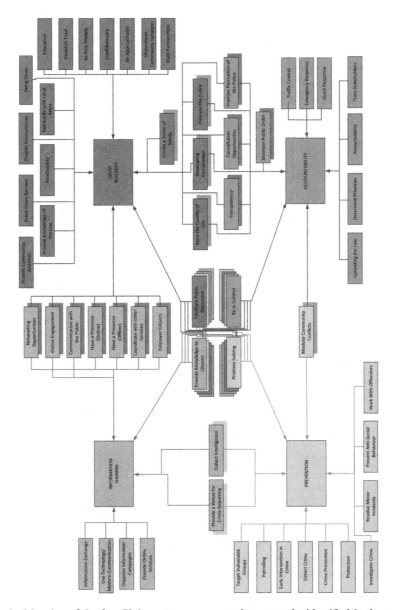

Fig. 1. Mapping of the four Unity outcome areas to the core tasks identified in the research

4.2 Police Activities Glossary Link to CP

We have used the Police Activities Glossary (PAG) as an initial framework to map the tasks and processes identified within Unity. The PAG [2] was developed by the National Police Improvement Agency to standardise the roles and responsibilities that exist within UK policing. The next step in our modelling process was to take the PAG

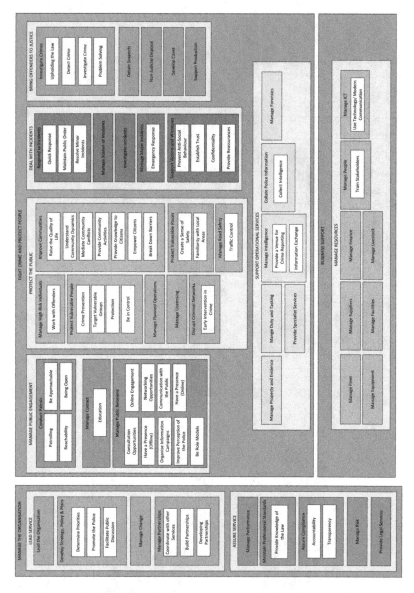

Fig. 2. Mapping of the Unity core tasks to the Police Activities Glossary

and map our previously identified core tasks to the PAG. The PAG is broken down into three main areas (managing the organisation, fight crime and protect people, and business support) and then divided into smaller subsections. For example, fight crime and protect people is then divided into manage public engagement, protect the public, deal with incidents, bring offenders to justice, and support operational services. Each of these subsections is then further sub-divided. It is at this third level that we then map the core CP tasks identified within the research to these third tier activities. These are shown in Fig. 2.

4.3 Stakeholders and Communication Channels

Information was also gathered on CP stakeholders and their CP communication channels. In Unity, stakeholders consist of: police, community members and groups, and intermediaries. Police members may include officers, community policing officers (such as PCSOs in the UK), police volunteers and support staff all who may come into contact with the CP process. Communities may include young people, migrants, geographic communities, victims of crime, offenders, various subcultures and, even, virtual communities that have no fixed location. Part of the CP process also involved intermediary organisations who may provide a bridge between the communities and police, or they may have reason to interact with the CP process directly. These intermediaries can be as diverse as specific community groups, support groups, local businesses, health and other social services, the education sector, and other blue light services. Many of these stakeholders will, or have the potential to be, involved in the majority of core CP tasks. In some tasks the police may be the instigator of the process and in others the CP process will be initiated due to a particular need, requirement or incident within the community.

A vital component of successful CP is ensuring that the communication channels between the police, citizens and intermediaries are always open and bi-directional. Within Unity's research a number of communication channels have been identified including traditional direct communication methods such as telephone, and face-to-face meetings, and new media communications such as websites, email, and social media. The police may also disseminate information through posters, notice boards, TV, public groups, education visits, lectures, neighbourhood watch, and other community meetings. By identifying both stakeholders and communications channels we can begin to figure out between who and through what mediums communication does or does not flow between the police and the communities they serve, identifying bottlenecks, inefficiencies, and where technologies such as mobile applications and social media may be well placed to improve and contribute to the CP process.

5 Discussion

In this paper, we have demonstrated how, within Unity, we are working towards developing an architecture for community policing. The next stages will require further analysis of existing data obtained through the Unity project from the police, intermediaries and communities to facilitate the refinement and expansion of the models for the communication and information flows for the core tasks. This will enable us to develop a clear vision and model for CP in the future.

Acknowledgements. This work has received funding from the European Union's Horizon 2020 Research and Innovation programme under Grant Agreement No. 653729.

References

1. ISO/IEC/IEEE: ISO/IEC/IEEE 42010: Systems and Software Engineering Architecture Description (2011)
2. Robinson, O.: Driving Strategic IT Through Business Architecture (2011)
3. Skogan, W.G., Williamson, T.: An overview of community policing: origins, concepts and implementation. In: The Handbook of Knowledge-Based Policing: Current Conceptions and Future Directions, pp. 43–58 (2008)
4. The Open Group: The Open Group Architecture Framework, version 9 (2011)

A Scalable Malware Classification Based on Integrated Static and Dynamic Features

Tewfik Bounouh[1], Zakaria Brahimi[1], Ameer Al-Nemrat[2],
and Chafika Benzaid[3(✉)]

[1] Department of Computer Science, USTHB, Bab Ezzouar, Algeria
[2] Architecture, Computing, and Engineering School, UEL, London, UK
ameer@uel.ac.uk
[3] Division Sécurité Informatique, CERIST, Ben Aknoun, Algeria
cbenzaid@cerist.dz

Abstract. This paper presents a malware classification approach which aims to improve precision and support scalability. To this end, a hybrid approach combining both static and dynamic features is adopted. The hybrid approach has the advantage of being a complete and robust solution to evasion techniques used by malware writers.

The proposed methodology allowed achieving a very promising accuracy of 99.41% in classifying malware into families while considerably reducing the feature space compared to competing approaches in the literature.

Keywords: Malware classification · Static features · Dynamic features · Coarse-grained modeling

1 Introduction

With millions of malicious programs in the wild, and more encountered every day, malware analysis is critical for anyone who responds to computer security incidents [23].

Over the past few years, an increased interest has emerged in developing automated malware classification systems [5, 6, 9, 14, 18–21, 25, 27, 28]. The existing classification systems basically rely on two analysis techniques: static and dynamic. The static analysis refers to examining the malware code without executing it, whereas the dynamic analysis consists in observing and monitoring actions performed by the malware during its execution. While static analysis provides important insights into the detection and classification of malware, its main weakness lies in coping with packing and obfuscation [17]. As a result, dynamic analysis has recently received remarkable attention as it is significantly less vulnerable to code obfuscating transformations. However, dynamic analysis has its own weaknesses. Indeed, dynamic analysis techniques monitor the malware execution in a controlled environment (e.g., a sandbox). Hence, environment-aware malware may detect the controlled environment and then prevent themselves from performing malicious behavior. Furthermore, dynamic analysis is not designed to explore all possible execution paths [17] which leads to an inaccurate picture of the malware behavior. Due to the limitations of static and dynamic analysis, relying only on one of them is insufficient to correctly classify malware.

© Springer International Publishing AG 2016
H. Jahankhani et al. (Eds.): ICGS3 2017, CCIS 630, pp. 113–124, 2016.
DOI: 10.1007/978-3-319-51064-4_10

Consequently, researchers [10, 13, 20] have most recently adopted a hybrid technique which combines both static and dynamic features for better malware detection and classification. The major issues of these approaches is the size of the feature space which grows in proportion with the number of samples under examination. This might induce a scalability issue and incur high performance penalties for the classification process.

In this study, a malware classification system is developed which aims to improve precision and support scalability. With this in mind, a hybrid approach combining both static and dynamic techniques is adopted. The hybrid approach has the advantage of being a complete and robust solution to evasion techniques used by malware writers. Indeed, the static analysis overcomes the shortcomings of dynamic analysis by extracting relevant features even if the malicious software does not execute its payload during the dynamic inspection. Meanwhile, the dynamic analysis allows to collect the malicious behavior of a malware even if its code is distorted by obfuscation and protection techniques. The proposed classification framework exploits two static features; that are: printable string information due to its precision in malware detection and function length frequencies for their contribution in dissimilarity between malware families. Moreover, the dynamic features used consists in the set of actions on the system resources modeled in coarse-grained manner which allows to bound the feature space.

The rest of the paper is organized as follows. Section 2 summarizes related work in the literature. Section 3 presents the proposed malware classification framework. Section 4 discusses the experimental results. Finally, Sect. 5 concludes the paper.

2   Related Work

Over the past few years, an increased interest has emerged in developing automated malware detection and classification systems. To this end, various data mining and machine learning approaches [5, 6, 9, 14, 18–21, 25, 27, 28] have been applied to categorize malware into families based on different features derived from the analysis of the malware. Indeed, malware analysis involves two fundamental techniques: static and dynamic. The static analysis refers to examining the malware code without executing it, whereas the dynamic analysis consists in observing and monitoring actions performed by the malware during its execution. In this section, we review some relevant work.

Features that are commonly gleaned from a static analysis of malware include Portable Executable (PE) header metadata such as Dynamic Link Library (DLL) [21] and API calls [28], bytes sequences (or n-grams) [14, 21, 29], Operational Codes (OpCodes) [19, 22, 24], strings [12, 21, 25], and function length and function length frequency [26]. Strings-based techniques were shown to achieve high detection and classification accuracy compared to PE and n-grams based techniques [21, 25]. Moreover, function length frequency features are significant in identifying the malware's family [13]. While static analysis provides important insights into the detection and classification of malware, its main weakness lies in coping with packing and obfuscation. In fact, Moser et al. [17] proposed an obfuscation scheme that is provably NP-hard to analyze statically.

As a result, dynamic analysis has recently received remarkable attention as it is significantly less vulnerable to code obfuscating transformations. The prominent techniques tailored to extract dynamic features are n-gram analysis [16], non-transient state changes [5], taint analysis [6, 30], system call trace analysis [7, 9, 18], and API calls [8, 27]. Dynamic approaches can further be categorized into fine-grained (e.g., [6, 15, 30]) and coarse-grained (e.g., [9]) behavior modeling approaches. The fine-grained behavior modeling approach yields precise information for executed codes, though comes with the cost of a huge feature space which might incur high performance penalties. In the other hand, coarse-grained analysis has proven its effectiveness in accurately capturing the malicious characteristics while reducing the feature space as well as the amount of noise in the extracted features [9]. In dynamic analysis techniques, malware samples typically require to be executed in a controlled environment (e.g., a sandbox). Hence, environment-aware malware may detect the controlled environment and then prevent themselves from performing malicious behavior. Furthermore, dynamic analysis is not designed to explore all possible execution paths [17] which leads to an inaccurate picture of the malware behavior.

Due to the limitations of static and dynamic analysis, relying on only one of them is insufficient to correctly classify malware. Most recently, the researchers' interest has turned to combine both static and dynamic features in the detection and classification approaches. Santos et al. [20] combine the frequency of occurrence of OpCodes sequences with the information of the execution trace of an executable. Islam et al. [13] classify binaries into malicious and benign files using function length frequency, printable string information, and API calls along with their parameters. The approach proposed in [10] distinguishes malware from cleanware based on suspicious section count, function call frequency and network and file activities along with their parameters. The major issues of these approaches is the size of the feature space which grows in proportion with the number of samples under examination. This might induce a scalability issue and incur high performance penalties for the classification process.

In this work, we adopt a hybrid approach which uses both static and dynamic characteristics. But unlike existing solutions, the proposed approach focuses on classifying malware into families rather than distinguishing between malware and cleanware. We aim to develop a classification system with a significant precision and scalability that allows the processing of large samples of malware in reduced delays. To this end, we exploit printable string information due to its precision in malware detection, function length frequencies for their contribution in dissimilarity between malware families, and the set of actions on the system resources modeled in coarse-grained manner which allows to bound the feature space.

3 Malware Classification Process

Our study focuses on implementing a malware classification framework. The classification system requires the succession of three distinct stages, namely: Feature extraction, feature abstraction, and then classification using a machine learning algorithm.

Firstly, static and dynamic features of each executable are collected during the extraction process. Afterward, the extracted data, which are presented in linguistic form (e.g., "Creation of file A"), will be transformed into vectors of integers during the abstraction process. These vectors represent the Cartesian coordinates of each executable in a space of n-dimensions. Finally, the feature vectors are passed to machine learning algorithms for malware classification.

In what follows, the different stages of the proposed system will be presented.

3.1   Feature Extraction

The data extraction process is the starting point of our malware classification framework. To this end, we adopt a hybrid approach which combines the extraction of static and dynamic features.

Static Feature Extraction. From each disassembled binary code, the *printable strings* and the *function length frequency* information are collected.

1. **Strings**
   A string is defined as a consecutive sequence of printable characters. In this work, the strings are extracted using *Hexdive* tool [3]. It is worth to mention that much of strings included in malware are irrelevant. Indeed, they are deliberately maintained in the code in order to confuse malware detection process. In order to remove noises (i.e., impertinent strings) without biasing the analysis, the *Hexdive* filter was configured to keep only strings whose the minimal length is 4 characters. Moreover, only strings related to system's actions and objects (e.g., *recv*, *ReadFile*, *GetProcAddress*) are selected. For the sake of optimizing the system's response time, the strings selected are the most dominant. That is, the strings with an apparition frequency of at least 80% in each malware family are maintained. For instance, if we have 50 malware belonging to family A, we will select strings whose apparition frequency is higher than 40. By applying the aforementioned selection recommendations, a global list is constructed, containing all printable strings extracted from the malware dataset.
   The strings feature consists in identifying for each malware sample the total number of distinct strings found within its code and a binary report on the presence of each string in the global list, where a '1' represents the fact that the string is present and a '0' that it is not.
2. **Function Length Frequency**
   The length of a function is defined as the number of bytes in the function's code. To construct the function length frequency feature, a set of length ranges are defined in order to obtain a satisfactory precision while keeping a suitable computation time. Indeed, more the number of ranges increases, more the classification precision will be increased but at the cost of an in- creased computation time. The function length frequency feature consists in counting the number of functions in different length ranges. The *IDA Pro* disassembler [2] was used to extract the length of functions. *IDA Pro* stands out from other disassembling tools by being programmable and by its ability to execute scripts (IDC, Python, · · · etc.) from Command Line Interface

(CLI). In our case, this contributes greatly in automating the extraction process of function lengths. To this end, an IDC script was developed to retrieve lengths of all functions identified in a given malware code.

From a practical point of view, upon completion of extraction, the extracted strings and their occurrence frequencies as well as the extracted function names and their lengths are saved in a MySQL database. Once the database is filled, its content is carefully studied in order to select relevant strings and define function length ranges to be used in the abstraction phase. The selected strings and the identified function length ranges are saved in two separated files. Those files represent the constitutional dimensions of static vectors to generate during the abstraction phase.

Dynamic Feature Extraction. Secondly, behavioral features are extracted from the reports generated after executing malicious software in a confined environment. This process is done by submitting the malware samples to Anubis [1] sandbox. Behavioral reports generated from Anubis sandbox are presented in XML format, which is by default structurally readable and platform independent suitable for a fast-paced and automated investigation.

Each report contains the execution trace of a program represented by system calls invoked to perform the program's tasks (file and registry manipulation, processes, and network communication). Recall that we adopted the approach proposed by Chandramohan et al. [9] to extract dynamic features from XML reports. The approach has the advantage of fixing the number of features while keeping a high accuracy rate. It is based on the assumption that the identification of malware families requires analyzing the types of security-sensitive actions performed on system resources. Thereby, the system resources and the actions performed on those resources are extracted. We limited our study to four system resources, namely file, registry, process, and network. Those resources are identified as the most security-critical system resources that are widely attacked by malware [9]. The dynamic features are based on the set of actions performed on the system resources. For sake of scalability, only non-identical set of features are kept. For instance, a set of identical actions performed on two different resource objects (e.g., files A and C) are considered as a single malware feature. Such behavior modeling reduces the amount of noise in the malware's features space while accurately capturing the underlying malicious characteristics [9].

1. **File Features**

   The possible actions performed by a malware on a *file* resource are: (1) *Create* action which creates a new file/directory or opens an existing file; (2) *Modify* action which modifies the file's content; (3) *Read* action which reads the file's content; (4) *Delete* action which deletes the file/directory; and (5) *Memory-mapped* action which maps the file into a virtual memory that can be shared by several processes. Thus, a malware has a maximum of $(2^5 - 1)$; that is 31 possible combinations of actions that could be performed on a file resource. Each of these combinations is modeled as a "*file*" feature. Consequently, there are 31 possible file features of a malware.

2. **Registry Features**

The six potential actions that a malware can perform on registry are as follows: (1) *Create a key* which creates a new registry key/sub-key; (2) *Delete a key* which deletes an existing registry key/sub-key; (3) *Monitor a key* which monitors the parameters of registry key/sub-key; (4) *Modify a value* which modifies the value of a registry key/sub-key; (5) *Read a value* which reads the value of a registry key/sub-key; and (6) *Delete a value* which deletes the value of a registry key/sub-key. This makes a total of ($2^6 - 1$); that is 63 possible registry features of a malware.

3. **Process Features**

The potential combinations of actions on a process are formed of: (1) *Create_a_process* which creates a process to execute a program; (2) *Delete_a_process* which terminates the process and kills all its threads; (3) *Create_a_thread* which creates a new thread to run within an executing process; (4) *Read_shared_memory* which allows the process to read the shared memory; and (5) *Write_shared_memory* which allows the process to write to the shared memory. This yields a total of ($2^5 - 1$); that is 31 possible process features of a malware.

4. **Network Features**

To identify the potential actions that a malware can perform on a network, both XML reports and the packet capture (pcap) files are analyzed. For network resource, we identified 9 possible actions that are as follows: (1) *TCP_Conversation* which establishes a TCP conversation with the destination; (2) *SMTP_Conversation* which initiates a conversation with a mail server; (3) *UDP_Traffic* which allows to exchange an UDP traffic; (4) *HTTP_Traffic* which allows to exchange an HTTP traffic; (5) *FTP_Traffic* which allows to exchange an FTP traffic; (6) *Ping_Requests* which checks whether a remote target is available over the network; (7) *DNS_Query* and (8) *socket* which allow to modify the target machine's information in order to compromise its integrity; and (9) *DATA* which indicates the potential transmission and reception of data. Hence, a malware has a maximum of ($2^9 - 1$); that is 511 possible combinations of network actions that could be performed on network resources. Consequently, there are 511 possible network features of a malware.

Unlike syntactic features, the extraction of behavioral features does not require a prior study. We just need to compare the extracted features with the set of possible combinations of each behavioral feature type. The possible combinations of actions performed on the four resources are saved in four separated files. The total size of the four files represents the constitutional dimension of dynamic vector to generate during the abstraction phase.

The result of the extraction process for each binary is a set of data including the function length distribution according to defined ranges, the strings present in code and their total number, as well as the combinations of actions performed on files, registry, processes, and network resources.

3.2   Data Abstraction

Data abstraction is the formalization process of the features collected during the extraction process. The choice of the formalism is closely related to the type of data supported by the classification algorithm. In our case, the classification algorithms used support Cartesian data. Hence, we chose to abstract the features as integer vectors. The vector encoding is used to represent the extracted features of a given malware as a point in an n − dimension space.

Firstly, dynamic features are represented with a vector of length $636 = 31 + 63 + 31 + 511$ for each malware. The first 31 bits are used for file features; the following 63 bits are used for registry features, the following 31 bits are used for process features and the last 511 bits represent the network features.

Formally, let F, R, P, and N be the set of file features, registry features, process features and network features respectively. Let $Z^{1-31} = \{x_1 | 1 \leq x_1 \leq 31, x_1 \in Z +\}$, $Z^{32-94} = \{x_2 | 32 \leq x_2 \leq 94, x_2 \in Z +\}$, $Z^{95-125} = \{x_3 | 95 \leq x_3 \leq 125, x_3 \in Z +\}$ and $Z^{126-636} = \{x_4 | 126 \leq x_4 \leq 636, x_4 \in Z +\}$. Let f, r, p and n be the mapping $F \rightarrow Z^{1-31}$, $R \rightarrow Z^{32-94}$, $P \rightarrow Z^{95-125}$, $N \rightarrow Z^{126-636}$ to assign a file, registry, process and network features respectively to a positive integer in the respective range that serves as the bit position in the feature vector to represent the feature. For a malware M, the dynamic feature vector V_D is defined as follows:

$$V_D[k] = \begin{cases} 1 \ if \ 1 \leq k \leq 31 \ and \ M \ has \ the \ feature \ x \in F, \ such \ as \ f[x] = k \\ 1 \ if \ 32 \leq k \leq 94 \ and \ M \ has \ the \ feature \ x \in R, \ such \ as \ r[x] = k \\ 1 \ if \ 95 \leq k \leq 125 \ and \ M \ has \ the \ feature \ x \in P, \ such \ as \ p[x] = k \\ 1 \ if \ 126 \leq k \leq 636 \ and \ M \ has \ the \ feature \ x \in N, \ such \ as \ n[x] = k \\ 0 \ Otherwise \end{cases} \quad (1)$$

In the same way, static features form two vectors. The first vector is for strings and the second one is for function length intervals. Let S and I be the set of strings and the set of function length intervals, respectively. Let $Z^{1-|S|} = \{x | 2 \leq x \leq |S|, x \in Z +\}$. Let s be the mapping $S \rightarrow Z^{2-|S|}$. For a malware M, the string feature vector V_{Ss} is defined as follows:

$$V_{Ss}[k] = \begin{cases} V_{Ss}[1] = number \ of \ strings \ found \\ 1 \ if \ 2 \leq k \leq |S| \ and \ M \ has \ the \ string \ x \in S, such \ as \ S[x] = k \\ 0 \ Otherwise \end{cases} \quad (2)$$

Let $Z^{1-|I|} = \{x | 1 \leq x \leq |I|, x \in Z +\}$. Let i be the mapping $I \rightarrow Z^{1-|I|}$. For a malware M, the function length frequencies feature vector V_{Sf} is defined as follows:

$$V_{Sf}[k] = \begin{cases} number \ of \ |function| \in interval \ x, \forall 1 \leq k \leq |I|; and \ x \in I, such \ as \ i[x] = k \\ 0 \ Otherwise \end{cases}$$

$$(3)$$

Finally, the obtained vectors V_D, V_{Ss}, and V_{Sf} are concatenated ($V_D\|V_{Ss}\|V_{Sf}$) to form the V vector, which represents, in an n-dimension space, the Cartesian data of the considered malware.

4   Classification Process and Evaluation

4.1   Malware Dataset

The test is conducted on a set of 1515 malware, previously classified and labeled by VXheaven [4]. The malware samples span a period of 8 years (from 2007 to 2015) and belong to 26 families with more than 30 individuals per family. All malware have been designed for Windows 32 bits platform. Table 1 lists the different families and number of samples per family.

Table 1. Experimental dataset

Malware family	# of samples	Malware family	# of samples
Backdoors	130	Trojan-DNSChanger-Win32	31
DoS-Win32	87	Trojan-Banker-Win32	43
Email-Worm	42	Trojan-Clicker-Win32	90
Exploit-Win32	39	Trojan-DDoS-Win32	48
Flooder-Win32	45	Trojan-Downloader-Win32	50
HackTool-Win32	117	Trojan-Dropper-Win32	37
Net-Worm-Win32	40	Trojan-Proxy-Win32	44
Packed	55	Trojan-Ransomware-Win32	42
P2P-Worm-Win32	49	Trojan-Spy-Win32	56
Rootkit-Win32	40	Trojan-Spy-KeyLogger	37
SpamTool-Win32	38	Trojan-Spy-BotNet	48
Trojan-Win32	94	Virus-Win32	59
Trojan-Dialer-Win32	52	Worm-Win32	102

4.2   Classification Process

We assessed the efficiency of the integrated approach using different classification algorithms from the Machine Learning toolbox WEKA [11]. The classification algorithms are: Support Vector Machine (SVM), Nearest Neighbor (NN), Decision Tree (DT), and Random Forest (RF). After the feature extraction and abstraction steps, the feature vectors are stored as ARFF (Attribute-Relation File Format) files and passed to WEKA for classification. It should be noted that all classifiers were evaluated by utilizing 10-fold cross-validation as it is a well-accepted and the standard method of classification.

4.3   Evaluation Metrics

To evaluate the proposed system, True Positive Rate (TPR), False Positive Rate (FPR), Precision, Recall and Accuracy are measured. TPR is the rate of malware samples correctly classified. FPR is the rate of malware samples falsely classified. Precision is the percentage of predicted malware classes that are actually the correct malware classes. Recall is the percentage of actual malware classes predicted correctly by the model. The formulas of Precision and Recall are given by Eqs. 4 and 5, respectively:

$$Precision = \frac{TP}{TP + FP} \tag{4}$$

$$Recall = \frac{TP}{TP + FN} \tag{5}$$

Where TP is the number of malware samples correctly classified in their class, FP is the number of malware samples incorrectly classified in another class, FN is the number of malware samples incorrectly classified in their class, and TN is the number of malware samples correctly classified in other classes.

4.4   Experimental Results and Discussion

Table 2 shows the weighted average results when only static features are used. It is worth to note that the weighted average is used in order to deal with the imbalance in the number of samples per malware family. Meanwhile, Table 3 presents the weighted average results when both static and dynamic features are used.

Table 2. Weighted average classification results on the data set using the static method

Classifier	TPR	FPR	Precision	Recall
NN	0.691	0.014	0.695	0.691
DT	0.979	0.001	0.979	0.979
RF	0.964	0.002	0.964	0.964
SVM	0.674	0.015	0.689	0.674

Table 3. Weighted average classification results on the data set using the hybrid method

Classifier	TPR	FPR	Precision	Recall
NN	0.631	0.017	0.636	0.631
DT	0.994	0.001	0.994	0.994
RF	0.957	0.002	0.958	0.957
SVM	0.747	0.011	0.751	0.747

The obtained results show that the hybrid method, where both static and dynamic features are used, achieves the best results with DT and SVM classifiers. Indeed, an average accuracy of above 99% is reached using DT classifier, with an improvement of 1.52% compared to using only static features. A gain of 1.52% may appear insignificant for a dataset of 1515 samples as it represents only 23 malware. However, considering a malware corpus of 1000000 samples, this gain will enhance the classification of 15200 malware samples.

Apart from accuracy, the main advantage of the proposed hybrid approach consists in the considerable reduction of the feature space thanks to the rules used to select the most dominant static features and the coarse-grained modeling of dynamic features. To confirm this claim, we compared the number of features generated by our approach against the one proposed by Islam et al. [13]. Table 4 reports the comparison results.

From Table 4, we notice that the proposed approach achieves a better classification accuracy compared to [13] while considerably reducing the feature space. In fact, the feature space is reduced by 98.73% which shows the effectiveness of the coarse-grained modeling of features.

Table 4. Weighted average classification results on the data set using the hybrid method

	# of samples	Accuracy	# of features	Features used
Islam et al. [13]	2939	97.05%	498	**Static:** printable strings + function length frequency
			72259	**Dynamic:** API calls and parameters
			Total = 72757	
Ours	1515	99.41%	289	**Static:** printable strings + function length frequency
			636	**Dynamic:** actions on system resources
			Total = 925	

5   Conclusion

In this paper, we have proposed a malware classification system which aims to improve classification accuracy while supporting scalability. The accuracy goal was achieved by adopting an hybrid approach where both static and dynamic features are combined. In the other hand, the scalability objective was achieved by reducing the feature space thanks to the rules used to select the most dominant static features and the coarse-grained modeling of dynamic features.

An experimental study was conducted on a dataset of 1515 malware samples. The obtained results showed that the proposed approach reaches an average accuracy of above 99%. Moreover, the feature space was reduced by 98.73% compared to a competing approach.

References

1. Anubis. http://anubis.seclab.tuwien.ac.at
2. Hex-Rays. IDA Pro. https://www.hex-rays.com/products/ida/
3. Hexcorn Ltd. HexDive. www.hexacorn.com
4. Vxheaven. www.vxheaven.org
5. Bailey, M., Oberheide, J., Andersen, J., Mao, Z.M., Jahanian, F., Nazario, J.: Automated classification and analysis of internet malware. In: Kruegel, C., Lippmann, R., Clark, A. (eds.) RAID 2007. LNCS, vol. 4637, pp. 178–197. Springer, Heidelberg (2007). doi:10. 1007/978-3-540-74320-0_10
6. Bayer, U., Comparetti, P.M., Hlauscheck, C., Kruegel, C., Kirda, E.: Scalable, behavior-based malware clustering. In: Proceedings of the 16th Symposium on Network and Distributed System Security (NDSS 2009), February 2009
7. Canzanese, R., Mancoridis, S., Kam, M.: Run-time classification of malicious processes using system call analysis. In: Proceedings of the 10th International Conference on Malicious and Unwanted Software (MALWARE 2015), pp. 21–28. IEEE, October 2015
8. Cesare, S., Xiang, Y., Zhou, W.: Malwise-an effective and efficient classification system for packed and polymorphic malware. IEEE Trans. Comput. **62**(6), 1193–1206 (2013)
9. Chandramohan, M., Tan, H.B.K., Shar, L.K.: Scalable malware clustering through coarse-grained behavior modeling. In: Proceedings of the ACM SIGSOFT 20th International Symposium on the Foundations of Software Engineering (FSE 2012), pp. 27:1–27:4. ACM, November 2012
10. Gandotra, E., Bansal, D., Sofat, S.: Integrated framework for classification of malwares. In: Proceedings of the 7th International Conference on Security of Information Networks (SIN 2014), pp. 417:417–417:422. ACM (2014)
11. Hall, M., Frank, E., Holmes, G., Pfahringer, B., Reutemann, P., Witten, I.H.: The weka data mining software: an update. SIGKDD Explor. Newsl. **11**(1), 10–18 (2009)
12. Islam, R., Tian, R., Batten, L., Versteeg, S.: Classification of malware based on string and function feature selection. In: Proceedings of 2nd Cybercrime and Trustworthy Computing Workshop (CTC 2010), pp. 9–17. IEEE, July 2010
13. Islam, R., Tian, R., Batten, L.M., Versteeg, S.: Classification of malware based on intergrated static and dynamic features. J. Netw. Comput. Appl. **36**, 646–656 (2013)
14. Kolter, J., Maloof, M.: Learning to detect malicious executables in the wild. In: Proceedings of the 10th ACM International Conferernce on Knowledge Discovery and Data Mining (SIGKDD 2004), pp. 470–478. ACM, August 2004
15. Lee, T., Mody, J.J.: Behavioral classification. In: Proceedings of the 15th Annual Conference of the European Institute for Computer Antivirus Research (EICAR 2006), April 2006
16. Mekky, H., Mohaisen, A., Zhang, Z.-L.: Separation of benign and malicious network events for accurate malware family classification. In: Proceedings of the IEEE Conference on Communications and Network Security (CNS 2015), pp. 125–133. IEEE, September 2015
17. Moser, A., Kruegel, C., Kirda, E.: Limits of static analysis for malware detection. In: Proceedings of the 23rd Annual Computer Security Applications Conference (ACSAC 2007), pp. 421–430. IEEE, December 2007
18. Rieck, K., Holz, T., Willems, C., Düssel, P., Laskov, P.: Learning and classification of malware behavior. In: Zamboni, D. (ed.) DIMVA 2008. LNCS, vol. 5137, pp. 108–125. Springer, Heidelberg (2008). doi:10.1007/978-3-540-70542-0_6

19. Santos, I., Brezo, F., Nieves, J., Penya, Y.K., Sanz, B., Laorden, C., Bringas, P.G.: Idea: opcode-sequence-based malware detection. In: Massacci, F., Wallach, D., Zannone, N. (eds.) ESSoS 2010. LNCS, vol. 5965, pp. 35–43. Springer, Heidelberg (2010). doi:10.1007/978-3-642-11747-3_3

20. Santos, I., Devesa, J., Brezo, F., Nieves, J., Bringas, P.G.: OPEM: a static-dynamic approach for machine learning based malware detection. In: Herrero, Á. (ed.) International Joint Conference CISIS'12-ICEUTE'12-SOCO'12 Special Sessions. AISC, vol. 189, pp. 271–280. Springer, Heidelberg (2013)

21. Schultz, M., Eskin, M., Zadok, E., Stolfo, F.: Data mining methods for detection of new malicious executables. In: Proceedings of the 22nd IEEE Symposium on Security and Privacy (S&P 2001), pp. 38–49. IEEE, May 2001

22. Siddiqui, M., Wang, M.C., Lee, J.: Data mining methods for malware detection using instruction sequences. In: Proceedings of the 26th IASTED International Conference on Artificial Intelligence and Applications (AIA 2008), pp. 358–368, February 2008

23. Sikorski, M., Honig, A.: Practical Malware Analysis: The Hands-On Guide to Dissecting Malicious Software, 1st edn. No Starch Press, San Francisco (2012)

24. Stolfo, S., Wang, K., Li, W.-J.: Towards stealthy malware detection. In: Christodorescu, M., Jha, S., Maughan, D., Song, D., Wang, C. (eds.) Malware Detection, pp. 231–249. Springer, Heidelberg (2007)

25. Tian, R., Batten, L., Islam, R., Versteeg, S.: An automated classification system based on the strings of trojan and virus families. In: Proceedings of 4th International Conference on Malicious and Unwanted Software (MALWARE 2009), pp. 23–30. IEEE, October 2009

26. Tian, R., Batten, L.M., Versteeg, S.C.: Function length as a tool for malware classification. In: Proceedings of the 3rd International Conference on Malicious and Unwanted Software (MALWARE 2008), pp. 69–76. IEEE, October 2008

27. Tian, R., Islam, R., Batten, L., Versteeg, S.: Differentiating malware from cleanware using behavioural analysis. In: Proceedings of the 5th International Conference on Malicious and Unwanted Software (MALWARE 2010), pp. 23–30. IEEE, October 2010

28. Wang, C., Pang, J., Zhao, R., Liu, X.: Using API sequence and Bayes algorithm to detect suspicious behavior. In: Proceedings of the International Conference on Communication Software and Networks (ICCSN 2009), pp. 544–548. IEEE, February 2009

29. Ye, Y., Li, T., Chen, Y., Jiang, Q.: Automatic malware categorization using cluster ensemble. In: Proceedings of the 16th ACM International Conference on Knowledge Discovery and Data Mining (SIGKDD 2016), pp. 95–104. ACM, July 2010

30. Yin, H., Song, D., Egele, M., Kruegel, C., Kirda, E.: Panorama: capturing system-wide information flow for malware detection and analysis. In: Proceedings of the 14th ACM Conference on Computer and Communications Security (CCS 2007), pp. 116–127. ACM (2007)

Source Camera Identification Using Non-decimated Wavelet Transform

Ahmad Ryad Soobhany[(✉)], Akbar Sheikh-Akbari,
and Z. Cliffe Schreuders

Cybercrime and Security Innovation Centre,
Leeds Beckett University, Leeds, UK
{r.soobhany, csi}@leedsbeckett.ac.uk

Abstract. Source Camera identification of digital images can be performed by matching the sensor pattern noise (SPN) of the images with that of the camera reference signature. This paper presents a non-decimated wavelet based source camera identification method for digital images. The proposed algorithm applies a non-decimated wavelet transform on the input image and split the image into its wavelet sub-bands. The coefficients within the resulting wavelet high frequency sub-bands are filtered to extract the SPN of the image. Cross correlation of the image SPN and the camera reference SPN signature is then used to identify the most likely source device of the image. Experimental results were generated using images of ten cameras to identify the source camera of the images. Results show that the proposed technique generates superior results to that of the state of the art wavelet based source camera identification.

Keywords: Sensor pattern noise · Non-decimated wavelet transform · Source identification · PRNU · Digital forensics · SPN

1 Introduction

With the decrease in cost of digital cameras, cell phones and tablets with cameras, the proliferation of digital photographs has reached epic proportions. Some of these imaging devices and the photographs that they produce are used in the commission of crime. A method to link the digital images, recovered by law enforcement agencies, to the source imaging device that created these photographs would be helpful in linking suspects to crimes. Within the digital camera image creation pipeline, described in [1], artifacts are left in the created image at each processing stage. These artifacts can be from processing inside the device or characteristics of the device itself [2] and can be extracted as features from images in order to link to the source imaging device. Some of the artifacts from the camera pipeline that can be used for source device identification are demosaicing algorithm of Color Filter Array (CFA), quantization tables for JPEG image compression, EXIF header of JPEG image, lens aberration and sensor noise. The first three techniques can identify the make and/or model of the source device whereas the last two techniques can identify a specific source device.

Within the scope of this paper, we will concentrate on sensor noise to identify the source device. The sensor noise, so-called sensor pattern noise (SPN), is a deterministic

© Springer International Publishing AG 2016
H. Jahankhani et al. (Eds.): ICGS3 2017, CCIS 630, pp. 125–133, 2016.
DOI: 10.1007/978-3-319-51064-4_11

artifact left in any image created by an imaging sensor. The SPN consists mainly of the photo response non-uniformity (PRNU) and to a lesser extent the fixed pattern noise (FPN) [3]. The PRNU occurs due to manufacturing imperfections and inhomogeneity in the silicon chips of the charge-coupled device (CCD) or complementary metal oxide semiconductor (CMOS) imaging sensors and the PRNU is unique to an individual sensor. The slight variation in conversion of light energy to electrical energy by each sensor pixel also contributes to the PRNU [4]. The FPN occurs due to dark currents when the sensor is not exposed to light and is eliminated by some cameras. Lukas et al. [3] proposed the extraction of SPN as a digital signature to identify the source imaging device and most subsequent extraction methods proposed by other researchers extract the SPN and use its main component PRNU as digital signature. The process for identification consists of creating a reference SPN signature for the camera sensor and matching the reference fingerprint against SPN signatures from suspect digital photographs.

The most common SPN extraction method is performed using wavelet transform in the frequency domain. The SPN, n, is a medium to high frequency signal, which can be separated from the image, I, using a high-pass filter [3]

$$n = I - f(I) \tag{1}$$

where f is denoising function that performs as a low-pass filter to extract the required signal. To the knowledge of the authors, all the wavelet extraction method uses a Wiener filter as the low-pass filter. Some methods based on wavelet SPN extraction have been proposed to improve the underlying SPN signature. Chen et al. introduced the maximum likelihood estimator (MLE) for the SPN combined from multiple images [5]. They set the mean of the rows and columns of the SPN signature to zero in order to attenuate the linear pattern. They apply Wiener filtering after performing the Discrete Fourier Transform (DFT) of the SPN signature to remove blockness artifacts. Another method assumes that the strong components in the SPN signature are caused by image scene details and thus attenuates all strong components [6].

There have been other methods of extracting the SPN from photographs. A two dimensional Gaussian filter in the spatial domain can be used by altering the variance of the filter to find a trade-off between the level of scene details and SPN details [7]. A simplified version of the Total Variation based noise removal algorithm has been used to extract the PRNU [8]. Singular Value Decomposition (SVD) was used to extract the PRNU of images by first estimating the PRNU energy of each image and then converting the PRNU to an additive noise to facilitate extraction using the SVD method [9]. Kang et al., proposed an SPN predictor based on context-adaptive inter-polation algorithm to suppress the effect of image scene [10].

All the existing wavelet based SPN extraction methods are based on decimated wavelet decomposition, where the details of the decomposition are down sampled. Non-decimated wavelet transform have been applied in edge detection algorithms for iris segmentation [11]. In this paper, an SPN extraction method is introduced based on non-decimated wavelet transform. All the details of the different sub bands are kept during the wavelet decomposition in order to retain more information about the SPN, which is already a weak signal. Experimental results on a mixture of images from digital cameras and camera phones show promising results for identification of imaging source devices. The rest of the paper is organized as follows: in Sect. 2, the proposed SPN extraction method is explained; in Sect. 3, a description of the experiments conducted together with the results obtained is detailed. Finally, Sect. 4 concludes the paper.

2   Proposed SPN Extraction Method

Non-decimated wavelet transform keeps all the details of the wavelet sub-bands during the decomposition process, which allows more information to be retained. Whereas decimated wavelet transform performs down sampling of the sub-bands, most often halving the size of the decomposed signal. Figure 1 shows the block diagram of the proposed algorithm applying non-decimated wavelet transform to an input image in order to extract the SPN.

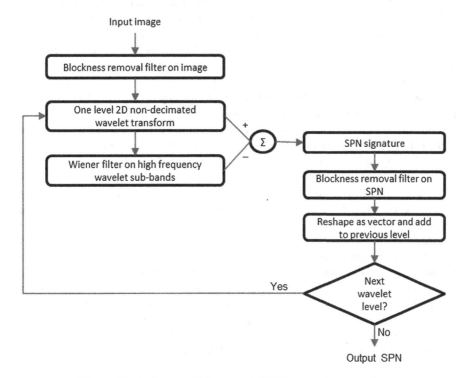

Fig. 1. Block diagram of the proposed SPN extraction algorithm.

The algorithm takes an input color image and applies a 2D Wiener filter in the frequency domain by applying DFT (Discrete Fourier Transform). This step is performed to reduce periodical patterns and other artifacts that occur in JPEG images. These patterns are also called blockness artifacts and cause false positives between SPN signatures from different cameras of the same brand or model. A one level non-decimated wavelet transform is applied first on the rows then the columns of the image. The process produces two-dimensional wavelet decomposition where the sub-bands are as shown in Fig. 2.

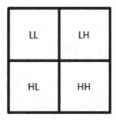

Fig. 2. Two dimensional wavelet sub-bands, where LL is LowLow, LH is LowHigh, HL is HighLow and HH is HighHigh coefficients frequency respectively.

The LL – LowLow, LH – LowHigh, HL – HighLow and HH – HighHigh wavelet sub-bands details represent the High and Low frequencies of the wavelet decomposition of the image. The LL is the approximation details that contain a low frequency representation of the image. The other three sub-bands contain the high frequency coefficients of the wavelet decomposition. The denoising of the three sub-bands of interest is done by applying a low pass filter, in the form of a 2D Wiener filter. The denoising process eliminates all medium to high frequency details from the sub-bands. The SPN signature is obtained by subtracting the low-passed wavelet sub-bands from the original decomposed wavelet sub-bands as shown in Eq. 1 in the first section of the paper. This process retains only the high frequency details from the non-decimated wavelet decomposition. The SPN extraction stage is performed on the three sub-bands of interest and does not include the approximation details (LL).

Some denoising errors can be introduced in the SPN signature by the denoising filtering process [12]. Most often periodic patterns are formed in the SPN signature. The blockness removal filter is applied to the SPN signature in order to attenuate any blocking artifacts that may have been inserted in the SPN by the denoising function. The SPN is reshaped from a 2D signal to a vector. All the SPN elements are concatenated and form the final SPN signature with information from each level of wavelet decomposition. If another level of wavelet decomposition is required the algorithm will perform the one level 2D non-decimated wavelet decomposition on the approximation details (LL) from the current level decomposition. The level of wavelet decomposition for SPN extraction is passed as a parameter to the algorithm. If the last level of wavelet decomposition has been reached, the output SPN signature is obtained.

3   Experiments and Results

The performance of the proposed source device identification algorithm was assessed by running a set of experiments on an image dataset to test a predefined hypothesis. The results of the algorithm were compared against the state of the art wavelet extraction method.

3.1 Hypothesis and Performance Measure

The identification of a source device using SPN can be formulated as the following binary hypothesis testing:

$$H_0 = \text{Image was not created by camera}$$
$$H_1 = \text{Image was created by camera} \tag{2}$$

where H_0 is the null hypothesis and H_1 is the alternative hypothesis. The correlation match is performed between the camera reference SPN and each individual image SPN in the dataset. If the correlation coefficient is above a predetermined threshold, the null hypothesis can be rejected. The threshold is pre-set empirically to 0.01, and it has been shown in previous research in source device identification that a threshold of 0.01 for the cross correlation coefficient was reasonable [6]. If the null hypothesis is rejected, it can be inferred that the photo originates from the camera fingerprint being tested. If the null hypothesis is not rejected, it can be inferred that the photo does not originate from the camera fingerprint under test.

The results obtained from the proposed scheme were compared against the state of the art in wavelet SPN extraction method [13] and the source code was downloaded from [14]. The experiments were designed so that the SPN extraction methods will be able to identify the source device of an image and that the proposed method can differentiate between devices of the same make and model.

3.2 Experimental Setup

For the purpose of our experiments, a total of 100 images were chosen from 10 imaging devices comprising of digital cameras and camera phones. Each device contributed 10 images. Table 1 shows the list of cameras used, where the camera make and models are

Table 1. Cameras used in experiment showing their makes, models and picture resolution

Device name	Device type	Make	Model	Picture resolution (px)
Agfa_DC-733s_0	Digital camera	Agfa	DC-733	3072 × 2304
Canon_Ixus70_0	Digital camera	Canon	Ixus70	3072 × 2304
Canon_Ixus70_1	Digital camera	Canon	Ixus70	3072 × 2304
Canon_Ixus70_2	Digital camera	Canon	Ixus70	3072 × 2304
Rollei_RCP-7325XS_0	Digital camera	Rollei	RCP-7325XS	3072 × 2304
Samsung_L74wide_0	Digital camera	Samsung	L74wide	3072 × 2304
samsung_galaxy_S2_A	Camera phone	Samsung	Galaxy S2	3262 × 2448
samsung_galaxy_S2_B	Camera phone	Samsung	Galaxy S2	3262 × 2448
zte_orange_sanfrisco_A	Camera phone	ZTE	Orange sanfrancisco	1536 × 2048
zte_orange_sanfrisco_B	Camera phone	ZTE	Orange sanfrancisco	1536 × 2048

listed together with the resolution of the pictures from these devices. The pictures for the digital cameras were selected from the Dresden public image dataset [15]. All cameras that had pictures with the same resolution (3072×2304 pixels) were chosen, in order to show that our method could differentiate between cameras that would have similar SPN synchronization pattern. The images from the camera phones were used in the experiments of [9] and they include four phones, with two phones from the same make and model. Furthermore, there are three Canon_Ixus70 cameras in the dataset so that the experiments can further demonstrate the differentiation between camera models. The fact there are three cameras of the same make and model (Canon Ixus70), it was decided to use one of the cameras (*Canon_Ixus70_0*) as the camera reference SPN signature.

To create the camera reference SPN signature, 50 flatfield pictures, pictures of white wall with no scene details, from the *Canon_Ixus70_0* camera were downloaded separately from the natural scene images. The SPN of the 50 images were extracted and averaged into one camera reference SPN. All the 100 images, including the 10 images originating from the *Canon_Ixus70_0* camera was matched against the camrea reference SPN. To ensure generality, the 100 pictures were natural images consisting of a mixture of outdoor and indoor scenes. The Dresden dataset contains natural pictures with similar scenes from different cameras, which ensures that the matching of the SPN is performed in more controlled conditions. To reduce computational complexity, all the images were cropped to a size of 512×512 pixels from the centre.

3.3   Results

In order to compare the performance of the proposed algorithm with the state of the art technique, firstly the camera reference SPN of the *Canon_Ixus70_0* camera was created using both algorithms. Secondly, the SPN signatures of the 100 images were extracted using both algorithms and matched against the camera reference SPN. Our proposed method is called 'non-decimated' and the state of the art method is called 'decimated' in the results section. The results obtained are shown in Fig. 3, where the *Canon_Ixus70_0* reference SPN signature and correlated with 100 images from 10 cameras. Images 11 to 20 come from this camera and rest of images from the other 9 cameras. Both non-decimated and decimated correlation coefficient results are displayed. All the images from the *Canon_Ixus70_0* camera were positively matched to the camera reference SPN by rejecting the null hypothesis, above the threshold of 0.01, when using both methods of extraction as the correlation coefficient values for images 11 to 20 shows in Fig. 3. The non-decimated method gave higher positive matching results than the decimated method for the 10 images from the *Canon_Ixus70_0* camera. The mean correlation coefficient values for the non-decimated method was 0.0411 and for the decimated method was 0.0407 respectively. The variance in values for images 11 to 20 were 0.00024 and 0.00030 for the non-decimated and decimated methods respectively. The decimated method had more variation in results for positive matchings and the non-decimated method provided more consistent results.

The correlation coefficient values for the other two Canon Ixus cameras (*Canon_Ixus70_1*, *Canon_Ixus70_2*), which were images 21 to 30 and 31 to 40

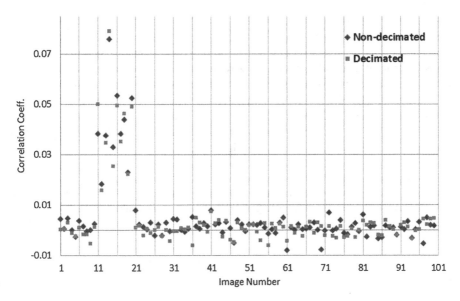

Fig. 3. *Canon_Ixus70_0* reference SPN signature and correlated with 100 images from 10 cameras. Images 11 to 20 come from this camera and rest of images from the other 9 cameras. Both non-decimated and decimated correlation coefficient results are displayed.

respectively, were close to zero for the non-decimated method similar to the decimated method. These results show that our proposed method was able to differentiate between cameras from the same make and model. The correlation coefficient values for the rest of the images from the other 7 cameras were all below the threshold, with no false positive and not rejecting the null hypothesis. The variance in correlation values was 0.00001 for both the non-decimated and decimated methods. Based on the variance of the correlation coefficients obtained it can be seen that the non-decimated method provided a more consistent identification result for the dataset used.

The decimated method can extract the SPN from an image with 4 levels of wavelet decomposition. While performing the experiments with different levels of wavelet decomposition it was found that the non-decimated method managed to extract the SPN signature from an image after the first level of wavelet decomposition. This may be due to the fact that the non-decimated wavelet transform retain more information about the SPN signal, so that it can be extracted after the first level of decomposition.

4   Conclusion

This paper presented a non-decimated wavelet based source camera identification method for digital images. The proposed algorithm applies a non-decimated wavelet transform on the input image and split the image into its wavelet sub-bands. The coefficients within the resulting wavelet high frequency sub-bands are denoised to extract the SPN from the picture. Cross correlation of the image SPN and the camera reference SPN signature was then used to identify the source camera of the image. Experimental results were generated using images of ten cameras to identify the source device of the images. Results showed that the proposed technique generates superior results to that of the state of the art wavelet based source camera identification. A secondary benefit with non-decimated wavelet transform is that the SPN signature can be extracted after the first level of wavelet decomposition as opposed to decimated method where a reliable SPN can only be extracted after 4 levels of wavelet decomposition. Further works to improve the quality of the extracted SPN is underway as well as reduce the dimensionality of the SPN signature.

Acknowledgements. This work, as part of the CARI project, is supported by the Police Knowledge Fund, which is administered by the College of Policing, the Home Office, and the Higher Education Funding Council for England (HEFCE). Special thanks to Sofia Soobhany for her insightful comments on the paper.

References

1. Soobhany, A.R., Leary, R., Lam, K.P.: On the performance of Li's unsupervised image classifier and the optimal cropping position of images for Forensic Investigations. Int. J. Digital Crime Forensics (IJDCF) **3**, 1–13 (2011)
2. Gloe, T., Kirchner, M., Winkler, A., Böhme, R.: Can we trust digital image forensics? In: Proceedings of the 15th International Conference on Multimedia, Augsburg, Germany, pp. 78–86 (2007)
3. Lukas, J., Fridrich, J., Goljan, M.: Digital camera identification from sensor pattern noise. IEEE Trans. Inf. Forensics Secur. **1**, 205–214 (2006)
4. Fridrich, J.: Digital image forensic using sensor noise. IEEE Signal Process. Mag. **26**, 26–37 (2009)
5. Chen, M., Fridrich, J., Goljan, M., Lukas, J.: Determining image origin and integrity using sensor noise. IEEE Trans. Inf. Forensics Secur. **3**(1), 74–90 (2008)
6. Li, C.-T.: Source camera identification using enhanced sensor pattern noise. IEEE Trans. Inf. Forensics Secur. **5**, 280–287 (2010)
7. Alles, E.J., Geradts, Z., Veenman, C.J.: Source camera identification for low resolution heavily compressed images. In: International Conference on Computational Sciences and its Applications, (ICCSA), pp. 557–567 (2008)
8. Gisolf, F., Malgoezar, A., Baar, T., Geradts, Z.: Improving source camera identification using a simplified total variation based noise removal algorithm. Digital Investig. **10**(3), 207–214 (2013)
9. Soobhany, A.R., Lam, K.P., Fletcher P., Collins, D.: Source identification of camera phones using SVD. In: IEEE International Conference on Image Processing, Melbourne, VIC, pp. 4497–4501 (2013)
10. Kang, X., Chen, J., Lin, K., Anjie, P.: A context-adaptive SPN predictor for trustworthy source camera identification. EURASIP J. Image Video Process. **2014**(1), 1–11 (2014)
11. Akbari, A.S., Zadeh, P.B., Behringer, R.: Iris segmentation using a non-decimated wavelet transform. In: Proceedings of the 2nd IET International Conference on Intelligent Signal Processing. Savoy Place, London (2015)
12. Lin, X., Li, C.-T.: Enhancing sensor pattern noise via filtering distortion removal. IEEE Signal Process. Lett. **23**(3), 381–385 (2016)

13. Goljan, M., Fridrich, J., Filler, T.: Large scale test of sensor fingerprint camera identification. In: Proceedings of SPIE Electronic Imaging, Media Forensics and Security XI, vol. 7254, pp. 0I-01–0I-12 (2009)
14. MATLAB implementation of digital camera fingerprint extraction. http://dde.binghamton. edu/download/camerafingerprint/
15. Gloe, T., Böhme, R.: The 'dresden image database' for benchmarking digital image forensics. In: Proceedings of the 25th Symposium on Applied Computing (ACM SAC), vol. 2, pp. 1585–1591 (2010)

Content Discovery Advertisements: An Explorative Analysis

Raghavender Rao Jadhav Balaji[✉], Andres Baravalle,
Ameer Al-Nemrat, and Paolo Falcarin

University of East London, London, UK
{r.jadhav-balaji,a.baravalle,a.al-nemrat,
falcarin}@uel.ac.uk

Abstract. Content discovery advertisements are type of native ads which have gained traction for driving ad traffic. These advertisements are being hosted on supposedly reputed websites and their popularity has been growing however it has been reported in the media that these ads are deploying click bait ads. In this research, these ads were evaluated for a period of one month to study and examine their credibility. It was found that significant percentage of these ads were malicious in nature.

1 Introduction

Online advertising has been the one of the significant factors behind the rise of internet marketing and promotion. Online advertisements range from banner ads, widgets, pop-up ads, flash based ads, content ads etc., One of the driving force of the online advertisements it's easy to place and their reach to millions of users with minimal cost. Online ads have grown in billions in numbers and with ad syndications it has become a complex task to monitor the authenticity of these ads where hackers and malicious persons are able to place deceiving ads on supposedly reputed websites to lure users for commercial gains [1]. Malicious advertising has been a challenge to tackle for internet marketing companies, as malicious ad creators have been able to evolve and evade detection, victimizing millions of gullible users. In this paper we look into content discovery Ads also referred as content recommendation platforms. These advertisements fall under the category of native advertising which have gained more traction and seen on majority of the news and content publishing websites.

1.1 Native Advertising

Native advertising refers to displaying ads that look native to the website and integrate with the content of the webpage. Native ads include sponsored content, branded content, content marketing, and related content [2]. These native ads tend to be more desirable because of the way they are displayed which makes them attracted to companies and users. In 2013 it was noted that 75% of the Online Publishers Association used Native ads [2]. Content recommendation/discovery platforms are new means of

© Springer International Publishing AG 2016
H. Jahankhani et al. (Eds.): ICGS3 2017, CCIS 630, pp. 134–143, 2016.
DOI: 10.1007/978-3-319-51064-4_12

advertisements on the webpages. These advertisements are tailored to the contents of the webpages and they blend with the contents of the webpages.

1.2 Content Discovery Ads

These ads are commonly found on news and major publishers' websites. They are, usually, wrapped around the contents of the webpages which makes them look as a natural part of the webpage. Figure 1 is a screen shot taken from the popular news website the Telegraph. It showed the content discovery ads on the webpage. The top three articles are content discovery ads while the three articles in the bottom are the news stories from the website itself. These ads look like contents from the Telegraph's website itself but they are, in fact, ads promoted by the content discovery platform providers. These ads can be typically recognized by looking at the URLs of the destination pages (and sometimes also by a small print wrapped around them stating phrases like "from the web" or "promoted stories" and the provider name). The origin of these ads is not always evident to the non-technical users. Content discovery platforms have gained popularity and are often displayed on the supposedly reputed websites. These ads now, as mentioned above, could be seen on many news websites and other content publishing websites. Table 1, illustrates some of these newspapers consumed online that display content discovery ads.

Fig. 1. Example of a content discovery advertisement (Source: www.telegraph.co.uk)

Currently the two major content providers are "Taboola" and "Outbrain". There are also many other content providers however with a smaller market share [3]. Taboola and Outbrain dominate the content discovery platforms, as of May 2016, with Taboola on at least 24,860 websites and Outbrain on at least 17,746 websites [4] and content discovery ads (CDA) are mostly placed in the category of websites like News, Entertainment, Sports, Technology, business, Media and Forums with ads placed mostly in US followed by the UK [5].

Table 1. Top news papers consumed online in the UK (Source: www.pressgazette.co.uk)

News websites	Users
Daily Mail	10.7 Million
The Guardian	10.5 Million
The Telegraph	9.4 Million
Independent	5.5 Million
Mirror	5 Million
The Express	2.5 Million
Metro	2.5 Million
Huffington Post	1.2 Million
The Sun	0.87 Million

Taboola has become one of the fastest growing content discovery platform company where it reached 1.1 billion clicks in a month and 1 billion unique desktop users [6, 7] and followed by Outbrain, draws clicks from 557 million unique desktops users [8].

1.3   Content Discovery Platform Working Model

The content discovery platforms enable small content publishing websites or start up websites to boost their traffic by placing their content as CDA on supposedly reputed news websites such as The Daily Mail, The Daily Telegraph, The Guardian, Forbes, The Sun, CNN, Daily Express, and other similar websites.

One of the boosting feature of these platforms is that the content ads placed on the supposedly reputed websites is tailored to match the relevance of the webpage. Wordings as "related story", "sponsored story", or "promoted story" is typically used and may induce the user to click on that particular ad. At the same time, as the ads are included in large traffic, reputable websites, this offers a convenient platform for small or start up content publishing websites to boost their traffic.

These small websites need to pay a fee to the content discovery platforms to place their content. For instance, Taboola operates Cost per click (CPC) model where Taboola charges $ 0.50 per click [9].

1.4   Credibility of the Content Ads

As noted earlier in this paper about the growing trend of these ads, several claims have been made by websites and news outlets as the BBC, The Washington Post, The Verge, Fortune, who have reported that these ad platforms are serving malicious advertisements, as click bait scams [10], and generally low quality content.

Initially CDA were blocked by adblockers as AdblockPlus, Adblock and uBlock. Adblock Plus, one of the most popular adblockers with 100 million active users is now including Taboola's ads in their acceptable ad whitelist [11].

In this paper, we carry out a critical evaluation of content discovery platforms and their ads on four supposedly reputed news websites from UK. We conducted our analysis in month of April 2016.

2 Methodology

In order to conduct an investigations of the content ads, as mentioned above, four websites that display content discovery platforms, namely: Dailymail, The Daily Telegraph, Daily Express, and The Sun were chosen.

These news websites were chosen for their reputation and popularity, as reflected in their Alexa ranking in April 2016. For our study, we chose top two tiered and bottom two-tiered news website according to the data from Table 2.

Table 2. Alexa ranking (UK)

Website	% of users	Ranking
Dailymail	19.9	19
The Telegraph	27.6	40
Daily Express	36.7	110
The Sun	28.9	156

Taboola ads were displayed on Dailymail website and Outbrain ads were displayed on The Telegraph, Daily Express and The Sun. After identifying the websites to evaluate, we identified content ads on these websites. On each article, Dailymail hosted up to 10 content ads, The Telegraph hosted 3 content ads, Daily Express hosted 6 content ads and The Sun hosted 5 content ads. We examined each ad on all the websites (see Fig. 2) and followed the links, and on those links, we identified further content ads, which were sponsored by Taboola, Outbrain and other three companies namely Revcontent, ContentAd and Earnify. On these link pages we identified that content ads were sometimes sponsored by more than one provider.

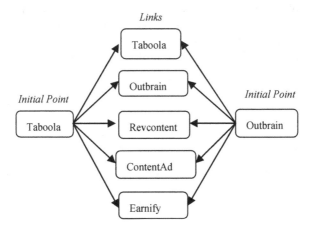

Fig. 2. Content ad providers on hosting page (initial point) and on landing page (Links)

2.1   Data Collection

The first step for the data collection was to scrape the web sites we selected for advertisements. A number of approaches and technologies are described in the litera- ture; from the use of basic string functions and regular expressions to automated extraction of loosely structured data [12].

Due to the dynamic nature of the web sources that we needed to scrape, the use of string functions and regular expressions itself was not sufficient. Instead, JavaScript had to be interpreted and the Selenium library was used for this task. The spider we developed mimicked the user interaction to collect ad data.

We identified the core elements of the main web pages on each website and we identified markers for the spider to locate and capture the advertisement data, using XPath. For instance, the content ad provider Taboola had the following relative XPath: (".//*[contains(@id,'internal_trc_')]") which remained same across all the websites hosting Taboola ads. Once the core markers were identified, we proceeded with our data collection (Table 3).

Table 3. Examples of the markers.

Content ad providers	Relative XPath
Taboola	(.//*[contains(@id,'internal_trc_')])
Outbrain	(.//*[contains(@id,'outbrain_widget_')
Revcontent	(.//*[contains(@id,'rc_w_')
ContentAd	(.//*[contains(@id,'ac_')
Earnify	(.//*[contains(@id,'earnify-widget-')

2.2   Sequence of Data Collection

To run and gather data we set up a Microsoft Windows machine, with no ad block protection. A "real", scripted browser was used for data collection. Basing on [13], the software stack included Python, the Selenium webdriver, Beautiful Soup for data extraction and MySQL to store the results.

The spider did run its sequence for each of the websites under examination every 30 min for the period of one month (Fig. 3).

Fig. 3. Sequence of data collection

3 Results and Analysis

During the period of our data collection we gathered over hundred thousand content ads. See Table 4.

Table 4. No. of Ads collected for each website

Websites	Total number of ads
Daily Mail	30057
Daily Express	35219
The Sun	31680
Telegraph	5167

3.1 Taxonomy of the Content Ads

In our preliminary analysis we identified that the content ads were displaying different kinds of click bait ads, which we classified with five categories: Money, Sex, Health, Trash and Other.

Money:	money scam ads luring users to invest small amount of money in return for high profits in millions
Sex:	sexual content, as fake dating opportunities
Health:	ads luring users to buy products promising to cure variety of body and health related issues
Trash:	ads related to website offering gossip stories; the ad web page hosted further ads related to money, sex, and health
Other:	the ads contained in this category displayed genuine ads.

3.2 Classifying the Ads

In our ad classification we used the title of the ads to classify the hundred thousand ads and we implemented Naïve Bayes classifier. In order to train and test the data, we manually classified 1896 out of 30057 ads from Daily Mail, 1708 out of 35219 ads from the Express, 1205 out of 31680 ads from the Sun and 1036 out of 5167 ads from the Telegraph.

3.3 Preparing the Data for Training and Testing

In the Naïve Bayes classifier, we created text corpus for the training data and cleaned the corpus by removing punctuations, numbers and also created file of stop words to be removed from the corpus. Once the corpus was clean we created document text matrix. Then we created training and test data and the Tables 5, 6, 7, 8 shows the results for the respective ads pool.

Table 5. Daily Mail

Total observations in Table: 565

predicted	actual health	money	other	sex	trash	Row Total
health	9	1	3	0	1	14
	0.429	0.045	0.011	0.000	0.005	
money	1	17	4	2	2	26
	0.048	0.773	0.015	0.036	0.010	
other	10	3	221	4	49	287
	0.476	0.136	0.831	0.071	0.245	
sex	0	0	10	31	10	51
	0.000	0.000	0.038	0.554	0.050	
trash	1	1	28	19	138	187
	0.048	0.045	0.105	0.339	0.690	
Column Total	21	22	266	56	200	565
	0.037	0.039	0.471	0.099	0.354	

Table 6. Daily Express

Total observations in Table: 508

predicted	actual health	money	other	sex	trash	Row Total
health	33	2	2	1	1	39
	0.892	0.048	0.017	0.010	0.005	
money	0	23	3	0	4	30
	0.000	0.548	0.025	0.000	0.019	
other	4	12	90	9	22	137
	0.108	0.286	0.750	0.094	0.103	
sex	0	2	1	73	18	94
	0.000	0.048	0.008	0.760	0.085	
trash	0	3	24	13	168	208
	0.000	0.071	0.200	0.135	0.789	
Column Total	37	42	120	96	213	508
	0.073	0.083	0.236	0.189	0.419	

3.4   Classification Model

In our classification model (see Table 9) we were able to achieve the detection rate of an average 70% across all categories on all the four websites with an exception in health, sex and money category in the Daily Mail, Daily Express respectively.

3.5   Results

Once the classifier was trained, we applied it to the respective pool of ads we collected, the Tables 10, 11, 12, 13 shows the results.

Table 7. The Sun

```
Total observations in Table:  361

           | actual
predicted  |  health |   money |   other |     sex |   trash | Row Total |
-----------|---------|---------|---------|---------|---------|-----------|
   health  |    14   |     0   |     1   |     0   |     1   |      16   |
           |  0.737  |  0.000  |  0.008  |  0.000  |  0.008  |           |
-----------|---------|---------|---------|---------|---------|-----------|
    money  |     0   |    26   |     2   |     0   |     3   |      31   |
           |  0.000  |  0.743  |  0.015  |  0.000  |  0.025  |           |
-----------|---------|---------|---------|---------|---------|-----------|
    other  |     1   |     5   |   101   |     2   |    12   |     121   |
           |  0.053  |  0.143  |  0.765  |  0.037  |  0.099  |           |
-----------|---------|---------|---------|---------|---------|-----------|
      sex  |     1   |     2   |     5   |    37   |     8   |      53   |
           |  0.053  |  0.057  |  0.038  |  0.685  |  0.066  |           |
-----------|---------|---------|---------|---------|---------|-----------|
    trash  |     3   |     2   |    23   |    15   |    97   |     140   |
           |  0.158  |  0.057  |  0.174  |  0.278  |  0.802  |           |
-----------|---------|---------|---------|---------|---------|-----------|
Column Total |   19  |    35   |   132   |    54   |   121   |     361   |
           |  0.053  |  0.097  |  0.366  |  0.150  |  0.335  |           |
```

Table 8. The Telegraph

```
Total observations in Table:  263

           | actual
predicted  |  health |   money |   other |     sex |   trash | Row Total |
-----------|---------|---------|---------|---------|---------|-----------|
   health  |    16   |     0   |     0   |     0   |     1   |      17   |
           |  0.800  |  0.000  |  0.000  |  0.000  |  0.015  |           |
-----------|---------|---------|---------|---------|---------|-----------|
    money  |     0   |    18   |     1   |     1   |     1   |      21   |
           |  0.000  |  0.720  |  0.008  |  0.045  |  0.015  |           |
-----------|---------|---------|---------|---------|---------|-----------|
    other  |     4   |     4   |   101   |     2   |    18   |     129   |
           |  0.200  |  0.160  |  0.783  |  0.091  |  0.269  |           |
-----------|---------|---------|---------|---------|---------|-----------|
      sex  |     0   |     0   |     5   |    17   |     5   |      27   |
           |  0.000  |  0.000  |  0.039  |  0.773  |  0.075  |           |
-----------|---------|---------|---------|---------|---------|-----------|
    trash  |     0   |     3   |    22   |     2   |    42   |      69   |
           |  0.000  |  0.120  |  0.171  |  0.091  |  0.627  |           |
-----------|---------|---------|---------|---------|---------|-----------|
Column Total |   20  |    25   |   129   |    22   |    67   |     263   |
           |  0.076  |  0.095  |  0.490  |  0.084  |  0.255  |           |
```

Table 9. Detection rate in %

	Health	Money	Other	Sex	Trash
Daily Mail	42.90	77.30	83.10	55.40	69.00
Daily Express	89.20	54.80	75.00	76.00	78.90
The Sun	73.70	74.30	76.50	68.50	80.20
The Daily Telegraph	80.00	72.00	78.30	77.30	62.70
Average	71.45	69.60	78.23	69.30	72.70

Table 10. Daily Mail in %

health	money	other	sex	trash
1561	1554	8579	5255	13107

health	money	other	sex	trash
5.2	5.2	28.5	17.5	43.6

Table 11. The Daily Express in %

health	money	other	sex	trash
4797	5825	6779	6051	11766

health	money	other	sex	trash
13.6	16.5	19.2	17.2	33.4

Table 12. The Sun in %

health	money	other	sex	trash
4817	3994	10313	3104	9456

health	money	other	sex	trash
15.2	12.6	32.5	9.8	29.8

Table 13. The Telegraph in %

health	money	other	sex	trash
927	931	1749	827	732

health	money	other	sex	trash
17.9	18.0	33.9	16.0	14.2

In the results we identified that once the users clicked on the content ads on the four news websites they were exposed to an average 70% of click bait ads of the category Money, Sex, Health and Trash.

Genuine ads were underrepresented: only 28.5% on the Dailymail, 19.2% on the Daily Express, 32.5% on the Sun 32.5% and 33.9% on the Telegraph.

4   Conclusion

The content discovery ads, from analysis demonstrated above, are the new gateways for malicious and click-bait websites. In this undergoing work, our aim was to focus on both an exploratory analysis and in the classification of the content discovery ads displayed on the supposedly reputed websites. We also identified that the websites with click bait ads were also hosting malicious ads. Our future work will involve exploring the content ad networks and detecting with precision the malicious ads in this criteria.

References

1. Li, Z., Zhang, K., Xie, Y., Yu, F., Wang, X.: Knowing your enemy: understanding and detecting malicious web advertising. In: Proceedings of the ACM Conference on Computer and Communications Security, pp. 674–686. ACM (2012)
2. Levi, L.: A faustian pact: native advertising and the future of the press. Ariz. L. Rev. **57**, 647 (2015)
3. WSJ. http://www.wsj.com/articles/outbrain-taboola-make-their-mark-on-online-advertising-industry-1426765357
4. Datanyze. https://www.datanyze.com/market-share/content-syndication-networks/outbrain-vs-taboola
5. Builtwith. http://trends.builtwith.com/ads/Outbrain/Market-Share
6. https://www.taboola.com/drive-traffic-and-leads-content-discovery
7. FastCompany. http://www.fastcompany.com/3054205/fast-feed/with-1-billion-monthly-clicks-taboola-is-the-worlds-biggest-content-discovery-tool
8. http://www.outbrain.com/
9. https://www.taboola.com/advertiser-help-center/bidding-and-budget-recommendations
10. BBCNews. http://www.bbc.co.uk/news/business-29322578
11. http://www.ft.com/cms/s/0/80a8ce54-a61d-11e4-9bd3-00144feab7de.html
12. Walther, M.: Unsupervised extraction of product information from semi-structured sources. In: IEEE 13th International Symposium on Computational Intelligence and Informatics (CINTI), pp. 257–262 (2012)
13. Lawson, R.: Web Scraping with Python. Packt Publishing, Birmingham (2015)

Phishing-Deception Data Model for Online Detection and Human Protection

Phoebe Barraclough$^{(\boxtimes)}$ and Graham Sexton

Computing, Engineering and Information Sciences, University of Northumbria,
Newcastle upon Tyne NE1, UK
{Phoebe.a.Barraclough,g.sexton}@northumbria.ac.uk

Abstract. The construction and interaction procedure of phishing and user in the deception mode is presented. We analyses phishing behavior when tempting human in order to construct a phishing-deception human-based data model (PDHDM) based on frequent associated events. The proposed phishing-deception human-based data model is utilized to generate association rules and to accurately classify between phishing and legitimate websites. This approach can reduce false positive rates in phishing detection systems, including a lack of effective dataset. Classification algorithms is employed for training and validation of the model. The proposed approach performance and the existing work is compared. Our proposed method yielded a remarkable result. The finding demonstrates that phishing-deception human-based data model is a promising scheme to develop effective phishing detection systems.

Keywords: Phishing behavior · Phishing-human interaction · Phishing websites · Association classification

1 Introduction

A number of phishing detection systems have been developed in Cybersecurity to detect phishing website attacks. However, no work has focused on constructing data model using phishing-deception based on human. As a results, there is still false positives and false negatives rates causing inadequacy in online transactions [1, 2]. Phishing attacks have almost doubled with a cost of 1.5 billion in 2012 alone [3]. The existing approaches utilizes either whitelist or blacklist to detect phishing websites. In general, Blacklist approaches have low error rates. Even so they are not able to generalize well with new automatically generated phishing websites because blacklist focused specifically on URL feature-set which handle specific part of websites [2, 4–8]. For example, Sheng [12] investigation blacklist toolbars and identified that blacklist-based toolbars can detect phishing websites 15% to 40% accurately. Feature-based approaches can generalize well to new phishing attacks. However, they need updated regularly to be ahead of phishing strategies [9–11]. Main contribution of this paper include analyzing phishing behavior when attempting human users to construct Phishing-deception Human-based data model.

© Springer International Publishing AG 2016
H. Jahankhani et al. (Eds.): ICGS3 2017, CCIS 630, pp. 144–154, 2016.
DOI: 10.1007/978-3-319-51064-4_13

1.1 Aim and Objectives

The aim of this paper is to analyse phishing while attempting users to construct phishing-deception Human-based data model to generate fuzzy rule in order to classify emerging phishing and suspicious sites with higher accuracy in real-time. This can strengthen phishing detection systems and protect user in online transaction.

Specific Objectives are:

- To identify feature sources and select 100 phishing email and 300 phishing websites,
- To extract data-set based on Phishing-deception human-based that can be used to discriminate between legitimate and illegitimate websites
- To design a phishing-deception Human-based model
- To train and to validate the model based on Random tree algorithm in order to assess its merit.
- Compare the propose results with the existing results

The remaining sections is structures as follows: Sect. 2 reviews the existing related literature in using feature-based approaches, classification algorithms and other approaches. Section 3 describes phishing-deception Human-based approach proposed methodology. It also discusses data sources identification and data extraction. Section 4 presents experimental procedure and covers training and testing process. Section 5 provides the results. It also provides discussions and Evaluation together with limitations of the proposed work. Section 6 concludes the paper and provide future work.

2 Related Work

2.1 Blacklist-Based Approach

This section focuses in reviewing existing literature. Various approaches employed blacklist-based toolbar approaches. For instance, Xiang and Hong [4] explored blacklist-based and content-based to strengthen human-verified blacklist and whitelist. Their techniques employed probabilistic to obtain high accuracy. Their experiment obtained 87.42% true positive, but suffered 4.34% false positive error rates, which is a higher risk for users. Xiang and Ma's work are related to this work because both works applied URL feature-based approach. Ma [13] investigated and found that Xiang's approach [4] is not capable of handling new domains.

Similarly, Internet Explorer (IE) Phishing Filter [6] also utilizes server-side blacklist of known phishing URLs maintained by Microsoft. Other toolbars utilizing a list of known phishing URLs maintained in a remote server of a community database such as PhishTank also exists to detect phishing attack. However, the degree of accuracy is not provided.

In addition, Toolbars using Phishing URL includes EarthLink was developed [8]. EarthLink uses a combination of heuristics, using ratings and manual verification. The toolbar enables users to report phishing websites where sites are verified and added to blacklist. However, less information about the toolbar was presented.

McAfee [16] was developed which runs on Microsoft Windows, Linux and Mac operating software. The SiteAdvisor detects phishing websites and spams. When a suspicious website is detected, users have choices of using the features to report phishing websites.

GeoTrustWatch toolbar [17] was developed that works with many third party services and certificate authorities to verify websites as legitimate. It also enables users to store a customer image and small text which is displayed consistently in order to know that the toolbar is not phishing. TrustWatch runs on MS Windows 98/NT/ 2000/XP/7 with Internet Explorer. However, it does not provide any information about how TrustWatch decides if a site is phishing or not.

eBay toolbar Account Guard [18] is a Microsoft Internet explorer extension. It is based on server-side blacklist, using similarity heuristics of website content to help protect against phishing eBay websites. The toolbar compares the content of the URLs of a given web page with blacklist. If the website a user has visited is verified to be eBay or PayPal, the account guard button displays green. If the site is suspicious, grey is displayed. If a phishing website is detected, a red button is displayed [20]. The problem with eBay toolbar is that it detects phishing attempts on eBay or PayPal only, while all other phishing websites are ignored.

The Netcraft toolbar [7] approach utilizes various methods to decide whether a website is legitimate or not. The Netcraft toolbar checks suspicious URLs that carry characters which deceive and display browser navigation controls in every windows to protect against pop-up windows that try to hide the navigational controls that display websites hosting locations including countries that helps to evaluate fake URLs [7].

SpoofGuards anti-phishing toolbar approach was developed utilizing heuristics to detect phishing websites [19]. It first checks the current domain name and compares it with websites that have been visited recently by the user to catch phishing websites with a similar looking domain name. The URL is analysed to detect obfuscation and non-standard port numbers. Then it analyses links in the websites using heuristics approach. It finally examines images on the website by hashing them to check if similar images are found on sites the user has visited. If two identical images are found, then a fake website has copied images from a legitimate website. As a result, a score is calculated for each website. If the score surpasses a certain threshold, the toolbar displays a red icon as an indicator of a phishing site. If some of the heuristics are triggered which are not enough to exceed the threshold, a yellow icon is displayed to indicate unknown site. If no heuristics are triggered, a green icon is displayed to indicate a safe website [25].

2.2 Content-Based Approaches

Other work also employed content-based approach. Afroz and Greenstadt presented PhishZoo to identify phishing attacks [14]. Their method utilized website contents including images and HTML elements and applied Scaling Invariant Feature Transformed (SIFT) algorithm with fuzzy hashing to identify phishing websites. While fuzzy hashing method can identify a new phishing website, this approach can easily be broken through by restructuring HTML elements with no alteration of appearance to the websites.

2.3 Features-Based Using MCAR and Association Classification Approaches

Feature-based approach was also applied. Aburrous and Khelifi also [15] developed a plug-in toolbar to detect phishing website. Their approach combined fuzzy reasoning in assessing imprecise and dynamic phishing features. The toolbar was tested and successfully recognized 86% phishing websites correctly. However, this approach misclassified 14% false alarms which is a high risk for users.

In the attempt to improve the approaches, Aburrous applied Fuzzy-Data mining that include: JRip, RIPPER, PART, PRISM, C4.5, Classification Based-Association (CBA) and priori algorithms (except MCAR) with 27 features and a case study [5]. This approach obtained 83.7% accuracy, but suffered 16.3% error rates which are either caused by less features or poor parameter tuning. Additional features and proper parameter tuning could alleviate the problem.

A study by [23] adopted 27 features from Aburrous et al., and employed MCAR and AC classification algorithm to present phishing detection method. Their method can classify webpages with more than 98.5% accuracy, but they did not mention in their study how many rules were generated by employing the MCAR algorithm.

Other researchers also investigated the same study, using rule-based classifications in detecting phishing webpages [24, 25]. Study by [24] proposed a model (a set of conventional features) and summarized the prediction error rate produced by a set of Associative Classification (AC) algorithms. The results indicated that C4.5 outperformed all algorithms with 5.76% average error-rate. They achieved 97.5% accuracy, which is relatively putting users in to 2.5% risk when faced with phishing attacks.

Our approach is based on phishing-deception human-based data model, using an Association Classifier algorithms based employed to generate association rules and to train and validate the model using Ten-fold cross-validation for a robust result.

3 Phishing-Deception Human-Based Proposed Methodology

Phishing-deception human-based is a malicious user in a cyber with an intention to manipulate legitimate users into surrendering sensitive information. phishing-deception human-based is composed of three main components as shows in Fig. 1:

- A phishing email that initiate interaction and direct a user to a phishing website
- a user as a target
- a phishing website which carries a form that captures user's sensitive information.

The phishing email and a phishing website is jointly referred to as phishing.

Phishing Email. phishing email is a channel for spreading text message to target users in the form of spam [22]. It comes in the form of a genuine email with a link to illegitimate website. It utilizes deception to get users' confidence to visit an illegitimate website and to fill a phishing form with their sensitive information. The messages may sound attractive rather than threatening or threatening rather than attractive. Email is used because it is the initiator of the deception which directs users to a website link. An

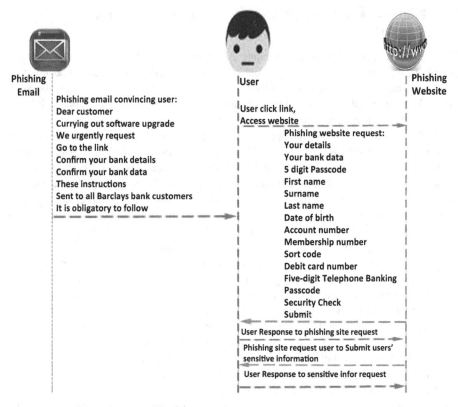

Fig. 1. User interacting with phishing email and phishing websites

example of such phishing email that imitate Barclays bank emails is shown in Fig. 3 in the appendix.

User. user is a person that uses computer programs and online services and networks including websites, internet and email.

Phishing website. phishing site is an exact copy of legitimate website from an organisation which is well-known to a user. It uses spoofed identity of the company to make them look like it comes from the company it claims to be. It imitations contents of a genuine website such as text, images, logos to make it look genuine. Also, it uses similar tone, words and links as it is in a genuine website to obtain user's confidence. It contains forms to that is intended to collect users' sensitive information where these forms are similar to that in the genuine website. For instance, such phishing website that mimic Barclays bank website is shown in Fig. 4 in the appendix.

3.1   Data Sources and Data Identification

To classify phishing websites accurately, detection systems need to use exact data that phishing website-forms requests users to fill. This data-set can be found from a large number of phishing emails and websites. 100 emails and 300 phishing websites were collected from SmillerSmiles website [19]. In total, 400 sources are used for data extraction in this paper. MillerSmile is an archive in which phishing scam is maintained. We used the SmillerSmile archive because it carries the most recent phishing sites and it can be accessed freely by public. Any number of sources can be selected, but 400 is selected randomly as a representative of the phishing sites without bias. Examples of enticing phishing phrases are as follows: {Confirm your bank data, your Bank detail, Five Digital Telephone Banking}. More of these phrases can be found in Fig. 1.

3.2 Data Extraction

After data sources are identified, finding the most frequent terms appearing on emails and websites is performed using an automated 'Find Function' and expert knowledge. Specifically, nine most frequent phishing phrases are identified from the collected 100 phishing emails. Likewise, fifteen most frequent phishing website phrases are spotted from 300 phishing websites. A total of 23 data-set is identified. The number of features to be used to build detection systems can be any number that can produce desirable results [20]. Previous work by Barraclough [11] extracted 288 features from five different sources also known as 5 inputs. Basic data-set to detect phishing website effectively are the data from website-forms requests for users to fill, which are presented in phishing-deception human-based data model in this paper.

It is important to prepare data-set to eliminate redundancy and to assign weight to data-set which is a value range between [0, 1]. 0 (zero) indicates legitimate sites, 1 (one) indicates phishing sites, while any number between [0, 1] represents suspicious.

4 Experiment Procedure

Experimental work is based on data-set from Phishing-deception Human based data Model (PDHDM), applying Random Tree as shown in Fig. 2.

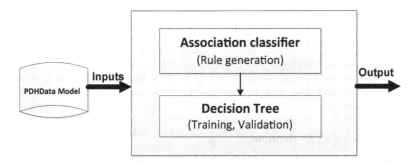

Fig. 2. Training and testing procedure flow

Data-set are text which are extracted while phishing email and phishing website interact with human users to entice human to surrender their sensitive information to attacker.

Association Classification algorithm is used to find relations between features by analyzing frequently used features [26]. Association rules is applied in other field such as web usage and intrusion detection.

Random Tree is an algorithm for producing a tree while considering randomly selected attributes at every node. It cannot perform pruning and has an option to enable estimation of probabilities base on a hold-out set.

4.1   Training and Validation

The model is measured for its accuracy and validity using 2-fold cross-validation. 23 data-set is randomly split into 60% training-set and 40% validation-sets. Training-set is used only ones to train the model and test the model on a testing-set. The role is changed so that the training is performed using testing-set and validation is carried out using training-set. A number of methods can be used for training and testing the model. However, 2-fold cross-validation is utilized in this paper for accuracy and robust results.

5   Results

The experiment is run based on Random tree algorithm with 23 data-set. The parameters are set to 0.05 delta which is the amount at which the support reduces eat time of iteration. The results achieved is 100% True Positive. That means all data-set are correctly classified without any error or overfitting. This suggest that the data-sets are free from noise. The result achieved demonstrates best performance. The result is summarized in Table 1.

Table 1. Results based on classifier using random tree

Classification	Numbers	Percentage
Correctly classified	17	100%
Incorrectly classified	0	0%
Relative absolute error	-	0%
Root relative squared error	-	0%
True Positive (TP)	1	100%
False Positive (FP)	0	0%

5.1   Discussions and Evaluation

One of the objective of this study is to compare the results of the proposed work with the previous work to enable the demonstration of the best performance. Our proposed work applied Random Tree algorithm using 23 data-set. 2-fold cross-validation method was chosen for a robust evaluation. Data-set was split randomly into 60% training-set and 40% testing-set. A set was used ones for training and testing. Our experiment achieved 100% accuracy. To compare our results with the existing feature-based approaches using Association Classification algorithms. Table 2 presents the results and shows clearly in the second row that our proposed approach out-performed existing work by 1.5%. The work by [15] under-performed by 1.4%.

Table 2. Comparison of proposed work and existing work

Proposed work & Previous work	Features based approaches	Algorithms	Accuracy results
Proposed work	23	Random tree	100%
Aburrous and Khelifi (2013)	-	toolbar	86%
Aijlouni et al., (2013)	27	MCAR	98.5%
Rami et al., (2014)	-	C4.5	97.5
Mohammad et al., (2014)	-	C4.5	94%

5.2   Propose Approach Limitation

Propose approach have best performance. Identifying 400 sources may be a representative for the whole phishing attacks, but considering the numbers of phishing websites reported in PhishTank [21] per year. Additional new data sources could be extracted to keep-up with emerging phishing attacks.

6   Conclusion and Further Work

The main contribution of this paper include constructing phishing-deception human-based data model of frequent phishing phrases by analyzing phishing deceiving users. This is the first study that demonstrated the approach of constructing phishing-deception human-based data model. The aim of this study was to analyze phishing while attempting users to construct phishing-deception human-base data model in order to classify emerging suspicious and phishing sites with higher accuracy in real-time. Based on the objective, the results demonstrate that phishing websites can be detected using Phishing-deception based-human data-set with a higher accuracy. In general, our results show that relationship between phishing-deception based on human responses plays a big role in extracting effective data-set.

6.1   Further Work

Phishing attacks evolve rapidly, more new sources of data-set to represent the population of phishing attack could be identified to extract additional data-set. feature work will also look at the new area called Internet of Things. How data used to detect phishing websites can be used to secure Internet of Things.

Appendix

Phishing Email Imitation

The email in Fig. 3 is an example of a phishing email that imitate Barclays bank legitimate email. It looks a genuine email with a link to illegitimate website. It also Copied contents of a legitimate website such as logos, text, images to make it look authentic, but in reality it is not legitimate.

Fig. 3. Copy of a phishing email imitating legitimate Barclays bank email

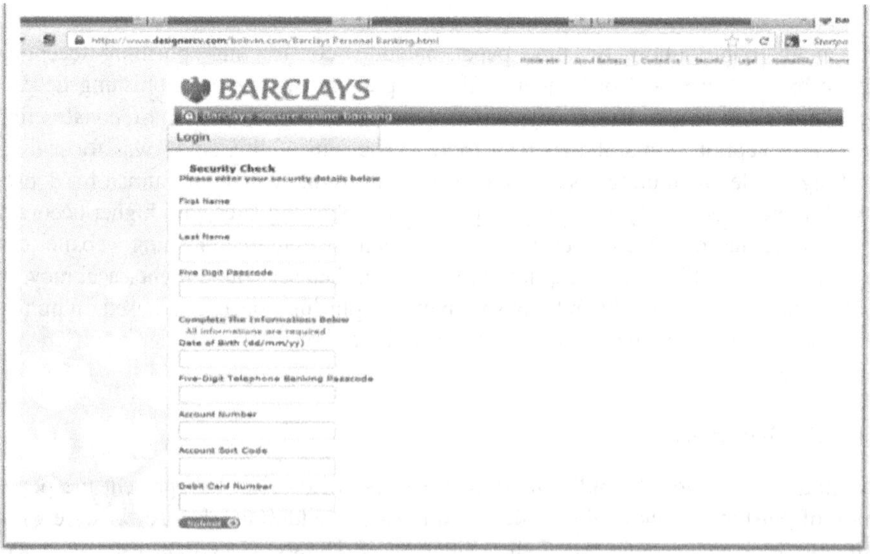

Fig. 4. Phishing website imitating legitimate Barclays bank website.

Phishing Website Copy

The website in Fig. 4 is a phishing website that mimic Barclays bank legitimate website. It carries a forms to collect users bank detail in which this form is similar to that in the legitimate website, but in real it is not a legitimate form.

References

1. Ead, W., Abdelwahed, W., Abdul-Kader, H.: Adaptive fuzzy classification- rule algorithm in detection malicious web sites from suspicious URLS. Int. Arab. J. eTechnol. **3**(1), 1–9 (2013)
2. Dong, X., Clerk, J.A., Jacob, J.L.: Defending the weakest link: Phishing Website Detection by analysing User Behaviours. IEEE Telecommun. Syst. **45**, 215–226 (2010)
3. RSA Anti-Fraud Command Center. www.rsa.com. Accessed 20 Sept 2013
4. Xiang, G., Hong, J.: A hybrid phish detection approach by identity discovery and keywords retrieval. In: Proceedings of the 18th International World Wide Web Conference (WWW 2009), pp. 571–580 (2009)
5. Jain, A., Richariya, V.: Implementing a web browser with phishing detection techniques. World Comput. Sci. Inf. Technol. J. (WCSIT) **1**(7), 289–291 (2011)
6. Microsoft Corporation: Internet Explorer 7 (2014). http://www.microsoft.com/windows/ie/default.mspx. Accessed 9 Nov 2006
7. Netcraft. Netcraft Anti-Phishing Toolbar. http://toolbar.netcraft.com/. Accessed 13 June 2006
8. EarthLink Inc. EarthLink Toolbar (2014). http://www.earthlink.net/software/free/toolbar/. Accessed 9 Nov 2006
9. Xiang, G., Pendleton, B.A., Hong, J., Rose, C.P.: A hierarchical adaptive probabilistic approach for zero hour phish detection. In: Gritzalis, D., Preneel, B., Theoharidou, M. (eds.) ESORICS 2010. LNCS, vol. 6345, pp. 268–285. Springer, Heidelberg (2010)
10. Aburrous, M., Khelifi, A.: Phishing detection plug-in toolbar using intelligent fuzzy-classification mining techniques. Int. J. Soft Comput. Softwa. Eng. (SCSE 2013) **3** (2013). Special Issue
11. Barraclough, P.A., Hossain, M.A., Tahir, M.A., Sexton, G., Aslam, N.: Intelligent phishing detection and protection scheme for online transactions. Expert Syst. Appl. **40**, 4697–4706 (2013)
12. Sheng, S., Wardman, B., Warner, G., Cranor, L., Hong, J., Zhang, C.: An empirical analysis of phishing blacklists. In: 6th Conference Proceeding, CEAS, Mountain View, Califonia, USA (2009)
13. Ma, J., Saul, L., Savag, S., Voelker, G.: Beyond blacklists: learning to detect malicious web sites from suspicious URLs. In: Proceedings of the 15th International Conference on Knowledge Discovery and Data Mining, Paris, France, pp. 1245–1254 (2009)
14. Afroz, A., Greenstadt, R.: PhishZoo: detecting phishing websites by looking at them. In: Proceedings of the IEEE Fifth International Conference on Semantic Computing (ICS 2011) (2011)
15. Aburrous, M., Khelifi, A.: Phishing detection plug-in toolbar using intelligent fuzzy-classification mining techniques. Int. J. Soft Comput. Softw. Eng. (JSCSE) **3**, 54–61 (2013)
16. McAfee Inc. McAfee SiteAdvisor (2014). http://www.siteadvisor.com/. Accessed 9 Nov 2006

17. GeoTrust Inc. TrustWatch Toolbar (2014). http://toolbar.trustwatch.com/tour/v3ie/toolbar-v3ie-tour-overview.html. Accessed 13 June 2006
18. eBay Inc. Using eBay Toolbar's Account Guard (2014). http://pages.eBay.com/help/confidence/account-guard.html. Accessed 13 June 2006
19. Millersmiles (2016). http://www.millersmiles.co.uk/. Accessed 20 Oct 2016
20. Huange, G.B., Zhu, Q.Y., Mao, K.Z., Siew, C.K., Saratchandran, P., Sundararajan, N.: Can threshold networks be trained directly. IEEE Trans. Circ. Syst. II **53**(3), 187–191 (2006)
21. PhishTank: Join the fight against phishing (2013). http://www.phishtank.com/. Accessed 5 July 2013 and 10 July 2013
22. Laorden, C., Ugart-Pedrero, X., Santos, I., Sanz, B., Nieves, J., Alvarez, P., Bringas, G.: Study on the effectiveness of anomaly detection for spam filtering. Inf. Sci. **277**, 421–444 (2014)
23. Ajlouni, M., Hadi, W., Alwedyan, J.: Detecting phishing websites using associative classification. Eur. J. Bus. Manage. **5**(15), 36–40 (2013)
24. Abdelhamid, N., Ayesh, A., Thabtah, F.: Phishing detection based associative classification data mining. Expert Syst. Appl. **41**(13), 5948–5959 (2014)
25. Rami, M., Thabtah, F.A., McCluskey, T.: Intelligent rule based phishing websites classification. IET Inf. Secur. **8**(3), 153–160 (2014)
26. Agrawal, R., Ramakrishnan, S.: Fast algorithms for mining association rules in large database. In: Proceedings of the 20th International Conference on Very Large Data Bases (VLDB), Santiago, Chile, pp. 487–499 (1994)

Cyber Attacks Analysis Using Decision Tree Technique for Improving Cyber Situational Awareness

Sina Pournouri[1(✉)], Babak Akhgar[1], and Petra Saskia Bayerl[2]

[1] Sheffield Hallam University, Howard Street, Sheffield S1 1WB, UK
Sina.pournouri@student.shu.ac.uk,
Babak.akhgar@shu.ac.uk
[2] Rotterdam School of Management, Erasmus University, Burgemeester
Oudlaan 50, Bayle Building, 3062 PA Rotterdam, Netherlands
bayerl@rsm.nl

Abstract. Cyber Security experts are trying to find solutions to prevent cyber-attacks and one of the main solutions is improving cyber situational awareness which leads to an extensive overview of the current situation in cyber space and gives prediction ability to managers to prevent future cyber threats. In this paper we aim to improve cyber situational awareness by analysing past cyber incidents in 2015 and for this purpose Open Source Intelligence has been chosen as main source of initial dataset and also Decision tree method has been used as a classification technique and a predictive approach in order to analyse the data.

Keywords: Cyber situational awareness · Cyber-attack · Open source intelligence · Decision tree

1 Introduction

Cyber-attacks are becoming the main concern of managers in any business and in larger scale they are becoming a significant threat to countries' security. Security experts try to defend different sections from cyber-attacks in different ways, however, there is always a need of framework to predict cyber-attacks and be prepared in order to prevent them in early stages. From a technical point of view, they are attempting to increase the efficiency and accuracy of security devices and software such as Intrusion Detection Systems and anti-viruses and this technical approach is considered as low level of cyber situational awareness (Barford et al. 2010). On the other hand, high level cyber situational awareness combats against cyber breaches in more general way by analysing cyber attackers' behaviour in terms of type of attack, type of victim and etc. (Barford et al. 2010). This ongoing study highlights usage of decision tree as a data mining technique to analyse cyber-attacks and give a more comprehensible overview of past cyber-attacks in 2015 and profile them in order to increase cyber situational awareness from high level point of view.

© Springer International Publishing AG 2016
H. Jahankhani et al. (Eds.): ICGS3 2017, CCIS 630, pp. 155–172, 2016.
DOI: 10.1007/978-3-319-51064-4_14

2 Background

In this section most recent and relevant approaches in terms of cyber-attack analysis will be explained and reviewed and also because this research benefits from decision tree algorithm as a classification technique, Classification and decision trees will be described.

2.1 Related Works

Cyber Situational Awareness (CSA) is a broad subject that each researcher can have different approaches. In this section we have reviewed some of them by type of analysis, type of their data and type of CSA that they want to deal with.

Ahn et al. (2014) design a framework for decision makers covering low level of CSA. Figure 1 shows their proposed framework. They form their framework into 4 main components. The first component has the task of collecting the raw data from Intrusion Detection System, Firewall, Data base and so on then feeding them into the next component which Big data appliances. This component then cluster the obtained data into different appliances based on their nature and type of analysis that will be applied to them in next stage. The third component then analyse the data based on needs and requests. This data analysis includes 3 different techniques:

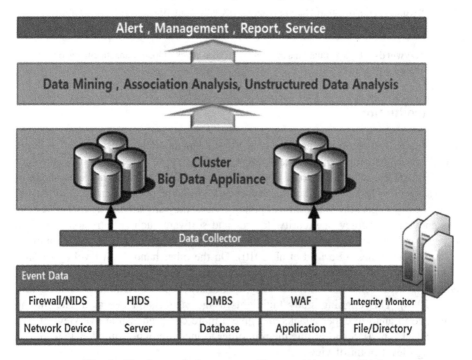

Fig. 1. Big data analysis system architecture (Ahn et al. 2014)

1. Classification: cyber experts can define the current level and predict the future of CSA by using classification techniques as predictive technique.
2. Regression analysis: By using this method, similar behaviour can be detected among the collected data from the past in terms of cyber breaches and discover a pattern and extend it as a prediction for future.
3. Relation Rules: this technique can be used in order to detect anomaly behaviour among the collected data.

The fourth component deals with presenting the outcome of analysis to decision makers and managers and make the results more understandable for them and help them to make effective decisions.

Feasel and Ramos (2013) suggest another model which cover both high and low level CSA. The important factor in their study is usage of Open Source Intelligence for their analysis, however, they did not mention how they are going to analyze the data and make predictions.

Musliner et al. (2011) propose another method to improve CSA by using Fuzzy logic as an Artificial Intelligence method in order to make an automated defense shield against future cyber-attacks. Their method is divided into two main section; Proactive and Reactive. Proactive section is concerned with identification of vulnerabilities and weaknesses in the system and Reactive section looks for countermeasures against different cyber-attacks. The data of these two then will be correlated by using fuzzy logic interference system and outcome will be a set of rules and facts. Therefore in case of an attack incident, an automated defense shield will be built based on those rules and facts. Figure 2 shows their proposed framework.

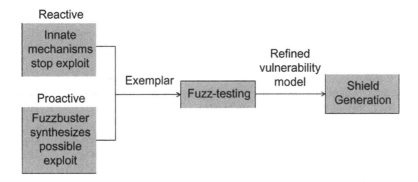

Fig. 2. Fuzzy buster (Musliner et al. 2011)

Wu et al. (2012) suggest another model improving low level of CSA based on Bayesian network. The initial data in this model is obtained from 4 environmental criteria:

1. Identify Vulnerability: This will be done through the scanning the network system.
2. The usage situation of network: This criterion should be measured and it is defined as the load of traffic on each node in the network.

3. The value of assets in the network: Value of each node should be measured by evaluating type of service and type of data and information that they stored in themselves.
4. Attack history: This factor should be investigated and gained from each node.

There are more studies around the subject of CSA and Table 1 shows more recent one and significant ones as a distillation.

Table 1. Distillation of previous researches

Researchers	Framework	Type of data and collection	Type of analysis	Type of CSA
Ahn et al. (2014)	Designed for decision making process	Log, IDS alarms and so on	Generalized Linear Model	Low level
Das et al. (2013) (i-HOPE)	Designed for resource allocation as a result of CSA understanding	Estimating the cost of cyber-attacks to different businesses through CSI/FBI annual report	Not applicable	High level
Wu et al. (2012)	Designed for decision making process	Past historical attacks, usage of network services, value of assets in the network and vulnerabilities of the system	Bayesian network	Low level
Fayyad and Meinel (2013)	Designed for protection against cyber-attacks based on past information	IDS data base, attack graphs	Correlation algorithms	Low level
Feasel and Ramos (2013)	Designed for decision making process	OSINT and blogs	.Not applicable	High level and Low level
Schreiberehl and Koch (2012)	Designed for decision making process	Attack signatures and methods	JDL data fusion method	Low level
Dutt et al. (2013)	Designed for decision making process based on internal behaviours	Attacker and Defender behaviours	Instance Based Learning Theory (IBLT)	High Level
Morris et al. (2011)	Designed for task management based on different missions of different levels within the network system	Each level task	Not applicable	High level and Low level
Musliner et al. (2011)	Designed for identifying technical elements in CSA	Past cyber-attack signature and common countermeasures against them	Fuzzy Logic algorithm	Low level

2.2   Classification and Decision Tree

Bhardwaj and Johari (2015) define classification as a data mining approach which tries to classify objects into different subgroups. Classification is mainly used for predictive purposes and it includes two main division; Decision Tree and Naïve Bayes. Decision trees is also known as prediction trees and include sequence of decisions and their outcomes as consequences. If inputs are a set of variables $x_1, x_2, x_3, \ldots, x_i$, the goal is to predict a set of result including $y_1, y_2, y_3, \ldots, y_i$. The prediction process can be done through making a decision tree with nodes and their branches. Each node represents a specific input variable and each branch means a decision making process. Leaf node refers to those nodes that they do not have branch and return class labels and in some occasion they generate probability scores. Decision trees are being used in most data mining application with predictive purposes due to the fact that they are easy to implement, visualize and present. Input variables can be categorical and continuous.

Decision trees are divided into two types; classification and regression. When output variables are categorical, the decision tree is called classification tree and when the outcome is continues such as numbers, they are called as regression trees (EMC education service 2015).

Decision trees always get the best available option to split by using greedy algorithm, however, that option might be the most desirable option at that stage and not in overall process. Therefore, if a bad split chosen, it will be permeate through the rest of the tree.

There are different ways to investigate whether the obtained decision trees are the desirable. They are as follows (EMC education service 2015):

1. Checking whether the splits make sense or not by validating them with domain experts.
2. Investigating of nodes and depth of the tree. Existence of too many layers and nodes can be an indication of an overfit model. In this case the model fits training set well, but it underperforms on test set. To address this issue of overfitting in decision trees, one must stop the tree growth before it gets to the stage when all training set is classified well or using post prune option to reduce errors can be considered.

3   Method

Our method has three main stages which are as follows:

1. Data collection and pre-process
2. Data analysis
3. Evaluation and interpretation of predictive models

3.1   Data Collection and Pre-process

One of the limitations of this study is getting access to the data of historical cyber-attacks which is collected by official authorities and law enforcement agencies.

It has been decided to use Open Source Intelligence (OSINT) which they are publicly available and free to use. The resource of the data is a blog (http://www. hackmageddon.com) collecting all cyber-attacks incidents from newspapers, websites, other blogs and etc. In this study, 2015 cyber-attacks are analysed using decision tree algorithm. The initial dataset has 750 records of cyber-attacks in 2015, however, data pre-processing is needed to clean and make the data ready for further analysis. The pre-processing stage has following steps:

In the first step of data pre-processing, cyber-attacks need to be categorized so then each of them will have different features and characteristic. All cyber-attacks will be categorized based on their attacker, type of threat that they pose, type of their target, type of their activity, the country of target and the date of incident. Table 2, shows an example of the categorized cyber-attacks in this study.

Table 2. Example of categorized cyber-attack.

Date	Author (Attacker)	Type of threat	Type of target	Country of target	Type of activity
2/12/2015	Syrian Electronic Army	Account Hijacking	NGO and Non-profit organization	Syria	Hacktivism

The data will be categorized based on their features. We categorized cyber-attacks based on their type of activity and purpose of the attack which can be considered as the following forms:

1. Cyber Crime: traditionally cybercrimes refer to usage of computer technology to commit a crime, however, in this study cybercrime is defined as usage of computer devices and systems to gain unauthorized access to computer systems to steal information or any type of minor hacking which happens in small scale (Gordon and Ford 2006).
2. Cyber Espionage: it refers to usage of computer systems to steal industrial, political, economic, military and other sensitive information about victims. In other words, it is an attempt to evaluate the security of defence strategies and systems of enemies or adversaries (O'Hara 2010).
3. Cyberwar: it is defined as a state sponsored cyber-attacks mainly to destroy enemies' critical infrastructure, however, sometimes these cyber-attacks can be done by terrorist groups against critical and sensitive infrastructure. So in our definition Cyber terrorism will be a subcategory of cyberwarfare. It needs to be mentioned that cyberwar is the largest form of cyber-attacks in terms of scale and damage that they can cause in comparison with cybercrime and cyber espionage (Lewis 2002).
4. Hacktivism: this form of cyber-attacks defines a cyber-attack which can lead to send a political or social message to public or victims. Mostly intention of hacktivism is not stealing sensitive information or damaging computer networks of target (Himma 2005).

In the next stage the attacks will be categorized based on type of threats posing to different section. The most common threats in 2015 according to our dataset are as follows:

1. Account hijacking: this type of threat refers to unauthorized access to email account, social media accounts or any type of account which they belong to single individuals, companies, groups and etc. (Endler 2002).
2. Defacement: these attacks happen when attackers can gain unauthorized access to web server of a company and they change the first page of victim's website and try to send message to public or damage reputation of victim (Householder et al. 2002).
3. DNS hijacking: Domain Name Resolution has the task of resolving URL in the internet browsers and address on computers into IP addresses. In this type of threat, cyber-attacks try to get control of DNS server to hijack browser or a session which leads to a fake website or session (Jackson et al. 2009).
4. DDOS: Distributed Denial of Service is a type of threat when attackers send loads of requests to servers constantly in order to target their availability, take them down and stop them from their offered service (Yaar et al. 2003).
5. SQL injection: it refers to type of threat compromising the data base of victim by injecting malicious codes and using other techniques (Boyd and Keromytis 2004).
6. Malware: it refers to general threat to computer devices and networks including viruses, Trojan horses, adware, spyware and etc. (Kumar et al. 2006).
7. POS Malware: these type of malwares are mainly written by cyber attackers to extract and steal payment information of customers from Point of Sale in retail shops (Bond et al. 2014).
8. Targeted Attacks: targeted attacks refer to type of threat which is carried out with series of different threats and illegitimate attempts from cyber criminals who have long term plan to attack to the victim (Estrada 2006).
9. XSS: XSS or Cross-site scripting is type of threat when attackers inject some form of script in a trusted website and gather information about cookies, session tokens or generally any type of critical and sensitive information gained by the victim's website (Grossman 2007).
10. Zero day attack: Zero day is a type of threat which attackers use unknown security bugs to penetrate to the systems. These security bugs are often unknown to developers and producers of systems or they have not been fixed yet (Kumar et al. 2006).

Table 3 shows the type of threat and their acronyms used in the data analysis section.

Next step would be categorizing targets and victims based on their business. Table 4, shows these categories and their acronyms in order to make data ready for analysis.

Table 3. Type of attack categories

Acronyms	Type of threat
AH	Account Hijacking
BT	Backdoor and Trojan
DF	Defacement
DH	DNS Hijacking
DS	DDOS
IF	iFrame Injection
MW	Malware
PM	POS Malware
SQ	SQL injection
TA	Targeted Attack
UN	Unknown Attacks
XSS	XSS vulnerability
ZD	0day

Table 4. Type target categories

Acronyms	Type of target
AI	Adult Industry
BP	Broadcast and Publishing
ED	Education
EN	Entertainment
ES	Energy Section
FB	Finance and Banks
GO	Government
HC	Healthcare
HT	Hospitality and Tourism
IO	Internet and Online Services
MD	Military and Defense Section
MU	Multiple
NN	NGO and No Profit
RT	Retail
SI	Single Individual
SN	Social Network
TC	Telecommunication
THS	Technology Hardware and Software
TM	Terrorism
TP	Transportation
UT	Utility

The second step is to deal with missing, doubles and vague values. Open refine has been used as powerful tool developed for cleaning messy data. Open refine known as Google refine initially developed by Google as a project in May 2010 (Verborgh and De Wilde 2013). Open refine is easy to use and implement and it is also open source and free to use. This step has following sub steps:

1. Dealing with vague records: By investigating the data and using Open Refine which gives better overview of the data, those records that they have more than two unknown and missing values will be eliminated from the data set.
2. Dealing with missing values: If in any record, there is one missing values, "un-known" or "Unidentified" will be put. Although in some case by cross referencing the missing value can be found in the data resource.
3. Outliers' removal: outliers can make the result less accurate, so removing outliers is an important stage. It has been decided to use WEKA as a data analysis tools which has specific filters for removing outliers in order to prepare them for decision trees.

After taking all the steps, 489 records are left and they are ready and perfect for further analysis.

3.2   Data Analysis

In this stage it has been decided to use R as a tool for data analysis. R is a programming language mainly used for data mining, machine learning and statistical analysis purposes. R is an open source programming environment and has different powerful packages making data analysts able to analyse their data more effectively and based on their needs (EMC Education Services 2015).

There are different packages for decision tree algorithm, in this study, Party package will be used due to the fact that it gives better and more understandable overview of the decision tree which leads to make prediction and it includes Ctree function which is provided for making decision trees.

We decided to classify cyber-attacks in 2015 based on their type of activity, type of threat, type of target and country of targets. For this purpose, the data will be divided into two sets of training and test set. 66% for training set which the classifier will be trained and 34% for test set to evaluate the performance of the obtained classifier. The reason of this type of splitting is

Classification Based on Type of Activity

As it mentioned in Sect. 3.1, the data will be categorized based on their features. Now we want to make our model based on above definitions of cyber activities. The structure of decision tree by R is as follows:

Response: Activity   Inputs: Threat, Target. Section, Country Number of observations: 306

1) Country == {AZ, KR, PK, TR}; criterion = 1, statistic = 334.754
  2)* weights = 7
1) Country == {AM, AU, BB, BD, BE, BR, CA, CN, DE, ES, FI, FR, IE, IL, IN, INT, IT, JP, KZ, LT, PL, PT, RU, SA, SE, SEVERAL, SY, TW, UK, US, VE, ZA}
  3) Threat == {TA}; criterion = 1, statistic = 296.75
    4)* weights = 27
  3) Threat == {AH, DF, DH, DS, MW, PM, SQ, UN, ZD}
    5) Country == {AM, AU, BB, CA, IL, INT, IT, JP, PT, SA, SEVERAL, SY}; criterion = 1, statistic = 219.792
      6) Threat == {AH, DH, MW, UN}; criterion = 0.979, statistic = 17.639
        7)* weights = 11
      6) Threat == {DF, DS, SQ}
        8)* weights = 23
    5) Country == {BD, BE, BR, CN, DE, ES, FI, FR, IN, KZ, LT, PL, SE, UK, US, VE, ZA}
      9) Threat == {DF}; criterion = 1, statistic = 129.882
        10) Country == {UK, US}; criterion = 0.993, statistic = 30.57
          11) Target.Section == {ED, FB, HC, SI}; criterion = 0.998, statistic = 19
            12)* weights = 9
          11) Target.Section == {GO}
            13)* weights = 11
        10) Country == {BD, CN, IN, LT, ZA}
          14)* weights = 8
      9) Threat == {AH, DH, DS, MW, PM, SQ, UN, ZD}
        15) Country == {BE, DE, ES, FI, KZ, PL, SE}; criterion = 1, statistic = 112.128
          16)* weights = 7
        15) Country == {BR, FR, IN, UK, US, VE}
          17) Target.Section == {BP, ED, EN, FB, GO, HC, HT, IO, NN, RT, SI, TC, THS, TM, TP}; criterion = 1, statistic = 123.787
            18) Country == {BR, FR, IN, VE}; criterion = 1, statistic = 48.682
              19)* weights = 8
            18) Country == {UK, US}
              20)* weights = 188
          17) Target.Section == {AI, ES, MD}
            21)* weights = 7

Some of the significant predictions based on the decision tree are as follows:

1. If Defacement happens in government section is UK or US then the activity is considered as Hacktivism.
2. Attacks are considered Cybercrime if they target Broadcasting and Publishing companies, educational sections and Banks and Financial services in Brazil, France, Indonesia and Venezuela in form of Account Hijacking, Malware, SQL injection and Zero Day.
3. Targeted Attacks happens in countries like US, UK, Japan and Russia are labelled as Cyber Espionage.

Classification Based on Threat

In this part, the data will be classified based on type of threat of cyber-attacks. The purpose for this operation is to find out which threats are likely to get posed to different businesses. Following codes illustrate the structure of decision tree based on type of threat:

```
Response:  Threat    Inputs:  Target.Section, Activity,
Country
Number of observations:  306

1) Activity == {CC, CW, HA}; criterion = 1, statistic =
335.844
  2) Activity == {CW, HA}; criterion = 1, statistic =
329.623
    3) Country == {CA, FR, IT, JP, SA, TR}; criterion =
1, statistic = 177.624
      4)* weights = 15
    3) Country == {AM, AU, AZ, BB, IL, IN, INT, KR, PK,
PT, SEVERAL, SY, UK, US}
      5) Country == {AM, IL, PT, UK}; criterion = 1, sta-
tistic = 117.288
        6)* weights = 8
      5) Country == {AU, AZ, BB, IN, INT, KR, PK,
SEVERAL, SY, US}
        7) Country == {AZ, SEVERAL}; criterion = 0.999,
statistic = 86.88
          8)* weights = 8
        7) Country == {AU, BB, IN, INT, KR, PK, SY, US}
          9)* weights = 41
```

```
  2) Activity == {CC}
    10) Country == {BD, CN, IN, LT, ZA}; criterion = 1,
statistic = 318.622
      11)* weights = 8
    10) Country == {BE, BR, CA, DE, ES, FI, FR, IE, JP,
PL, SE, SEVERAL, UK, US, VE}
      12) Target.Section == {AI, BP, ED, EN, ES, FB, GO,
HC, HT, IO, MD, MU, NN, RT, TC, THS, TM, TP}; criterion =
0.999, statistic = 233.826
        13) Country == {IE, JP, SEVERAL}; criterion =
0.982, statistic = 180.196
          14)* weights = 8
        13) Country == {BE, BR, CA, ES, FI, FR, PL, SE,
UK, US, VE}
          15)* weights = 178
      12) Target.Section == {SI}
        16)* weights = 17
  1) Activity == {CE}
    17) Country == {JP, RU, SEVERAL, TW}; criterion =
0.973, statistic = 26.675
      18)* weights = 9
    17) Country == {KZ, US}
      19)* weights = 14
```

Some of the significant predictions based on this decision tree are as follows:

1. If US and Kazakhstan are attacked by cyber espionage activity then the type threat can be highly likely predicted as Targeted Attack.
2. If cyber war or hacktivism happens in countries like Japan, France, Italy, Saudi Arabia, Turkey and Canada then attack will be mostly likely DOS.
3. SQL injection as a type of threat will be predicted when an act of hacktivism or cyber war takes place in Israel, UK, Portugal and Armenia.

Classification Based on Target Section

In this part of study, we try to model cyber-attacks based on their target categories in order make prediction about which targets are most favorable by cyber attackers. Following codes are showing our obtained model:

```
Response:  Target.Section
Inputs:  Threat, Activity, Country
Number of observations:  306

1) Country == {SEVERAL, ZA}; criterion = 1, statistic =
1067.179
  2)* weights = 19
1) Country == {AM, AU, AZ, BB, BD, BE, BR, CA, CN, DE,
ES, FI, FR, IE, IL, IN, INT, IT, JP, KR, KZ, LT, PK, PL,
PT, RU, SA, SE, SY, TR, TW, UK, US, VE}
  3) Country == {BE, FR, JP}; criterion = 1, statistic =
932.7
    4)* weights = 8
  3) Country == {AM, AU, AZ, BB, BD, BR, CA, CN, DE, ES,
FI, IE, IL, IN, INT, IT, KR, KZ, LT, PK, PL, PT, RU, SA,
SE, SY, TR, TW, UK, US, VE}
    5) Threat == {AH}; criterion = 1, statistic = 666.646
      6)* weights = 43
    5) Threat == {DF, DH, DS, MW, PM, SQ, TA, UN, ZD}
      7) Country == {AZ, CA, KR, PK, VE}; criterion = 1,
statistic = 667.924
        8)* weights = 15
      7) Country == {AM, AU, BB, BD, BR, CN, DE, ES, FI,
IE, IL, IN, INT, IT, LT, PL, PT, RU, SA, TR, TW, UK, US}
        9) Country == {AM, AU, BB, BD, BR, CN, DE, ES,
FI, IE, IL, INT, IT, LT, PL, PT, RU, SA, TR, TW, UK, US};
criterion = 1, statistic = 563.228
          10) Country == {ES, INT, UK}; criterion = 1,
statistic = 508.513
            11)* weights = 15
          10) Country == {AM, AU, BB, BD, BR, CN, DE, FI,
IE, IL, IT, LT, PL, PT, RU, SA, TR, TW, US}
            12) Threat == {MW, PM}; criterion = 1, sta-
tistic = 383.728
              13)* weights = 39
            12) Threat == {DF, DH, DS, SQ, TA, UN, ZD}
              14) Threat == {TA, ZD}; criterion = 1, sta-
tistic = 336.858
                15)* weights = 18
              14) Threat == {DF, DH, DS, SQ, UN}
                16)* weights = 142
        9) Country == {IN}
          17)* weights = 7
```

Following predictions are interpreted based on the generated decision tree:

1. In countries like Azerbaijan, Canada, Pakistan, Korea Republic and Venezuela, governments are the first potential targets for cyber criminals who employ Defacement or DDOS or Malware or SQL injection or Targeted attacks or Zero day techniques.
2. Energy Sections are the most favourable targets for cyber attackers in countries like France, Japan and Belgium.
3. Health Care sections are the most potential type of targets in Indonesia for attackers who use Defacement, DNS hijacking, DOS and SQL injection.
4. Educational section in countries like US, Taiwan, Russia and Saudi Arabia are the weakest section against Defacement, DNS hijacking, DDOS and SQL injection.

Classification Based on Country

In this section, the data will be classified using decision tree based on the victims' countries in order to profile cyber-attacks based on country of victims and also make prediction about the most vulnerable countries in terms of cyber breaches. Following codes explain structure of our decision tree:

```
Response:  Country
Inputs:  Threat, Target.Section, Activity
Number of observations:  306

1) Target.Section == {AI, MU, TM}; criterion = 1, statis-
tic = 1067.179
  2)* weights = 19
1) Target.Section == {BP, ED, EN, ES, FB, GO, HC, HT, IO,
MD, NN, RT, SI, TC, THS, TP}
  3) Activity == {CW}; criterion = 1, statistic = 799.879
    4)* weights = 12
  3) Activity == {CC, CE, HA}
    5) Target.Section == {ES, TC}; criterion = 1, statis-
tic = 809.119
      6)* weights = 8
    5) Target.Section == {BP, ED, EN, FB, GO, HC, HT, IO,
MD, NN, RT, SI, THS, TP}
      7) Activity == {CC, CE}; criterion = 1, statistic =
478.846
        8) Threat == {AH, MW, PM, UN, ZD}; criterion = 1,
statistic = 358.093
          9) Target.Section == {ED, FB, HC, HT, IO, NN,
RT, SI, TP}; criterion = 1, statistic = 127.866
            10)* weights = 109
          9) Target.Section == {BP, EN, GO, MD, THS}
            11)* weights = 26
```

```
      8) Threat == {DF, DH, DS, SQ, TA}
         12) Target.Section == {BP, ED, EN, GO, HT, IO,
NN, SI}; criterion = 1, statistic = 357.047
            13) Threat == {DS}; criterion = 0.999, sta-
tistic = 96.887
               14)* weights = 17
            13) Threat == {DF, DH, SQ, TA}
               15) Threat == {DH, SQ}; criterion = 0.998,
statistic = 72.352
                  16) Target.Section == {ED, IO}; criterion
= 1, statistic = 58
                     17)* weights = 19
                  16) Target.Section == {BP, EN, GO, HT,
NN, SI}
                     18)* weights = 11
               15) Threat == {DF, TA}
                  19)* weights = 18
         12) Target.Section == {FB, HC, MD, THS, TP}
            20)* weights = 16
      7) Activity == {HA}
         21) Target.Section == {FB, HT, MD, SI}; criterion
= 1, statistic = 262.101
            22)* weights = 9
         21) Target.Section == {BP, ED, EN, GO, HC, IO,
NN, TP}
            23) Target.Section == {EN, IO, NN, TP}; crite-
rion = 1, statistic = 193.11
               24)* weights = 9
            23) Target.Section == {BP, ED, GO, HC}
               25) Target.Section == {GO}; criterion =
0.977, statistic = 38.382
                  26)* weights = 18
               25) Target.Section == {BP, ED, HC}
                  27)* weights = 15
```

Some of the important predictions illustrated by this decision tree are as follows:

1. If type of activity is cyber espionage, cybercrime and hacktivism and type of target is Telecommunication and Tourism and Hospitality, then the most vulnerable countries are US, UK and Russia respectively.
2. If type of activity is cyber espionage or cybercrime or hacktivism and type of target is Energy Section, Military and Defence companies, then the most favourable countries for attackers are US and Israel. Type of attacks can be Account Hijacking, Defacement, DOS, Malware, SQL injection, Targeted Attacks and XSS Vulnerability.

3. If type of activity is Hacktivism, type of Target is BP or Entertainment or Financial and Bank Services and type of threat is Defacement or Denial of Service or Malware or SQL injection, then US and Canada are the most vulnerable countries.

3.3   Evaluation of Models

In order to evaluate the accuracy and reliability of the predictive model, the test set should be fed into the trained classifier to calculate the misclassification rate. As it was mentioned in previous sections, four models are trained based on decision tree as a classification technique. The result of misclassification rates are shown in Table 5.

Table 5. Misclassification rate of decision trees

Model	Misclassification rate
Activity	% 10.78
Threat	% 63.04
Target section	% 53.26
Country	% 24.40

As it is shown in the Table 5, the "Activity" model performs better than others and it is 89.22% accurate on test set and this will lead to better prediction of type of activity in cyber-attacks. The next accurate and reliable model is "Country" model which has reliability of 75.6% in classify test set. On the other hand, Threat and Target Section model did not perform very well on test set. It can be because of there is need of more variables to predict type of target and type of threat. In addition, other classification methods such as Naïve Bayes or Neural network might perform better than decision trees on our data set. It should be mentioned that this is an ongoing investigation and research in future work it will be discussed.

4   Conclusion and Future Works

According to Pournouri and Craven (2014) prediction is a crucial factor in prevention of cyber-attacks. From governments to any type of businesses need to be prepared against growth of cyber-attacks in order to protect not only their financial benefits and assets but also their reputation. This research is trying to address the issue of prediction of cyber-attacks from different point of view. One of the highlight of this research is using of Open Source Intelligence (OSINT) as main resource of initial data which is open to public and free to use and generally these days OSINT is one of the resource of information for intelligence services (Steele 2007). It also applies some limitations to this research such as inaccuracy of the data. The inaccuracy in the data can include different factors such as irrelevant and incomplete information. In order to overcome these issues we use Google Refine, Weka and R to remove outliers and deal with inaccurate data. In this study 4 different classifiers are trained by decision tree algorithm in order to make prediction about cyber-attacks. Our model performs accurate with almost 90% reliability in prediction of cyber activity which helps law enforcements and also different companies to see what type of cyber-attack targeting them in terms of type of activity. The second best feature of our model is accurate performing in prediction of weak and vulnerable countries against cyber-attacks and can support governments, decision makers and strategist to plan efficient countermeasures against ongoing and future cyber-attacks. On the other hand, the model does not do an acceptable job in prediction of type threat and type of target. Therefore, future work can be done in order to increase accuracy of predictive models and also add more variables to dataset of past cyber-attack. Also, there is a ne ed of applying more predictive techniques in order to investigate which approaches are faster, more efficient and more accurate. It should be mentioned our research is an ongoing work and in future work we try to address weaknesses and issues in this field of study.

References

Ahn, S.H., Kim, N.U., Chung, T.M.: Big data analysis system concept for detecting unknown attacks. In: 16th International Conference on Advanced Communication Technology, pp. 269–272. IEEE, February 2014

Barford, P., Dacier, M., Dietterich, T.G., Fredrikson, M., Giffin, J., Jajodia, S., Wang, C.: Cyber SA: Situational Awareness for Cyber Defense, pp. 3–14 (2010)

Bhardwaj, V., Johari, R.: Big data analysis: issues and challenges. In: 2015 International Conference on Electrical, Electronics, Signals, Communication and Optimization (EESCO), pp. 1–6. IEEE, January 2015

Bond, M., Choudary, O., Murdoch, S.J., Skorobogatov, S., Anderson, R.: Chip and Skim: cloning EMV cards with the pre-play attack. In: 2014 IEEE Symposium on Security and Privacy, pp. 49–64. IEEE, May 2014

Boyd, S.W., Keromytis, A.D.: SQLrand: preventing SQL injection attacks. In: Jakobsson, M., Yung, M., Zhou, J. (eds.) ACNS 2004. LNCS, vol. 3089, pp. 292–302. Springer Berlin Heidelberg, Berlin, Heidelberg (2004). doi:10.1007/978-3-540-24852-1_21

Das, S., Mukhopadhyay, A., Shukla, G.K.: i-HOPE framework for predicting cyber breaches: a logit approach. In: 2013 46th Hawaii International Conference on System Sciences (HICSS), pp. 3008–3017. IEEE, January 2013

Dutt, V., Ahn, Y.S., Gonzalez, C.: Cyber situation awareness modeling detection of cyber attacks with instance-based learning theory. Hum. Factors J. Hum. Factors Ergon. Soc. 55(3), 605–618 (2013)

EMC Education Services, Data Science and Big Data Analytics: Discovering, Analyzing, Visualizing and Presenting Data. John Wiley & Sons (2015)

Endler, D.: The evolution of cross site scripting attacks. Technical report, iDEFENSE Labs (2002)

Estrada, E.: Network robustness to targeted attacks. The interplay of expansibility and degree distribution. Eur. Phys. J. B 52(4), 563–574 (2006)

Fayyad, S., Meinel, C.: Attack scenario prediction methodology. In: 2013 Tenth International Conference on Information Technology: New Generations (ITNG), pp. 53–59. IEEE, April 2013

Feasel, J., Romas, G.: Visualization, Modeling and Predictive Analysis of Internet Attacks, vol. 8768, pp. 1–6 (2013)

Gordon, S., Ford, R.: On the definition and classification of cybercrime. J. Comput. Virol. 2(1), 13–20 (2006)

Grossman, J.: XSS Attacks: Cross-site scripting exploits and defense. Syngress (2007)

Himma, K.E.: Hacking as Politically Motivated Digital Civil Disobedience: Is Hacktivism Morally Justified? SSRN 799545 (2005)

Householder, A., Houle, K., Dougherty, C.: Computer attack trends challenge Internet security. Computer 35(4), 5–7 (2002)

Jackson, C., Barth, A., Bortz, A., Shao, W., Boneh, D.: Protecting browsers from DNS rebinding attacks. ACM Trans. Web (TWEB) 3(1), 2 (2009)

Kumar, V., Srivastava, J., Lazarevic, A. (eds.): Managing Cyber Threats: Issues, Approaches, and Challenges, vol. 5. Springer Science & Business Media, Heidelberg (2006)

Lewis, J.A.: Assessing the Risks of Cyber Terrorism, Cyber War and other Cyber Threats. Center for Strategic & International Studies, Washington, DC (2002)

Minelli, M., Chambers, M., Dhiraj, A.: Big Data, Big Analytics: Emerging Business Intelligence and Analytic Trends for Today's Businesses. John Wiley & Sons, New York (2012)

Morris, T.I., Mayron, L.M., Smith, W.B., Knepper, M.M., Ita, R., Fox, K.L.: A perceptually-relevant model-based cyber threat prediction method for enterprise mission assurance. In: 2011 IEEE International Multi-Disciplinary Conference on Cognitive Methods in Situation Awareness and Decision Support (CogSIMA), pp. 60–65. IEEE, February 2011

Musliner, D.J., Rye, J.M., Thomsen, D., McDonald, D.D., Burstein, M.H., Robertson, P.: Fuzzbuster: towards adaptive immunity from cyber threats. In: 2011 Fifth IEEE Conference on Self-Adaptive and Self-Organizing Systems Workshops (SASOW), pp. 137–140. IEEE, October 2011

O'Hara, G.: Cyber-Espionage: a Growing threat to the american economy. CommLaw Conspectus 19, 241 (2010)

Pournouri, S., Craven, M.: E-business, recent threats and security countermeasures. Int. J. Electron. Secur. Digit. Forensics 6(3), 169–184 (2014)

Schreiber-Ehle, S., Koch, W.: The JDL model of data fusion applied to cyber-defence—a review paper. In: 2012 Workshop on Sensor Data Fusion: Trends, Solutions, Applications (SDF), pp. 116–119. IEEE, September 2012

Steele, R.: Open source intelligence. In: Handbook of Intelligence Studies, pp. 129–147 (2007)

Verborgh, R., De Wilde, M.: Using OpenRefine. Packt Publishing Ltd. (2013)

Wu, J., Yin, L., Guo, Y.: Cyber attacks prediction model based on Bayesian network. In: 2012 IEEE 18th International Conference on Parallel and Distributed Systems (ICPADS), pp. 730–731. IEEE, December 2012

Yaar, A., Perrig, A., Song, D.: Pi: A path identification mechanism to defend against DDoS attacks. In: Proceedings of 2003 Symposium on Security and Privacy, pp. 93–107. IEEE, May 2003

ITAOFIR: IT Asset Ontology for Information Risk in Knowledge Economy and Beyond

A. Kayode Adesemowo[(✉)], Rossouw von Solms,
and Reinhardt A. Botha

School of ICT, Centre for Research in Information and Cyber Security,
Nelson Mandela Metropolitan University, Port Elizabeth, South Africa
{Kayode.adesemowo, Rossouw.VonSolms,
ReinhardtA.Botha}@nmmu.ac.za

Abstract. As more and more organisations continue to rely on information and innovate through advancement in technology, the role and nature of IT assets as assets would keep evolving. It does not appear that this evolving nature of IT assets is understood or thoughtfully considered. More so, there is no universal taxonomy for such an important asset. This paper advances knowledge in information risk in the knowledge economy and beyond in two ways. Firstly, the OWL based IT assets ontology is the first ontology to present IT assets in a flexible, structured, dynamic, and modular view. Secondly, our ontology balances the "asset" and "possibility of threat" elements of risk in a coherent manner. It is expected that the IT assets ontology would contribute immensely toward the goal of a complete and integrated security ontology as being advocated by researchers in the field as-well-as points us towards the path of a definitive definition.

Keywords: IT assets · Ontology · Information risk · Security ontology · Knowledge economy

1 Introduction

It is now common knowledge that information is a driver of the knowledge economy and beyond (the 21st century). As a driver, it is increasingly being regarded as an organisational asset, and rightly so. As an organisational asset, information assets can be safely classified as intangible assets whose value must be preserved in an organisation [1]. As a driver, information assets must be processed upon in order to increase an organisation's business value (bottom line profit). As with other organisational assets that enhance an organisation's value, there are risks. It is then imperative that risks that might impact on the value of an asset must be mitigated.

We will now narrate the theoretical lens of risk's uncertainty. Then, the research approach and literature review are presented followed by related work. Our ontology is introduced after this and thereafter discussion on the merit of the ontology. Although the terms information technology (IT) and information, communication technology (ICT) are often used to define slightly different concepts, we adopt a wide-angled view of the notion and will thus use the two terms inter-changeably.

© Springer International Publishing AG 2016
H. Jahankhani et al. (Eds.): ICGS3 2017, CCIS 630, pp. 173–187, 2016.
DOI: 10.1007/978-3-319-51064-4_15

2   Research Domain

Before embarking on presenting our IT assets' Ontology, we firstly present the underlying theory underpinning the research work, and the basis for this paper. We then give a summary of the methodology and a brief review of classification systems as they relate to IT assets.

2.1   Theoretical Framework

Risk has for long been an important topic and more so in the knowledge economy and beyond, where the nature of assets keeps evolving. At the very heart of risk theory, is the provisioning of frameworks that allows for risk mitigation and dealing with uncertainty [2, 3]. Typically, this uncertainty is attributed to the 'probability of threats' to an asset in the risk analysis equation. The point of departure for this research project is that in information risk, which encompasses IT risk domain, epistemic uncertainty [4] can also apply to assets (IT assets) themselves and not just the threats.

Two challenges we are faced with is that information security and IT risk focus on only a part of the problem of information risk, (– the probability of threats –), and even at that still fail in protecting organisations adequately [5]. Secondly, reliably assessing information security and IT risks can be more challenging than assessing other types of risks in an organisation. A possible contributory factor (for this unreliable assessing of information risk) might be that one of the elements of the risk component, assets, in this instance that of IT assets and the underlying information assets, keep evolving in the knowledge economy. There seems to be a cloud of uncertainty and deep grasp of what IT assets are (as well as that of the embedded information assets). Practitioners have varying and subjective opinions [1, 6–11].

On the balance sheet, assets equate to liability and equity [12]. The definition for information risk by Riedl and Serafeim [12] shows that should "asset" be substituted by "IT asset", then the inability to ascertain the valuation parameters underlying an IT asset constitutes a risk. What then needs to be studied is the characterisation and componentisation of IT assets. In effect, what constitute an IT asset? A plausible approach might be to outline the components of IT assets, possibly by means of an ontology, from a classification system point of view.

2.2   Research Aim and Rationale

In the information risk world, it is common for organisations to ... "mostly fall back on best-practices, information security standards, or domain experts when conducting the risk assessment and mitigation phases" [6]. Typically standards, frameworks and best-practices include CRAMM, NIST SP 800-30, CORAS, OCTAVE, EBIOS, German IT Grundschutz Manual, ISO 27005, ITIL and COBIT5 amongst others as outlined in [1, 6]. Through these standards, frameworks and best-practices, 'Threat Models' for risk have relatively been well developed. The focus on threat models is also the trend seen in literatures [4, 10, 13, 14].

In [5], it was made clear that failures of information security are clearly adverse events which cause losses to an organisation. In effect, information security (in IT risk) can be construed to be a risk management discipline. Risk is calculated by multiplying the ratings assigned to risk likelihood and the potential impact [6] on assets.

Information security risk management is a crucial element for ensuring long-term business success because it provides an effective approach for measuring the security through the identification and valuation of assets, threats, and vulnerabilities and offers methods for the risk assessment, risk mitigation and evaluation [15].

Therefore, it can be said that risk (and by inference information risk, information security risk and IT risk) is made up of two components, those of threat likelihood and potential impact on asset [6]. The focus of this research project is on the asset leg, specifically IT asset (a type of asset).

Successful risk analysis and the subsequent assessment and mitigation of risks depends on the availability of (reliable) asset information [16]. In essence, Birkholz et al. [16] are of the view that in the case of IT assets, the information about the IT asset and its components, are crucial for the assessment of potential threats and impacts (magnitude of harm) associated with a threat exercise on a vulnerable IT asset.

More so, [1], in their search for a definitive definition for information asset across standards, frameworks and legislations, highlighted a concern similar to [16] regarding an IT asset and its components. [1] noted that a commonly held, universal definition for information asset is lacking. They also posited that information is an integral sub-element of IT assets. With this said, there is therefore a need to understand the elements of an IT asset and derive a classification system such as an ontology to arrive at a common representation of what an IT asset is, as it relates to risk.

The objective of this research project as presented herein is to architect an IT asset ontology that can assist with IT assets definition/description and therefore can be used as a methodological approach towards information risk management.

2.3   Methodology

A number of frameworks and approaches have hitherto focused on threat models. The goal of our research work is to develop a methodological framework that assists with IT assets risk value calculation or assessment in the knowledge economy and beyond. The IT assets ontology presented in this paper aims to assist in determining inherent attributes of IT assets that can assist in the process of IT assets risk value assessment. With this goal in mind, this research work is situated in the 'Critical Realism' research philosophy [17]. In critical realism, one can combine and reconcile ontological realism, epistemological relativism and judgmental rationality [17]. In essence one might be able to meta-critically extend a concept to object or structure.

We are therefore provided with a platform for ontological analysis and logical reasoning inferences. The research strategy is hinged on argumentation that glues together literature review and reasoning [18]. The logical reasoning (as an instance of procedural argumentation) need not be proved in the absolute [18], nor does it has to be entirely correct in every single respect. This is more apt in this context (developing a methodological framework in the form of an ontology for IT assets to assist in risk) rather than approaching from an "artefact" point of view. In essence, we carried out the following: literature review, development (ontology), logical reasoning (argumentation), and use case (review of two scenarios).

2.4 Related Ontologies

From literature and search on both the Semantic Web search – Swoggle (www.umbc. edu) and Stanford University's WebProtégé page (webprotege.stanford.edu), we identified a number of related ontologies. Five of them are reviewed herein.

Media Asset Ontology. A media asset ontology [19] that was published by the World Wide Web Consortium (W3C), defines the Ontology for Media Resources 1.0. The ontology is a critical milestone in the drive towards a common vocabulary, descriptive properties for media resources. Following from this, a Semantic Web compatible implementation of a RDF/OWL based abstract ontology (for media assets) is available for all to use and aligned to. Even though the media asset ontology does not cover the generality of IT assets, it is essential in our research work as it emphasises the importance of a common representation of a phenomenon – IT assets in the knowledge economy. More so, media assets can be said to be a subclass of information assets.

Cybersecurity Operational Information Ontology. The notion of cybersecurity is that it is a threat beyond the borders of a country. As such, cybersecurity information exchange must be shared on a global scale [9]. The ontology proposed by Takahashi et al. [9] is a specification of abstracted world of cybersecurity operational information that could assist with automated response to cyber threat.

Their ontology included an 'IT Asset Management Domain' alongside 'Incident Handling Domain', and 'Knowledge Accumulation Domain' as the three domains. In the IT asset management domain, there exists an asset database that acts as the repository for information on the assets of each organisation. The focus is on IT systems alongside cloud service lists, and surrounding external network topologies. It can then be said that there is a notion of ITIL's service asset to an extent. However, the gathering of assets' information is left to the forte of ICT administrator and infrastructure provider. This does not suffice in gathering and articulating IT assets of the knowledge economy.

The ontology in [9] is of interest to us as it highlights the need for "organisations to share information amongst one another in the absence of a globally common format and framework for cybersecurity information exchange". In our case this global format and framework will be for IT assets in the knowledge economy and beyond.

Ontology-Based Security Management. The security ontology (SO) by Tsoumas and Gritzalis, dubbed "an ontology that elaborates on the security aspects of an information system", is an attempt towards an automated process that supports the Information System (IS) security management [8]. They used "Asset, Stakeholder, Vulnerability, Countermeasure and Threat concepts in the construction of the SO". More specifically, they envisaged that "a stakeholder (i.e. an entity with a valid interest) possesses an asset, which in turn can be compromised by a vulnerability. In addition, a threat initiated by a threat agent targets an asset and exploits a vulnerability of the asset in order to achieve its goal" [8]. The concept of stakeholders was further re-enforced in [10].

Although assets were classified as a class, the instances of assets were 'hard-coded' into the ontology. Assets was sub-divided into 'Personnel', 'Network', 'Services', 'Data', 'Hardware', 'Software', and 'Information'. Flexibility was not allowed for in the nature of an asset. This is an area of concern for us as their ontology might require a lot of adaptation effort when being adopted in organisations.

We are of the view that this lapse (in modelling IT assets) in the ontology by [8] must be viewed against the backdrop of reliance on widely-accepted standards and frameworks at the time. As shown in [1], even these standards, and frameworks (and their updated versions) are lacking in common understanding of what information assets are.

IO Interconnected Asset Ontology. Similar to the ontology in [8], is the proposed interconnected asset ontology by Birkholz et al. [16]. In designing their ontology, which focusses on IT assets taxonomy, they relied on the fact that IT asset information is crucial for IT risk [16]. To us, this is a welcome development. However, it appears that like others, they see IT assets from what we will call from the *eye-sight of threat* rather than threat from the *eye-sight of asset*. This implies the focus, as shown in literature, is geared towards vulnerabilities to assets rather than the impact of assets value to organisational imperatives. Nonetheless, the noble concept of narrowing down to IT network components/devices level and their inter-relationships, we are of the view that in the knowledge economy and beyond, there is more to IT assets than just tangible IT assets and the tangible components of IT assets thereof.

AURUM. In an attempt to address a gap of risk management strategy in IT security domain, Ekelhart et al. [15] published a SO as a framework for their risk management tool that they called AURUM [6]. Their SO publicly available on the Stanford University's WebProtégé page (as at the time of writing this paper), is able to blend the IT security environment and the organisational environment. Their SO also classified assets as tangible and intangible. By using the AURUM toolkit, the populating of the SO with the organisation's tangible IT assets can be fairly automated through the use of network scanners. Through a wizard-driven process, the snapshot of the organisational environment is then mapped to the inventory of IT-related infrastructure elements to build a knowledge base for the purpose of security risk management processes [15].

It would appear that the objective of their SO is to assist with asset-specific threat probability. As with most work on IT risk management, the focus is not on asset importance [20]! Nonetheless, the extensibility and vastness of their SO is duly acknowledged. Their SO (similar to [8]) covers 'Asset', 'Threat', 'Vulnerability', 'Controls' and 'Organisation'. Mapping 'Stakeholder' from ontology by [8] and 'interconnected asset' from [16] to [15], would be a drive towards a global, integrated SO [21]. There is bound to be challenges though. Even then, there is a need to address the dynamic nature of IT assets in the knowledge economy. Our IT assets ontology which seeks to fill the gap can then be unified with the global and integrated SO.

Related Work Summary. In this section, we have reviewed five ontologies. We highlighted the lapses in each of the reviewed ontologies. Although our review is not as robust as that of [21], we included two ontologies (media assets and cybersecurity) which were missing in earlier reviews. Our review has also shown a missing aspect in the already reviewed security ontologies – that of dynamic nature of IT assets in the knowledge economy.

We duly acknowledged the need for a complete security ontology in the security community [21]. We also acknowledge that the criteria for a universally agreed information security taxonomies (concepts, relations, axioms, ontological agreements …) are missing [21]. More so, we acknowledge that defining an integrated SO would be a highly complex challenge which in any case the scientific community has not yet completely fulfilled [21]. These all imply that there is an important challenge and there is a need for research in the area of an ontology for information security. Other attempts made towards an ontology for information security [22] and ontology-based evaluation of ISO 27001 [23] only emphasis the dire need.

However, in the journey towards this universally acceptable integrated SO, the IT assets element of risk factor that has not been looked into in-depth deserves attention. Hence, this paper presents an ontology that seeks to address this. This would be a much valued and needed contribution to the envisaged integrated SO.

It has been shown that none of these ontologies addresses the components of IT assets from the viewpoint of information assets being integral part of IT assets [11] in the knowledge economy. The closest is the "Security Ontology" built for AURUM, which splits assets into tangible and intangible. However, the identified IT assets were 'hardcoded' as instances of IT assets, rather than being inferred or dynamically logically grouped.

It can thus be argued that there is a need for a more structured, flexible and adaptive IT assets ontology. We will now review classification systems per the ISO 22274 standard and thereafter present our adaptive IT assets ontology for information risk.

3   Classification System: ISO 22274

The ISO 22274 standard (systems to manage terminology, knowledge and content) establishes basic principles and requirements for ensuring that classification systems are suitable for worldwide application [24]. In a complex world such as the knowledge economy and beyond, where knowledge sharing is of the essence, the role of classification systems can hardly be overestimated [24].

In this research project, terms and definitions drawn from ISO 22274 are used inter-alia with World Wide Web Consortium's (W3C) specification for OWL (Web Ontology Language). See Ontology_ISO22274_Mapping_ITAOFIR_v0.1.1.pdf at www.researchgate.net/project/ISO-22274-mapping-to-World-Wide-Web-Consortiums-W3C-specification-for-OWL-Web-Ontology-Language.

Noting that ontology is a formal specification of a shared conceptualisation or inter-relationship of concepts in a domain of interest [25], in this instance the impact of IT assets in information risk, the authors are of the view that this mapping is of the essence. A plausible reasoning is that information risk practitioners relates with the philosophy and theory of risk as well as systems and concepts of risks. These two can be related to by means of a standard and a representation. More so, ISO 2700x suite of information security standards are a common denominator in most of the security ontologies. As ISO standards normatively reference other ISO standards, it would make logical sense that there should be alignment between the ISO 22274 standard that focuses on classification systems and the framework for security ontologies.

In ISO 22274, the viewpoint of a concept system is that, the relations between the concepts are formalized and the characteristics that delimit related concepts are identified [24]. In ontology, the concepts are not only formalised taxonomically-wise, their inter-relationship can be brought to fore by inference. Knowledge is then expressed and can be shared. The knowledge derived from the concept system can invariably address different user communities or stakeholders or interest of domain experts who might have different requirements for granularity of their classification system. The ontology is no longer simply a model, but a modelling of a classification system as a means to expressing knowledge – methodological framework.

4   IT Assets Ontology

We will now present our IT assets ontology that was built using the Stanford University's Protégé ontology development environment [26]. Protégé is a widely used software (desktop and web) system for building and maintaining ontologies. The desktop system (Protégé 5) which we used, enables the construction and management of our OWL based IT asset ontology [26]. The choice of Protégé was based on preference, its availability and popularity. We used three reasoners for drawing logical inferences from our ontology. These are HermiT, Pellet and FaCT++. We will refer back to these in the discussion section.

4.1   IT Assets Ontology for Risk

Having noted the asset section (class) of other ontologies (as reviewed earlier) and literature on IT assets in the knowledge economy, we proceed to design an IT asset ontology that would:

1. Be dynamic (noting that IT assets and information assets are dynamic, having different state during their lifecycle);
2. Show that risk is available only when there is a possibility of threat and the asset has a value; and
3. Be modular (allow categorisation to be added and integrate with other ontologies).

4.2   IT Assets Ontology Tangible and Intangible Concept

In our ontology, IT assets are positioned as a sub-class of the assets domain, even though our domain of interest is IT assets. We created an ontological equivalent ITAsset class for the IT asset class ('IT asset'). We are of the belief that this will support portability and integration of our ontology onto other ontologies.

The 'IT asset' class is divided into "tangible" and "intangible" by means of equivalence. This was realised by denoting tangible and intangible based on the equivalence of 'IT asset' and hasAssetTypeFormat property to be either tangible or intangible. In the current iteration the class IntangibleITAsset is disjoint with

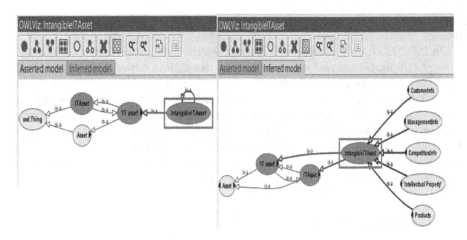

Fig. 1. IT assets ontology showing IntangibleITAsset as asserted and inferred

TangibleITAsset. Figure 1 shows the asserted state and the inferred state of intangible IT assets.

For purpose of clarity, the sample views of the ontology presented in this paper are based on a stripped-down iteration of our IT assets ontology.

4.3   IT Assets Ontology Risk Concept

Subscribing to the notion that risk is a function of possibility of threat and impact on an asset, we introduce the risk class as an intercession of 'IT asset' class and hasRisk property having a value for AssetThreatPossibility and AssetValue. More so, risk will hold true if the intercession is true and hasRiskLevel property has been denoted a value from AssetRiskLevel as can be seen in Fig. 2.

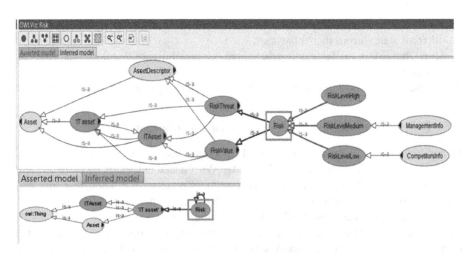

Fig. 2. Asserted and Inferred view of risk in the IT assets ontology

As shown in Fig. 3, the IT assets ontology would only flag a risk if there is a threat to an IT asset that has an asset value and for which a risk level has been assigned (through a risk assessment).

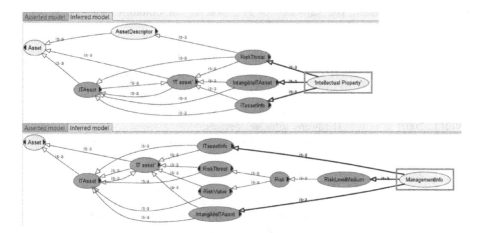

Fig. 3. Risk is denoted only when the three elements (of threat, value and level) are true

4.4 IT Assets Ontology Summary

In this section, the modular and dynamic nature of our IT assets ontology was evident by the use of 'equivalence', structured layout of classes and innovative use of 'properties'. These are based on the design considerations at the beginning of this section. The inferences or rather the reasoning made from the assertions are made possible through the properties that have been defined in the ontology.

In the next section, we will discuss the usefulness of our ontology by highlighting some of the logical reasoning. We shall then relate this to two scenarios.

5 Discussion

We have highlighted the need for a complete security ontology and that it is lacking a common criteria for building a complete integrated SO. The things that exist, which are in good step, are standards, frameworks and best practices. The 'universal' adoption of these standards, frameworks and best practices is another discussion that needs to take place. This is outside the scope of this research work at this instant.

Given that in information security, risk is inevitable, the elements of risk must be looked into critically in order to develop a complete and integrated ontology. The two elements of risks are fundamentally those of threats and assets. We have highlighted that there is a body of work looking into the threats element of risk. The second building block, assets, must be structurally developed as well.

5.1   IT Assets Elements

A cursory look through literature, as summarised in Table 1, indicates that there are different opinions on what constitute IT assets. However, in order to build an integrated SO that is universally accepted, there has to be some level of consensus on what are the elements of IT assets. The sub-class of IT assets in our ontology, see Fig. 4, were derived from literature.

Table 1. Collation of IT assets elements in literature

	IT ASSETS ELEMENTS (O = ONTOLOGY)	
[11] *(IN ARAL & WEILL, 2007)	Tangible, intangible; Hardware, software, services; *IT Capability: HR Capabilities, Management Capability, Internal Communications, Communications with Suppliers, Internet Capability	
[9]	IT systems, cloud service, external network topologies; Asset database: software/hardware list, configurations, resource usage status, security policies, security level assessment result, topology; Resources: data center and SaaS, usage status/history of the resources, contract information of the resource usages	O
[8]	Personnel; Network; Services; Data; Hardware; Software; Information;	O
[16]	Network; Network Component;Interface; Address; ACL;	O
[15]	Tangible, intangible; data, software concepts; IT-related infrastructure; Telecommunication	O
[22]	Countermeasure; Credential; Human; Technology: Hardware, data, process, Network;	O
[23]	A thing of value deserving protection	
[1] *(FROM ITIL 2011)	Tangible, intangible Information asset; Software, software license; Hardware; Data; *Resource; *Capability;	

The authors with over fifty years aggregated IT and information risk experience, further fine-tuned the many disparate part into the logical grouping in the IT assets ontology. The fine-tuning was done with dynamic and modular nature of IT assets in the knowledge economy at mind. We replaced data with information and differentiate between data/information that are stored and data/information that are used for specific purposes (competitors, customers, management and product information).

The concept of IT systems was based on line-of-business use, such as ERP (Enterprise Resource Planning), EAM (Enterprise Assets Management), CRM (Customer Relationship Management) et al. IT infrastructure refers to platforms that are sub-divided into two main parts; data centre and cloud computing. We were able to refer to IT assets based on their format, such as tower, rack or blade server. Thereby,

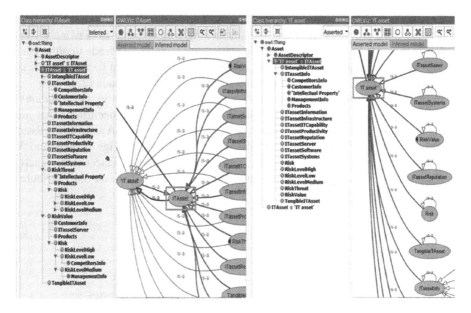

Fig. 4. Layout of classes in the IT assets ontology in assert and inferred mode

being able to identify elements within a rack/cabinet. More so, IT assets were classified on the basis of productivity where elements such as desktops, laptops, mobile devices and even BYOD were classified. We kept the software category to cover distinguishable software and software licenses. Depending on the prevalent accounting system within an organisation, software can switched between tangible and intangible.

It is our belief that this modular approach that allows for sub-categories and the dynamic nature of IT assets throughout their lifecycle is more apt for the knowledge economy. In effect, IT assets can be classified based on the properties they possess rather than just being 'hardcoded' into a fixed category.

5.2 Argumentation

"Let us now consider non-necessary reasoning. This divides itself, according to the different ways in which it may be valid, into three classes: probable deduction; experimental reasoning, which I now call Induction; and processes of thought capable of producing no conclusion more definite than a conjecture, which I now call Abduction." - Charles Sanders Peirce

The premise of the logical argumentation [18] as applied in this research project from the viewpoint of abductive reasoning, are as follows:

1. Risk is a function of possibility of threat and impact on asset;
2. IT assets are a type of asset;
3. In the knowledge economy and beyond, IT assets wholly or collectively consist of two parts (tangible and intangible); and
4. The intangible part are integral part of tangible IT assets.

Even though abductive reasoning/argument or abductive inference [17, 27] can at times be *erroneous* (infers an erroneous conclusion), it is valuable in drawing a conclusion on one of the possibility of consequences on a claim that leads to a/the conclusion. Through (1) an iterative process, and (2) constraining set of facts or argument attacks in a plausible hypothesis, a more exact inference can be made [27].

In our ontology, the set of facts on IT assets were constrained by the *'relations'* that we have defined (as properties). The inferences or logical conclusions that are drawn from the assertions in our ontology is then able to support the earlier listed four premises of our logical argumentation. This is evidenced in Figs. 2, 3, 4, and 5. The web of 'relations' has been carefully constructed such that instances (individuals) of IT assets are wholly linked to tangibility and risk based, on the attributes ("AssetDescriptor") of the IT asset.

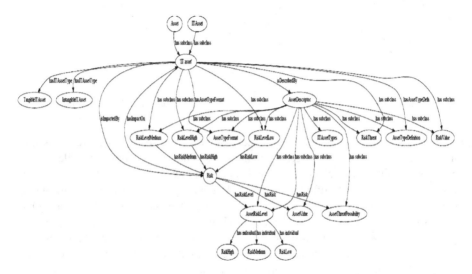

Fig. 5. The 'stripped-down' IT assets ontology showing relations to risk

5.3 Abstract Usage Scenario

Having shown that our ontology supports the arguments and conversely that abductive reasoning can be made from our ontology, we will now look at two scenarios.

BCBST Discarded Hard Drives. It is now common knowledge that Blue Cross Blue Shield of Tennessee (BCBST) left behind some hard-drives in a warehouse. They were deemed to be of no value and have no risk to BCBST. The theft of the hard-drives however proved otherwise. The hard-drives that have no accounting value have resulted in BCBST having to spend more than US$17 million on 'corrective' actions relating to the security breach. These include HIPAA violation fee, legal costs amongst others [28].

When an ontology is integrated into a risk register or risk management process [15, 16], it is possible to constrained (through OWL restrictions) the set of facts about an entity (such as the BCBST's hard-drives). The BCBST's hard-drives consisted of tangible parts that have their own value and threat(s). They also have intangible parts, in this case customer health-related information, linked to the hard-drives. In the ontology, the value of and threat(s) to the intangible customer information would be constrained to the hard-drives.

Our ontology would have been able to highlight that there yet exists a risk on the hard-drives (linked to customer information). Therefore, the hard-drives' risk value would have to be looked into and the resulting risk appropriately mitigated. Even if the hard-drives are deemed not to have "accounting value", the ontology would have shown that they have risk value on the contrary.

At the moment, threat countermeasures are not defined in our ontology. However, because our ontology is a means to an end (methodological framework), it can be integrated with other security ontologies reviewed herein that would assist with the threat countermeasures.

What BCBST suffered is not just a careless mistake but what [1] referred to as the lack of appropriate controls on (information) assets premised on the fact that assets of the knowledge economy are not properly understood, properly defined, properly identified, and hence not properly controlled, and/or properly retired.

Discarded Laptop. In [29], a laptop containing sensitive information was discarded. Forensic analysis showed that the laptop contained go-to-market marketing and contract information. The analysis also showed that the laptop was sent for repair and from there ended up being disposed.

The isITassetInfo property in the ontology would have possibly link the laptop to management information and product information. As with the BCBST hard-drives, the associated risk would have been flagged before disposal. The time for this flagging (of risk) is not necessarily at the time of disposal, rather it should have been at a time of referral for repair. Nonetheless, risk assessment could still have been carried out when the laptop is being discarded after being found 'unrepairable'.

The two cases have highlighted an important aspect of information risk yet seemly overlooked in practice. This relates to the value of assets and the internal controls that are applied to them. The value of assets are generally taken to be the financial accounting value. In information risk, there might possibly be a mis-match between the accounting value (which is linked to some depreciating factor) and risk value (which is more of a function of "impact"). This seems to be the case with the BCBST's hard-drives. What needs to be done is to have an ontology such as ours in place as a means towards linking up all the elements of an IT asset. The asset value that would be derived from this would then be used for the purpose of putting in place risk controls to mitigate risks.

6 Conclusion

This paper has advanced knowledge in information risk in two ways. Firstly, the OWL based IT assets ontology is the first ontology to present IT assets in a flexible, structured, dynamic, and modular view. Secondly, our ontology balances the "asset" and "possibility of threat" elements of risk in a coherent manner.

Our contribution puts into action a gap that was identified. That of a need for an ontology of information security – "What the field needs is an ontology—a set of descriptions of the most important concepts and the relationship among them. ... Maybe we [the community of security professionals] can set the example by building our ontology in a machine-usable form in using XML and developing it collaboratively." [Donner 2003 in 22]. With this in place, we might as well be en-route towards a *universal definition* and *security ontology* for IT assets.

Acknowledgement. This work was supported by the institutional research development fund of the Nelson Mandela Metropolitan University, South Africa. The ontology work was conducted using the Protégé resource, which is supported by grant GM10331601 from the National Institute of General Medical Sciences of the United States National Institutes of Health.

References

1. Adesemowo, A.K., Von Solms, R., Botha, R.A.: Safeguarding information as an asset: do we need a redefinition in the knowledge economy and beyond? SA J. Inf. Manag. **18**, 1–12 (2016). doi:10.4102/sajim.v18i1.706
2. Roeser, S.: Handbook of Risk Theory: Epistemology, Decision Theory, Ethics, and Social Implications of Risk. Springer Science & Business Media, Heidelberg (2012)
3. Borch, K.: The theory of risk. J. R. Stat. Soc. **29**, 432–467 (1967)
4. Aven, T., Baraldi, P., Flage, R., Zio, E.: Uncertainty in Risk Assessment. Wiley, Chichester (2014)
5. Blakley, B., McDermott, E., Geer, D.: Information security is information risk management. In: Proceedings of the 2001 Workshop on New Security Paradigms - NSPW 2001, p. 97. ACM Press, New York (2001)
6. Ekelhart, A., Fenz, S., Neubauer, T.: AURUM: a framework for information security risk management. In: Proceedings of the 42nd Hawaii International Conference on System Sciences – HICSS, pp. 1–10. IEEE Computer Society, Waikoloa (2009)
7. Ahmad, A., Bosua, R., Scheepers, R.: Protecting organizational competitive advantage: a knowledge leakage perspective. Comput. Secur. **42**, 27–39 (2014)
8. Tsoumas, B., Gritzalis, D.: Towards an ontology-based security management. In: 20th International Conference on Advanced Information Networking and Applications (AINA 2006), vol. 1. pp. 985–992. IEEE, Vienna (2006)
9. Takahashi, T., Fujiwara, H., Kadobayashi, Y.: Building ontology of cybersecurity operational information. In: Proceedings of the Sixth Annual Workshop on Cyber Security and Information Intelligence Research - CSIIRW 2010, pp. 1–4. ACM Press, New York (2010)
10. Poller, A., Türpe, S., Kinder-Kurlanda, K.: An asset to security modeling? Analyzing stakeholder collaborations instead of threats to assets. In: Proceedings of the 2014 workshop on New Security Paradigms Workshop – NSPW, pp. 69–82. ACM Press, Victoria (2014)

11. Saunders, A., Brynjolfsson, E.: Valuing information technology related intangible assets. Manag. Inf. Syst. Q. **40**, 83–110 (2016)
12. Riedl, E.J., Serafeim, G.: Information risk and fair values: an examination of equity betas. J. Account. Res. **49**, 1083–1122 (2011)
13. Chen, Y., Boehm, B., Sheppard, L.: Value driven security threat modeling based on attack path analysis. In: 2007 40th Annual Hawaii International Conference on System Sciences (HICSS 2007), p. 280a. IEEE, Walkoloa (2007)
14. Calder, A., Watkins, S.G.: Information Security Risk Management for ISO27001/ISO27002. IT Governance Ltd, Ely (2010)
15. Ekelhart, A., Fenz, S., Neubauer, T.: Ontology-based decision support for information security risk management. In: 2009 Fourth International Conference on Systems, pp. 80–85. IEEE, Porto (2009). doi:10.1109/ICONS.2009.8
16. Birkholz, H., Sieverdingbeck, I., Sohr, K., Bormann, C.: IO: an interconnected asset ontology in support of risk management processes. In: 2012 Seventh International Conference on Availability, Reliability and Security, pp. 534–541. IEEE, Prague (2012). doi:10.1109/ARES.2012.73
17. Archer, M.S., Bhaskar, R., Collier, A., Lawson, T., Norrie, A. (eds.): Critical Realism: Essential Readings. Routledge, London (2013)
18. Walton, D.N.: Methods of Argumentation. Cambridge University Press, New York (2013). 10013
19. Lee, W., Bailer, W., Bürger, T., Champin, P.-A., Evain, J.-P., Malaisé, V., Michel, T., Sasaki, F., Söderberg, J., Stegmaier, F., Strassner, J. (eds.): Ontology for Media Resources 1.0 (2012). https://www.w3.org/TR/mediaont-10/
20. Fenz, S., Neubauer, T.: How to determine threat probabilities using ontologies and Bayesian networks. In: Proceedings of the 5th Annual Workshop on Cyber Security and Information Intelligence Research Cyber Security and Information Intelligence Challenges and Strategies - CSIIRW 2009. pp. 1–3. ACM Press, New York (2009)
21. Blanco, C., Lasheras, J., Fernández-Medina, E., Valencia-García, R., Toval, A.: Basis for an integrated security ontology according to a systematic review of existing proposals. Comput. Stand. Interfaces **33**, 372–388 (2011). doi:10.1016/j.csi.2010.12.002
22. Herzog, A., Shahmehri, N., Duma, C.: An ontology of information security. Int. J. Inf. Secur. Priv. **1**, 1–23 (2007). doi:10.4018/jisp.2007100101
23. Milicevic, D., Goeken, M.: Ontology-based evaluation of ISO 27001. In: Cellary, W., Estevez, E. (eds.) I3E 2010. IAICT, vol. 341, pp. 93–102. Springer, Heidelberg (2010). doi:10.1007/978-3-642-16283-1_13
24. ISO/IEC: ISO 22274:2013 - Systems to manage terminology, knowledge and content - concept-related aspects for developing and internationalizing classification systems, Geneva, Switzerland (2013)
25. Gruber, T.R.: Toward principles for the design of ontologies used for knowledge sharing? Int. J. Hum. Comput. Stud. **43**, 907–928 (1995)
26. Musen, M.A.: The protégé team: a look back and a look forward. AI Matters **1**, 4–12 (2015)
27. Walton, D.N.: Abductive, presumptive and plausible arguments. Informal Log **21**, 141–169 (2001)
28. Edwards Wildman Palmer: Edwards Wildman Privacy and Data Breach Risk Report, Boston, MA (2013)
29. Adesemowo, A.K., Thomson, K.-L.: Service desk link into IT asset disposal: a case of a discarded IT asset. In: 2013 International Conference on Adaptive Science and Technology, pp. 1–4. IEEE, Pretoria (2013)

Information Systems Security Management

Disaster Management System as an Element of Risk Management for Natural Disaster Systems Using the PESTLE Framework

Dilshad Sarwar[⊠], Muthu Ramachandran, and Amin Hosseinian-Far

Leeds Beckett University, Leeds, UK
{D. Sarwar, M. Ramachandran,
A. Hosseinian-Far}@leedsbeckett.ac.uk

Abstract. Recently, we have witnessed so many natural catastrophes such as earthquakes in Japan, severe floods in the UK, US and many other parts of the world. Consequently businesses have been losing tens of billions of dollars as a result of various natural and man-made disasters. Disaster Management System (DMS) have proven to be important means for reducing risks associated with such damages to businesses. A DMS can minimize and in some cases, eliminates the risks through technical, management or operational solutions (risk management effort). However, it is virtually impossible to eliminate all risks. Information technology systems are vulnerable for a variety of disruptions (e.g. short-term power outage, disk drive failure) as a result of natural disasters to terrorist actions. In many cases, critical resources may reside outside the organizations control (such as telecommunications or electric power), and the organization may be unable to ensure their availability. This paper proposes a model for Disaster Management System as an Element of Risk Management using the PESTLE framework. Thus, an effective Disaster Management System in the form of contingency planning, execution and testing are essential to mitigate the risk of system and service availability. We have developed a global model for disaster recover planning and management based on the PESTLE framework which can be customised and applied to a variety of disasters prone systems such natural, emergency, IT/Network/Security, Data recovery, and incident-response systems. To summarise, this paper aims to maximise the benefits of PESTLE analysis it should be used on a regular basis within an organisation to enable the identification of trends.

Keywords: Disaster preparedness · Disaster management system · Recovery/reconstruction · Risk identification · Emergency management and early warning · PESTLE

1 Introduction

PESTLE analysis is not a new phenomenon within business environments however; it is something that has not been largely explored within the context of Disaster Management Systems. PESTLE focuses on political, environmental, social, technological, economical and legal aspects of any given organizational environment (Al-Marri and

© Springer International Publishing AG 2016
H. Jahankhani et al. (Eds.): ICGS3 2017, CCIS 630, pp. 191–204, 2016.
DOI: 10.1007/978-3-319-51064-4_16

Ramachandran 2009). It is widely known that many businesses have in the last few years suffered greatly and lost tens of thousands of dollars on account of both man-made and natural disasters. Man-made disasters have included: the bombing of the World Trade Centre and the Oklahoma City Government Building as well as the corruption and damage to various Information Technology systems and their data, information and processing.

Threats and risks are increasing and becoming more complex. These threats are multifaceted and have been increasingly difficult to address. The threats faced today can be placed under the following key areas:

- Transitional threats due to terrorism
- Globalised disease outbreaks
- Infrastructure
- Cyber attacks

The issues and concerns raised within this paper will highlight the level of severity and scope which need to be considered in terms of addressing disaster management in relation to human and economic loss (Deutsche 2004).

This paper aims to take a very different approach to Disaster Management System as it is uses the basic principles of PESTLE and applies those to a DMS in order to improve the overall disaster management processes (Thomson and Martin 2010). This paper will look at carrying out a PESTLE analysis for a disaster management system looking particularly at the political, environmental, social, technological, legal and economic requirements to implement an effective disaster management system (Daniel et al. 2003).

Politically to implement a DMS there are a number of considerations which need to be addressed. There is a need to have a consistent political agenda which is in align with the DMS agenda. Politically there needs to be adequate consideration in terms of the processes that are required to be followed by individual countries, when such disasters occur (Chandrasekhar et al. 2014).

With regards to DMS implementation it is essential to strengthen the focus of resilience that allows for a holistic and integrated approach which includes an effective implementation of a DMS. The focus here is on the prevention and mitigation, preparedness, response and recovery factors. The concepts of disaster management systems approach to co-ordinate a clear structure across the government bodies (Thomson and Martin 2010). A clear DMS model is are required to address and initially allow for the objectives for governmental approaches which are imperative to understand threats and hazards for each country.

DMS enables an institution or environment to consider links associated with its external environment (Thomson and Martin 2010). Systems are thus implemented in an organisational construct which are fundamentally based on internal organisational factors. The general distinction between internal and external aspects of systems, have to be considered and applied to organisational theories (Johnson et al. 2008). The focus on internal and external factors associated with DMS when used within the business impact analysis which requires consideration to be applied to the environment in terms of risk in association with DMS planning (Johnson et al. 2008). Documentation at strategic level does need to be limited in terms of length so as to minimise confusion.

An effective DMS would not need to have a complicated set of documentation. It is however, necessary to create a high level plan which looks at addressing emergency planning at operational level (Chandrasekhar et al. 2014). Numerous global organisations have specific and detailed planning documentation. The employment of a DMS needs to complement existing plans which are in place (Al-Marri and Ramachandran 2009). In particular, the integration of DMS in accordance with disaster management requirements is essential.

1.1 Why PESTLE?

Existing work in this research are interesting with different approaches to DMS (Al-marri and Ramachandran 2009; Chandrasekhar et al. 2014). Existing literature within this research area illustrates a different approach to as seen in works by Chandrasekhar et al. (2014) have proposed nontraditional approach of participation by local people and communities to speed up the recovery (Rothearmel 2012). However, for creating a systematic approach to disaster planning, we need to use precise means of analysis with each countries critical parameter such as strengths, challenges, future planning and risks (natural disasters). Therefore a PESTLE analysis would be deemed popular for large communities such as the whole nation (MarketLine 2015). Organisations find themselves functioning in an environment which is constantly changing and evolving. The need to analyse the concerns and the method the organization uses to address these concerns is based around a fundamental organizational strategy. It is essential to analyse the organisations external environment (Fallara 2003). An organisation needs to identify external factors within the environment which could impact on the organisation (Thomson and Martin 2010).

The PESTLE tool is a powerful technique for analysing the organisational environment. Once the PESTLE is used within an organisational construct it clearly identifies areas that focus on internal changes to the organisation (Fledrich and Burghardt 2007). The following section will provide an overview of a PESTLE for DMS.

Political: It is essential to keep abreast of potential policy changes in any government. There may-be a change in government priorities for example environmental regulations.

Economic: Considering the economic investment for the types of disaster management systems in place is an essential activity which needs to be considered (Chandrasekhar et al. 2014).

Social: Issues which have an impact on the market and population growth are required for DMS as it is imperative to gain understanding of the societal impact on the environment for which the DMS is being developed (Rothearmel 2012).

Technological: Technological factors can be divided into key areas such as automation, cost saving, outsourcing, growth of networking capabilities, the evasive side of the growth of technology.

Legal: Focus on current and impending legislation. There is a view of ensuring organisations understand the notion of how laws can have an impact on DMS.

Environmental: The concerns focused on the environment protection ae considerably important especially in todays' ever changing environment; particularly in areas such as weather, climate, and geographical location. For example natural disasters, weather cycles such as monsoons; Physical conditions with the extent and maturity of a country's infrastructure; Weather conditions could cause logistical problems at certain times of the year.

As with the other PESTLE factors there is a requirement to look at potential changes to weather patterns (Johnson et al. 2008). These ecological and environmental aspects can have consequences that are on a social and economic level. MarketLine (2015) provides an extensive application of PESTLE model for structures in Japan (PESTLE - Macro Environmental Analysis 2012). Each factor which has been explored is on four main parameters that are current strengths, challenges, future prospects, and future risks (Marketline 2015). Environmental factors include infrastructure, cyclical weather, disposal of materials, energy availability and cost and the ecological consequences of production processes (Van de Walle and Turoff 2007). The impact of a certain external factor may have more severe consequences for a particular division. The PESTLE technique can help clarify why change is needed and identify potential options.

Natural disasters have included: the earthquakes in Southern California and the San Francisco Bay Area; Hurricane Hugo and Andrew; and floods in the mid-west (Aljazeera 2005). Disasters like these could clearly take place in the future and it is for this reason that one needs to consider if the incorporation of a Disaster Management System (DMS); and system could be an effective means of protecting businesses from different types of disasters (Deutsche 2004). It is possible to argue that all businesses and Information Technology departments should be involved in Disaster Management System, implementing, testing and updating. Furthermore, the use of DMSs should be encouraged so that in time all Information Technology departments come to accept such systems as a necessity (Deutsche 2004). At times, certain information technology and automated information systems are prone to interruptions that can greatly disrupt the efficient running of such systems. If the Information Technology Contingency Plan was to be adopted by businesses, this problem could be resolved and would put in place useful technical procedures that ensure systems recover quickly from any troublesome disruptions (Thomson and Martin 2010). It is the DMS that determines what planning practices should be implemented by businesses in order to create an efficient Information Technology contingency plan (Al-Marri and Ramachandran 2009). Although such practices are on the whole sufficient for most business, it is important to acknowledge that some businesses may need to make use of other practices to deal with certain extra needs (Johnson et al. 2008). This article does not take into account the DMS for supercomputers and wireless networks, but even so the majority of the practices put forth are applicable to these systems (Chandrasekhar et al. 2014).

Earlier work has focused on a more generic mode for emergency-response system and contingency planning for natural disaster and IT security management systems (Al-marri and Ramachandran 2009; Ramachandran and Orange 2008). In this work, we have developed a global model for Disaster recover planning and management which can be customized and applied to a variety of disasters prone systems such natural, emergency, IT/Network/Security, Data recovery, and incident-response systems.

International human actions – the risk associated with chemical, nuclear or other hazards, resulting from deliberate actions – e.g. terrorism, sabotage (Rehak 1994). Unintentional human actions – the risks associated with chemical, nuclear or other hazards, resulting from accidents – e.g. hazardous materials, spill or chemical release, explosion, fire, water control, structure, building and dam. Environmentally – analysing consequences/impacts – that affect many set objectives. Does the risk have the potential to impact on large scale geographical areas? Does the risk have the potential to impact the health of the population – does the risk have the potential to identify impact on the borders, and the impact on the environment in the long run? Develop strategic emergency management planning – building blocks, strategic emergency management plan – the step focuses on an informed emergency management approach for the institution (Rehak 1994). Inputs should include emergency management planning considerations and assumptions. All hazard risk assessment establishes an emergency management structure. Each institution should establish an emergency management governance structure. Confirming strategic priorities it is important to ensure that the country's governance structure is aligned to the overall governance structure (Thomson and Martin 2010). This is a requirement to identify assumptions, constraints and limitations. The planning team should aim to clearly identify the planning constraints and institutional limitations that will influence the subsequent development. Identify prevention/mitigation, preparedness response and recovery requirements and opportunities.

2   A Model for Disaster Management System and Risk Management Process Using PESTLE

Risk management has been widely used in various projects. However, risk management for national disasters is more complex and harder to predict. Therefore, this section aims to structure DMS as part of risk management process for national disasters. A variety of procedures are adopted to appropriately identify, control and reduce risks to Information Technology systems. Fallara (2003) has proposed a similar approach to disaster recovery planning as part of the risk management as they are crucial to any disaster recovery. However, we have proposed a more structured approach to Disaster Management System as an element of risk management (Fledrich and Burghardt 2007). In order to effectively manage risks to Information Technology contingency planning, it is necessary that the following risk management actions are taken:

Firstly, it is important to investigate whether the concerned system has any weaknesses that could lead to it being damaged or destroyed and subsequently to take the required precautions (Fledrich and Burghardt 2007). There are three types of threats in particular that could harm weaken or deem the system insecure:

- Terrorism – cyber attacks
- Threats to the infrastructure

- Natural disasters
- This could include disasters under the areas of:
- Natural: this includes fires, floods, tornados and hurricanes.
- Human: this involves terrorist attacks, human mistakes, and risk from hackers.
- Environmental: this includes software gaining errors, equipment ceasing to work and power failures.

Secondly: it is essential to asses any residual risks in order to form an effective contingency plan. Figure 1 illustrates the Disaster Recovery System: which shows the process of putting into place the necessary security precautions, forming a contingency plan and putting the DRS into action when any incident occurs.

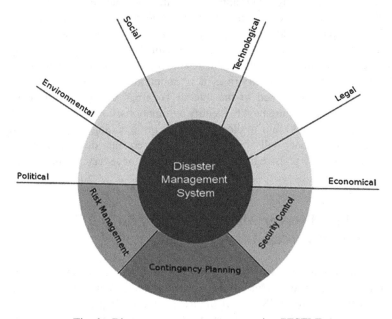

Fig. 1. Disaster management system using PESTLE

It is important that analyses of risks to Information Technology systems are taken to ensure that the risks to Information Technology systems are properly identified. In this way, it is possible for risks to be allocated with a risk level that predicts how high at risk systems are to various threats and how serious such threats may be to systems (Fallara 2003). The measures put in place to deal with risks clearly have to be constantly examined and updated by the people who are dealing with the Information Technology contingency planning since Information Technology systems may constantly be forced to face new dangers from various threats (Fallara 2003). Information Technology contingency planning involves a larger range of measures than DMS to help Information Technology systems survive disasters (Van de Walle and Turoff 2007). In particular, Information Technology contingency planning need to be focused on guaranteeing that organisations and businesses are able to survive disasters as well as plans for ways of dealing with any disasters that may hit Information Technology systems, business processes and facilities (Deutsche 2004). Although there has been no general consent on what would constitute effective Information Technology contingency planning, the fact that there is an inbuilt link between Information Technology systems and business processes shows that every plan should consider the two at the same time to ensure that both work effectively alongside one another. Generally, Fig. 2 shows the Disaster Risk Management Process (cycle). The DRMP consists of four main processes/stages such as identifying and analysing risks (Rehak 1994). It is composed of the following elements:

Fig. 2. Disaster risk management process

- Risk location and examination: this involves assessing the cause, nature and behaviour of the threat and, in particular, determining how serious it is.
- Knowledge management: this involves raising awareness about potential risks, putting in place education and training programs, extensive research on ways of preventing disasters.
- Political commitment to a disaster reduction policy: this includes ensuring that laws are drawn up to ensure that such policies are adhered to.
- Taking active measures to reduce risks: this could include planning and building protective structures like dams and dikes.

- Cautionary methods for disasters: this could include ensuring that people are supplied with the knowledge and information required (ESPON 2005); to take the necessary precautions against disasters.
- Preparation for disasters: this includes making sure that people are able to cope with any disasters that may occur. For example, this could involve creating a suitable plan to evacuate people from buildings.
- Repairs and rebuilding: this includes seeing to it that areas that have been hit by disasters are repaired and that the people affected by disasters are given the required assistance so that they may deal with whatever situation they may be in.

The above main elements can lead one to conclude that disaster recovery management involves firstly actions taken prior to a disaster. It is essential to assess what risks businesses or places may be prone to and to put in place the required measures (Fledrich and Burghardt 2007). Secondly, disaster risk management involves actions taken at the time of a disaster including assisting those areas and people involved in disasters. Thirdly, it must involve taking action after disasters occur and it must ensure that the necessary repairs and reconstructions are put in place to improve the areas hit by disasters. It is essential to take into account technical capabilities, costs and the social and environmental consequences when assessing ways of reducing risks (Committee 2005) and not just the actions taken prior to disasters, which is at times the only concern of disaster risk management (Deutsche 2004).

The Business Continuity Plan (BCP) may be designed generally for all the main business processes or specifically for a single business process (Marketline 2015). It also takes into account the value of Information Technology systems to business processes. Although the DMS does not take into account small disruptions that Information Technology contingency plans often treat, it does very often include a plan designed for Information Technology systems and can be used as a way of restoring target systems, applications or facilities in more suitable locations (Marketline 2015). If required by a business or organisation, several DMSs may be included with the BCP. Risk management template is one the structured means of identifying risk elements, impact factors, and relevant actions required as seen in (Table 1). Our impact factor consists of a number risk levels:

Critical which is a highest form of risk and therefore immediate action is required.

- High
- Medium
- Low

Table 1. Risk assessment template for recovery

Critical Aspects	Impact Factor	Recover/Contingency Plan	Team Responsible
Evacuate people from the place of incident such as a building	Critical	Call emergency evacuation team of professional experts such as Army personals.	Establishment Manager

3   Effective Disaster Recovery System Plan (DSP)

It is clear that teamwork is essential for the creation of effective disaster recovery programs. This section proposes disaster recovery plan, which is essential to structure DSR activities. It is essential that teams working on such programs must adhere to health and safety guidelines and must be briefed on exactly what the requirements are for the businesses or systems that need protection from disasters (Johnson et al. 2008). It is crucial that teams constantly monitor what protection is needed by examining whether there are any new potential threats; this means that teams must constantly be assessing whether the resources they have to deal with disasters are sufficient for creating effective disaster recovery systems. It is important that there are three separate teams to deal with the three separate phases of Disaster Management System (Fallara 2003). One team examines what requirements are needed to prepare systems and businesses for disasters; another team that actually puts in place and manages a Disaster Management System; and a third implementation team that carries out the action. Table 2 shows DMS Team Management and the detailed phases are:

- Phase 1 Requirements what is meant and what is to be done
- Phase 2 team to create and manage a Disaster Management System
- Phase 3 Implementation team to take action

Table 2. Effective disaster management system planning cycle

DMS Management Team		
Phase 1: Requirements	Phase 2: Planning	Phase 3: Implementation
DMS Requirement Team	DMS Planning Team	DMS Implementation Team

It is essential that an assessment is made of what sort of skills need to be possessed by the team members of each phase and also what resources are required by every team (Rehak 1994). A coherent structure also needs to be put in place so that every team know exactly what its objectives and responsibilities are; this is essential for the smooth and effective running of the Disaster Management System (Fledrich and Burghardt 2007). Various developments to traditional disaster recovery business took place in the 1980s, which were partly due to the fact that computer hardware was becoming cheaper and that technology was centered largely on personal computers (Rehak 1994). Although these plans in the 1980s were able to deal with the use of mainframe computers, it was not until later that plans were put in place to take into account communication networks (Chandrasekhar et al. 2014). Indeed the plans designed today differ greatly from the 1980s as it is now a requirement that managers prepare themselves for any potential risks and computer systems. If any disaster should occur, it is essential that the systems affected are restored in a number of hours instead of days and that any lost data is fully restored (Chandrasekhar et al. 2014). Such changes are mainly due to various government regulations, union contracts and the demands from customers. Today, technology plays a massive role on most businesses with various companies having both local and remote basis connections to their main computer.

Additionally government institutions are responsible for conducting mandate specific risk assessments, including risks to critical infrastructure. The key to any emergency planning is awareness of the potential situations that could impose risks on the organisation and to assess those risks on the organisation and to assess those risks on the terms of their impact and potential mitigation measures (Fledrich and Burghardt 2007). Assess the internal environment. Understanding the internal context is essential to confirm that the risk assessment approach meets the needs of the institution and of its internal stakeholders. It is the environment in which the institution operates to achieve its objectives and which can be influenced by the institution to manage risk (Fledrich and Burghardt 2007). The internal context may include the capabilities, understood in terms of resources and knowledge, capital, time, people, processes, systems, technologies, including capability improvement process, information systems, information flows and decision making processes, internal risks and vulnerabilities (Fallara 2003). It is important to identify, appraise and prioritise all institutional assets. Assets can be both tangible and intangible and can be assessed in terms of importance, value and sensitivity. With respect to known threats and hazards vulnerability exists when there is a situation or circumstance that if left unchanged may result in loss of life or may affect the confidentiality, integrity or availability of other mission critical systems. Examples of conditions that maybe considered include vulnerabilities – personal issues, high turnover, insufficient secondary or support processes and existing disaster management systems that are immature and have not been tested (ESPON 2005). Each institution has its own risk assessment process of informing decision making. Each organisation has its own strategic and operational objectives with each being exposed to its own unique risks and each having its own information and resource limitations (ESPON 2005). Therefore the risk assessment process is tailored to each institution. Risk translates into events or circumstances that if they materialise, could negatively affect achievement and objectives.

The hazard risk domain is divided into three risk areas –

- Natural hazards
- Intentional human actions and
- Unintentional human actions.

Natural hazards come under the umbrella of risks associated with natural geographical, meteorological or biological – e.g. landslides, flood, drought, pandemic influenza, foot and mouth disease and insect infestation (ZIKA Virus).

4 Evaluation and Validation of the Model

This section will explain the evaluation model. According to Fledrich and Burghardt (2007) the focus is on gathering data about the usability of a design or product by specific group of users for a particular activity with a specified environment or work context. The Environmental problems can be considered as a contributed element of causing instability. It hinders economic development; displaces populations; contributes in the increase of weapons of mass destruction; and enhances the growth of undesirable elements. Some countries are considered as environmental troubled regions

(Deutsche 2004). They suffer from water shortages, hazardous materials, oil spills in the Gulf, shipping incidents, and transmission of new diseases (Deutsche 2004). Disaster recovery Management Activity Model and the contingency and continuity-planning model for recovery actions have been discussed (Fallara 2003).

The requirements of workforce safety will be also explored. In addition to that, suggestion on how the emergency managers could be developed, and the way to create excellent communication and co-operation with involved organizations and individuals has been presented. This PESTLE DMS model provides an explanation of the use of emerging technology, the role of people and their culture, and global support (Fledrich and Burghardt 2007). It is vital to understand and analyze the operation of power within the context of evaluation in order to identify the approaches, tools and methods which can contribute in improving the practice of information system evaluation. According to Ramachandran and Orange (2008), Less that, 25% of the managers believe that the organisation did very well in handling the disaster contingency and around 14% only said the organisation very poor in handling the disaster contingency (Ramachandran 2009).

This paper encourages emergency managers to apply business continuity planning and Disaster Management System along with other newer technologies in the work. It offers ideas and possible actions, which can be adopted by the emergency managers when dealing with disasters. For that reason, the paper will present issues such as business continuity plan (BCP), Disaster Management System (DMS), workforce, education, and information technology facilities and insurance (Al-Marri and Ramachandran 2009). It gives example of how to apply business continuity plan and Disaster Management Systems at lowest cost within a PESTLE framework.

An environmental scan is necessary to gather and analyse information and typically consider both internal and external factors. Scanning can be done on a regular scheduled basis, such as annually or a continuous basis for environmental factors, that are dynamic or that are of greatest interest to the organisation. As part of the environmental scan, the organisation defines the internal and external parameters to be taken into account when managing the risk and setting the scope and risk criteria for the remaining risk assessment process (Al-Marri and Ramachandran 2009). It sets the time, scope and scale and contributes the adoption of an approach that is appropriate to the situation of the institutions and to the risks affecting the achievement of its objectives.

5   Conclusions

Today Disaster Management Systems have developed significantly since their early days when it was the company data centre that provided the most protection (Chandrasekhar et al. 2014). They are now able to ensure that all the main operating components are protected by the innovative usage of a corporate-wide risk management approach. Many lives and vast amounts of money can be saved if a disaster plan is designed efficiently for a company's so long as all the phases of the planning procedure are stuck to and developed (Chandrasekhar et al. 2014). Indeed emergency and security management programs may only be truly effective if the plan is properly designed. Teamwork and cooperation between all members of an organisation is essential for preventing disasters and it is clear that good contingency business planning effectively depends on everyone preparing for disasters and responding immediately to them.

On the whole DMS's are implemented to be aligned to existing plans, procedures and internal procedures and internal processes which are required to address the emergency support functions in line with other policy documentation (Rehak 1994). Additional to this DMS's are implemented to focus on hazards, which look at risk management measures which are applied to preventing and mitigation, preparedness, response and recovery (Van de Walle and Turoff 2007). There is a further requirement to ensure that greater understanding can be achieved from these systems and typically in line with an emergency, which additionally refers to an immediate event, including events under the umbrella of an IT incident, which requires immediate co-ordination of actions which are related to individuals in relation to property, which is required to protect the health, safety or welfare of individuals or in line with limiting damage to property or the environment (Al-Marri and Ramachandran 2009).

There are some risked based functions which are aimed at addressing the DMS which is required to support the prevention and mitigation of ensuring there is readiness for response to and recovery from emergencies (Fallara 2003). The areas addressed here are in line with functions undertaking DMS's in areas such as environmental scans and updates of environmental factors; additionally there should be on-going regular all hazard risk assessments which additionally underpin the whole government approach to the whole government approach and the collection and analysis of government response. There are additional steps to consider before the implementation of a DMS can occur. These are in relation to identifying training and skills requirements analysis.

It is necessary to carry out an environmental scan, which is required to look at assessing both the internal and external environment factors (Thomson and Martin 2010). There is a need to look at stakeholder positions and concerns they may have in line with positions and issues that arise. There is a need to identify the existing plans and address the openings in gaps in meeting institutional requirements and looks at the positions and issues of stakeholders. Additionally there is a need to address the assets and services list to complete and update critical assets and services (Thomson and Martin 2010). Completion of threats and hazards need to be identified in terms of vulnerabilities that are required to identify current safeguards. Conducting hazards and risk assessments are needed to outline the hazards applied to conducting all hazards. To identify risks, establishing a risk register, analysing risks, evaluating probability, likelihood of occurrence and analyse the probability to evaluate the likelihood of occurrence, where it is necessary to analyse the consequences and impacts (Daniel et al. 2003). Evaluating risks and prioritising risks to identify risk prevention with mitigation options. Evaluating risks prioritise risks and identify risk prevention/mitigation in line with preparedness and in the main focusing on opportunities with the notion of addressing requirements which encompass threats, hazards and specific plans. It is essential for far more engagement with the internal and external stakeholders, in order that information can be updated and refined within the DMS. The process of planning and recognising responsibilities in terms of DMS processes is necessary for the DMS to be used effectively in line with the PESTLE framework model (Daniel et al. 2003).

Thus establishing a governance structure requires confirming priorities for strategic assumptions, constraints and the overall limitations. The DMS needs to be focused on central activities which provide clear integration and inter departmental DMS. The DMS can trigger the planning stages of the system with clear links to integration and co-ordinating of other internal DMS plans (Fledrich and Burghardt 2007). The DMS can vary between government institutions, and in terms of the composition of the DMS following the PESTLE framework. The planning stages should consist of the necessary skills and experience to develop and apply key skills and experiences necessary to develop the DMS.

The areas to consider would entail the following:

- Identify team members and fundamental areas
- Establish authority and skills set requirements
- Establish authority and terms of reference

The DMS planning team needs to have a clear level of authority and direction. The DMS process should be carried out as part of an institutions strategic and business planning process which will be applied to allow for the alignment. Following this the next focus is on implementation at specific documentation.

References

Aljazeera (2005). http://english.aljazeera.net/NR/exeres/A46E0B05-1DC7-4852-83A1-5B6C1D 9521E3.htm

Al-Marri, S., Ramachandran, M.: Global emergency response system using GIS. In: Enterprise Information Systems and Implementing IT (2009)

Chandrasekhar, D., Zang, Y., Xiao, Y.: Nontraditional participation in disaster recovery planning: cases from China, India and the U.S. Am. Plann. Assoc. **80**(04), 373–384 (2014)

Daniel, L.M., Guttorm, S., Teqje, B., Arne, S.: Evaluating the quality of information business contingency planning models. Empirical Testing of a Conceptual Model Quality Framework (2003). Retrieved from Evaluating the Quality of Information Business Contingency Planning Models

Deutsche, G.F.: Guidelines: Risk Analysis - A Basis for Disaster Risk Management. Eschborn, Eschborn (2004)

ESPON: The spatial effects and management of natural and technological hazards in Europe. Eur. Spat. Obs. Netw. (2005)

Fallara, P.: Disaster recovery planning. IEEE Potentials **22**(5), 42–44 (2003)

Fledrich, F., Burghardt, P.: Agent-based systems for disaster management. Commun. ACM **50** (3), 41–42 (2007)

Johnson, G., Scholes, K., Whittington, R.: Exploring Corporate Strategy, pp. 55–57. FT Prentice Hall, Upper Saddle River (2008)

Marketline: Japan In-Depth PESTLE insights, 18 April 2015. http://www.marketline.com. Accessed 2016

PESTLE - Macro Environmental Analysis (2012). Retrieved from Oxford Learning Lab: http://www.oxlearn.com/arg_Marketing-Resources-PESTLE-Macro-Environmental-Analysis_11_31

Ramachandran, M.: The role of information technology managers in the significant company in case of natural deisasters in Qatar. In: Handbook of Software Engineering Researh and Productivity Technologies, Implications of Globalisation (2009)

Ramachandran, M., Orange, G.: Information systems model for global emergency-response system in context of natural disaster recovery management system. Geo-Information Technology for Natural Disaster Management and Rehabilitation, Bagkok (2008)

Rehak, R.H.: Disaster recovery then and now: considerations for contingency planning. Risk Manag. 41(1), 14–23 (1994)

Rothearmel, F.T.: Strategic Management: Concepts and Cases. McGraw-Hill, New York (2012)

Thomson, J., Martin, F.: Strategic Management: Awareness and Change. Cengage Learning EMEA, Boston (2010)

Van de Walle, B., Turoff, M.: Emergency Response Systems: Emerging Trends and Technologies. Commun. ACM 50, 29–31 (2007)

A Review on Privacy Issues in Hotels: A Contribution to the Definition of Information Security Policies and Marketing Strategies

Maria José Magalhães[1,2], Sérgio Tenreiro de Magalhães[2,3,4(✉)],
Kenneth Revett[5], and Hamid Jahankhani[6]

[1] GOVCOPP, Universidade de Aveiro, Aveiro, Portugal
mjmagalhaes@ua.pt
[2] Faculdade de Filosofia e Ciências Sociais da Universidade Católica
Portuguesa, Braga, Portugal
{mjmagalhaes, stmagalhaes}@braga.ucp.pt
[3] ALGORITMI Research Center, University of Minho, Guimarães, Portugal
psmagalhaes@dsi.uminho.pt
[4] Department of Computer Science, University of Beira Interior,
Covilhã, Braga, Portugal
stmagalhaes@di.ubi.pt
[5] Anastamose International, Boston, MA, USA
Ken.revett@gmail.com
[6] GSM London, London, UK
hamid.jahankhani@gsmlondon.ac.uk

Abstract. Hotels are a home away from home, with many similarities but also with many differences. This work reviews the existing knowledge on privacy issues in the hotel industry and concludes that this is a field of increasing attention from researchers all over the world but there is still much to do in order to help the industry to adopt the best practices that can maximize profit while protecting their clients' privacy rights. From the existing knowledge it is possible to conclude that privacy issues are not only a legal requirement in many countries, but are also a managerial and marketing opportunity for hotels, but there aren't clear indications to this industry on how to create, implement and publicize adequate information security policies or on how to align the marketing strategies to the importance of privacy assurance.

Keywords: Privacy · Security · Hotel · Tourism · Hospitality

1 Introduction

Security is a broad field that includes many types of concerns, some of them sometimes isolated in the concept of safety. However, in the context of this work, there will be no formal distinction between those concepts, once the focus is given to privacy, which is related, indirectly, both to security and to safety. The notion of Privacy is complex and subjective, once the information that one considers to be in need of some confidentiality assurance varies from person to person and most recently there is a generalization of the idea that the needs for privacy have come to an end. In fact, John and

© Springer International Publishing AG 2016
H. Jahankhani et al. (Eds.): ICGS3 2017, CCIS 630, pp. 205–217, 2016.
DOI: 10.1007/978-3-319-51064-4_17

Peters [1] have found 101 papers published between 1990 and 2012 declaring the end of privacy, but those authors have also concluded that this idea has persisted along time while the concept of privacy is changing with the change of the world, resulting in a consistent need for some type of privacy.

Privacy is also a concept deeply related to confidentiality, one of the three pillars of information security (confidentiality, integrity and availability). Hotels store personal information, both on the clients and on the clients' behaviors, both for general operation's management as for marketing purposes, and the organizational knowledge includes even more information, gathered in informal ways.

The information stored in the hotels information systems include, at least, the client's name, home address, nationality, phone number and/or e-mail address, passport number (or another identification document). This information is enough to forge an identity and identity theft is a growing crime. For instance, in the United States, the Federal Trade Commission has reported as increase in identity thefts complains from 86.250 in 2001 to 490.220 in 2015, ranking this type of crime as the second highest in their consumer complaints records (16% of the total), next to debt collection (29%) and above Impostor Scams complaints (11%) [2]. Data also show that it is frequent that the perpetrator of identity theft either works or has access to someone who works in a company of which the victim is a costumer [3].

Hotels also have information on the behaviors of their clients, either stored in the information system or simply in the organizational knowledge available, once the employees have access to relevant information of this nature. This type of information includes information of the hotel client as a costumer, like drinking habits (room's mini-bar and hotel bar) or video-on-demand choices (for instance, porn movies). But the information stored in the hotel organization as a whole also includes information about other types of behavior, like the use of escort services, the existence of adultery, or even the sexual tendencies of the hotel guests.

Depending on the local culture and type of hotel, these sex related aspects can be more or less determinants of the general quality of the service provided. For instance, in Japan there is an important segment of the hotel business called "love hotels", deeply rooted in the Japanese culture acceptance of the erotic, in which privacy assurance in fundamental for the success of the business [4].

Some food restrictions are also indicators of some diseases and many times hotels have that type of information [5]. Food restrictions can also be an indication of the guests' religion. Asking for Kosher food or for Halal food is an indicator of being, respectively, Jewish or Muslim, which can be a private information and, in the current sociocultural context, leaking of that information can be very problematic in many countries.

Hotels often provide clients with Internet services, operating as an Internet Service Provider to their clients. Therefore, hotels can have access to a lot of information resulting from the use of the Internet. The hotel can have access to the navigation habits of their guests and from there obtain a profile of the client. This profile can classify the client on the level of income (from online purchases), hobbies, tastes, etc. Hotels can, technically, have access to the contents of much of the information that is communicated through the provided Internet Services, like the content of e-mail messages or the conversations made through messaging services or VOIP (Voice over IP) services. In the past years many of these services started to be encrypted, providing the client with some level of privacy assurance and making it harder for providers to access information, but those systems are not unbreakable and even if we choose to believe that the hotels wouldn't invest time and money to obtain that information, it is necessary to understand if the hotel has the right, or even the obligation, to pass that data to third parties in certain situations, for instance to help the police, with or without a warrant, on an ongoing criminal investigation.

Therefore, the hotel's information system, that is not limited to the CRM (Customer Relationship Management) software and/or the hotel general management software, typically has specific characteristics that make it a repository of private information and, especially if combined with the organizational knowledge, can be a powerful marketing tool, but simultaneously represents a serious threat to the privacy of the hotel clients.

Marketing is also becoming increasingly simultaneously personalized and through digitalization, massified. Therefore, privacy issues can be a limitation for the possible strategies. On the other hand, if clients value privacy and the hotel can assure, to a relevant extent, the client's privacy, then that can be a relevant characteristic of the hotel and, therefore, can become one of the key aspects of the marketing strategy.

In order to study the existing knowledge in these domains, a literature review was conducted. The next section presents the method used to conduct that review. Section 3 presents the obtained results, divided in results on the level of research in the topic and in the analyses of the contents of the existing research; finally, this work ends with the conclusions that can be drawn from the research currently available in peer-reviewed indexed (Scopus and/or ISI Web of Science) publications.

2 Method

For this work we made several queries in Scopus and Web-of-Science, the two most relevant indexers in peer-reviewed academic publishing in the beginning of August 2016.

In the Scopus search portal, the queries were made using the terms presented in Table 1, limiting to the fields of "Physical Sciences" (which includes Computer Science and Information Systems) and "Social Sciences and Humanities" (which includes the several domains of Tourism and Hospitality, like Business, Economics and Social Sciences) and excluding any books, reviews or editorials, due to the nature of these type of scientific productions.

Table 1. Search queries and number of papers found in Scopus

Terms used in the query	Number of items found
Privacy + Information + Hotel	25
"Information security" + Hotel	5
"Privacy" + Hotel	67
"Privacy requirements" + Hotel	0
"Privacy policy" + Hotel	3
"Privacy policies" + Hotel	3
"Personal information" + Hotel	15
"Personal information" + Hotel + disclosure	1

Many of the papers found related to algorithms designed for communications/storage security and, therefore, are out of the scope of this work. In order to focus the results on the field in study, the queries were reproduced but the papers classified in fields considered to be out of the scope of this work were removed. After removing the papers classified as being in the fields of Computer Science and/or Engineering and/or Nursing and/or Energy and/or Biochemistry and/or Physics and Astronomy and/or Medicine and/or Chemical Engineering, the number of papers was substantially reduced, as presented in Table 2.

Table 2. Search queries and number of papers found in Scopus after refining the subject field

Terms used in the query	Number of items found
Privacy + Information + Hotel	12
"Information security" + Hotel	3
"Privacy" + Hotel	28
"Privacy requirements" + Hotel	0
"Privacy policy" + Hotel	3
"Privacy policies" + Hotel	3
"Personal information" + Hotel	4
"Personal information" + Hotel + disclosure	1

After combining all the queries (through a OR operator), in order to eliminate the repetition of papers, 28 papers were found and analyzed, allowing for the conclusion that all other queries resulted in a subset of the query Privacy AND Hotel.

The next stage was to read the abstracts in order to eliminate papers that, despite the use of the relevant keywords in their title, abstract or paper keywords, were clearly out of this work's scope. This lead to the exclusion of two papers, leaving 26 papers for a deeper analysis.

The procedure was replicated in the Web-of-Science search portal, making the queries in the "Topic" fields (title, abstract and keywords) and excluding all non-relevant scientific domains (for instance, medicine). The number of papers found is presented in Table 3 and the number of papers found that was not indexed by Scopus is presented in Table 4.

Table 3. Search queries and number of papers found in Web of Science

Terms used in the query	Number of items found
Privacy + Information + Hotel	4
"Information security" + Hotel	3
"Privacy" + Hotel	26
"Privacy requirements" + Hotel	0
"Privacy policy" + Hotel	1
"Privacy policies" + Hotel	1
"Personal information" + Hotel	6
"Personal information" + Hotel + disclosure	1

Table 4. Search queries and number of papers found only in Web of Science

Terms used in the query	Number of new items found
Privacy + Information + Hotel	1
"Information security" + Hotel	0
"Privacy" + Hotel	10
"Privacy requirements" + Hotel	0
"Privacy policy" + Hotel	0
"Privacy policies" + Hotel	0
"Personal information" + Hotel	3
"Personal information" + Hotel + disclosure	0

Once again, after reading the abstracts some papers were excluded for being out-of-scope. For instance, one of the papers was excluded because the search term "hotel" appeared in a reference to the Habbo Hotel, an online social game.

All together 31 papers were analyzed and a few more were found to be out-of-scope for this work, resulting in 22 papers to be reviewed.

On the 22 relevant papers found two studies were made: the first on the scientific domain, through a study of the types of publication, countries of the authors and evolution through time of the number of publications; the second on the contributions of these papers, in order to summarize the respective state-of-art. The obtained results are presented in the next section.

3   Results

3.1   The Evolution of Research on the Topic

With the exception of one paper, that was published in 2000 [4], all other works analyzed were published after 2006, with more than 2/3 (17 papers out of 22) being published in the past six years, which shows an increasing interest in the topic, what

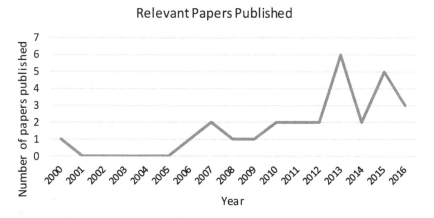

Fig. 1. Evolution on the publication of papers from 2000 to 2016

can also be seen through the tendency of evolution along the years in the number of publications (Fig. 1).

The topic has captured the interest of researchers worldwide, with researchers from thirteen countries and four continents (Africa, America, Asia and Europe) contributing to the development of the knowledge in this field (Fig. 2)[1]. It is also symptomatic that the contributions come from six different scientific domains (Fig. 3)[2].

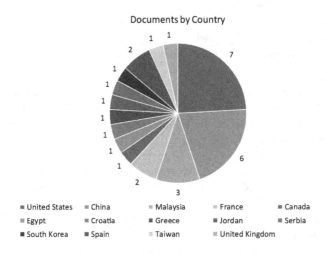

Fig. 2. Papers published by country of origin

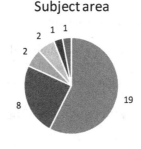

Fig. 3. Subject areas of classification of the papers analyzed

---

[1] Note that some papers have authors from more than one country and some countries are repeated in many papers. Therefore, the sum of number of papers per country is different than the total number of papers analyzed.

[2] Note that some papers are classified in more than one subject area. Therefore, the sum of number of papers in the subject areas is bigger than the total number of papers analyzed.

3.2 Contributions Found

One of the major findings of this literature review is that privacy is a relevant factor for hotels and hospitality in general as a business.

In [6] the author, while arguing that the ethical standards of hotel staff have a fundamental role in the way guests perceive the hotel service, has identified the factors that determine what he calls of questionable job-related behavior. The conclusion was that any perturbation of property or privacy strongly penalizes the guest's perception, especially in female guests. Nevertheless, the hotel clients are willing to stand a certain amount of privacy violation if in turn they feel that they are being well treated. But there is always a limit to the amount of privacy that they are willing to abdicate. In [7] Bakhtier et al. have analyzed the implementation of environmental policies in hotel, a subject that could easily be seen as not related to privacy concerns. But the conclusions are quite different. In general, guests welcome this type of measures and will increase positive Word-of-Mouth (WoM), as long as they don't affect three aspects: privacy, personal preferences and hygiene. So, once again, privacy presents itself as a critical factor of success in the hotel industry. Also in [8] privacy concerns are proven to be critical for this industry, once the authors have concluded not only that information security breaches have a negative impact on client satisfaction and consequent (WoM), but also that promoting hotel achievements in PCI-DSS (Payment Card Industry Data Security Standards) have a positive impact on the clients' future decisions (WoM, decision to return, etc.).

In [9, 10] the authors have analyzed the critical factors of success of SPA (Salute per aqua) facilities, a major income for many hotels, and found that a high level of privacy, both in the treatment rooms as in common spaces, is one of the most important factors for the clients. Privacy in second only to the therapist's qualification and is more important than the price and much more important than the facilities or the SPA product branding.

Even for hostels, privacy is important, once [11] has proved, in a study that combined 20 interviews and 385 questionnaires, that as age increases backpackers increasingly value privacy and are willing to pay for it, what should alter the current hostel business, namely in what relates to room configurations.

Also in [12] the authors have analyzed the importance of Information Security (in general) for four and five stars' hotel and concluded of its relevancy, despite the different approaches/focus in different types of hotel, according both to the number of stars (five stars' hotels tend to focus more in the organizational aspects while four stars' hotels tend to focus more in technical aspects) and to the type of management (local or domestic hotels tend to have proprietary software and focus on the network's penetration resistance and data leakage, while hotels that are part of a hotel chain tend to focus on business continuity aspects).

Also of importance to the hotels' business model is the adoption of technologies, but the willingness of the guests to adopt them is also related to privacy.

In [4] the authors have developed and validated a model for the intention of guests to use Near Field Communication Mobile Payments (NFC-MP), concluding that:

1. There is a negative correlation between general concerns with privacy and the willingness to use NFC-MP in hotels;
2. There is a negative correlation between concerns with privacy in NFC-MP and the willingness to use NFC-MP in hotels;
3. There is a positive correlation between general concerns with privacy and concerns with privacy in NFC-MP;
4. There is a positive correlation between general the perception of security in NFC-MP and the intention to use them;
5. There is a negative correlation between the perception of security in NFC-MP and the privacy concerns with NFC-MP.

Considering this results, the authors recommended that hotel maintain an active communication policy, which should explain, in simple terms, the hotel rules for privacy preservation, the relevant advantages and disadvantages in using NFC-MP, that the credit card number is not stored by the hotel and the steps for the guests to insure privacy in their own devices. In this way, the authors believe that a higher perception of security can be achieved and, through that, a higher adoption of this type of technology.

In [13] the authors have analyzed the conditions of adoption of another type of technology in use in many hotels: self-service services. The conclusions, once again, emphasize privacy as a main factor for adoption, once they have concluded that privacy is a relevant factor in the perception of utility of this types of services. It is also interesting that the authors found, on the other hand, that many guests like to interact with the hotel staff and, therefore, only with a high perception of utility, which implies the existence of privacy gains, they are willing to adopt this type of technologies.

Another important type of technologies for hotels are those related to the Internet, like the website and/or booking platforms. In [14, 15] the studies (one with more than 1000 tourists and the other with 759 Internet users) showed that the client choice of the reservation channel is related to the perception of risk. The clients choose the platform that is perceived has having the lower risk. A similar conclusion arises from [16] where, based on a business analyze, the authors recommend the use of electronic commerce and, for that, the user's experience must be improved, including in the protection of trust and privacy. Also in [17] security and privacy issues are found to be the most important factor for refusal to use online booking platforms, overcoming issues related to usability.

Privacy is also a legal right of the hotel clients in many clients. In [18] Radolovic conclude that the Croatia law does not explicitly protected (2010) the privacy of hotel guests but he has also analyzed the legislation of France, Italy, Germany, United Kingdom and United States of America (USA) and concluded that there are several widely recognized rights, namely:

- The respect of the guest's room privacy: protected in all the mentioned countries;
- Registration under false name for privacy reasons: despite the general obligation of presenting to the hotel the true identity of the guest, the registration under a false name is permitted explicitly by the German law and in the USA is forbidden only in case of obstruction to a criminal inquiry
- Refuse of people/guests in the hotel for security/privacy reasons: permitted in all the mentioned countries

- Discretion of hotel staff: this obligation is presumed in all the mentioned laws, and there are sentenced cases of violation of this obligation.

The author has also identified several situations that are clearly a contractual liability for non-proprietary damage to violation of guest's privacy, namely:

- Intrusion of staff in the guest's room (with exception for emergency situations and cleaning if the "do not disturb" sign is not in the door);
- Release of persons in the guest's room;
- Recording, wiretapping and/or spying
- Giving third parties information about the guests.

The European Union (EU) as also issued a directive on data protection (directive CE 1995/46), that is being adopted/adapted across the EU and that fails to identify specific issues in the hotel business.

In what concerns to the privacy of the hotel room, [19] has even discussed the possibility of providing access to law enforcement agents in the USA. The discussion in centered in the issue of data protection when the client provides information to the service provider (the hotel or the hotel management and/or staff), doing so on his own risk. The authors challenges this commonly accepted idea and concludes that the information that is provided to the hotel, either explicitly or by having it in the hotel room, is not provided voluntarily, but is a *sine qua non* for the contractualization of a service that is absolutely necessary to satisfy the demands of a full life as it is understood today. Being so, the information is not provided because with the base of trust but with the base of need, therefore an eventual leakage is not the result of a misjudgment of the client. The authors concluded in this work that even if the hotel managers have the right to access the rooms of their clients they cannot grant that right to law enforcement only on the basis of collaboration with the authorities.

Considering both the European Union Directive on data protection [20] and the Federal Trade Commission's recommendations (USA) [21], O'Connor [22] analyzed 97 websites of major hotels operating in Europe to study their information gathering and data protection information policies. The author concluded that, despite frequently publishing information on the gathering and use of data, none of the hotels comply with all the existing legal requirements. Most of the websites collects information on name, e-mail address, phone number and title of the potential client, as well as bed preference, smoking preference and room preference. Furthermore, over one third of the hotels collected information on date of birth, credit card number, company name and annual nights in hotels. Less frequent, but still present in over one fourth of the hotels, is the collection of information on job title, language preference and frequent flyer number. All the websites complied with at least one of the categories of privacy practices (notice, choice, onward transfer, access, security, integrity and accountability) but one of them failed at least in complying with one of them. Most of the website comply with the "notice" practice (48% fully complied and 43% partially complied) and most of the websites did not comply with the "onward transfer" practice (72%) and/or with the "access" practice (51%).

The data presented in [22] is even more important when Tinggi et al. [23] concluded that most of the clients have high confidence in the hotels' privacy policies and that there is a revenue advantage in insuring clients' data protection. But this should be taken in consideration by hotels when designing their websites, but this importance to privacy policies is notice essentially in Asian hotels [24].

Despite the proven importance of privacy for the hotel industry, there is a lack of research in the field of privacy requirements and recommendations that can be considered in an information security policy. Other than the framework of the legal obligations and of technical algorithms for information security (that don't belong in an information security police and, therefore, are out of the scope of this work), we found only four papers with these type of recommendations, both for digital information security practices and physical information security practices. As shown in Table 5, the large majority of the analyzed papers are focused on the relevance of privacy for business and/or marketing strategies.

Table 5. Distribution of the analyzed papers by research topic.

Topic	Number of papers
Importance of privacy for the business/marketing strategy	15
Legal aspects	3
Physical and digital requirements to insure privacy	4
Recommendations for privacy related contents for Information Security Policies of hotels (other than legal recommendations/obligations concerning construction/disclosure of privacy policies)	0

In the class of physical information security practices, Dallabona [25] analyzes the different privacy requirements of different parts of the hotels, just like in a home but with the difference of having to consider not only the spatial dimension but also the time dimension. For instance, there is no need for privacy in a hotel room after one guest's check-out and before the next guest occupying that room check-in. Furthermore, there is a kind of privacy invasion, limited in time, when the staff enters the room to clean it. The recommendations of Dallabona are the creation of delimited zones in the common areas (but not with walls), increasing the sensation of privacy; and the use of background music and sound-absorbing materials in the public areas, to increase the level of comfort while increasing the level of auditive privacy, which is related to the privacy of the information being communicated in the conversations that happen in those spaces.

Also in the physical protection of information are the conclusions presented in [26]. The authors have evaluated the factors considered by guests of high star rated hotels as more relevant for the comfort of the rooms, concluding that, among 44 factors considered, the privacy of the guests is ranked in fourth place *ex aequo* with the softness of the bed linen. The second and third more important factors were the quality of the air and the service attitude. And the most important factor for the comfort of the room was the existence of a sound proofing effect, which is related to rest but is also, once again, related to privacy. So, the obvious recommendation for hotel managers of this type of hotels (high stared) is to insure sound proofing of the rooms.

On the digital protection of information privacy, two papers were found: [27] proposes that CCTV (Closed Circuit Television) may be less used in VIP (Very Important People) surveillance, by using agents made invisible through the emerging technology designated as "cloak of invisibility"; finally, Lee et al. [28] have studied the effect of the format of policy statements in websites in the client's trust, concluding that there is an advantage in presenting the document in the form of a video, instead of text, and recommending that those videos should be placed in a relevant part of the website, like the center or the main menu, instead of being relegated to the footnote.

4   Conclusions

From this work it is possible to conclude that privacy is a key aspect in the marketing strategy of the hotel industry, once privacy concerns are related simultaneously to difficulties in acquiring clients through web-based booking platforms (including the hotel own website), to leading the guests to use hotel technologies that represent part of the hotel income, like SPA services and self-service services (mini-bar, vendor machines, etc.), to the perception of comfort of the rooms and to the intention to return to the hotel.

Privacy assurance is also a legal obligation in many countries, with a tendency to become more and more relevant, and, therefore, must also be a business requirement.

Despite the relevance of privacy issues to the business in the hotel industry and despite the increase in this field of research in the past six years all over the world, there is a lot to be done and the current research lacks in indications for the definition of security policies that can, in an effective manner, provide hotel with business continuity assurance, while simultaneously increasing the number of clients, the rate of clients' return, the profit per client and avoiding legal problems related to liability for non-proprietary damage.

The matter of staff training, namely in security awareness and ethical/deontological aspects, is only mentioned in general, stating there the staff should act in a privacy preserving way, which is clearly not enough. There is a need for research both on the development of a deontological code for hotel staff as for training strategies for effective privacy oriented services.

Researchers from the information security fields and from the Hospitality fields, together, should therefore invest on studies that can help the industry to create, implement and publicize adequate information security policies and to align the marketing strategies to the importance of privacy assurance.

Acknowledgments. This work has been supported by COMPETE: POCI-01-0145-FEDER-007043 and FCT – Fundação para a Ciência e Tecnologia within the Project Scope: UID/CEC/00319/2013.

References

1. John, N.A., Peters, B.: Why privacy keeps dying: the trouble with talk about the end of privacy. Inf. Commun. Soc. **20**, 1–15 (2016)
2. Federal Trade Commission: Consumer Sentinel Network Data Book for January–December 2015 (2016)
3. Wang, W.J., Yuan, Y., Archer, N.: A contextual framework for combating identity theft. IEEE Secur. Priv. **4**(2), 30–38 (2006)
4. Basil, M.: Japanese love hotels: protecting privacy for private encounters. In: E-European Advances in Consumer Research, vol. 8 (2007)
5. Morosan, C., DeFranco, A.: Disclosing personal information via hotel apps: a privacy calculus perspective. Int. J. Hosp. Manag. **47**, 120–130 (2015)
6. Wong, S., Keung, C.: Tourists' perceptions of hotel frontline employees' questionable job-related behaviour. Tour. Manag. **21**(2), 121–134 (2000)
7. Bakhtiar, M.F.S., Azdel, A.A., Kamaruddin, M.S.Y., Hamad, N.A.: Perception of environmental strategies in hotels and the influence towards future behavior intention: locals' perspective in Malaysia. In: Theory and Practice in Hospitality and Tourism Research, p. 343 (2014)
8. Berezina, K., et al.: The impact of information security breach on hotel guest perception of service quality, satisfaction, revisit intentions and word-of-mouth. Int. J. Contemp. Hosp. Manag. **24**(7), 991–1010 (2012)
9. Kucukusta, D., Guillet, B.: Measuring spa-goers' preferences: a conjoint analysis approach. Int. J. Hosp. Manag. **41**, 115–124 (2014)
10. Kucukusta, D., Pang, L., Chui, S.: Inbound travelers' selection criteria for hotel spas in Hong Kong. J. Travel Tour. Mark. **30**(6), 557–576 (2013)
11. Hecht, J.-A., Martin, D.: Backpacking and hostel-picking: an analysis from Canada. Int. J. Contemp. Hosp. Manag. **18**(1), 69–77 (2006)
12. Kim, H.-b., Lee, D.-S., Ham, S.: Impact of hotel information security on system reliability. Int. J. Hosp. Manag. **35**, 369–379 (2013)
13. Oh, H., Jeong, M., Baloglu, S.: Tourists' adoption of self-service technologies at resort hotels. J. Bus. Res. **66**(6), 692–699 (2013)
14. Yusta, A.I., Ruiz, M.P.M.: Análisis de los factores que condicionan la elección del canal de compra por parte del consumidor: evidencias empíricas en la industria hotelera. Cuadernos de Economía y Dirección de la Empresa **12**(41), 93–122 (2009)
15. Yusta, A.I., Ruiz, M.P.M., Zarco, A.I.J.: Condicionantes económicos de la adopción de una innovación por parte del consumidor: análisis de la compra de servicios online. Innovar **20**(36), 173 (2010)
16. Azizan, N.A., Said, M.A.A.: The effect of E-eommerce usage of online business performance of hotels. Int. Bus. Manag. **9**(4), 574–580 (2015)
17. Essawy, M.: Egyptians' hotel booking behavior on the internet. Int. J. Hosp. Tour. Adm. **14**(4), 341–357 (2013)
18. Radolović, O.: Hotel guest's privacy protection in tourism business law. Interdisc. Manag. Res. **6**, 699–708 (2010)
19. Brennan-Marquez, K.R.: Fourth Amendment Fiduciaries. Fordham Law Rev. **84**(2) (2015)
20. European Parliament and Council: 95/46/EC of the European parliament and of the council of 24 October 1995 on the protection of individuals with regard to the processing of personal data and on the free movement of such data. Off. J. EC **23**(6) (1995)
21. Federal Trade Commission: Privacy online: fair information practices in the electronic marketplace: a federal trade commission report to congress. FTC, Washington DC (2000)

22. O'Connor, P.: Online consumer privacy an analysis of hotel company behavior. Cornell Hotel Restaur. Adm. Q. **48**(2), 183–200 (2007)
23. Tinggi, M., et al.: Customers? Confidence and trust towards privacy policy: a conceptual research of hotel revenue management. Int. J. Revenue Manag. **5**(4), 350–368 (2011)
24. Ting, P.-H., et al.: Website evaluation of the top 100 hotels using advanced content analysis and eMICA model. Cornell Hosp. Q. **54**(3), 284–293 (2013)
25. Dallabona, A.: At home with the Missoni family: narratives of domesticity within hotel Missoni Edinburgh. Home Cult. **13**(1), 1–21 (2016)
26. Zou, Y., Huang, J.: An importance-performance analysis of influencing factors of guestroom comfort in high star-rated hotels. In: ICSSSM 2012. IEEE (2012)
27. Goh, C.K.L., Law, R.: Applying the "cloak of invisibility" technology to security and privacy in the hotel industry. Int. J. Contemp. Hosp. Manag. **19**(7), 600–605 (2007)
28. Lee, H., Au, N., Law, R.: Presentation formats of policy statements on hotel websites and privacy concerns: a multimedia learning theory perspective. J. Hosp. Tour. Res. (2012). doi:10.1177/1096348012436384

Tor Marketplaces Exploratory Data Analysis: The Drugs Case

Alessandro Celestini[1], Gianluigi Me[2]($^{(\boxtimes)}$), and Mara Mignone[3]

[1] Institute for Applied Computing, IAC-CNR, Via Dei Taurini 19, Rome, Italy
a.celestini@iac.cnr.it
[2] CERSI, Luiss Guido Carli University, Viale Romania 37, Rome, Italy
gme@luiss.it
[3] RISSC, Research Centre on Security and Crime, Via Casoni 2,
36040 Torri di Quartesolo (VI), Italy
mara.mignone@rissc.it

Abstract. The anonymous marketplaces ecosystem represents a new channel for black market/goods and services, offering a huge variety of illegal items. For many darknet marketplaces, the overall sales incidence is not (yet) comparable with the correspondent physical market; however, since it represents a further trade channel, providing opportunities to new and old forms of illegal trade with worldwide customers, anonymous trading should be carefully studied, via regular crawling and data analysis, in order to detect new trends in illegal goods and services (physical and digital), new drug substances and sources and alternative paths to import socially dangerous goods (e.g. drugs, weapons). Such markets, based on e-commerce retail leaders model, e.g. Amazon and E-bay, are designed with ease of use in mind, using off-the-shelf web technologies where users have their own profiles and credentials, acting as sellers, posting offers, or buyers, posting reviews or both. This lead to very poor data quality related to market offers and related, possible feedback, increasing the complexity of extraction of reliable data.

In this paper we present an approaching methodology to crawl and manipulate data for analysis of illicit drugs trade taking place in such marketplaces. We focus our analysis on AlphaBay, Nucleus and East India Company and we will show how to prepare data for the analysis and how to carry on the preliminary data investigation, based on the Exploratory Data Analysis.

Keywords: Tor · Marketplaces · Dark web · Exploratory data analysis

1 Introduction

More than 20 anonymous marketplaces[1] are currently active in the *dark web*, a share of the so-called deep web. Specifically, anonymous marketplaces are mainly implemented as hidden services in The Onion Router (Tor) network,

---

[1] On 9-9-2016, www.deepdotweb.com.

© Springer International Publishing AG 2016
H. Jahankhani et al. (Eds.): ICGS3 2017, CCIS 630, pp. 218–229, 2016.
DOI: 10.1007/978-3-319-51064-4_18

an overlay network providing anonymity to its users. The Tor network reroutes user's connection through multiple anonymous servers (onion routers), masking the original IP address of the user. Anonymity of both administrators and participants is ensured by the use of different technologies: electronic payments are carried out through the use of the virtual *cryptocurrencies* (Bitcoin is the most popular of near 100 cryptocurrencies), *Tor* is used for network communication and the *Pretty Good Privacy (PGP)* cryptosystem is often used to exchange e-mails. Darknet marketplaces operate on the same model as eBay, with three main actors: *vendors, buyers* (both *participants* of the Marketplace) and *market administrators*, taking a 5–10% cut of each sale and providing the web-platform, the escrow service and the basic rules under which all market participants must operate. Active running marketplaces are continuously varying in number, due to scams or taking downs, offering a plethora of illegal goods services, e.g. weapons, drugs, pharmaceuticals, C&C systems, digital identities, counterfeited goods, contraband. In particular, according to the Global Drug Survey[2], online markets still account for a small share of illicit drug sales, although they are growing fast and turnover has risen from an estimated $15m–17m in 2012 to $150m–180m in 2015.

In spite of both the escrow and feedback systems (like those in Amazon and eBay), where buyers rate their purchases and leave comments to help to choose a trustworthy supplier, scams are not rare between vendors and buyers, and among administrators and users (both vendors and buyers): in this case, administrators quit&close the marketplace (so called *exit scam*), frauding the users by keeping their escrowed money, as in the case of Evolution marketplace, disappeared in March 2015 with $12m-worth of customers Bitcoin. The frauds enabling factor, as in the most cases of digital and real life, is based on the basis of social engineering techniques, relying on the trustful, sometimes naive, behavior of the ICT user, which can easily access TOR and marketplaces due to popular *GUI's look and feel*. In fact, the success of darknet marketplaces has been facilitated by the development of usable interfaces to anonymous networks, (e.g. the "Tor browser bundle") that made it easy for anybody to browse the Internet anonymously. Moreover, anonymous marketplaces integrate many structural features of popular web marketplaces, providing a searchable listings of products for sale where buyers are leave feedback on their purchases, regardless of the trustworthiness of the comments posted by other users. Consequently, many vendors are taking the risks of shipping internationally and we can expect this trend to continue moving forward with the expansion of cryptomarkets, as shown in [14]. Based on the above-mentioned facts TOR marketplaces can be considered outsiders in the market drug, offering a new sales channel very hard/expensive to cope with in the single transaction: therefore, the importance of the preventive approach by monitoring the activities on cryptomarkets, enables the early warning on changes in the evolution of drug use in different countries and prepares the development of prevention programs that target the drugs being sold.

---

[2] https://www.globaldrugsurvey.com/wp-content/uploads/2016/06/TASTER-KEY-FINDINGS-FROM-GDS2016.pdf.

2   Related Works

Several recent works focused on the study of Internet organised crime [1,15], in particular the study of on-line drugs marketplaces [11,12] has become quite popular, e.g. focusing on the analysis of vendors' behavior [8] or identifying new challenges for LEAs [4].

Soska and Christin in [14] present an analysis of the anonymous marketplace ecosystem evolution. Their study is a long-term measurement analysis: in more than two years, they collected data from 16 different marketplaces, without focusing on a specific products' category. With respect to this work, our study focuses on illicit drugs trade, setting a short-term analysis on a reduced set of marketplaces. The results of their study suggest that marketplaces are quite resilient to law enforcement take-downs and large-scale frauds. They also evidence that the majority of the products being sold belongs to the drugs category. Several research works about anonymous marketplaces focuses on Silk Road, in particular on the drug selling: in [9,10] the authors present interesting studies about Silk Road user's experiences, in both cases the analysis concerned drug purchasing. In [10] they monitored and observed the market's forum for four months and collected anonymous on-line interviews of adult 'Silk Road' users. In [9] they present a single case study, reporting the motivations, experiences and usage of the website of a single 'Silk Road' user. Christin in [5] presents a comprehensive analysis of the Silk Road marketplace. For the study the author gathered and analyzed data over eight months, obtaining a detailed picture of the type of goods being sold. The analysis, among the others results, shows that Silk Road was mainly used as a market for controlled substances and narcotics. In [7,13] a similar study has been done for Silk Road 2, a new marketplace launched to replace Silk Road after its shut down in October 2013 by the FBI. The main objective of these works is to compare the two markets, the old one e the new one, in particular the authors analysed the structure of the two markets and the typology of their users. The authors of [3] analyze consumer motivations for accessing marketplaces and the factors associated with their use. They recruited an Australian national sample that was asked about purchasing substances from dark net marketplaces and the reasons for doing so. In [2] the authors present an overview of the Canadian illicit drug market, providing information about how vendors are diversifying and replicating across marketplaces. Their study gives an insight into the structure and organization of distribution networks existing online. They collected data about listings and vendor profiles on eight anonymous marketplaces between August and September 2014.

3   System Description

The typical structure of anonymous marketplaces offer a list of products and their individual pages where authorized vendors can set up a virtual shop and place listings. Items for sale are organized in categories and subcategories, the organization vary from market to market, but there is large agreement on mains product categories (e.g. drugs, weapons, frauds). Usually it is possible to search products for sale both by product categories and by keywords, but the last option is not always available. Buyers and sellers are able to leave feedback about their transactions, these are usually composed of a rating (e.g., good/bad or a value between 0 and 5), a comment and the obfuscated user' nickname who leaves the feedback. Such information are used to construct users' reputations inside the market both as sellers and as buyers. The main difference with surface market is the regulation of market access: users accounts of anonymous marketplaces are needed not only to carry out transactions, but they are required to access the market itself, this isn't true for surface markets.

For our analysis we focused our attention on three marketplaces: AlphaBay, Nucleus and East India Company. The Nucleus market[3] was established on November 24, 2014, the AlphaBay[4] market was established on December 22, 2014 and the East India Company[5] market was established on April 28, 2015. Two of these three markets are not anymore active, only AlphaBay is reachable and active, the shut down of Nucleus and East India Company have been reported as cases of exit scam by market administrators. In such cases, administrators lock users' funds on the market, taking as much money as possible just to shut down the market soon after. The shut down of Nucleus was quite unexpected because it was one of the major market with AlphaBay and largely trusted by users.

For the creation of our dataset we crawled regularly the three marketplaces, visiting each market every month for four months. We focused our attention on illegal drug trade, collecting all items' pages concerning drugs and their related images. Gathered data form a dataset of 36 GB in size, each crawl of each market ranged from 1,682 to 18,831 pages/images, and crawling time took from several hours up to few days. For each market we designed and implemented a custom spider using the *scrapy*[6] framework, spiders are configured to use Tor [6] in order to have the capability of reaching anonymous marketplaces. Figure 1 shows the logical workflow of our system for the collection, elaboration and analysis of anonymous marketplaces data.

3.1 Spiders

The crawling of anonymous marketplaces raises several challenges, such as the login and session cookies management, the avoidance of undesired actions execution and the monitoring of requests frequency. As described below, we designed and implemented our spiders trying to face all these challenges.

For each marketplace we created an account, which is mandatory to enter any marketplace. Since our spiders are able to authenticate them-self and to

---

[3] nucleusoitxmebfx.onion.

[4] pwoah7oh4jlgdwri.onion.

[5] g4c35ipwiutqccly.onion.

[6] Scrapy: A Fast and Powerful Scraping and Web Crawling Framework http://scrapy. org.

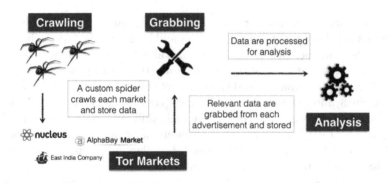

Fig. 1. System workflow

manage session cookies, the crawling of the marketplace after authentication is automatic. In particular, only the login phase is supervised, indeed in most marketplaces a CAPTCHA is used to protect login form, and often a double check is required by the market web site. A first CAPTCHA is used for bot exclusion and protects the login page, a second CAPTCHA protects the login procedure. We manually resolve CAPTCHA and provides to spiders the session cookies obtained. After authentication each spider is able to manage session cookies and automatically crawl each market. Concerning requests frequency, in order to not overwhelm marketplaces with requests, we fix a random interval for each request to each marketplace. Thus, spiders request pages with different waiting times between each request, we also deny the possibility of sending concurrent request to marketplaces, clearly these precautions increases the crawling time for each market. Such settings are natively supported by *scrapy*, and we resort on them for spiders' configuration. Finally, in order to prevent undesired actions execution, such as adding items to cart or sending messages, each spider is designed to request only URL of interest. Specifically, we crawl only listings' pages and items' pages. Spiders scrape listing pages to collect items' pages URL, but they store only item's pages, together with items' images.

In order to check the outcome and accuracy of each crawling we proceed as follows: first, we manually check the number of items for sale available in each section of each market. Then, for each crawl we record all the url of items for sale in each section of each market found by spiders. Finally we count the number of item's pages gathered by each spider. If these three values coincide we are reasonable sure of the completeness of our crawling.

3.2   Data Grabbing and Reduction to Table

From each item's page we extract the information necessary to fulfill the table fields reported in Table 1. To grab such information we take advantage of the HTML structure of each page. A generic HTML page is enclosed in a main <html> tag and divided in two sections identified by the tags <head> and <body>. Tags inside the <body> contain information we look for, the data

Table 1. Extracted fields

Field Name	Field Type	Field Name	Field Type
name	text	product_type	text
vendor_name	text	description	text
quantity_g	decimal	product_review	text
price_bc	decimal	refund_policy	text
marketplace	text	shipping_options	text
index	int	quantity_t	text
escrow	tinyint	price_t	varchar
payment	text	ships_from	text
date_visti	date	ships_to	text
raw_material	tinyint	url	text

we want to extract are enclosed in different tags at different level of the HTML structure. Every single marketplace has a different tree structure of HTML pages, thus we implemented a customized parser for each marketplace:hence, the related parser identifies the nodes within the Document Object Model (DOM), through a Xpath selector.

The objective of data grabbing is to *reduce* items advertisement to *tuple*, containing the relevant field for the analysis, as shown in the following Table 1. Actually, the most valuable fields, with regard to the outcomes presented in this paper, are related to shipments, as the <shipping_option, ships_from, ships_to>.

3.3 Why the User Feedback Field Has Not Been Included

While several characteristics of electronic markets serve to facilitate trade, online transactions also involve greater uncertainty and increased opportunities for fraud. Unlike buyers in traditional settings, online customers are physically unable to inspect products for sale and must rely on pictures and descriptions provided by the seller (information asymmetry). Buyers can determine the quality of a product only when they receive it, after the purchase has been made, thus sellers have less incentive to provide high quality products (e.g. lemons market). Electronic marketplaces like eBay have attempted to reduce fraud and assess sellers' reliability by allowing participants to post feedback about their transactions (signal). Tor marketplaces are characterized by higher information asymmetry: illegal trade of goods/services reinforces information asymmetry due to the poor reliability of the criminal activity of the vendor, increasing the fraud risk. Online legal markets (e.g. eBay) try to protect customers with signals like vendor reputation (feedback), but such mechanisms do not completely protect from fraud. Tor Marketplaces replicate these mechanisms and reinforce them by offering escrow services and sometimes, by denying the *finalized early* (pay the goods before shipping) option. However, several examples show that even vendors with high reputation scores decide for exit scam (e.g. 9THWonder). In conclusion, non-negligible fake feedback reviews rate, exit scams and out-of-marketplace finalization of transaction pose several doubts to the reliability of feedbacks as a metric to estimate vendors sales volume and her/his reliability, considering that every single purchase can be a black swan event.

4   Data Preparation

The marketplace mechanism to place offers makes the overall raw dataset quality very poor. In fact, every vendor can place his offer regardless of almost any input data check, leading to the creation of empty or duplicated offers (in the raw dataset), mistakes in key-text fields, and non-uniform metrics/currencies. Moreover, the offers can be misplaced in the different categories, leading to mismatching the overall amounts of offers. Hence, for the above mentioned reasons, the data preparation phase assumes a strategic role in order to achieve correct analysis results. Former phase relies on *data scrubbing*, also called *data cleansing*, which is the process of correcting or removing data in a dataset that is incorrect, inaccurate, incomplete, improperly formatted, or duplicated. The result of the data analysis process not only depends on the algorithms, it also depends on the quality of the data, that is why the accuracy of the data scrubbing process is crucial after data collection. Hence, in order to avoid dirty data, the dataset should be characterized by *correctness, completeness, accuracy, consistency and uniformity*. Dirty data (e.g. outliers) can be detected by applying statistical data validation methods and by parsing texts, deleting duplicate values and missing data contribute to bad analysis results. After the collected dataset has been loaded into the data preparation database, containing all the raw data to be manipulated, some statistical methods have been applied to find values that are unexpected and thus erroneous, even if the data type match but the values are out of the range, it can be resolved by setting the values to an average, Median, and Range Constraints.

Resuming, the data preparation phases applied to the raw dataset are:

- *Data cleansing and wrangling* represents a core process in this work to prepare data, which are directly inserted by vendors without strong data validation constraints. In this phase incomplete, incorrect, inaccurate, irrelevant, etc. parts of the data are replaced, modified or deleted. In fact, offer attributes as <weight>, <price> and <description> can be found in different metrics (e.g. ounce, gram or BTC, LTC, USD).
- *Data Transformation*, where the mapping of the data from its given format into the format expected by the analysis tool. This phase includes value conversions or translation functions, as well as normalizing numeric values to conform to minimum and maximum values;
- *Data Exploration*, applying Exploratory Data Analysis (EDA) which represents a critical part of the data analysis process because it helps us to detect mistakes, determine relationships and tendencies, or check assumptions;

– *Modeling*, which represents the most important stage in the analysis with selection, application, evaluation of results and possibly model tuning;
– *Visualize and interpret results*, which represents the key phase to let the results understandable, improving their overall impact.

Data cleansing, wrangling and exploration phases have been implemented by the use of Rapidminer[7].

The above mentioned data collection and preparation processes have been carried out in order to answer the following questions:

1. How many offers (overall/Novel Psychoactive Substances)?
2. How many vendors?
3. Where do they ship from?(Possible drug stocking place)
4. Which is the world share distribution?
5. Which is the European countries' distribution map?
6. Which market share of the overall categories is holding the half of offering vendors?
7. How many possible scams?
8. Which vendors are cross-sellers on categories?

The following preliminary indicators fulfill the above requirements, putting EDA in practice and supporting for data cleansing and wrangling:

– *Offers*: the overall number of offers considered (1)
– *Number of Vendors*: the overall number of vendors (2)
– *Median*: the value of the number of offers of the vendor splitting halfway into the set of vendors
– *Offers to median*: overall number of offers to median value
– *Market polarization* (%):

$$MP = \frac{\text{offers to median}}{\sum \text{offers}}$$

– *Possible scam* (%): the ratio between the number of vendors offering one or two items and the total number of vendors (7)
– *European share* (%): the ratio between the European offers and the total amount of offers

Although in the following section the authors will present some sample charts, the overall results analysis is out of the scope of this paper.

5   Data Analysis

The obtained dataset is ready for EDA, providing results (presented in this paper only in a sample) in the form of both uni and multi-variate graphical statistics. We used EDA to extract important variables, discover underlying structure in

---

[7] https://rapidminer.com.

order to further develop appropriate models. One limit of this methodology is related to the reliability of the offers, since the only way to verify if an offer is a fake or a scam is to proceed with the purchase of the item and wait the shipment. During data exploration we recognized vendors with high-volume of offers in different markets, we can assume that these are not fake vendors (although we can never avoid the scam), while nothing can be said about vendors with low-volume of offers. Hence, we assumed that fake offers can be placed by vendors with less than 3 different offers, as shown in Sect. 4.

As shown in Fig. 2, the most recurrent offers on the Eastindia, Nucleus and Alphabay markets are in the cannabis category (natural, not synthetic), followed by the ecstasy and stimulants categories. This ranking is repeated individually for the three markets, showing which are the most requested substances in each market.

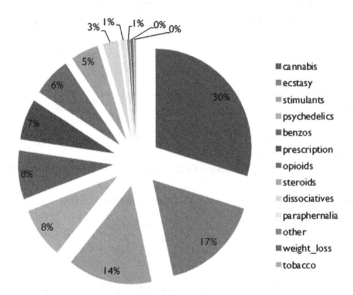

Fig. 2. Overall shares of drugs market

The Fig. 3 shows, for Eastindia market, which are the top European countries labeled as shipping departure places for drugs. These data are mostly reliable due to the fact that shipping expenses change with respect to the destination continent/country. Moreover, from these data we can infer what is the country where the item is located, while nothing can be said regarding vendor's location (which in many cases resides in the shipping source).

Finally, in Fig. 4 small bubbles indicate low number of countries selling items in the related category. Showing that *cannabis, stimulants, benzodiazepines* and *opioids* offers are widespread all around the world, probably related to facilitated access to the substances, while *prescription, steroids, tobacco* and

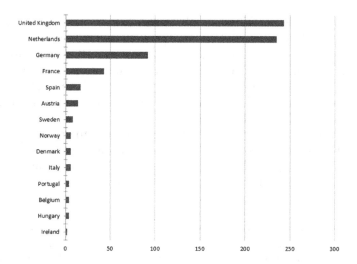

Fig. 3. Eastindia offers by origin country

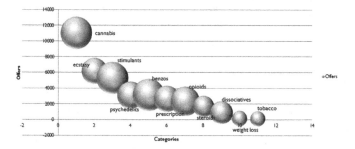

Fig. 4. Categories size vs cross market vendors

weightloss are concentrated in few countries, probably related to facilitating legal framework. Ecstasy represents an anomaly with a very high number of offers concentrated on average number of countries, but most of the offers are from the Netherlands.

6   Conclusions

Illegal trading sites on the Darknet represent cross-cutting crime enablers. In particular, recent studies [8] showed that drug market represents the biggest offers share in every TOR marketplace, due to reinforced motivation provided by the greater anonymity afforded by the Tor Network. The huge size of the listings enables multiple trading opportunities, e.g. retailing (dealer-to-customer transactions). Since the impact of these new dynamics in the overall drug market (or in some categories/segments) is not yet completely clear, monitoring trends and behaviors represent a crucial cornerstone to cope with this phenomenon, as confirmed, e.g., by the marketplace take-downs (e.g. operation Onymous), not representing an effective response to this phenomenon, since the underground community regularly recovers to some degree, showing resiliency to this counter-measure. In order to determine characteristics of vendors, substances, countries and prices and to determine significant differences in trends among all these drug offers features, we presented a methodology to automatically surf and prepare data from offers on Tor marketplaces in order to target a preliminary EDA on drug offers data and, consequently, providing hypothesis to drive further refined analysis of the phenomenon. In fact, our ultimate, ambitious objective is to understand the underlying *modus operandi* and to detect criminal mechanisms representing the base of the illicit drugs trade phenomenon taking place in the Tor marketplaces.

Acknowledgement. This work has been supported by the Drug Prevention and Information Programme of the European Union under the EPS/NPS Project -Enhancing Police Skills concerning Novel Psychoactive Substances, with the financial support of the European Commission – Targeted call on cross border law enforcement cooperation in the field of drug trafficking – DG Justice/DG Migrations and Home Affairs (grant JUST/2013/ISEC/DRUGS/AG/6429). The authors would like to thank Dr. Mara Mginone and RISSC EPS-NPS researchers for supporting this work with discussions and ideas.

References

1. The internet organised crime threat assessment (IOCTA). Technical report, EUROPOL (2015)
2. Brosus, J., Rhumorbarbe, D., Mireault, C., Ouellette, V., Crispino, F., Dcary-Htu, D.: Studying illicit drug trafficking on darknet markets: structure and organisation from a Canadian perspective. Forensic. Sci. Int. **264**, 7–14 (2016). Special Issue on the 7th European Academy of Forensic Science Conference
3. Buskirk, J.V., Roxburgh, A., Bruno, R., Naicker, S., Lenton, S., Sutherland, R., Whittaker, E., Sindicich, N., Matthews, A., Butler, K., Burns, L.: Characterising dark net marketplace purchasers in a sample of regular psychostimulant users. Int. J. Drug Policy **35**, 32–37 (2016)
4. Buxton, J., Bingham, T.: The rise and challenge of dark net drug markets. Policy Brief 7 (2015)
5. Christin, N.: Traveling the Silk Road: a measurement analysis of a large anonymous online marketplace. In: Proceedings of the 22nd International Conference on World Wide Web, WWW 2013, pp. 213–224. ACM, New York (2013)
6. Dingledine, R., Mathewson, N., Syverson, P.: Tor: the second-generation onion router. Technical report, DTIC Document (2004)
7. Dolliver, D.S.: Evaluating drug trafficking on the tor network: Silk Road 2, the sequel. Int. J. Drug Policy **26**(11), 1113–1123 (2015)
8. Dolliver, D.S., Kenney, J.L.: Characteristics of drug vendors on the Tor network: a cryptomarket comparison. Victims & Offenders, pp. 1–21 (2016)
9. Hout, M.C.V., Bingham, T.: 'Silk Road', the virtual drug marketplace: a single case study of user experiences. Int. J. Drug Policy **24**(5), 385–391 (2013)

10. Hout, M.C.V., Bingham, T.: 'Surfing the Silk Road': a study of users experiences. Int. J. Drug Policy **24**(6), 524–529 (2013)
11. Laura, L., Me, G.: Searching the web for illegal content: the anatomy of a semantic search engine. In: Jahankhani, H., Carlile, A., Akhgar, B., Taal, A., Hessami, A.G., Hosseinian-Far, A. (eds.) ICGS3 2015. CCIS, vol. 534, pp. 113–122. Springer, Heidelberg (2015). doi:10.1007/978-3-319-23276-8_10
12. Mignone, M., Bosio, E.: Criminological analysis of the NPS market. Technical report RISSC (2016)
13. Munksgaard, R., Demant, J., Branwen, G.: A replication and methodological critique of the study "Evaluating drug trafficking on the Tor network". Int. J. Drug Policy **35**, 92–96 (2016)
14. Soska, K., Christin, N.: Measuring the longitudinal evolution of the online anonymous marketplace ecosystem. In: 24th USENIX Security Symposium (USENIX Security 2015), pp. 33–48 (2015)
15. Thomas, K., Huang, D., Wang, D., Bursztein, E., Grier, C., Holt, T.J., Kruegel, C., McCoy, D., Savage, S., Vigna, G.: Framing dependencies introduced by underground commoditization. In: Workshop on the Economics of Information Security (2015)

User Acceptance of Information Technology: A Critical Review of Technology Acceptance Models and the Decision to Invest in Information Security

Patrice Seuwou$^{(\boxtimes)}$, Ebad Banissi, and George Ubakanma

School of Engineering, Division of Computing and Informatics,
London South Bank University, London, UK
{seuwoup, banisse, george.ubakanma}@lsbu.ac.uk

Abstract. In today's fast changing world, technology is increasingly influencing and having a major impact on all aspect of our daily life. For decades, the user acceptance of technology has been a vital field of study. Despite numerous models being proposed to explain and predict the use of a system or to assist in decision making to invest in information security, the latest models and theories are still not been able to fully capture the complexity of the relationship between humans and technology. This paper provides a historical overview and a critical review of technology acceptance models (TAM) and theories. It also explores external variables influencing information security investment. It is concluded that although TAM and associated theories are well-established concepts in the information systems community, further research will be required to capture other important elements influencing public acceptance of technology which are not currently represented in existing models.

Keywords: Technology acceptance model · Unified theory of acceptance and use of technology · Theory of reasoned action · Information security · IT decision making

1 Introduction

In the field of Information Systems, it is known that information technology is underutilised in many organisations producing massive financial losses. Information technology acceptance and use is a subject that has attracted practitioners as well as researchers for several decades. Their interest is about exploring the models and theories that demonstrate potential in explaining and predicting behaviour across various fields. The aim of their studies is mainly to investigate how to promote usage and also examine the barriers obstructing usage and intention to use technology. It can be observed that a number of social and psychological factors influence the interaction between humans and technology. Therefore, due to the complexities involved in predicting human behaviour, several studies have generated a variety of models and theories to assist in explaining patterns of adoption and use of technologies.

© Springer International Publishing AG 2016
H. Jahankhani et al. (Eds.): ICGS3 2017, CCIS 630, pp. 230–251, 2016.
DOI: 10.1007/978-3-319-51064-4_19

Each noticeable technology acceptance model or theory which has not been superseded by more recent research has different properties and benefits. It is therefore essential to study them intentionally, since it is expected that theoretical concepts from these theories will help to provide a sound basis for the theoretical framework for creating a research model that could properly demonstrate the acceptance of technology. This paper provides a critical review of the prominent technology acceptance works. This review identifies major technology acceptance models and theories in order to make explicit their major assumptions. Furthermore, we also discuss the external variables influencing decisions to invest in information security.

2 Concept Underling User Acceptance

In an attempt to explain system use, various academics initially developed tools for analysing and measuring computer user satisfaction. As highlighted by Bailey and Pearson in 1983 [1], it was logical to look for answers from psychologists who spent a great deal studying satisfaction. Presently, user acceptance can be defined as the demonstrable willingness within a user group to employ information technology for the tasks it is designed to support [1]. Thus, the concept is not being applied to situations in which users claim they will employ it without providing evidence of use, or to the use of a technology for purposes unintended by designers or procurers. Observably, there is a degree of fuzziness here since actual usage is always likely to deviate slightly from idealized, planned usage. The principle of user acceptance theory is that such deviations are not significant; that is, the process of user acceptance of any information technology for intended purposes can be predicted and modelled. Indeed, on several instances, users are not willing to use information systems which if used will produce remarkable performance gains. Thus, user acceptance has been regarded as the central factor in determining the failure or success of any information system project. Several technology acceptance models have been developed in the past and they all follow the very same concept. Figure 1 below illustrates the basic concept underlying user acceptance models and theories. They each have their own specific characteristics which will be reviewed and discussed in chronological order.

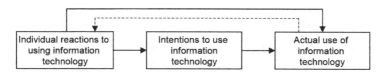

Fig. 1. Basic concept underlying user acceptance models [2]

3 Acceptance Models Historical Timeline

3.1 Theory of Reasoned Action

The theory of reasoned action (TRA) originates from learning theory and assumes that behaviour toward a specific object is approximated by an intention to perform that behaviour. The model was developed by Ajzen and Fishbein initially in 1975 and then in 1980 as an improvement over information integration theory [3–5]. It integrated various studies on attitudes from social psychology with the aim of developing an integrated conceptual framework to explain and predict an individual's behaviour towards adoption in a broad situational setting. The originators of this theory suggested that an individual's behavioural intention is the direct determinant of behaviour, their attitude and their subjective norm are facilitated through behavioural intention and their behavioural and normative beliefs are mediated through attitude and subjective norm. The TRA model can be seen as one of the earlier prediction models, but was not specifically aimed at the acceptance of technology, although it operated as a starting point for technology acceptance models [5]. TRA was adopted in several studies and is a strong predictor of actual behaviour in different locations, but it has been criticised since it does not take into consideration the individual's ability to control [6]. Figure 2 below shows the Theory of Reasoned Action model.

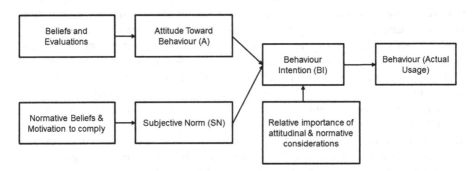

Fig. 2. Theory of Reasoned Action (TRA) [4]

3.2 Social Cognitive Theory

The social cognitive theory (SCT) was introduced by Albert Bandura in 1986. It states that learning occurs in a social context with a dynamic and reciprocal interaction of environmental factors, personal factors, and behaviours [7]. This theory is used in psychology, communication and education. It embraces portions of an individual's knowledge acquisition that can be directly related to observing others within the context of experiences, outside media influences, and social interactions. Furthermore, it posits that social environment in which behaviour is developed is considered when users acquire and maintain behaviour. It gives prominence to the concept of self-efficacy [8]. The theory speculates that people remember the sequence of events and use the information to guide following behaviours when they observe a model performing behaviour and the consequences of that behaviour. The social cognitive theory suggests that personal factors, behaviours and environmental factors are determined reciprocally [9]. SCT is a theory with emphasis on social influence and on external and internal social reinforcement which are its unique features. However, some of its limitations include the fact that it assumes changes in the person will automatically be led by changes in the environment, which may not always be true. Furthermore, SCT massively concentrates on processes of learning therefore disregards hormonal and biological predispositions that may have an impact on behaviours, irrespective of past experience and expectations. Figure 3 below shows, the social cognitive theory.

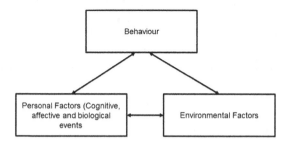

Fig. 3. Social Cognitive Theory (SCT) [7]

3.3 Technology Acceptance Model

Technology Acceptance Model (TAM) was developed by Davis in 1989. TAM was introduced to help in predicting technology usage behaviour. It was an adaptation of the TRA and specifically tailored for modelling user acceptance of information systems. Its goal was to provide an explanation of the constructs of computer acceptance which is generally also capable of explaining user behaviour across a broad range of end-user computing technologies and the population [5]. Figure 4 below shows Technology Acceptance Model.

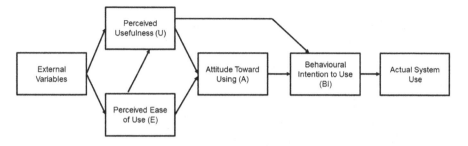

Fig. 4. Technology Acceptance Model (TAM) [5]

Two significant factors are perceived ease of use and perceived usefulness. Shroff stated system developers can have better control over users' beliefs about the system by manipulating these two determinants. Therefore enabling the ability to predict their behavioural intention and actual usage of the system [10]. TAM provided an explanation of the constructs of technology acceptance that made possible an explanation of user behaviour across an extensive scope of end-user information technologies and user populations [5]. As opposed to TRA, subjective norms are not included in TAM because of the weak psychometric results which are generated [5, 11]. The TAM system can be seen as a theoretical foundation for a number of different technology acceptance models, which are following different streams of technology acceptance research. One of these streams leads to models that are slightly modified or extended models of the TAM with a number of added determinants to come to a more accurate prediction within a specific setting. Other streams of research are aimed to be more unified and thereby making use of some of the TAM determinants. In a critical review of TAM, it was found that TAM is a useful theoretical model to understand and explain usage behaviour in IT implementation, [12] although many scholars have criticised this model for not including subjective norms.

3.4   Theory of Planned Behavior

The Theory of Planned Behaviour (TPB) is a theory that links behaviour and beliefs. This concept was introduced by Ajzen [13] to improve on some of the limitations of the theory of reasoned action (TRA) with the introduction of perceived behaviour. The theory examined the factors of subjective norms, attitude, perceived behavioural control, and intentions on actual behaviour. It was then concluded that TPB had a superior ability to predict behaviour that TRA [14, 15]. Figure 5 below shows the theory of planned behaviour.

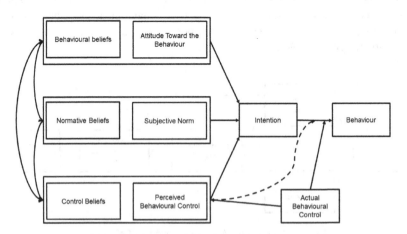

Fig. 5. Theory of Planned Behaviour (TPB) diagram [16]

Ajzen argued that some behaviour that is not under a person's volitional control might be problematic due to the differences in individuals' abilities and in external forces. It is noticeable people are expected to carry out their intentions when the opportunity arises once when given a sufficient degree of actual control over their behaviour that when given a sufficient degree of actual control over their behaviour, people are expected to carry out their intentions when the opportunity arises. Some examples of studies that can be conducted with TPB include whether to check oneself for disease and whether to wear a seat belt. Therefore, it has been concluded that TPB has a superior ability to predict behaviour than TRA [14, 15].

3.5   Model of PC Utilization (MPCU)

Thompson, Higgin and Howell in 1991 established MPCU to explain problems of PC utilization. According to them, "Behaviour is determined by what people would like to do (attitudes), what they think they should do (social norms), what they have usually done (habits), and by the expected consequences of their behaviour" [17]. This model resulted from Individual Behaviours model by Triandis in 1971 [18]. The Individual Behaviours model held that factors determining one's behaviours included attitudes, social norm, habits and expected results of the behaviours. Attitudes cover cognitive, affective and behavioural components. In MPCU factors affecting PC utilisation include perceived consequences, effect, social factors and facilitating conditions. Perception results cover complexity, job fitness and long-term consequences. Thompson et al. in 1991 conducted empirical studies of knowledge workers in the manufacturing industry [17]. The findings show only society, complexity, job fitness and long-term results have significant influence on PC utilization. Though MPCU relations were not proved to exist, scholars still had gained valuable studies based on the MPCU framework (Fig. 6).

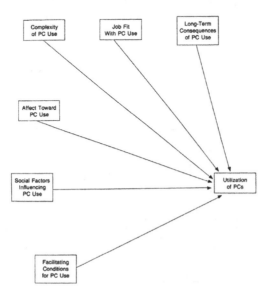

Fig. 6. The Model of PC utilization [17]

3.6   Motivation Model (MM)

Davis et al. in 1992 apply motivational theory to study information technology adoption and use [19]. The Motivation Model suggests that extrinsic and intrinsic motivations are the basis of individuals' behaviour. Extrinsic motivation can be defined as the perception that users want to perform an activity "because it is perceived to be instrumental in achieving valued outcomes that are distinct from the activity itself, such as improved job performance, pay, or promotions" [19]. The perceived ease of use, perceived usefulness and subjective norm are examples of extrinsic motivation. In this model, enjoyment and computer playfulness are determinants of intrinsic motivation [19, 20] and perceived ease of use, perceived usefulness, and subjective norm are constructs of extrinsic motivation. This model is based on the psychological sides of technology acceptance and has supported the general motivation theory as an explanation for behaviour.

3.7   Innovative Diffusion Theory (IDT)

Innovations Diffusion Theory (IDT) has been used since the 1950s to describe the innovation-decision process. It studies why, how, and at what rate new thoughts and technology spread through cultures. The theory has progressively evolved until the best well-known innovation-decision process was introduced by Rogers [21–24]. IDT applies not just in information technology exclusively, but also to other diffusion processes throughout society such as the acceptance of new technological products, dressing style, music style, food, principles, political candidates, or services. Disciplines such as education, sociology, communication, agriculture, marketing, and information technology amongst other have seen the application of research on the diffusion of innovation [23, 25, 26]. Theoretically, there is no explicit relation between the diffusion of innovation perspective and TAM, but both share important determinants. Some findings shows that the relative advantage construct in IDT is similar to the

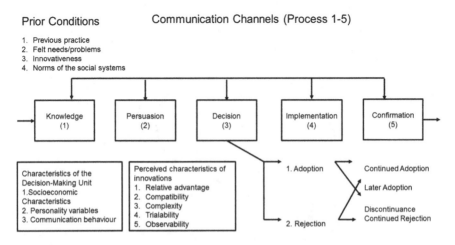

Fig. 7. A model of stages in the innovation-decision process [23]

notion of the PU in TAM, and the complexity construct in IDT captures the PEU in the technology acceptance model, although the sign is the opposite [27]. Figure 7 shows a model of stages in the Innovation-Decision Process.

3.8 Decomposed Theory of Planned Behavior (DTPB)

In 1995, Taylor and Todd introduced the Decomposed TPB (DTPB) also known as Combined TAM-TPB. DTPB was developed by linking the predictors of TPB with the determinant of perceived usefulness and ease of use from TAM [28, 29]. The theory explores the dimensions of subjective norm (i.e., social influence), attitude belief, and perceived behavioural control by decomposing them into specific belief dimensions [30]. DTPB proposes that behavioural intention is the main direct construct of behaviour. Attitude is decomposed to be influenced by perceived usefulness (relative advantage), perceived ease of use (complexity) and compatibility. The normative belief structure is affected by peer influence and superior influence. The control belief structure is affected by self-efficacy and facilitating conditions. Therefore, it seemed to have more capability in explaining usage behaviour although it is a less parsimonious theory when compared to TPB. Figure 8 below illustrates the decomposed theory of planned behaviour.

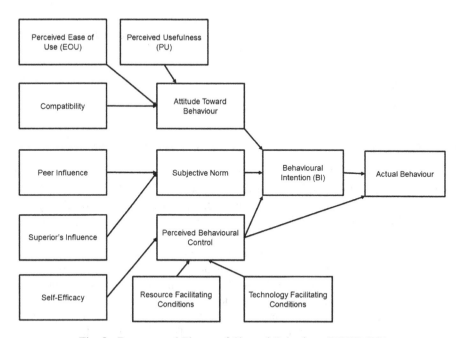

Fig. 8. Decomposed Theory of Planned Behaviour (DTPB) [30]

3.9 Technology Acceptance Model 2 (TAM2)

Venkatesh and Davis introduced TAM2 in 2000 as a theoretical extension of Technology Acceptance Model (TAM). This model included additional key constructs of TAM that explain perceived usefulness and usage intensions in terms of cognitive instrumental processes and social influence. Furthermore, it helped to understand how the effects of these constructs change with an increasing user experience of the target system over time. TAM2 keeps the concept of perceived ease of use from the original TAM as a direct construct influencing the perceived usefulness. All of these additional elements are believed to affect the acceptance of technology (Fig. 9).

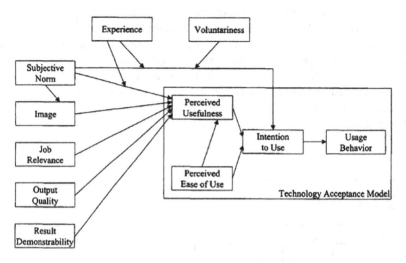

Fig. 9. TAM2 – Extension of TAM [31]

3.10 Unified Theory of Acceptance and Use of Technology (UTAUT)

In 2003, Venkatesh et al. introduced UTAUT which resulted from the integration of eight existing technology acceptance models and theories (TRA, TAM, MM, TPB, the combined TAM-TPB, the model of PC utilization, innovation diffusion theory and social cognitive theory). This theory has four main constructs of intention and usage, and up to four moderators of key relationships (performance expectancy, effort expectancy, social influence and facilitating conditions). Existing literature on technology acceptance has not given enough attention to age as a moderating factor although findings from the study of UTAUT indicate that age moderates all the main relationships in the theory. Additionally, gender is also a key moderating factor and has received some attention. These findings are consistent with other research conducted in social psychology and in sociology literature [32]. The UTAUT has been criticised because of the high number of independent variables used to predict intentions and behaviour towards the usage of technology. Nevertheless, it is considered to be more vigorous than other previous models used to evaluate and predict technology acceptance (Fig. 10).

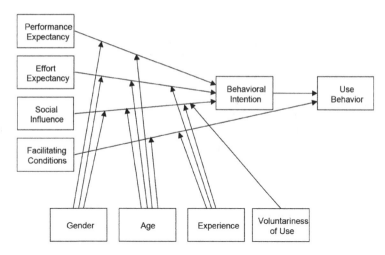

Fig. 10. Unified Theory of Acceptance and Use of Technology UTAUT [2]

3.11 Technology Acceptance Model 3 (TAM3)

In 2008 Venkatesh and Bala introduced TAM 3 [33]. The model was developed by combining TAM2 [31] and the model of the determinants of perceived ease of use [20]. TAM3, illustrated in Fig. 11 presents a complete nomological network of the constructs of individuals' IT adoption and use. The model suggests that perceived ease of use is influenced by computer playfulness, computer self-efficacy, computer anxiety, and perception of external control, perceived enjoyment and objective usability. The perceived usefulness is determined by job relevance, subjective norms, result demonstrability and image. Though, this model is criticised due to the high number of variables and the high number of relationship between variables.

3.12 Unified Theory of Acceptance and Use of Technology 2 (UTAUT2)

In 2012, Venkatesh et al. introduced UTAUT2 in order to extend the existing UTAUT model to other contexts [34]. This model is an updated version of the UTAUT which was initially introduced to explain employee technology acceptance and use [34], but because of its main focus on employees and organisations, its unified purpose is arguable. Since the numbers of technology devices and applications have an enormous value [35], the UTAUT model was extended with three additional determinants that are more customer oriented. The first of these determinants is the Hedonic Motivation, which can be seen as the extent to which a user experiences enjoyment from using a system. The second added determinant is Price Value, and is based on the idea that when consumers are responsible for costs, these costs can determine whether or not consumers will adopt the system [36, 37]. Finally, the Behavioural Intention, which in the UTAUT2 model is classified as 'Habit', is the last determinant and has shown in different research that habit has a direct impact on technology use. Similar to the original UTAUT model, age, gender and experience are taken into account, while the Voluntariness of Use has been removed and instead a line between Facilitating

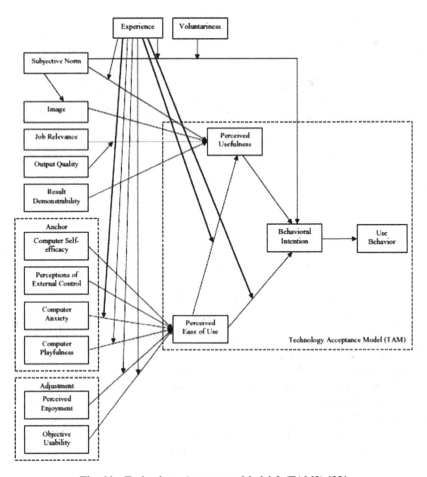

Fig. 11. Technology Acceptance Model 3 (TAM3) [33]

Conditions and Behavioural Intention was drawn, which is influenced by gender, age and experience. As the model Fig. 12 indicates, Hedonic Motivation is also moderated by gender, age, and experience, while the effect of Price Value is moderated by gender and age. Habit has both influence on Behavioural Intention and Use Behaviour, and is affected by age, gender and experience. Venkatesh et al. expand the whole framework with regard to technology use; however, voluntariness has been ignored.

3.13   UTAUT Extensions

There have been several UTAUT extensions in the past few years which can be classified in four main types: exogenous mechanisms, new endogenous mechanisms, new moderating mechanisms and new outcome mechanisms. Figure 13 illustrates the four types of UTAUT extensions at a more abstract level and Table 1 below summarises the four types of UTAUT extension studies.

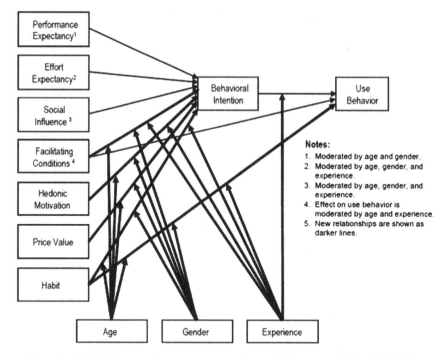

Fig. 12. Unified Theory of Acceptance and Use of Technology 2 (UTAUT2) [34]

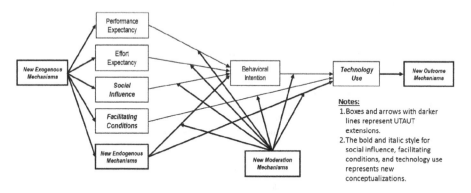

Fig. 13. Types of UTAUT Extensions [43]

Table 1. Types of UTAUT Extensions [43]

Source	New exogenous mechanisms	New endogenous mechanisms	New moderation mechanisms	New outcome mechanisms
Alaiad and Zhou (2013)		Trust		
Al-Gahtani, Hubona and Wang (2007)			Culture (Saudi Arabia vs. USA)	
Alshare and Mousa (2014)			Espoused culture values	
Borrero, Yousafzai, Javed and Page (2014)			Technology readiness	
Bourdon and Sandrine (2009)		Enriching social influences; enriching facilitations		
Brown et al. (2010)	Collaboration-related constructs: technology characteristics, individual characteristics, group characteristics, task characteristics, and situational characteristics			
Carter and Schaupp (2008)		Trust, self-efficacy, and experience		
Casey and Wilson-Evered (2012)	Trust and Innovativeness			
Chiu and Wang (2008)	Computer self-efficacy	Task value, task cost, and computer self-efficacy		
Dasgupta and Gupta (2011)	Organizational culture			
Eckhardt et al. (2009)		Enriching social influences	Adopter vs. non-adopter	
Im et al. (2011)			Culture (Korea vs. USA)	
Lallmahomed, Ab Rahim, Ibrahim and Rahman (2013)		Hedonic performance expectancy, enriching system use		
Liang et al. (2010)	Team climate for innovation			
Liew, Vaithilingam and Nair (2014)		Adoption perceived economic benefit, and perceived social benefit, enriching use	Ethnicity, religion, language, employment, income, education, and marital status	

(continued)

Table 1. (*continued*)

Source	New exogenous mechanisms	New endogenous mechanisms	New moderation mechanisms	New outcome mechanisms
		behavior(economic use and social use)		
Loose, Weeger and Gewald (2014)		Perceived threats		
Lu, Yu and Liu (2009)			Income and location	
Martins, Oliveira and Popovic (2014)	Perceived risk	Perceived risk		
McKenna, Tuunanen and Gardner (2013)	Adaptive service components, computational service components, collaborative service components, and networking service	Self-efficacy		
McLeod, Pippin and Catania (2009)		Tax performance expectancy; privacy and risk	Professionals vs. novices	
Neufeld et al. (2007)	Charismatic leadership			
Niehaves and Plattfaut (2010)			Income, education, and migration background	
Oh and Yoon (2014)		Trust and flow experience	E-Learning vs. online game	
Park et al. (2011)		Organizational facilitating conditions	Organizational facilitating conditions	
Saeed (2013)		Perceived financial control and ease of navigation		
Schaupp, Carter and McBride (2010)		Optimism bias and perceived risk	Schaupp, Carter and McBride (2010)	
Shibl, Lawley and Debuse (2013)	Professional development, time, cost, training, security, integration, and workflow	Involvement	Shibl, Lawley and Debuse (2013)	Professional development, time, cost, training, security, integration, and workflow
Sun et al. (2009)	Perceived work compatibility			Individual performance
Thong et al. (2011)			IT service type; Adoption vs. continued use	

(*continued*)

Table 1. (*continued*)

Source	New exogenous mechanisms	New endogenous mechanisms	New moderation mechanisms	New outcome mechanisms
Venkatesh and Zhang (2010)			Culture	
Venkatesh et al. (2008)		Behavioral expectation Duration, frequency, and intensity of use	Age, gender, and experience moderate the impacts of facilitating conditions on behavioral expectation; experience moderates the impacts of behavioral intention and behavioral expectation on use	
Venkatesh et al. (2012)		Hedonic motivation, habit, and price value	Age, gender, and experience moderating the impacts of hedonic motivation, habit, and price value on intention and use respectively	
Wang et al. (2012)		Trust	Type of recommender system; type of product	
Wang, Jung, Kang and Chung (2014)	Perceived innovativeness with IT and computer self-efficacy	Enriching social in fluence, knowledge sharing outcome expectancy, and security.	User groups (silent vs. social users)	
Weerakkody, El- Haddadeh, Aɪ-Sobhi,: Shareef and Dwivedi (2013)	Trust of Internet and trust of Intermediaries			
Xiong, Qureshi and Najjar (2013)		Job fit, attitude, self-efficacy, and anxiety		Economic development
Yuen, Yeow, Lim and Saylani (2010)		Attitude, anxiety, perceived credibility, and self-efficacy	Culture	

4 Comparative Study

See Table 2

Table 2. Technology Acceptance models and theories comparison study

Models and Theories	Characteristics	Core constructs	Reference and Applications
Theory of Reasoned Action (TRA) (1975)	• Developed by Ajzen and Fishbein in 1975 • Drawn from social psychology • One of the most important and influential theories of human behaviour • Links the perception, norms and attitudes to the intentions of a person in making a decision and from there predicts the person behaviour • The starting point of TAM • Does not consider the individual's ability to control	• Attitude toward behaviour • Subjective Norm	Fishbein and Ajzen 1975 [3]
Social Cognitive Theory (SCT) (1986)	• Developed by Albert Bandura • Proposes that environmental factors, personal factors and behaviours are determined reciprocally • Learning occurs in a social context with a dynamic and reciprocal interaction of personal factors, environmental factors, and behaviours	• Outcome Expectations Performance • Outcome Expectations Personal • Self-efficacy • Affect • Anxiety	Compeau and Higgins 1995b [8]
Technology Acceptance Model (TAM) (1986, 1989)	• Developed by Fred Davis in his doctoral study • TAM originated as an adaptation of the more generalised TRA and was developed more specifically later to predict and explain technology usage behaviour • TAM has been used to study the adoption of different technologies and it has become the most significant theory in this field • TAM is tailored to IS contexts and was designed to predict information technology acceptance and usage on the job	• Perceived Usefulness • Perceived Ease of Use • Subjective Norm	• The case of cellular telephone adoption (Kwon and Chidambaram 2000 [38]) • Behavioural intention to use e-books (Wen-Chia Tsai 2012 [39]

(continued)

Table 2. (*continued*)

Models and Theories	Characteristics	Core constructs	Reference and Applications
	• In contrast with TRA. the TAM does not include subjective norms because of the weak psychometric results which are generated • Researchers of ICT have criticised this model for not including subjective norms,		
Theory of Planned Behaviour (TPB) (1991)	• Developed by Ajzen in 1991 as an extension of TRA, with the additional determinant of intention perceived behaviour control • TPB has a greater ability to predict behaviour than TRA	• Attitude toward behaviour • Subjective Norm • Perceived behavioural control	• Ajzen 1991 [13] • Taylor and Todd 1995b [30]
Model of PC Utilization (MPCU) (1991)	• Thompson, Higgins and Howell (1991) predicted PC utilisation behaviour model • Derived largely from Triandis' (1977) theory of human behavior, this model presents a competing perspective to that proposed by TRA and TPB • However, the nature of the model makes it particularly suited to redict individual acceptance and use of a range of information technologies. It predicts usage behavior rather than intention	• Job-fit • Complexity • Long-term consequences • Affect towards use • Social factors • Facilitating conditions	Thompson et al. 1991. p.129 [17]
Motivation Model (MM) (1992)	• This model is based on the psychological aspects of technology acceptance	• Extrinsic Motivation • Intrinsic Motivation	Applied by Davis, Bagozzi and Warshaw to study ICT adoption and use (1992) [19]
Innovative Diffusion Tlieory (IDT) (1962, 1971, 1983, 1995)	• Developed by Rogers in 1995 • Grounded in sociology and has been used since the 1960s to study a variety of innovations, ranging from agricultural tools to organisational innovation • Appropriate in both an individual or organizational context • Is one of the most well -known theories associated with the adoption of new technology	• Relative advantage • Ease of use • Image • Visibility • Compatibility • Results demonstrability • Voluntariness of use	Moore and Benbasat 1991, p. 195 [27]

(*continued*)

Table 2. (*continued*)

Models and Theories	Characteristics	Core constructs	Reference and Applications
Decomposed Theory of Planned Behavior (DTPB) or Combined TAM - TPB (1995)	• Developed by Taylor and Todd in 1995.	• Attitude toward behaviour • Subjective Norm • Perceived Behavioral Control • Perceived Usefulness	Taylor and Todd 1995a [29]
Extension of TAM (TAM2) (2000)	• Developed by Venkatesh and Davis in 2000 by adding two more determinants to the original TAM (social influences and cognitive instrumental processes)	• Voluntariness • Experience • Subjective norm • Image • Job relevance • Output Quality • Result Demonstrability	Venkatesk and Davis 2000 [31]
Unified Theory of Acceptance and Use of Technology (UTAUT) (2003)	• Developed by Venkatesh, Morris, Davis, G. and Davis. F. in 2003 • Integrates the components of eight technology acceptance models and theories: TRA, TAM. the motivational model. TPB, combined TAM-TPB, the model of PC utilization, innovation diffusion theory, and social cognitive theory • It is considered to be more robust than other technology acceptance models in evaluating and predicting technology acceptance • This theory has been criticised for having too many	• Performance expectancy • Effort • Expectancy • Social Influence • Facilitating conditions	Venkatesh, Morris, Davis, G. and Davis, F 2003 [2]

5 Technology Acceptance and the Decision to Invest in Information Security

Information security refers to any process, activity, or task that protects the integrity, accessibility, and confidentiality of information [41]. In today's digital society with the increased abilities of hackers and information theft, security is becoming a crucial aspect of everyday life although its importance is well recognised by current information security literature [44]. Certainly, for any technology to be successfully acceptance in organisations, the security aspect has to be reviewed with a great level of detail. Information security is vital for protecting important assets of organisations, including the information resources and the organisation's reputation. In addition, some studies have reported that users' concern about security has increased and it has been known as one of the most significant factors for technology acceptance [42]. Furthermore, the paucity of empirical research exists to explain an organization's motivation to invest in (or not to invest in) information security. Since the introduction of e-mail and the World Wide Web, information security breaches have increasingly become a major threat to organizations. The Fig. 14 below is an adaptation based on TAM, information security investment and decision-making which explores information security investment decisions making and acceptance [44].

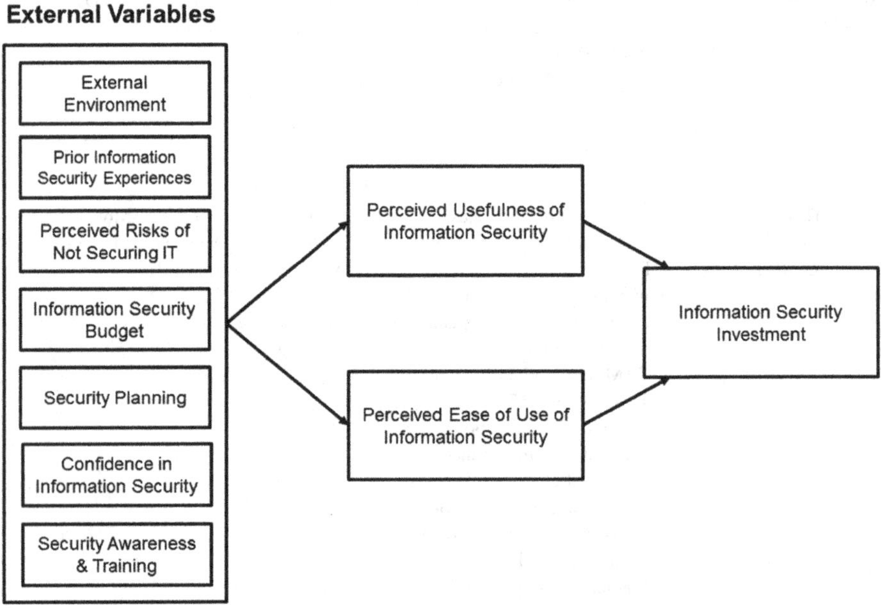

External Variables

Fig. 14. Conceptual model for decision to invest in Information security [44]

The proposed model identifies a set of external variables influencing perceived usefulness of information security and also affecting the perceived ease of use of information security, which are key factors playing a major role in any information security investment. In this list of external variables, security awareness and training are amongst the most important components of information security and acceptance as awareness about technology causes users to look forward to try technology while enjoying the various benefits that the system will provide. It might also provide guidance to managers in their efforts to justify and receive funding for information security.

6 Discussion

The UTAUT has proven to be a useful theoretical model in helping to understand and explain use behaviour in information system implementation. It has been tested in many empirical research studies and the tools used with the model have proven to be of quality and to yield statistically reliable results. In today's society, the globalization of business has highlighted the need to understand the effectiveness of IS that span different cultures and social classes. Multinational and trans-cultural organizations use IT to achieve economies of scale, coordinate operations, and facilitate collaborative work across locations and cultures. Cultural differences have become an important issue in the evaluation of computer applications and new technologies as a whole. To make valid comparisons, models should be robust across cultures. Culture is often partially blamed when organisations experience failure. For example, the Columbia and Challenger disasters experience by NASA were in part attributed to a culture that valued conformity to rules resulting in the overlooking of potential risks [40]. On the other hand, social class to some extent plays a major role in technology adoption. This may be related to the level of convenience, social/institutional safeguards, or the pursuit of social class membership. Therefore, developing new models that will take into consideration culture effect as a new construct on the basis of Hofstede's cultural dimensions and social class as a moderating factor possibly combined with the Actor Network Theory as a framework to analyse external variables influencing consumers' behavioural intention of using technology, would be our next challenge.

7 Conclusion and Future Work

TAM has been widely used in information and communication technology research to help understand as well as explain user behaviours. This paper has summarised technology acceptance models and theories. We made explicit the assumptions underlying these TA models and theories including factors relevant to each model, and have attempted to review the origins and the evolution of TAM from 1975 to 2016. TAM has succeeded in providing a robust model which is applicable across a broad range of end-user computing technologies. More importantly, we identified a significant body of literature that reports inconsistent results with these models and the lack of consideration of the cultural influence and social class in acceptance of new technology makes these models incomplete. It is suggested that future researchers shall start with simple or most fundamental models and then add new variables for different targets. Furthermore, it is essential to recognise that effective Information security management is critical in ensuring important assets of organisations, such as information and reputation, receive appropriate protection. Future work will be use a theory such as the actor-network theory to further explore external variables and other relevant entities influencing behavioural intention and use of technology.

References

1. Bailey, J., Pearson, S.: Development of a tool for measurement and analyzing computer user satisfaction. Manage. Sci. **29**(5), 530–575 (1983)
2. Venkatesh, V., Morris, M.G., Davis, G.B., Davis, F.D.: User acceptance of information technology: toward a unified view. MIS Q. **27**(3), 425–478 (2003)
3. Fishbein, M., Ajzen, I.: Belief, Attitude, Intention and Behavior: An Introduction to Theory and Research. Addison-Wesley, Reading (1975)
4. Ajzen, I., Fishbein, M.: Understanding Attitudes and Predicting Social Behavior. Prentice Hall, NJ (1980)
5. Davis, F.D., Bagozzi, R., Warshaw, P.: User acceptance of computer technology: a comparison of two theoretical models. Manage. Sci. (1989). doi:10.1287/mnsc.35.8.982
6. Yusuf, M., Derus, A.M.: Measurement model of corporate Zakat collection in malaysia: a test of diffusion of innovation theory. Humanomics **29**(1), 61–74 (2013)
7. Bandura, A.: Social Foundations of Thought and Action: A Social Cognitive Theory. Prentice- Hall Inc., Englewood Cliffs (1986)
8. Compeau, D.R., Higgins, C.A., Huff, S.: Social cognitive theory and individual reactions to computing technology: a longitudinal study. MIS Q. **23**(2), 145–158 (1999)
9. Bandura, A.: Social cognitive theory. In: Vasta, R. (ed.) Annals of Child Development, vol. 6. Six Theories of Child Development, pp. 1–60. JAI Press, Greenwich (1989)
10. Shroff, R.H., Deneen, C.C., Ng, E.M.W.: Analysis of the technology acceptance model in examining students' behavioural intention to use an e-portfolio system. Australas. J. Education. Tech. **27**(4), 600–618 (2011)
11. Wu, M., Chou, H., Weng, Y., Huang, Y.: TAM2-based study of website user behavior — using web 2. 0 websites as an example. Wseas Trans. Bus. Econ. **8**(4), 133–151 (2011)
12. Legris, P., Ingham, J., Collerette, P.: Why do people use information technology? a critical review of the technology acceptance model. Inf. Manag. **40**(3), 191–204 (2003)
13. Ajzen, I.: The theory of planned behavior. Organ. Behav. Hum. Decis. Process. **50**(2), 179–211 (1991)
14. Kok, G., DeVries, A., Muddle, N., Strecher, V.: Planned health education and role of self-efficacy: Dutch research. Health Educ. Res. **6**(2), 231–238 (1991)
15. Liang, T., Huang, J.: An empirical study on consumer acceptance of products in electronic markets: a transaction cost model. Decis. Support Syst. **24**(1), 29–43 (1998)
16. Ajzen, I.: Constructing a TpB Questionnaire: Conceptual and Methodological Considerations. World Wide Web (2006). http://www.people.umass.edu/aizen/pdf/tpb.measurement.pdf. Accessed 14 May 2016
17. Thompson, R.L., Higgins, C.A., Howell, J.M.: Personal computing: toward a conceptual model of utilization. MIS Quarterly **15**(1), 125–143 (1991)
18. Triandis, H.: Interpersonal Behavior. Brooke/Cole, Monterey, CA (1977)
19. Davis, F., Bagozzi, R., Warshaw, P.: Extrinsic and intrinsic motivation to use computers in the workplace. J. Appl. Soc. Psychol. **22**(14), 1111–1132 (1992)
20. Venkatesh, V.: Determinants of perceived ease of use: integrating perceived behavioral control, computer anxiety and enjoyment into the technology acceptance model. Inf. Syst. Res. **11**(4), 342–365 (2000)
21. Rogers, E.M.: Diffusion of Innovations, 1st edn. The Free Press, New York (1962)
22. Rogers, E.M.: Diffusion of Innovations, 3rd edn. The Free Press, New York (1983)
23. Rogers, E.M.: Diffusion of Innovations, 4th edn. The Free Press, New York (1995)
24. Rogers, E.M., Shoemaker, F.F. (eds.).: Communication of Innovations: A Crosscultural Approach. Free Press, New York (1971)

25. Karahanna, E., Straub, D.: The psychological origins of perceived usefulness and ease-of-use. Inf. Manag. **35**(4), 237–250 (1999)
26. Agarwal, R., Sambamurthy, V., Stair, R.M.: The evolving relationship between general and specific computer efficacy: an empirical assessment. Inf. Syst. Res. **11**(4), 418–430 (2000)
27. Moore, G.C., Benbasat, I.: Development of an instrument to measure the perceptions of adopting an information technology innovation. Inf. Syst. Res. **2**(3), 192–222 (1991)
28. Surendran, P.: Technology acceptance model: a survey of literature. Int. J. Bus. Soc. Res. **2** (4), 175–178 (2012)
29. Taylor, S., Todd, P.: Assessing it usage: the role of prior experience. MIS Q. **19**(4), 61–70 (1995a). Accessed 30 March 2016
30. Taylor, S., Todd, P.: Understanding information technology usage: a test of competing models. Inf. Syst. Res. **61**, 44–76 (1995b). Accessed 30 March 2016
31. Venkatesh, V., Davis, F.D.: A theoretical extension of technology acceptance model: four longitudinal field studies. Manage. Sci. **46**(2), 186–204 (2000)
32. Levy, J.A.: Intersections of gender and aging (1988). http://search.epnet.com/login.aspx?direct=true&db=aph&authdb=epref&an=SQ.BI.DGI.LEVY.IGA
33. Venkatesh, V., Bala, H.L: Technology acceptance model 3 and a research agenda on interventions. Decis. Sci. J. Innovative Educ. **39**(2), 273–315 (2008)
34. Venkatesh, V., Thong, J., Xu, X.: Consumer acceptance and use of information technology: extending the unified theory of acceptance and use of technology. MIS Q. **36**(1), 157–178 (2012)
35. Stofega, W., Llamas, R.T.: *Worldwide Mobile Phone 2009-2013 Forecast Update, IDC Document Number 217209*. IDC, Framingham (2009)
36. Brown, S.A., Venkatesh, V.: Model of adoption of technology in households: a baseline model test and extension incorporating household lifecycle. MIS Q. **29**(3), 399–426 (2005)
37. Coulter, K.S., Coulter, R.A.: Distortion of Price Discount Perceptions: the Right Digit Effect. Journal of Consumer Research **34**(2), 162–175 (2007)
38. Kwon, H.S., Chidambaram, L.: A test of the technology acceptance model-the case of cellular telephone adoption. In: Proceedings of the 33rd Hawaii International Conference on System Sciences (2000)
39. Wen-Chia, T.: A study of consumer behavioral intention to use e-books: the technology Acceptance Model perspective. Innovative Marketing **8**(4), 55–66 (2012)
40. Vaughn, D.: The Challenger Launch Decision: Risky Technology, Culture and Deviance at NASA. University of Chicago Press, Chicago (1996)
41. NIST (National Institute of Technical Standards) An introduction to computer security: the NIST handbook, Special Publication 800–12, (1995)
42. Vijayasarathy, L.R.: Predicting consumer intentions to use online shopping: the case for an augmented technology acceptance model. Inf. Manag. **41**(6), 747–762 (2004)
43. Venkatesh, V., Thong, J.Y.L., Xu, X.: Unified theory of acceptance and use of technology: a synthesis and the road ahead. J. Assoc. Inf. Syst. **17**(5), 328–376 (2016)
44. Johnson, A.M.: The technology acceptance model and the decision to invest in information security. In: Proceedings of the Southern Association of Information Systems Conference (2005)

Application of a Digraph for Behavioural Eye Tracking Biometrics

Bobby L. Tait[✉]

School of Computing, UNISA, Pretoria, South Africa
taitbl@unisa.ac.za

Abstract. Preliminary reports on the soon to be released Samsung note 7, suggests that the new device will incorporate an iris scanner to be used for biometric authentication. It is clear that over the past number of years, vendors of personal digital devices, consider biometric authentication of a human as a possible replacement for pin, password and pattern based authentication mechanisms currently in use.

Behavioural biometrics is often used to strengthen existing authentication mechanisms. A digraph is commonly associated with the behavioural biometric known as keystroke dynamics. A password is firstly tested for correctness against the reference password on file. This is followed by a second step, where the biometric behavioural aspect is tested. The unique rhythm that a user exhibits when the password is entered forms part of the authentication process by using a digraph approach.

This paper utilizes the EyeWriter to test if the digraph approach can be used in eye tracking to create a behavioural biometric to authenticate a person.

The test was performed on 20 candidates and the results from this test indicated clearly that the behavioural aspect can fundamentally be used for behavioural biometric authentication in a one-to-one biometric authentication approach.

Keywords: Behavioural biometrics · Eye tracking · Eye based authentication · Access control · Eye writer

1 Introduction

The five main information security services are defined as Identification, Authentication, Authorization, Confidentiality and Non-repudiation (Zissis and Lekkas 2012). It must be noted that if the Identification and Authentication services fail, the rest of the information security services cannot be trusted. A successfully authenticated human is authorized to perform specific actions in a computerized environment. If the authentic password is supplied, an encrypted cipher will decrypt correctly to yield the clear text. For the service of non-repudiation to succeed, all parties must be successfully identified and authenticated. Identification and authentication can be considered as the gate-keepers of the remaining three security services (Hummen et al. 2013).

© Springer International Publishing AG 2016
H. Jahankhani et al. (Eds.): ICGS3 2017, CCIS 630, pp. 252–265, 2016.
DOI: 10.1007/978-3-319-51064-4_20

The identification phase requires that a person provides certain information to assist in identifying the person. This information is usually in the form of a username (Almeshekah and Spafford 2014).

The authentication phase is a very crucial phase, as any person can make a claim during the identification phase to falsely claim a certain identity. During the authentication phase this claim must be tested and confirmed. In order to enforce the security service of authentication, some unique data must be presented that is unique for the person given the size of the particular population.

Firstly, this can be accomplished by the person presenting unique information such as a password, pass-phrase or pin (Bang et al. 2012).

Another approach that can be followed to confirm authenticity is by presenting a unique possession, such as a special key, unique card or any unique token (Dhillon et al. 2016).

Finally a person can be authenticated using some form of behavioral or physical aspect which is part of a human, also referred to as biometric authentication (Tait 2014).

Physical biometrics includes biometric characteristics such as fingerprints, iris, retina, handprint and facial thermography. These biometric characteristics are part of the human and are found to be unique among different humans (Weinberg 2015). A behavioural biometric as a unique human trait that a person exhibits. It is often used as a mechanism to strengthen other authentication systems (Monaco et al. 2013). Behavioural biometrics evaluates the way that a person behaves in order to make a decision about the authenticity of a person. The rhythm that a person exhibits when entering a password is measured, and apart from the password match, the rhythm used to enter the password is used for biometric authentication. The way that a person walks, referred to as a person's gait, is another example of behavioural biometric authentication (Liu et al. 2015). Behavioural biometrics is central to this paper, and will be discussed in further detail in the following section.

In the paper entitled "Behavioural Biometrics: Utilizing Eye-Tracking to Generate a Behavioural Pin Using the Eyewriter" the author presents an argument that the Eyewriter can be used to generate a behavioural profile of a person that uses an Eyewriter to present a 5 digit pin (Tait 2015).

This paper investigates and tests the feasibility of using the Eyewriter to generate a unique behavioural profile based on the way that a person selects the different digits associated with the person's pin.

The premise was tested using 20 candidates, in various experimental setups as described in this paper. It was concluded that the behavioural profiles are indeed unique enough to be used as a biometric authenticator, especially if the system is applied in a one-to-one biometric authentication environment.

The remainder of the paper is organized in the following way: Sect. 2 discusses the literature relating to the technology and concepts required to conduct the experiments. Section 3 describes the experimental setup followed by Sect. 4 that illustrates the results of the experiments conducted on the 20 candidates. Section 5 critically evaluates the results presented in Sect. 4, followed by the conclusion and further research presented in Sect. 6.

2 Literature Study

2.1 Biometrics

The notion to use biometric characteristics for authentication in order to uniquely confirm the identity of a person is not a novel proposal at all. Fingerprint biometrics as authentication mechanism can be traced back the biblical times, where potters would leave an imprint on articles that they manufactured as a seal of authenticity (Goren and Arie 2014). Fingerprints were required by Sir William Herschel, British Administrator in District in India, on civil contracts (Waits 2016). For forensic investigation methods utilized latent fingerprint information at crime scenes since 1891, when Juan Vucetich, Argentine police official initiated the fingerprinting of criminals. The proposal the use fingerprint information was first used for the Rojas homicide case in 1892. In this criminal case the latent fingerprint characteristics of the woman who murdered her two sons and then cut her own throat (in an attempt to place the blame on another person) was found on a door post at the crime scene. (Murphy and Morrison 2014).

The above mentioned example relies on humans to evaluate the latent biometric information for authenticity. In order to allow a computing system to evaluate the biometric data, the computing system must be equipped with special sensors, specifically developed to capture information from human beings.

Figure 1 illustrates a few physical biometrics which are often used for biometric authentication. For the various physical biometrics, a purposely developed sensor must be developed. Fingerprint scanners are developed to capture the fingerprint patterns found on human fingertips. A retina scanner has the ability to illuminate the dark retina of the human eye in order to capture the unique vascular structure of the retina inside the human eye. A photographic sensor has been developed to capture the unique characteristics of a human face. All these sensors allows a computing system to collect biometric data from a human and in a sense "perceive" a human more accurately if you may (Bolle et al. 2013).

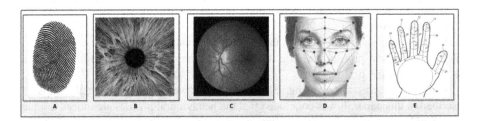

Fig. 1. Physical biometrics.

To record a behavioural biometric from a person, similar to physical biometrics, specialized sensors are required to allow a computing system to capture the behaviour of the person. Behavioural biometrics is concerned with the way that a person conducts a certain action (Liu et al. 2015).

When a person signs a document, the person will create a signature that has a specific visual uniqueness. However, during the creation phase of the signature, the way that the person creates the signature contains unique biometric information directly related to the person. For example, the behaviour of the person creating the signature can be measured in a number of ways. Aspects such as pressure of the pen, the pen acceleration, pen dwell times and pen flight times can all be recorded to create a behavioural profile of the person. These aspects have been proven to be useful during behavioural biometric evaluation (Sanchez-Reillo et al. 2015).

Figure 2 illustrates four behavioural biometric approaches. Keystroke dynamics using a digraph is illustrated in A, signature biometrics is illustrated by B, followed by voice authentication and gait illustrated by C and D respectively.

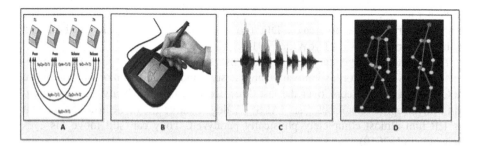

Fig. 2. Behavioural biometrics.

In order to capture the movements of human eye, a number of eye tracking technologies have been developed. The Tobii eye tracking system is a well-established eye tracking device, and used in various eye tracking related studies (Holland and Komogortsev 2012). Eye tracking has been developed to study where a person focuses their gaze in order to understand a number of questions relating to eye movement and human attention (Holland and Komogortsev 2012).

For the purpose of this paper the movement of the eye is studied in an effort to determine if the movement of the eye is unique enough to be used as a behavioural biometric. It was determined by (Tait 2015) that if an Eyewriter is used to capture the movements of the eye during the creation of a pin, enough behavioural biometric information is available to successfully authenticate a person.

The following section focuses of eye tracking as a behavioural biometric.

2.2   Eye Tracking as Behavioural Biometric

Humans move their eyes in order to bring the image of an inspected object onto the fovea (the small and high-resolution area of the retina). Once the image of the object is stabilized on the retina, the information can be extracted. Tobii manufactures a device known as Eye-tracker (Tobii 2016). Eye-tracker is a device that records the movements of the eyes. Most of the current eye-trackers use infrared light emitters, video image analysis of the pupil center and reflections from cornea to estimate the direction of gaze.

The movement of the pupil can be tracked with a high amount of accuracy. It is possible to record exactly where the person is looking or how the person's eyes are moving (Morgante et al. 2012).

In 2005, Bednarik et al. conducted research to establish the uniqueness of the movement of the eye designed specifically for the behavioural biometric purposes (Bednarik et al. 2005). They illustrated that 90% accuracy was found during the authentication process of the eye movement of 12 subjects. Bednarik et al. concluded that due to hardware limitations the micro movements of the eye it is difficult to capture with the technology available in 2005.

2.3   EyeWriter for Eye-Tracking

The EyeWriter project is an open source project. All software needed to allow the EyeWriter to function is freely available from the EyeWriter developer's website. The complete instructions set to create a DIY (do it yourself) Eyewriter, can also be found on the EyeWriter website (EyeWriter 2016).

Tony Quan is a legendary LA graffiti artist, social activist and publisher internationally. He is known for his innovative artistic style and his efforts to build and nurture the California graffiti scene over the last three decades. In 2003, Tony was diagnosed with Amyotrophic lateral sclerosis (ALS). A degenerative motor neuron disease that has left him almost completely physically paralyzed. Tony can still move his eyes (Bellucci et al. 2010).

In 2008, Mick and Caskey Ebeling became familiar with Tony's illness. In 2009 the "Not impossible Foundation" and "The new school of Design" set out to create a low cost ($\sim$50 US dollar) open source eye tracking system that allows an ALS patient to draw by just using their eyes. (Bellucci et al. 2010).

It was illustrated in previous research that the EyeWriter can successfully be used to generate a behavioral biometric pin (Tait 2015).

As confirmed in initial tests of the EyeWriter, it was concluded that the initial version of the EyeWriter is not accurate enough due to the movement of a normal person's head. An updated version of the EyeWriter was subsequently used for experiments conducted during the research presented in this paper. In the adapted version of the EyeWriter the Camera module is placed a bit closer to the eye and 4 IR LED's are incorporated to increase the contrast between the pupil and the iris. The result of the contrast increase from the view that was captured on the PS3 camera is illustrated in Fig. 3. Note the contrast difference and the very dark nature of the pupil in the picture. This near black result of the pupil can easily be tracked by the EyeWriter software.

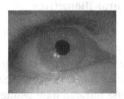

Fig. 3. a clear view of the pupil from PS3 camera's perspective.

In order to enter a pin using the EyeWriter, the user must select numeric values from a keypad by only using their eyes. The user must glance at the correct digit and then blink to indicate that the digit that is being glanced at, is the digit that the user wants to select. If the pin is for e.g. a 5 digit pin the user must select the correct 5 digits in the correct order. This process simply allows a user (even if paralyzed) to enter a pin by simply glancing at the keypad on the screen. It must be noted that at this stage the process does not include any biometrically measurable aspect.

The following section discusses the application of a Digraph to generate a behavioural biometric for the pin that the person enters. Keystroke dynamics relies on a digraph to evaluate the behaviour or typical rhythm exhibited by a user to enter a password (Banerjee and Woodard 2012).

2.4   Application of a Digraph for Eye Movement Biometrics

Keystroke dynamics, is detailed timing information that describes exactly when each key on a keyboard was pressed and when each key was released. The recorded timing data is then processed through a unique neural algorithm that determines a primary pattern for comparison (Bours 2012).

A digraph is used to measure the way that a person create a password or a pin rather than simply considering the actual password or pin supplied. The behavioral aspect of the pin creation is very important.

A digraph continually evaluates two aspects to be measured against each other (Shepherd 1995). For example: The time that the user took to select the first letter compared to the time that the user took to select the second letter, or the time it took from selecting the first key until the pin creation is completed (last key selected). Figure 4 illustrates the aspects that a digraph records during the entering of a pin.

For the presented example in Fig. 4, tsS7- tsS1 indicates the time taken from selecting key 7 until selecting the following key (key 1). The last measurement (tsS7-tsS3) refers to the total time that it took to create the full pin consisting of 5 digits.

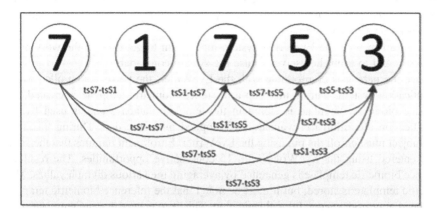

Fig. 4. Digraph for a pin supplied by the user.

As proposed, for the purpose of this paper, the EyeWriter is used to select the values from an onscreen keypad to create the pin. In order to measure the behavioral aspect resulting from the creation of the pin, the time aspect is measured.

To test the ability of the EyeWriter to capture the pin, a template of a keypad is provided. The user must focus on the relevant numerical value on the keypad and blink to indicate a selection.

For clarity, a colored dot is placed on the area of the numerical value that the person selected. For a secure application, the system will not indicate the value selected. It will only indicate that a selection was successfully made. As a test example this selection process for the numerical value 71753 is illustrated in Fig. 5.

Fig. 5. Keypad with values selected by the EyeWriter.

The following section discusses the experimental setup used to test if the EyeWriter can be used to authenticate a person based on the behaviour that each person exhibits during the selection of a pin from the onscreen keypad.

3   Experimental Setup

In order to test if the EyeWriter can be used for successfully authenticate the behavioral aspect of a pin supplied by a person, 20 candidates were tested during the experiment. The pin that the subjects used was the exact same pin for each namely 71753, and thus not a secret as a pin should be.

Each person used the EyeWriter system for 30 min to get used to the working of the system and to train themselves to use the system comfortably.

Once the person is comfortable with the EyeWriter, the person is enrolled to the authentication system. During this step a reference biometric template is created; the reference biometric template is stored in the template database and is used by the authentication algorithm for evaluation of supplied biometric data. During this step, each subject must enroll the pin using the EyeWriter. Enrollment requires that the same pin is entered using the EyeWriter with 15 consecutive opportunities. The resulting reference biometric template is generated by averaging the various digraph values. This biometric template is stored, but it must be noted that the reference biometric template is updated after each successful authentication. This is to ensure that the template stays up to date, as a person's behaviour does tend to change over time.

For the purpose of this experiment each person enrolled the same pin, resulting in only the recorded digraph data to differ among the 20 candidates.

All experiments were tested on the same EyeWriter system.

The candidates were not enrolled or tested on the same day and it must be noted that all 20 candidates were first enrolled on the EyeWriter system before any of the experiments were conducted.

For clarity during the tests conducted, the enrolled identity will be using the following naming convention:

User <Alphabet value A-T>, for Example "User A"

During the experiments conducted for this paper, when a person uses the system, the person is referred to using the following naming convention:

Candidate <Alphabet value A-T>, for example "Candidate A"

For this reason, "User A" (an enrolled user) and "Candidate A" (Test subject) is the same person. User A = Candidate A.

An important aspect that needed to be stested, was to determine the outcome of a one-to-one biometric match, compared to a one-to-many biometric matching approach.

3.1 One-to-One Biometric Match Experiments

In a one-to-one biometric match, a candidate is first identified - the candidate must offer a username to claim his or her identity. The system confirms that the username supplied is a valid user of the system. If the username is successfully identified and found amount the registered usernames of the system, the authentication data offered by the candidate is directly compared to stored reference authentication template in order to confirm the identity claim made (Quinn and Grother 2012).

The first aspect tested for behavioral digraph authentication using the Eyewriter, is to test if there is sufficient uniqueness among the candidates to accept and identify a user as authentic and to reject a user that is masquerading as another user.

3.1.1 Test 1: One-to-One Test of an Authentic User

In this experiment Candidate A presents his identity (rightfully) as User A. The candidate supplies the pin using the EyeWriter. During this experiment it is tested if the system correctly accepts Candidate A as User A.

3.1.2 Test 2: One-to-One Test of a Masquerading User

In this experiment Candidate L presents his identity as any of the other users for e.g. User A. The candidate then supplies the pin using the EyeWriter. During this experiment it is tested if the system correctly rejects Candidate L as User A.

3.2 Test 3: One-to-Many Biometric Match Experiment

In a one-to-many biometric match the user is not known, nor does the user supply a username. Only the biometric data is available to be tested in a search of the user that the biometric data belongs to. The biometric data is thus compared to all the reference biometric templates in the database. The accurate success of a one-to-many match is reliant on a number of factors such as type of biometric, biometric storage resolution and the size of the population stored in the reference database (Hamid 2015).

In this experiment, the candidate does not supply any identification information. Candidate A supplies the pin using the EyeWriter. The system is then tested to see if the behavioural biometric data supplied is matched to User A only.

Section 4 presents the results from the experiments conducted during the research.

4   Experimental Results

Due to length constraints on this paper, 5 randomly selected candidate's data is supplied as an example of data collected during the experimental phase. For all graphs presented the Y-axis relates to the number of Digraph measurements and the X-axis relates to the time dimension.

4.1   Results from Test 1

The first set of tests conducted, relates to the one-to-one experiments presented in Sects. 3.1.1 and 3.1.2, Table 1 presents the results relating to experiment Sect. 3.1.1. and Fig. 6 illustrates a comparison between the reference biometric data and the biometric data collected from the experiment for user D and user H.

Table 1. Results from one-to-one authentic user experiment.

	User A		User D		User H		User N		User R	
	Ref	Data	Ref	Data	Ref	Data	Ref	Data	Ref	Data
tsS7 - tsS1	0.7	0.71	0.41	0.44	0.59	0.54	0.92	0.86	0.77	0.71
tsS1 - tsS7	0.91	0.67	0.55	0.61	0.7	0.72	0.75	0.7	0.77	0.78
tsS7 - tsS5	0.6	0.75	0.63	0.58	0.82	0.73	0.84	0.86	0.71	0.74
tsS5 - tsS3	0.6	0.72	0.31	0.51	0.38	0.45	0.78	0.79	0.68	0.71
tsS7 - tsS7	1.61	1.38	0.96	1.05	1.29	1.26	1.67	1.56	1.54	1.49
tsS1 - tsS5	1.51	1.42	1.18	1.19	1.52	1.45	1.59	1.56	1.48	1.52
tsS7 - tsS3	1.2	1.47	0.94	1.09	1.2	1.18	1.62	1.65	1.39	1.45
tsS7 - tsS5	2.21	2.13	1.59	1.63	2.11	1.99	2.51	2.42	2.25	2.23
tsS1 - tsS3	2.42	2.09	1.73	1.8	2.22	2.17	2.34	2.26	2.25	2.3
tsS7 - tsS3	4.63	4.22	3.32	3.43	4.33	4.16	4.85	4.68	4.5	4.53
Outcome	Success		Success		Success		Success		Success	

4.2   Results from Test 2

The second set of tests conducted, relates to the experiment presented in Sect. 3.1.2. During this experiment all candidates were requested to masquerade as all other users. Table 2 lists the results from this experiment where candidate L masqueraded as User A, User D, User H and User R. Figure 7 illustrates a comparison between the reference biometric data and the biometric data collected from the experiment.

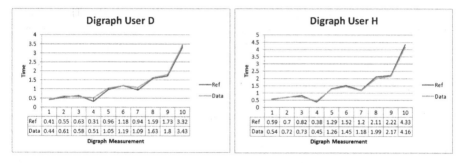

Fig. 6. Successful match User D and User H

Table 2. Results from one-to-one masquerading user experiment.

	User L		User L		User L		User L		User L	
	Ref A	Data L	Ref D	Data L	Ref H	Data L	Ref N	Data L	Ref R	Data L
tsS7 - tsS1	0.7	0.54	0.41	0.55	0.59	0.54	0.92	0.61	0.77	0.51
tsS1 - tsS7	0.91	0.86	0.55	0.81	0.7	0.81	0.75	0.84	0.77	0.75
tsS7 - tsS5	0.6	0.71	0.63	0.69	0.82	0.63	0.84	0.73	0.71	0.7
tsS5 - tsS3	0.6	0.79	0.31	0.75	0.38	0.71	0.78	0.76	0.68	0.8
tsS7 - tsS7	1.61	1.4	0.96	1.36	1.29	1.35	1.67	1.45	1.54	1.26
tsS1 - tsS5	1.51	1.57	1.18	1.5	1.52	1.44	1.59	1.57	1.48	1.45
tsS7 - tsS3	1.2	1.5	0.94	1.44	1.2	1.34	1.62	1.49	1.39	1.5
tsS7 - tsS5	2.21	2.11	1.59	2.05	2.11	1.98	2.51	2.18	2.25	1.96
tsS1 - tsS3	2.42	2.43	1.73	2.31	2.22	2.25	2.34	2.41	2.25	2.2
tsS7 - tsS3	4.63	4.54	3.32	4.36	4.33	4.23	4.85	4.59	4.5	4.16
Outcome	Fail		Fail		Fail		Fail		Fail	

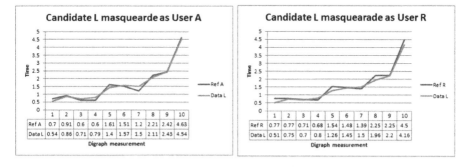

Fig. 7. Digraph for Candidate L masquerading as User A and User R.

4.3   Results from Test 3

The third test were conducted on all candidates to test the ability of the system to identify a user based on received biometric data only as outlined in Sect. 3.2. During this test a user will simply supply the pin using the EyeWriter system. The software then compares the received biometric data (denoted as "bio data") with all reference biometric templates in the database, if a match is found that falls within the tolerances of the matching algorithm, the match is indicated as for e.g. "Matched C". The result of this experiment is presented by Table 3.

Table 3. Results from one-to-many user experiment.

Bio data from:	Candidate C		Candidate F		Candidate G		Candidate T		Candidate D	
	Bio Data	Matched C	Bio Data	Matched Q	Bio Data	Matched G	Bio Data		Bio Data	Matched D
tsS7 - tsS1	0.56	0.58	0.42	0.48	0.7	0.74	0.88	-	0.42	0.41
tsS1 - tsS7	0.69	0.71	0.59	0.64	0.55	0.61	0.79	-	0.54	0.54
tsS7 - tsS5	0.77	0.8	0.66	0.68	0.48	0.5	0.51	-	0.61	0.63
tsS5 - tsS3	0.91	0.88	0.39	0.43	0.38	0.41	0.38	-	0.34	0.33
tsS7 - tsS7	1.25	1.29	1.01	1.12	1.25	1.35	1.67	-	0.96	0.95
tsS1 - tsS5	1.46	1.51	1.25	1.32	1.03	1.11	1.3	-	1.15	1.17
tsS7 - tsS3	1.68	1.68	1.05	1.11	0.86	0.91	0.89	-	0.95	0.96
tsS7 - tsS5	2.02	2.09	1.67	1.8	1.73	1.85	2.18	-	1.57	1.58
tsS1 - tsS3	2.15	2.22	1.84	1.96	1.58	1.72	2.09	-	1.69	1.71
tsS7 - tsS3	4.17	4.31	3.51	3.76	3.31	3.57	4.27	-	3.26	3.29
Outcome	Found User		Found User *		Found User		No Match		Found user	

Take note that the system incorrectly matched candidate F to User Q. Furthermore the system could not successfully match Candidate T the existing reference biometric template of User T. This is illustrated in Fig. 8.

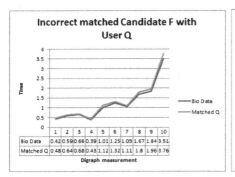
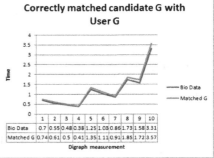

Fig. 8. One to many matching using behavioural pin data.

5   Evaluation of Test and Results

From the tests conducted, it is instantly clear that when a one-to-one biometric match is used, the system has no problem confirming the authenticity of each Candidate to their supplied user name. During this test the supplied biometric data is only checked against the reference biometric template to authenticate a user. The system does not consider if the supplied biometric data is a close match to any other data in the reference template database. It was found during the tests conducted in the first test (as outline in Sect. 3.1.1) the system had a 100% success rate to confirm the authenticity of each candidate in the system. One must keep in mind that the population on this test was limited to only 20 candidates as an initial proof of concept, but it should be noted that 20 candidates with a positive outcome is a good improvement to the 12 candidates tested 11 years ago by Bednarik et al. (2005).

For the second test conducted as described in Sect. 3.1.2, the results are equally positive. The system showed a clear ability to confirm that a candidate that endeavor to masquerade as any of the users in the system, did not succeed, and authentication of the masquerading user were rejected on every account. During the tests conducted, each candidate, tried to masquerade as one of the other 19 users in the system. On all accounts this attempt, by each candidate failed, resulting in a 100% success rate during this one-to-one test.

For the last test conducted, as described in Sect. 3.2, the system did not yield the same positive outcome as found for tests 1, and 2. During a one-to-many biometric match attempt the overall success of the system was only found to be 38.25% accurate. Considering the small number of users in the reference database, this figure is not a very promising value. The system would match the wrong user to the wrong candidate. In one instance, the system did not match the actual candidate with the actual user in the system at all. It is not currently entirely clear why this occurred during the test for that specific candidate, and it was suggested that during that specific attempt the candidate might have been tired, or distracted, however this outcome will be investigated further.

The results presented in this paper under Sect. 4.3 for the one-to-many tests conducted on the candidates showed "found user" only if a very certain match was made (98% certainty), however it must be noted that if a number of close matches were found the system would select the highest one as the possible match. If a wrong match was made it is often found that the actual user was the second closest match. This occurred 100% of the time when a wrong match was made – the correct user was the second listed user as a candidate for the biometric data supplied.

It must be noted that the bio reference data used for user D in the final experiment, in Table 3, differs slightly from the reference bio data presented for user D in Table 2. This is due to the fact that the reference biometric template in the database is constantly updated after every successful authentication, and thus correctly reflected in Table 3.

From the tests conducted; it is clear that the proposal made to use eye-tracking technology for the creation of a behavioural pin is indeed feasible if applied in a one-to-one biometric authentication system.

6 Conclusion

This paper investigated the feasibility of using Eye-Tracking to generate a behavioural pin using the Eyewriter.

In order to test the proposal the EyeWriter system was used, in all cases the candidates used the same pin to ensure that the behavioural aspect of the pin creation is the only aspect that is tested.

Three tests were developed, two of these tests related to one-to-one biometric matching and one test related to one-to-many biometric matching. A total of 20 candidates were tested during various intervals.

It was found that that the system managed to successfully authenticate a candidate if the candidate supplied the username linked to his or her identity. It was also illustrated that the system managed to detect a candidate that tries to masquerade as another user of the system. In all cases, test 1 and test 2 yielded a 100% success rate given the population for this test. This made is clear that the system is extremely capable of authenticating a candidate if a one-to-one approach for authentication is used.

On the other hand, the system was not very good at finding a user in the reference database, if the identity is not known. This is however in line with other biometric systems such as fingerprint biometrics, where an accurate persona is seldom found in a one-to-many biometric search effort (Quinn and Grother 2012).

Future research of this work will include tests to measure the uniqueness of the eye movement when a pin is selected from an onscreen keypad.

References

Almeshekah, M.H., Spafford, E.H.: Planning and integrating deception into computer security defenses. In: Proceedings of the 2014 Workshop on New Security Paradigms Workshop, pp. 127–138. ACM, September 2014

Banerjee, S.P., Woodard, D.L.: Biometric authentication and identification using keystroke dynamics: a survey. J. Pattern Recogn. Res. 7(1), 116–139 (2012)

Bang, Y., Lee, D.J., Bae, Y.S., Ahn, J.H.: Improving information security management: an analysis of ID–password usage and a new login vulnerability measure. Int. J. Inf. Manag. 32 (5), 409–418 (2012)

Bednarik, R., Kinnunen, T., Mihaila, A., Fränti, P.: Eye-movements as a biometric. In: Kalviainen, H., Parkkinen, J., Kaarna, A. (eds.) SCIA 2005. LNCS, vol. 3540, pp. 780–789. Springer, Heidelberg (2005). doi:10.1007/11499145_79

Bellucci, A., Malizia, A., Diaz, P., Aedo, I.: Human-display interaction technology: emerging remote interfaces for pervasive display environments. IEEE Pervasive Comput. 9(2), 72–76 (2010)

Bolle, R.M., Connell, J., Pankanti, S., Ratha, N.K., Senior, A.W.: Guide to Biometrics. Springer Science & Business Media, Heidelberg (2013)

Bours, P.: Continuous keystroke dynamics: a different perspective towards biometric evaluation. Inf. Secur. Tech. Rep. 17(1), 36–43 (2012)

Dhillon, G., Syed, R., Pedron, C.: Interpreting information security culture: an organizational transformation case study. Comput. Secur. 56, 63–69 (2016)

EyeWriter (2016). www.eyewriter.org. Accessed 1 Aug 2016

Goren, Y., Arie, E.: The authenticity of the Bullae of Berekhyahu son of Neriyahu the scribe. Bull. Am. Sch. Orient. Res. 372, 147–158 (2014)

Hamid, L.: Biometric technology: not a password replacement, but a complement. Biom. Technol. Today 2015(6), 7–10 (2015)

Holland, C., Komogortsev, O.: Eye tracking on unmodified common tablets: challenges and solutions. In: Proceedings of the Symposium on Eye Tracking Research and Applications, pp. 277–280. ACM, March 2012

Hummen, R., Ziegeldorf, J.H., Shafagh, H., Raza, S., Wehrle, K.: Towards viable certificate-based authentication for the internet of things. In: Proceedings of the 2nd ACM Workshop on Hot Topics on Wireless Network Security and Privacy, pp. 37–42. ACM, April 2013

Liu, Z., Zhang, Z., Wu, Q., Wang, Y.: Enhancing person re-identification by integrating gait biometric. Neurocomputing **168**, 1144–1156 (2015)

Monaco, J.V., Stewart, J.C., Cha, S.H., Tappert, C.C.: Behavioral biometric verification of student identity in online course assessment and authentication of authors in literary works. In: 2013 IEEE Sixth International Conference on Biometrics: Theory, Applications and Systems (BTAS), pp. 1–8. IEEE, September 2013

Morgante, J.D., Zolfaghari, R., Johnson, S.P.: A critical test of temporal and spatial accuracy of the Tobii T60XL eye tracker. Infancy **17**(1), 9–32 (2012)

Murphy, B.L., Morrison, R.D. (eds.): Introduction to Environmental Forensics. Academic Press, Cambridge (2014)

Quinn, G.W., Grother, P.: The one-to-many multi-modal fusion challenge. In: 2012 5th IAPR International Conference on Biometrics (ICB), pp. 408–412. IEEE, March 2012

Tait, B.L.: The biometric landscape–towards a sustainable biometric terminology framework 9. Int. J. Electron. Secur. Digit. Forensics **6**(2), 147–156 (2014)

Tait, B.L.: Behavioural biometrics: utilizing eye-tracking to generate a behavioural pin using the eyewriter. In: Jahankhani, H., Carlile, A., Akhgar, B., Taal, A., Hessami, A.G., Hosseinian-Far, A. (eds.) ICGS3 2015. CCIS, vol. 534, pp. 348–359. Springer, Heidelberg (2015). doi:10.1007/978-3-319-23276-8_31

Tobii Eye tracking technologies (2016). www.tobii.com. Accessed 1 Aug 2016

Sanchez-Reillo, R., Quiros-Sandoval, H.C., Liu-Jimenez, J., Goicoechea-Telleria, I.: Evaluation of strengths and weaknesses of dynamic handwritten signature recognition against forgeries. In: 2015 International Carnahan Conference on Security Technology (ICCST), pp. 373–378. IEEE, September 2015

Shepherd, S.J.: Continuous authentication by analysis of keyboard typing characteristics. In: European Convention on Security and Detection, pp. 111–114, 16–18 May 1995 doi:10.1049/cp:19950480

Waits, M.R.: The indexical trace: a visual interpretation of the history of fingerprinting in colonial India. Vis. Cult. Br. **17**(1), 18–46 (2016)

Weinberg, J.T.: Biometric identity. Commun. ACM **59**(1), 30–32 (2015)

Zissis, D., Lekkas, D.: Addressing cloud computing security issues. Future Gener. Comput. Syst. **28**(3), 583–592 (2012). Elsevier

Behavioural Biometrics for Authentication and Stress Detection – A Case Study with Children

Ana I. Azevedo[1], Henrique D. Santos[1,2], Vítor J. Sá[2,3(✉)], and Nuno V. Lopes[1,2]

[1] Department of Information Systems, School of Engineering, University of Minho, 4800 Guimarães, Portugal
{hsantos,vascolopes}@dsi.uminho.pt
[2] ALGORITMI Research Center, University of Minho, Braga/Guimarães, Portugal
[3] Faculty of Philosophy and Social Sciences, Catholic University of Portugal, 4700 Braga, Portugal
vitor.sa@braga.ucp.pt

Abstract. This article presents a stress detection model based on real time collection and analysis of physiological signals monitored by non-invasive and non-intrusive sensors. The assumption of a state of stress is made taking into account the validation of a certain number of biometric reactions to some specific situations. The biometric data collected is also used to create a method capable of guaranteeing user's authentication. To validate this model, an experiment was set, demonstrating that it is possible to infer stressful situations by monitoring some specific physiological signals.

1 Introduction

Nowadays, access to Wi-Fi and 4G-LTE wireless Internet is almost a lifestyle. This trend has promoted the emergence of new applications and increased the use of mobile devices. The evolution of ubiquity is evident, raising the need to create systems with improved safety, in particular, by building more robust authentication methods that can be applied continuously.

Recent advances in the development of wireless sensor networks have been allowing the improvement of sensors, turning them into smaller devices with lower power consumption and lower cost, increasing their use in several areas of research. Biometric data collection using wireless sensor networks emerged as one of the most promising technologies for creating a non deplorable authentication able to offer better privacy conditions. The physiological sensors can make collections in very short time intervals, which enables the implementation of a panoply of systems such as authentication, or monitoring health conditions in real-time, i.e., stress [1].

Stress is a public health problem that also affects children and can be indicated as a symptom of various diseases. A study published in The Journal of Immunology shows that stress may contribute to an imbalance in the child's immune response [2].

© Springer International Publishing AG 2016
H. Jahankhani et al. (Eds.): ICGS3 2017, CCIS 630, pp. 266–280, 2016.
DOI: 10.1007/978-3-319-51064-4_21

Such a biometric system requires a phase of information pre-collection, so that it can be created a profile of their biometric pattern. The user activity is monitored continuously and their interactions will be constantly compared with the predetermined profile, thus allowing proper authentication of the user and also the detection of its state of stress.

This work aims to develop a system capable of determining when a child is in stress through the use of a sensor network. The collected biometric data will also be used for authentication of the child to the system, thus providing better guarantees of privacy and security.

To achieve this purpose, the following tasks were performed: (1) definition of a functional architecture for the system; (2) creating a stress simulation environment for the child; (3) collection of data obtained by simulation and subsequent processing and extraction of the desired features for further development of a biometric data template; (4) classification of the collected samples, using *machine learning* algorithms; (5) system evaluation based on the results obtained in the previous point.

The research method adopted for the implementation of this work focused on three major tasks, namely: collection of biometric data; analysis and processing of the collected information; classification of data.

Samples were collected from 20 children aged 5 and 6 years. The processing of the signals was performed using the Matlab programming tool. Then, to make the data classification we used RStudio tool.

In Sect. 2 we present a set of concepts to contextualize the reader about the topic; in the following section we present how the system was implemented; in Sect. 4 the data collection, processing and analysis are presented; in Sect. 5 we have the results and, finally, some conclusions are drawn.

2   Related Knowledge

The development of a robust biometric system requires skills about several concepts that are applied in an integrated manner, starting with the appropriate procedure for data capture and evaluation, digital processing, feature extraction, classification algorithms and adequate result interpretation. The interdisciplinary and integration of various technological areas is thus a crucial aspect in the development of these systems and applications [6].

Biometrics is a technique of analysis and measurement of inherent and measurable characteristics of human beings that allow recognition of the identity of an individual, and can be classified into two types: physical and behavioural. Physical biometrics refers to characteristics and/or body responses of the user, such as fingerprints, hand geometry, face characteristics and any other unique features that may be associated with human body and measured by an automatic process [8, 9].

Behavioural biometrics consist in the analysis and measurement of behaviour patterns of human beings made in everyday life. Each individual expresses him self and interacts in a characteristic and unique way. Examples of behavioural biometrics are: speech, keystroke and mouse movement dynamics, signature, gait and all body movements that are typical and able to identify a particular user [18].

A biometric system is a pattern recognition system capable of performing the recognition of an individual based on their biometric information, by extracting a vector of physiological and/or behavioural characteristics and comparing them to a model of standard features stored in a database.

The feature vectors are used to classify the biometric data presented to the system in accordance with a set of decision rules designated classifier. There are many types of classification algorithms. These should be chosen according to the context of the application in order to provide better system performance [13].

The *machine learning* classification algorithms are divided into two groups: supervised learning and unsupervised learning. The unsupervised learning algorithms aim to group data by classes according to rules predefined by the system programmer. Supervised learning algorithms is a technique in which the system is set according to a training data set properly labelled. This kind of learning is comprised of two phases: a training phase and a testing phase.

The training phase consists in the creation of a data classification model based on a training data set. During the testing phase, the developed model is tested using data unknown to the system in order to measure the accuracy of the defined classification model [10]. Of the various existing data classification models such as the k-nearest neighbours, the Naives Bayes, or the Support Vector Machine, in this work was used the last one – SVM.

2.1 Stress and Behavioural Biometry

Stress is defined as a body response to external events that somehow modifies the internal balance of the individual or transmits the sense of threat. The body reacts to the stressor agent by producing hormones such as adrenaline into the blood stream, which allows an increase of concentration [11].

As mentioned earlier, the behavioural biometry defines an individual's behaviour patterns in different situations of daily life. In a stressful situation, it should be also possible to standardize the individual's physiological reaction.

The behavioural responses tend to vary widely according to the individual's personality. For example, speech problems, hesitation or difficulty in articulating words, interrupted sleep patterns or extreme fatigue levels become more evident when the person is in a stress situation [12].

A stress detection model appears to be the most suitable method to get a better understanding of the disposition of a user that tries to access or that is using the system. So, if the person has values outside the boundaries of their standard of stress, then something abnormal is happening with the individual and may compromise the system security.

Characteristics such as skin conductivity and temperature, eye pupil dilation and the heart rate are stress indicators that can easily be collected and processed in a non intrusive way, thus contributing to the construction of a biometric behavioural pattern capable of recognize unequivocally the user.

Skin Conductivity. Skin conductivity, also called galvanic skin response (GSR) means the measurement of the skin electrical resistance. Recently, the thermoelectric response has been described as a valuable and non-invasive physiological measurement. Once the skin becomes momentarily better conductive when exposed to external or internal stimuli, this can be very useful to indicate situations of pain or stress [13, 14]. It presents the advantage that it is not affected by ambient temperature or by the cardiorespiratory status of the individual. This is a reliable feature that can be applied to individuals of any age. Recently, GSR has been measured in response to heel puncture procedures in new-born infants of only 29 weeks [15].

Skin Temperature. The skin is the largest organ of the human body. This protects the body tissues from injury and helps to regulate body temperature making its pores larger or smaller. Skin temperature is a quantitative indicator that enables an objective evaluation of human sensations. It is controlled by the sympathetic nerve activity, which makes possible the analysis of information processing in the brain [16]. Exposure to stress results in endocrine, autonomic and behavioural response which enables the organism to adapt to the surrounding environment. From the analysis of these parameters became clear that the human body temperature changes in response to a stressful situation [17].

Photopletysmography. Measurement of blood volume pulse (BVP), also known as photoplethysmography (PPG) is an optical analysis method that allows to detect the changes of cardiovascular dynamics by studying blood translucency. When the heart pumps blood, the arteries become more opaque, decreasing the amount of transmitted light [18].

Researchers from various fields of science have demonstrated a growing interest in PPG signal analysis due to its numerous advantages, namely, non-invasiveness, low cost and convenience as medical diagnostic tool.

The PPG signal analysis allows to obtain the variation of the heart rate of the individual which represents a significant contribution to the study of potential stress situations.

Accelerometry. The accelerometry is a technique that consists in detecting and measuring the movement. Once obtained this measure, it is possible to infer a relationship between the user's health and his physical activity.

The measurement of the individual movements is performed using a portable, small, non-intrusive and easy to use sensor. The use of this sensor enables to set the default and motion intensity of the user, and to quantify their total activity in a given time period [19].

The study of stress reaction by the user requires the evaluation of several parameters. When certain stimuli cause anxiety or disturbs the user, he presents various physiological symptoms, one of them being the tremor. The use of an accelerometer sensor can be very important to detect and quantify the movement performed by the individual [20].

3 System Implementation

Knowing from the outset that the method to implement this project could not involve a high emotional charge to the child, it was agreed to induce a slight amount of stress on the child, proving that the given variables are effectively indicators of stress, allowing the development of a non-intrusive system for the child.

The whole procedure was done in a controlled environment, since the interaction with people outside the data collection could influence the obtained results. Participants were subject to the same evaluation conditions.

The adopted data collection scenario comprises the following two stages: definition of the typical child biometric pattern; definition of the child physiological response when exposed to a stressor. After the collection stage, came the data processing and subsequent extraction of the desired features. The data were analysed according to the two perspectives: stress analysis and data authentication.

According to the perspective of stress analysis, the data processing lists all the variables collected in the two phases of the procedure, because the idea is to determine which factors influence the stress and quantify how this affects each individual.

3.1 Procedure

The first stage aimed at achieving a small task that would allow the registration of the child's baseline values. Since we wanted to obtain data on children in their daily lives, it should be offered a relatively long task and where the child does not feel any kind of external pressure. It was proposed to the child, through the use of gouache paint, to perform a design on something of its liking.

The results of this first phase pointed to that initially the child had slightly altered stress levels, because the placement of the sensors in the child's hand could create a slight feeling of anxiety. However, as the child was drawing, these values tend to the normal values, once the child accustom to the presence of the sensors.

The execution time of this task was not the same for all children. Because the goal was the child to focus on the drawing without any indication or external pressure, it was defined that the child could take as long as considered necessary. When the child indicates that finished drawing the sensors are turned off and the second data collection phase is prepared.

The second phase aimed stress detection. To do this, the child was stimulated by an activity able to induce a small stress load. The proposed task is a computer game comprising several levels. This was a memory game where the child must find the existing matching cards on the screen. The game is timed and as the level increases, a greater number of cards are available. All participants are subject to the same game conditions. If the player loses, he has two more tries to play.

To play the child must use the computer mouse. As some children had difficulties in using the mouse, before starting the game, they made some exercises to learn how to use it and so all children could be evaluated under the same conditions.

The completion of the procedure resulted in sampling for 20 children. However, only 11 subjects were considered valid for integrating the model evaluation. The analysed population has aged 5 and 6 years. All participants were subjected to the same experimental environment. It should also be noted that all the children who participated in the procedure were right-handed.

3.2   Data Collection and Processing

After conducting the literature review, it was concluded that the sensors of PPG, skin temperature, accelerometry and thermoelectric conductivity could be good indicators of stress and allow the creation of a biometric pattern able to authenticate the user.

To enable the data analysis by these two perspectives were defined two data collection phases. Initially, it is intended to set the user default biometric profile. In the second data collection phase, the main objective is to evaluate the changes caused to the user due to the existence of a possible stress situation.

The user authentication model was tested crossing information from the legitimate user with several other users.

The stress detection model was defined by comparing the two stages of data collection, checking the differences between the user's pattern biometric profile with the presented biometric profile when subjected to a stressor agent.

The data collection process involved the use of various biometric sensors, has shown in Table 1.

Table 1. Device and sensors for data acquisition

BioPlux device	Triaxial accelerometer	GSR sensor	PPG sensor	Temperature sensor

After the data collection it is necessary to perform the processing of the acquired signals, removing noise to subsequently perform the feature vector extraction of each of the collected variables. For data processing we chose the Matlab tool, which has a high-level language with an interactive and easy to understand environment. It is a very versatile tool, used in various areas, particularly in signal and images processing, communications, control systems and computational finance.

A signal in the time domain can be converted to the frequency domain by calculating the Fourier transform. This transform decomposes the signal sampled in time in an infinite sum of complex sinusoids of known frequency being defined by the following expression:

$$X(j\Omega) = \sum_{n=-\infty}^{\infty} x[n]e^{-j\Omega Tn} \tag{1}$$

where x[n] represents a discrete signal in time, Ω means the analogue frequency and T the sampling period. For any computer solution the used signal is discrete, then the Fourier transform used is as follows:

$$X\left(e^{\frac{j2\pi k}{N}}\right) = \sum_{n=0}^{N-1} x[n]e^{-j\frac{2\pi}{N}kn} \tag{2}$$

Some systems are designed to allow to pass certain frequency range without making a significant distortion as eliminate or attenuate other frequencies. These systems are referred to as selective frequency filters, being widely used bandpass filter.

There are two important requirements for the use of digital filters: stability and linear phase response. The FIR filters (Finite Impulse Response) can easily fulfil these requirements, as they are stable (do not have poles outside the origin), and its linear phase response may be obtained by imposing that the coefficients of the impulse response are symmetric around its average point [21].

Another important procedure is the signal smoothing consisting in a filtering process in order to reduce fluctuations and noise. There are several methods which attenuate the signal, and the most common is the "moving average" filter. This type of filter is widely used in DSP (Digital Signal Processors) due to its ease of use and understanding [22].

For each used biometric sensor it has been implemented a data processing method which algorithm is briefly described in Table 2.

Table 2. Algorithm for values extraction (by biometric sensor)

Sensor	Operations flux
Photopletysmography	50 Hz noise removal; bandpass filter; removing the continuous component; data segmentation; conversion to BPM (beats per minute)
Skin temperature	50 Hz noise removal; moving average filter; conversion to Celsius degrees
Accelerometry	Removing of continuous component; calculation of the fundamental frequency; bandpass filter; moving average filter
Skin conductivity	50 Hz noise removal; moving average filter

3.3 Data Analysis

Once collected and processed all data the next step was the sample classification. We adopted the SVM algorithm because is widely used in pattern recognition applications, and known for good results compared to other approaches.

A classifier is responsible for the comparison between the user biometric profile stored in the database with the new set of data.

To train the classifier it is necessary to create a template with the samples related to the user biometric profile. Each user should have two templates associated with his profile. The first to perform the user authentication and the second to detect the individual stress pattern. To each user characteristics matrix it should be added a class attribute labeled "standard" or "stress" in the case of stress analysis, and "valid" or "invalid" in the case of user authentication.

It will be based on the analysis of this attribute that the SVM algorithm will build a model that allows the creation of a hyperplane able to separate the samples according to the class that the new set of user data belongs to.

A SVM classification is determined by the type, the kernel and the parameters associated with that classification. Since the objective was to make a pattern recognition we used a SVM algorithm of type classification. The kernel function calculates the dot product of two vectors x and x0 in a given characteristics map $\Phi: X \rightarrow H$. In library "kernlab" the kernels are objects S4 of class kernel which can be adjusted according to a set of hyperparameters.

The selected kernel to implement the SVM model was the Gaussian radial, which has a general purpose and is defined by the following function [23]:

$$k(x, x') = \exp(-\sigma \|x - x'\|^2) \tag{3}$$

The hyperparameter associated with this type of kernel is the 'sigma'. The results of a SVM classifier vary greatly with changing the parameters, so that an adjustment of these may be crucial to increase the system's accuracy. The values associated with the parameters vary according to the templates used in the system.

To find the best value for sigma was used the 'sigest' command from the 'kernlab' library. This command provides a range of values for the hyperparameter in the case of the Gaussian radial kernel. The estimation of value is based on the data matrix used for training. To create the SVM model was applied the 'ksvm' command of the package 'kernlab' applying the parameters obtained after using the 'siggest' command. In the case of the used kernel the 'kpar' parameter according to the result obtained by applying the 'sigest' command.

The test was the last stage of the data classification process. The same procedure was the basis for the construction of both the training and testing files because it was applied to all samples in the database. One half of the data was used for training and the remaining half for testing. Using the functions available in the 'kernlab' library, could be possible to use the 'predict' command responsible for testing the developed SVM model.

After the application of the mentioned command, we obtain a matrix with the results, indicating when a correct prediction was achieved. This matrix is called "confusion matrix" and allows to define the accuracy of the model, which we will discuss in the next section.

4 Results

To assess the robustness of the system, it was carried a detailed analysis of the results obtained during the process of data classification. The evaluation of a classifier is typically carried out by constructing a confusion matrix organized according to the parameters indicated in Table 3.

Table 3. Confusion matrix

Expected class	True class	
	True	False
Positive	True positive (TP)	False positive (FP)
Negative	False negative (FN)	True negative (TN)

The lines represent the prediction of the class to which belongs the information and the columns represent the true class. In the confusion matrix TP represents the number of real examples classified as positive or correct and FP is the number of examples that were wrongly classified as true. FN characterizes the number of samples incorrectly classified as false, and finally, TN represents the number of false examples correctly classified [24].

One of the most used performance evaluation parameters in *machine learning* is the accuracy. This is defined according to the following expression:

$$Precision = \frac{TP + TN}{TP + FP + TN + FN} \tag{4}$$

The main advantage of using this measure is the ease of interpretation of the result. The system accuracy can be affected if the training data file are unbalanced and/or the costs of several errors vary significantly, which is very common in the analysis of biological signals. The system error rate is obtained simply by subtracting to one the precision value.

The specificity and sensitivity represent the individual results of each class. Sensitivity is the ratio of the correct classifications of positive class by the total of all positives.

$$Sensibility = \frac{TP}{TP + FN} \tag{5}$$

Specificity is the ratio of true negatives by all the negative classifications.

$$Specificity = \frac{TN}{TN + FP} \tag{6}$$

The ROC curve (Receiver Operating Characteristic) is a normalized technique that summarizes the performance of the classifier by comparing the percentage of true positives and false positives. Analysing the data of this technique it is possible to set a value of AUC (Area Under the Curve) [24]. This is a simple scalar measurement that represents a benchmark widely used in the data classification process.

4.1 Stress Detection

After the data classification it was set a results evaluation model according to the fundaments mentioned before. This section will show the best and worst case obtained in the data analysis process for a threshold of 0.5.

Table 4 represents the confusion matrix for a threshold of 0.5 of the sample that got better precision in the developed model.

Table 4. Confusion matrix for a threshold of 0.5

	True	False
Positive	28	0
Negative	0	28

For the analysis of the confusion matrix shown above it is possible to verify that the model was able to perfectly distinguish all samples from this individual. Table 5 briefly presents all the information that can be drawn from the analysis of this matrix.

Table 5. Results evaluation for a threshold of 0.5

Parameter measured	Value (%)
Percentage of false positives	0%
Percentage of false negatives	0%
Precision	100%

Considering all possible thresholds, the accuracy of the defined model can be described according to Fig. 1 below represented.

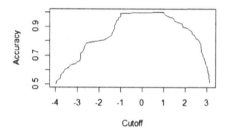

Fig. 1. System accuracy for various threshold values

The case mentioned above describes an optimal model for data classification where no samples classified incorrectly. However, this is a rare case in such systems. The following sample was the one that obtained the classification with most incorrectly classified cases, however, the results may be considered satisfactory.

Table 6 describes the confusion matrix obtained for threshold of 0.5 in the stress detection model.

Table 6. Confusion matrix for a threshold of 0.5

	True	False
Positive	4	25
Negative	0	29

The results obtained for threshold of 0.5 are shown in Table 7.

Table 7. Results evaluation for a threshold of 0.5

Parameter measured	Value (%)
Percentage of false positives	86%
Percentage of false negatives	0%
Precision	57%

Considering various thresholds, the model accuracy graph for this user can be described according to the following chart (Fig. 2).

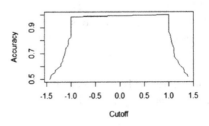

Fig. 2. Accuracy for various values of threshold

In the analysis presented above only were used the data from photopletysmography, skin temperature and thermoelectric conductivity. After performing the data classification, it was possible to conclude that the use of the accelerometer caused too much differentiation in data, vitiating the results. In the table below are the results for the individual who obtained a lower accuracy for threshold of 0.5, if it had been considered the accelerometer (Tables 8 and 9).

Table 8. Confusion matrix for a threshold of 0.5

	True	False
Positive	29	0
Negative	0	29

Table 9. Results evaluation for a threshold of 0.5

Parameter measured	Value (%)
Percentage of false positives	0%
Percentage of false negatives	0%
Precision	100%

4.2   User Authentication

Since in the analysis for detecting stress variations it was concluded that the accelerometer is found to vitiate the results, this variable was not used also in the user authentication analysis process.

This section will present the data obtained for better and worse accuracy for a threshold of 0.5. Tables 10 and 11 represent the confusion matrix and the model statistics defined for the mentioned threshold.

Table 10. Confusion matrix for a threshold of 0.5

	True	False
Positive	49	0
Negative	0	49

Table 11. Results evaluation for a threshold of 0.5

Parameter measured	Value (%)
Percentage of false positives	0%
Percentage of false negatives	0%
Precision	100%

Figure 3 represents the model accuracy curve for different threshold values.

As was verified, as in the stress detection by making analysis of the authentication data, also was obtained a model with good precision for a threshold of 0.5. The fact that in authentication has been also obtained an accuracy of 100% means that the characteristics used not only serve for the development of a good stress detection model, they can also be used in authentication.

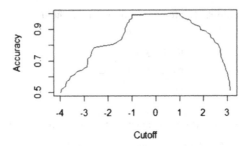

Fig. 3. Accuracy for various values of threshold

The confusion matrix shown below shows the results for a threshold of 0.5 in the process of authentication analysis (Tables 12 and 13).

Table 12. Confusion matrix for a threshold of 0.5

	True	False
Positive	33	0
Negative	29	4

Table 13. Results evaluation for a threshold of 0.5

Parameter measured	Value (%)
Percentage of false positives	0%
Percentage of false negatives	47%
Precision	56%

Through precision analysis for various threshold values it was possible to draw the following chart (Fig. 4).

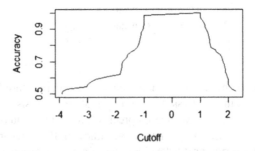

Fig. 4. Accuracy for various values of threshold

5 Conclusions

The constant development of sensor networks has allowed the improvement of them, making these devices smaller, with lower power consumption and with low cost. The use of biometrics appears then as a good solution to ensure user authentication. In this work it is also proposed the definition of a biometric system for detecting stress variations.

The obtained results are quite satisfactory allowing to concluded that the variables selected for stress detection are indeed good indicators and it is really possible to create a stress detection model based on them. In practice, an accuracy of 1 is not very common because this value is considered the optimum value of a data classification model. These results allow us to make many considerations in particular that individuals who participated in this work have very different biometric values and to achieve greater consistency of data would be necessary to increase the number of samples per individual as well as the number of individuals involved. The SVM model is a very sophisticated model typically used for pattern recognition and indicated for this type of application. However, given the amplitude of the collected data it could have been used any other classification model.

We can then conclude that the developed model is reliable but there are several tasks that can be perform to improve the project. As mentioned, to obtain a more complete biometric user profile the model should integrate accelerometry data. Once these have quite different values it should be established a classification scale of user movements, e.g., an indication whether or not the individual had jitter. By placing a binary value in the user accelerometry data template, it would be providing relevant information to the classifier and completing the individual characteristics matrix.

Acknowledgments. This work has been supported by COMPETE: POCI-01-0145-FEDER-007043 and FCT – Fundação para a Ciência e Tecnologia within the Project Scope: UID/CEC/00319/2013.

References

1. Jain, A., Bolle, R., Pankanti, S.: Biometrics: Personal Identification in Networked Society. Springer Science & Business Media, Heidelberg (2006)
2. Carlsson, E., Frostell, A., Ludvigsson, J.: Psychological stress in children may alter the immune response. J. Immunol. **192**(5), 2071–2081 (2014)
3. Nappi, M., Piuri, V., Tan, T., Zhang, D.: Introduction to the special section on biometric systems, applications. IEEE Trans. Syst. Man Cybern.: Syst. **44**(11), 1457–1460 (2014)
4. Jain, A.K., Nandakumar, K.: Biometric authentication: system security and user privacy. IEEE Comput. **45**(11), 87–92 (2012)
5. Long, L.: Biometrics: the future of mobile phones (2014)
6. Saeed, K.: Biometrics principles and important concerns. In: Saeed, K., Nagashima, T. (eds.) Biometrics and Kansei Engineering, pp. 3–20. Springer, New York (2012)
7. Prabhakar, S., Pankati, S., Jain, A.K.: Biometric recognition: security and privacy concerns. IEEE Secur. Priv. **1**, 33–42 (2003)

8. Jain, A.K., Ross, A., Prabhakar, S.: An introduction to biometric recognition. IEEE Trans. Circuits Syst. Video Technol. **14**(1), 4–20 (2004)

9. Uddin, M.N., Sharmin, S., Ahmed, A.H., Hasan, E., Hossain, S., Muniruzzaman: A survey of biometrics security system. IJCSNS Int. J. Comput. Sci. Netw. Secur. **11**(10), 16 (2011)

10. Derawi, M.O.: Smartphones and biometrics: gait and activity recognition. Ph.D. thesis, Gjøvik University (2012)

11. Sun, F.-T., Kuo, C., Cheng, H.-T., Buthpitiya, S., Collins, P., Griss, M.: Activity-aware mental stress detection using physiological sensors. In: Gris, M., Yang, G. (eds.) MobiCASE 2010. LNICSSITE, vol. 76, pp. 211–230. Springer, Heidelberg (2012). doi:10.1007/978-3-642-29336-8_12

12. Butler, G.: Definitions of stress. Occas. Pap. R. Coll. Gen. Pract. **61**, 1 (1993)

13. Liapis, A., Katsanos, C., Sotiropoulos, D., Xenos, M., Karousos, N.: Recognizing emotions in human computer interaction: studying stress using skin conductance. In: Abascal, J., Barbosa, S., Fetter, M., Gross, T., Palanque, P., Winckler, M. (eds.) INTERACT 2015. LNCS, vol. 9296, pp. 255–262. Springer, Heidelberg (2015). doi:10.1007/978-3-319-22701-6_18

14. Picard, R.W., Scheirer, J.: The galvactivator: a glove that senses and communicates skin conductivity. In: Proceedings 9th International Conference on HCI, August 2001

15. Harrison, D., Boyce, S., Loughnan, P., Dargaville, P., Storm, H., Johnston, L.: Skin conductance as a measure of pain and stress in hospitalised infants. Early Hum. Dev. **82**(9), 603–608 (2006)

16. Kataoka, H., Kano, H., Yoshida, H., Saijo, A., Yasuda, M., Osumi, M.: Development of a skin temperature measuring system for non-contact stress evaluation. In: Proceedings of the 20th Annual International Conference of the IEEE Engineering in Medicine and Biology Society, vol. 2, pp. 940–943, October 1998

17. Vinkers, C.H., Penning, R., Hellhammer, J., Verster, J.C., Klaessens, J.H.G.M., Olivier, B., Kalkman, C.J.: The effect of stress on core and peripheral body temperature in humans. Stress **16**(5), 520–530 (2013)

18. Elgendi, M.: On the analysis of fingertip photoplethysmogram signals. Curr. Cardiol. Rev. **8** (1), 14 (2012)

19. Rowlands, A.V.: Accelerometer assessment of physical activity in children: an update. Pediatr. Exerc. Sci. **19**(3), 252–266 (2007)

20. Heimberg, R.G.: Social Phobia: Diagnosis, Assessment, and Treatment. Guilford Press, New York (1995)

21. Liang, H., Bronzino, J.D., Peterson, D.R. (eds.): Biosignal Processing: Principles and Practices. CRC Press, Boca Raton (2012)

22. Smith, S.W.: The Scientist and Engineer's Guide to Digital Signal Processing. California Technical Pub, San Diego (1997)

23. Zeileis, A., Hornik, K., Smola, A., Karatzoglou, A.: Kernlab-an S4 package for kernel methods in R. J. Stat. Softw. **11**(9), 1–20 (2004)

24. Chawla, N.V.: Data mining for imbalanced datasets: an overview. In: Maimon, O., Rokach, L. (eds.) Data Mining and Knowledge Discovery Handbook, pp. 853–867. Springer, Heidelberg (2005)

Using Dual Trigger Handover Algorithm to Improve WiMAX Handover Delay

Imran Khan and Sufian Yousef[✉]

Faculty of Science and Technology, Anglia Ruskin University, Chelmsford, UK
imran.khan8@pgr.anglia.ac.uk, sufian.yousef@anglia.ac.uk

Abstract. WiMAX (worldwide interoperability Microwave access) IEEE 802.16 is an accepted standard for mobile networks and when we are discussing WiMAX mobility the most important factor involving the performance of WiMAX network is handover. There has been numerous papers published regarding handover. This work discusses the implementations of Dual-Triger Handover DTHO algorithm for WiMAX networks. This algorithm is based on SNR (Signal to Noise Ratio) computation which are received at Mobile stations. These measurements of SNR and free capacity for BS and MS improves the accuracy of reception level which in turn improves the handover decisions. The nodes such as BS and MS do not trigger handover and it is the mutual decision between nodes which decides and that is why it is implemented at both nodes. This work was simulated on OPNET Modeller version and the results have shown less delay in the handover process in WiMAX services.

Keywords: WiMAX · Handover delay · Dual trigger algorithm

1 Introduction

WiMAX (worldwide Interoperability for Microwave Access) is being considered for both fixed and mobile networks and The IEEE 802.16e standard supports 3.5–20 MHz [4] and it also supports 2,048 subcarriers.

WiMAX Standard supports link adaptation modulation and power control while PHY layer supports MIMO (multiple input and output), NLOS (Non-Line of Sight) and also hybrid automatic antennas [2–9].

In Mobile WiMAX there are two types of handovers

(a) Hard Handover (b) soft Handover

(a) Hard Handover
   Hard handover is also called break before make where the mobile station have to disconnect from previous before it connect to new.
(B) Soft Handover
   Soft handover depends mainly on MDHO (Macro Diversity Handoff) and FBSS (Fast Base Station Switching) and this improves QoS (quality of Service).

The process of handover initiation depends on many factors such as signal strengths by Mobile Station (MS) and different base stations (BS) while handover can also

© Springer International Publishing AG 2016
H. Jahankhani et al. (Eds.): ICGS3 2017, CCIS 630, pp. 281–289, 2016.
DOI: 10.1007/978-3-319-51064-4_22

happen due to network traffic load and channel fading etc. There are many algorithms which can help in handover by using factors such as Signal to Noise Ratio (SNR) and Received signal straight indicators (RSSI).

There are two main types of handover algorithms [1].

(a) The first type of handover algorithms where handover is decided mainly based on received signal strength of receiver base station to new target base station.
(b) The second type of algorithms where handover occurs when relative signal strength and the threshold between mobile stations and base stations is reached.

2 Handover Algorithm Used for Simulation

The algorithm which has been used in this simulation experiment is a combination of existing handover algorithms and can be considered to be based on both type of algorithms. That's why it is also called a hybrid which is based on initiated MS and Initiated BS [10].

This algorithm prevents an MS from starting Handover when the BS has no free Capacity while the negative side of this capacity handover is that BS has to force one MS to start handover before it accepts new MS.

This algorithm has two process
(a) Scanning (b) Handover

(a) **Scanning Algorithm:**
     The MOB_NBR-ADV message is used by BS to send PHY Layer parameters to Neighbouring BSs and MSs. This includes DCD/UCD and resources for Radio [1]. MS will start scanning process when it reaches its threshold by sending MOB_SCN REQ then MS starts calculating the signal strength using the required parameters to decide QoS level and send message to Recipient BS for Handover.
(b) **Handover Algorithm:**
     The handover process is decided by MS/BS using the Threshold Level and the algorithm provides a triggering system which is calculated with SNR and Free Capacity estimation. It is supposed to reduce the voice calls to be disconnected during the handover.

Mathematically this can be defined as Fallows [1].

$$SNR_{maxDT} - SNR_{DS} \geq H1$$
$$AND$$
$$C_{EF} \geq H_2 \text{ x } \quad C \text{ max,}$$

3 Network Model

In this simulation WiMAX network is simulated with OPNET simulator and this network consists of 7 cells covering 1000 m^2 and multiple BS and MS at different locations where the terrain is assumed to be clear line of sight and mobile stations are moving with speed with maximum speed of 72 Kmph in circular defined path. WiMAX

Table 1. [8] Attributes of different OFDMA Parameters used in WiMAX Simulation

Chosen values (s)					
System bandwidth (MHz)	1.25	2.5	5	10	20
Sampling frequency (Fs, MHz)	1.42	2.85	5.71	11.43	22.86
Sample time (1/Fs, ns)	700	350	175	88	44
FFT size (NFFT)	128	256	512	1,024	2,048
Subcarrier frequency spacing	11.160 kHz				
Useful symbol time (Tb = 1/f)	89.6 µs				
Guard time (Tg = Tb/8)	11.2 µs				
Symbol time (Ts = Tb + Tg)	100.8 µs				

networks are designed to support large numbers of MS and due to this there is high need for the network to be efficient. In order to resolve this efficiency problems this simulation will test dual trigger algorithm which in term is supposed to result in lower handover delay times which in turns increase mobility (Table 1).

4   OPNET Simulation Scenarios and Results

To test the efficiency in reducing the handover delay this dual trigger algorithm is tested with OPNET simulator in WiMAX Module. The network structure can be seen in Fig. 1. While Fig. 2 shows Where backbone network is connected to wired network.

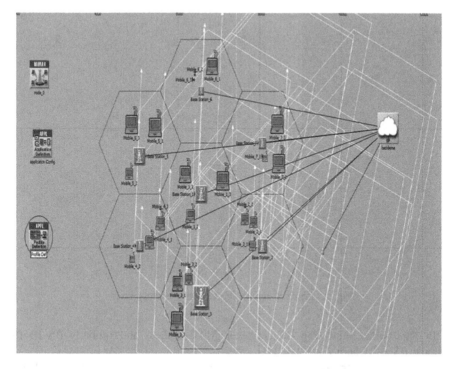

Fig. 1. WiMAX network model showing BS and MS station

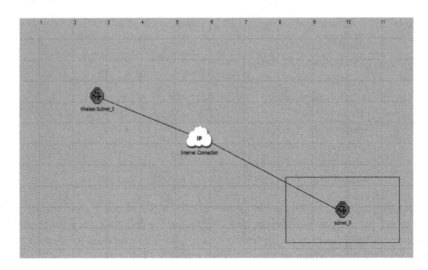

Fig. 2. Wireless subnet is connect to wired subnet

The Fig. 3 shows the wire path which connected to second subnet where service server
s are connected as shown in figure.

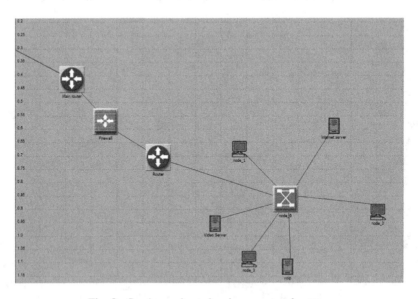

Fig. 3. Services subnet showing connected servers

In This Opnet simulation BS are given MAC address and similarly BS ID for
example BS = I where I = 1,2,3…

OFDMA = 512 frams with 5 ms duration with BS station traffic rate of 64 Kbps.

To achieve the best mobility and reduce the effects of factors standardized factors are used which have been tested to provide lowest handover times as follows:

Link going down factor 1.3
Scan iteration 5
Interleaving Interval 20
Timeout Parameter 20

The Fig. 1 it can be shown the complete subnet of WiMAX network where the WiMAX network is consists of 7 cells with similar number of base stations. While mobile stations are located at different locations with predefined trajectory and fulfilling both conditions of algorithm.

After running the simulations below the following are the simulation results for WiMAX delay which is found to be WiMAX delay is between .020 til .030 s as shown in the Fig. 4.

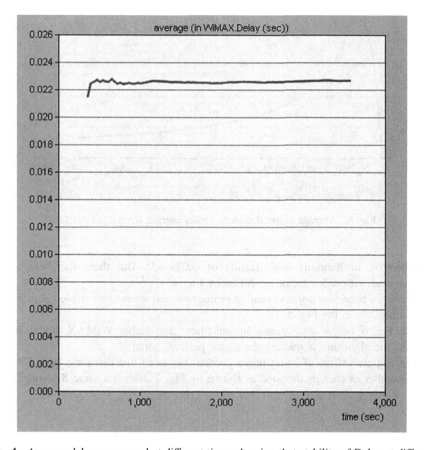

Fig. 4. Average delay per second at different times showing that stability of Delay at different times

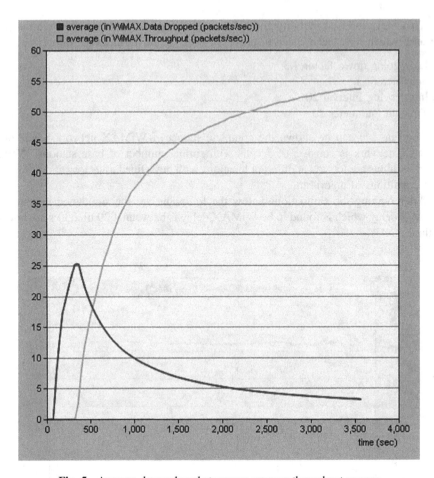

Fig. 5. Average dropped packets verses average throughput per sec

Which is in harmony with results of 0.029 [3]. But there has been some improvement with delay factor as shown by Fig. 4.

There has been also improvement in throughput and it has more stable value Which has can be seen in the Fig. 5.

The Fig. 6 below also shows improvement and stable WiMAX signal which Explains the algorithm is making the signal perform better.

The negative effect of using this algorithm has been that there has been Considerable number of packets dropped as shown by Fig. 7 describes same Situation.

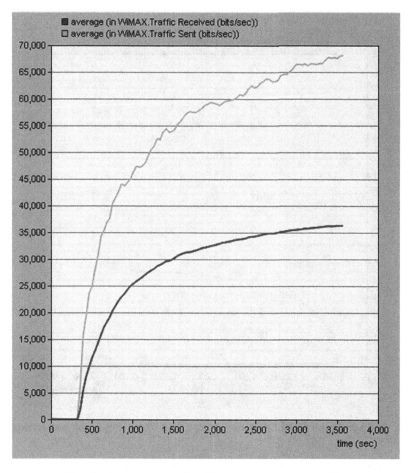

Fig. 6. Average received traffic verses average sent traffic

5 Conclusion

In this experiment OPNET modular was employed at WiMAX network which was standardized with adjusting. The parameters to level where WiMAX network had considerable low handover delay and then we implement Dual trigger algorithm to establish how the handover algorithm will improve the handover in WiMAX. This Simulation validated that there was improvement with handover and the WiMAX signal was performed better but there was also higher number of loss packets while throughput was improved. The SNR calculation had improved the triggering of the handover which in turn provided more stable WiMAX signal.

There is more need for signal improvement specially to reduce the packet loss which has been identified in this experiment. The future work should concentrate on reduction of packets loss by improving algorithm or using alternative algorithm to improve the efficiency of the signal. The future work calls for implementation of an

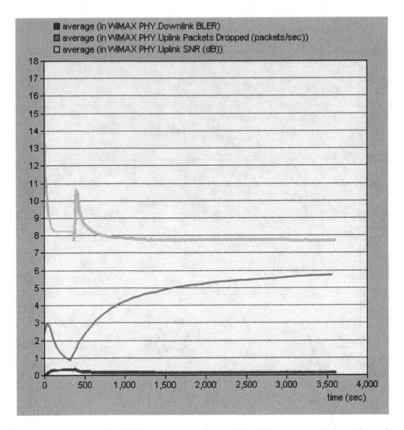

Fig. 7. Average downlink (BLER) verses average SNR (db) verses uplink packets dropped

adaptive mechanism for optimizing thresholds for the handover hysteresis values. A more novel work in handover is based on using the bit error rate (BER) as a main parameter instead of the signal level. This will be our next research trend.

References

1. Lee, B.G., Choi, S.: Broadband Wireless Access and Local Networks: Mobile WiMAX and WiFi. Artech House, Boston, London (2007)
2. Tarhini, C., Chahed, T.: On capacity of OFDMA-based IEEE802.16 WiMAX including adaptive modulation and coding (AMC) and inter-cell interference. In: Proceedings of the 15th IEEE Workshop on Local and Metropolitan Area Networks, LANMAN, Evry, France, June 2007, pp. 139–144 (2007)
3. Khan, I., Yousef, S., Cole, M.: Substantial reduction of handover delay for optimum mobility in WIMAX. IJET **6**, 203–252 (2016)
4. IEEE standard for local and metropolitan area networks part 16: air interface for fixed and mobile broadband wireless access systems, IEEE Standard 802.16 (2005)

5. Gudmundson, M.: Correlation model for shadow fading in mobile radio systems. Electron. Lett. **27**(23), 2145–2146 (1991)
6. Ashayeri, M.R., Taheri, H.: Mobile WiMAX capacity estimation in various conditions. In: Proceedings of the 18th Iranian Conference on Electrical Engineering, ICEE 2010, May 2010, pp. 483–488 (2010)
7. Al-Rousan, N., Altrad, O., Trajković, L.: Dual-trigger handover algorithm for WiMAX technology OPNETWORK 2011, Vancouver, August 2011
8. Andrews, J.G., Ghosh, A., Muhamed, R.: Fundamentals of WiMAX: Understanding Broadband Wireless Networking. Prentice Hall, Upper Saddle River (2007)
9. Understanding WiMAX Model Internals and Interfaces. http://coloftp.opnet.com/x/69eeff7ffd6dbeb8af5eacb13975bd08/1579/1579_pres.pdf
10. Erceg, V., Greenstein, L., Tjandra, S., Parkoff, S., Gupta, A., Kulic, B., Julius, A., Bianchi, R.: An empirically based path loss model for wireless channels in suburban environments. IEEE J. Sel. Areas Commun. **17**(7), 1205–1211 (1999)

Social Media and E-Voting – A Secure and Trusted Political Forum for Palestine

Fouad Shat[1] and Elias Pimenidis[2(✉)]

[1] Brunel University, London, UK
Fouadjf.shat@Brunel.ac.uk
[2] University of the West of England, Bristol, UK
Elias.Pimenidis@uwe.ac.uk

Abstract. Electronic Government applications are nowadays a common tool for governments across the globe. The success rate in gaining the trust of citizens/users and the rates of participation in democratic processes vary considerably from country to country. Social media have managed to capture the trust of people from all cultures and origins and appear to be the means through which e-participation can be enhanced and citizens can be attracted to engage in a secure and trusted e-democratic process. This could prove particularly useful for governments which need to serve citizens that are dispersed in locations across the world. The authors explore the level of trust shown in e-voting systems and social media among Palestinians residing in different countries and this on-going work attempts to assess the suitability of such systems in supporting a true e-democracy.

Keywords: E-Trust · Social media · E-Voting · Privacy · E-Democracy · Palestine

1 Introduction

Over the past two decades governments around the world have developed long term plans and have invested heavily in digitizing services and providing means and opportunities for citizens to engage in political debates online; while more recently the efforts have been concentrated to facilitate digital citizen participation in decision making. Many of these projects have delivered very successful results, while some governments and administrations are still struggling to establish facilities that would appear attractive and at the same time trustworthy to convince citizens to engage with. The overwhelming majority of such e-government services have enjoyed success in areas where the political and economic environments are stable and citizens can aspire to perform their daily tasks in a safe and secure environment, trusting the governments and administrations providing the services. Having overcome the technical and security issues of the earlier days of e-government services governments have often concentrated on the performance and effectiveness of the services that they deliver. It is this last property that often causes more challenges on a global scale and this will be the starting point of the work discussed here [1].

© Springer International Publishing AG 2016
H. Jahankhani et al. (Eds.): ICGS3 2017, CCIS 630, pp. 290–302, 2016.
DOI: 10.1007/978-3-319-51064-4_23

At present the United Nations confirm that the world is experiencing a major crisis with a record number of displaced people, often fleeing war, oppressive regimes and poverty [2]. The role of this work is not to engage in a political agenda as to the causes of such misfortunes, but to introduce and further explore the use of e-government services and social media to engage displaced people with the political developments in the home countries and involve them in a digital democratic process.

In Europe alone the arrival of refugees has been recorded in millions of people in the past three years alone. As efforts to support, feed, shelter and provide a sense of normality in life for all these people have proved a daily struggle, they cannot be the focus of our research but hopefully could benefit by the outcome of such work in the near future.

This work has focused on a different group of largely displaced people the majority of which live in more settled environments and find them more focused in political debates and the need to participate in democratic processes albeit for a distance, the Palestinians.

In previous work the authors have explored the necessity, potential and plans for e-government services offered by the Palestinian Authority to Palestinians around the world. More recently the case of e-voting has been the subject of a worldwide survey amongst Palestinians, exploring their trust, willingness and desire to participate in elections in Palestine using e-voting systems. The authors recognizing that the Pales-tinian diaspora might struggle to engage with e-government systems directly have sought to explore the option of engaging citizens in political debate via the use of social media and possibly through them accessing digital government systems. Thus a second worldwide survey among Palestinians is at the time of writing underway.

2   E-Democracy and Social Media

The term "e-democracy" refers to the use of the internet or other networks to maintain the access of political information and the participation of citizens in the political life [3]. Although e-democracy is widely associated with the participation of citizens in elections using electronic access platforms, it is not limited to the process of elections by any means. In this context, e-democracy could include the attempts of various stakeholders including governments, political parties, civil society organizations and activist groups to use information technologies as a means to communicate with citizens and to facilitate the exchange of information for meeting requirements for accountability and transparency in governance processes [4].

Trust is one of the concepts that have the potential to make e-democracy more effective or undermine the possibilities of having it as an alternative to traditional methods. The dependence of e-democracy on the use of technology in engaging citizens in the political process assumes the trust of these citizens in the use of ICT in this context and makes such trust one of its foundation stones [5].

With the development of information technologies in governmental contexts, e-trust has emerged as an increasingly important concept that links citizens to services offered by their governments through digital and online means. In this context, with the passage of time and the evolution of technological advancements, e-trust is nowadays one of the most important aspects to be considered in all stages of planning, implementing or assessing e-government services [6].

Besides, the incorporation of e-trust and e-democratic services along with the more traditional e-government services will empower governments and administrations in evolving their services towards including their citizens and the public institutions in direct evolvement in public decision making [1].

2.1 Social Media and E-Trust

In seeking to further develop the concept of e-trust, governments have often sought to engage social media in their attempts to enhance citizens' participation in their decision-making and policy processes. In order to understand the citizens' needs, the decision-makers need to know more about citizens' behaviours, preferences and ability to use e-government online services. Social media represents a strategic opportunity that can help governments to become more transparent by providing citizens with better services and enhancing information's access in a way that makes them more involved [7]. This surge in government involvement with social media has led researchers across the globe to attempt to formalize such approaches with many efforts resulting in the proposal of a model or a framework for integrating existing social media environments into a government's portal. Such approaches are not necessarily new as Lacigova et al. [8] had verified through a number of European Union funded projects that utilizing citizens' already preferred media channels has a higher chance of succeeding in engaging people. Other similar research has suggested that for a government or an administration using of existing social media applications is more efficient, both fiscally and in communicating with citizens, than creating a government social networking site. Although proponents of creating of such aforesaid sites have claimed that it does provide the government with more control over the content and structure, and might reduce concerns about privacy and trust; other studies have showed that creating dedicated websites for this purpose has less chance of succeeding in engaging people [9].

Other researchers though are warning that embracing social media without a proper strategy might backfire and lead to isolation for some citizens due to the widening of the Digital Divide in society. To avoid such undesirable effects Mousavi and Pimenidis [10] proposed a risk assessment approach to support the government body that offers such an engagement and involvement to its citizens in ensuring that trust is maintained and no citizen groups are alienated.

Complimentary to the above work other researchers have proposed a framework for use by governments to explore the profiles of social media users to allow them to enhance their understanding of their citizens' profiles. This in turn will enable the organization to improve and adapt public services, decision making, information sharing, transparency of their processes; improving citizens' trust in their systems and the quality of meeting the individual's current and relevant needs [7]. Such a framework can work in more stable societies that enjoy enhanced freedom of opinion, have benefited from long years of democratic processes and have very high affinity for technology. This is the case in the U.S.A. where the current presidential election campaign has seen both candidates' camps use social media to enhance their relationship with citizens/voters. This means gaining more trust from the citizens, which in the case of the U.S.A. is easier to gain as the public is more conditioned and keen to accept trade-offs for deals versus relinquishing some privacy and trust [11].

Different societies though react in a variety of ways and therefore might require different approaches and systems to capture the trust of citizens and to attract them to e-participation. Citizens believe that in the era of digital services they should be offered more opportunity to engage with decision making and participate more actively in government actions that affect present life and the future of a country or a small local entity. Voters find the representative system boring and low participation levels in elections in Portugal are an indicative phenomenon of disinterested and disappointed citizens. An e-participation platform that would allow citizens to engage more actively in decision making and also the direct evaluation of government actions, leading to more transparency and higher citizen control, has been proposed in [12].

3   E-Voting Systems

Over the period of the last decade there have been increasing debates about the use of ICTs in relation to practicing democracy and making it possible for citizens to participate in elections and voting using electronic means rather than traditional means. The term "e-voting" came to use referring to the electronic voting techniques and procedures that take place through the use of punched cards, optical scan voting systems and specialized electronic voting systems that would replace the use of ballot boxes and their accompanied tools [13].

This in particular has emerged as a result of attempts by governments to jeopardize the ill and the adverse effects of the traditional election systems. Here, e-voting has been seen as an effective solution that would improve the whole process of voting and help to avoid any miscellaneous taking place already.

3.1   Advantages of Electronic Voting Systems

One of the fundamental advantages of the use of online voting systems is that they eradicate the need to arrange the elections from scratch and securely save the ballots cast in electronic format. Moreover, e-voting systems can be considered as a source of reducing costs to the structure of the governmental body of a country [14].

As compared to traditional democratic systems, e-democratic systems would resemble a quick acquaintance with the supreme vigilance and monitoring in the societal, fiscal and the rational aspects' of governments' endeavors towards achieving success. Effective electoral voting systems would embrace the prevalent system with the provisions of jeopardizing the existing and uncertain problems relating to the security and confidentiality of the voting and polling ballots. Political, societal, infrastructural facilities and economic conditions of governments can be enriched due to the effectiveness inherent in e-voting systems accessed from home. Citizens in the countries that embrace the use of such systems are able to withstand challenges due to the progression in the electoral voting rights.

Since the early days of e-voting such systems had the potential of enhancing the democratic process by triggering an increase in voter turnout. Such a potential can be further enhanced by for instance providing ballots in multiple languages, accommodating lengthy ballots or facilitating early and absentee voting in addition to meeting the needs of those voters who have physical disabilities [15].

3.2   E-Trust and E-Voting Systems

Taking into consideration the various promises as well as implications that are related to the use of e-voting systems and e-democracy, it would be inevitable for governments and other stakeholders to try and work on the trust of citizens in these services. Here, the application of e-services including e-voting systems should be carried out while all factors are taken into consideration. [14] confirmed that secrecy and accuracy are amongst the key things that must be preserved by voting systems if they aimed to gain the trust of citizens. However, he adds that this should be carried out in a transparent way that would make citizens able to access all required information. As for the issue of accuracy, he argues, it is something that e-voting systems usually have the ability to deal with but when it comes to secrecy then these systems may prove some kind of inefficiency, and at the same time their potential for transparency is considerably doubted. In addition to the above, Schaupp et al. [16] adds that it is indicated that perceptions of users have a big impact on their willingness to use e-voting systems. These perceptions are mostly related to compatibility, usefulness, and trust.

4   The Case for E-Democracy for Palestine

Palestine is a geographical region in Western Asia between the Mediterranean Sea and the Jordan River, situated at a strategic location between Egypt and Jordan; the boundaries of the region have changed throughout history. Previously Palestine was under the rule of the Ottoman (Turkish) Empire. During the First World War, Britain promised to support "complete and final liberation" for the people of the wider region in return for them rebelling against the Ottomans [17].

However in 1948 Israel was established unilaterally with the Jewish population forming a minority of the local population. By 1949 Palestinians had started spreading into different countries across the world included in those societies as refugees. After this spread Israel became the ruler of more than 78% of the land. The remaining land (22%) called West Bank, Gaza Strip and East Jerusalem have been under an illegal Israeli military rule since they were occupied in the 1967 war, and today are referred to as the "Occupied Palestinian Territories" [17]. The Arab League Summit had created an organization called Palestinian liberation organization (PLO) in 1964 for the purpose of liberating Palestine and creating a state for its people. Later PLO was recognized as sole legitimate representative of the Palestinian people by many countries [18]. On 1993, Israel and PLO have signed Oslo accords. This agreement had offered Palestinian self-determination which had resulted to form a government for Palestinians called Palestinian authority(PA) [19] and since that time PA became responsible to serve Palestinian citizen in west bank and Gaza strip mainly and particularly across the world. Recently General Assembly of the UN has granted Palestine non-member observer State statue which has resulted to a first real recognition for Palestine as state [20].

4.1 The Need for E-Government for Palestine

Many Palestinians are currently denied from entering Palestine because of the occupation control. At present, Palestinians are living in different areas around the world where there are differences in terms of ICT infrastructure, Internet availability and IT literacy. This situation has resulted to significant problem in terms of accessing public services, communication with government agencies and participating in the general election. The Palestinian government has started an e-government initiative to cope with this problem in 2001.

Implementation of e-government in Palestine may solve most the problems for accessing public services and communication with government agencies. Considering the exceptional dispersion of the Palestinian population and Israel's control of the area, implementing of real electronic government may enable the government to perform their responsibilities and provide public services electronically to Palestinians and other stakeholders. Moreover, it will facilitate democracy by removing the need for physical voting stations which is one of the main barriers to holding conventional elections.

The Palestinian Government's policy over the past few years has included e-government as one of the top national priorities. President Abbas has assigned a Ministerial Committee for E-Government. This committee has prepared the first comprehensive E-government Strategic Plan in 2005, and this document was part of the PA vision "to provide a better life for our citizens by being a Government that: Empowers citizens to participate in government; Connects citizens, the private sector and institutions to drive economic growth and meet community challenges; and Delivers real public value through citizen-centric government services" [21].

According to the Organization for Economic Co-operation and Development (OECD), e-government vision and policies in Palestine at 2010 was including "a public sector that provides citizens with high quality services and value for money". This plan states that the e-government National strategy should, over time, work to increase efficiency and effectiveness of public service delivery; it also states that the Ministry of Telecommunications and Information Technology (MTIT) is main key players in terms of move this initiatives forward, moreover, the 13th government program (Ending the Occupation, Establishing the State and Homestretch to Freedom) has clearly mention that the use of ICT and e-government particular should help public sector reform and this is the most important national priorities. Currently, the e-government project in Palestine is still suffering from various factors such as administrative complexities, interior complexities, problems of cooperation and data exchange between government institutions and in data accessibility [22].

4.2 An E-Voting System for Palestinians

The forced diaspora of Palestinians has created challenges for the Palestinian Authority (PA) as it continues to gain international recognition as an emerging state. With the possibility of the requirement for democratic elections and a fully recognized Palestinian state in the horizon, it is a pressing need for the officials within the existing Palestinian Authority find new and innovative ways to engage a scattered constituency in the democratic process [23].

Due to the spread of Palestinians in different countries, Palestine has experienced a huge difficulty in enabling its citizens to elect their representatives. Using a democratic way to elect people representatives will be an ideal to solving the Palestinian leadership crisis. According to government officials many countries who are hosting Palestinian as refugees do not allow them to hold election activities in their territories; hence e-voting systems could offer a solution to overcome this problem [24, 25].

Palestinian activists across the world have started an initiative for general election for Palestinians across the world. Leaders from the main Palestinian parties and factions, in addition to independents and intellectuals, have also encouraged Palestinians around the world to register to vote in this civic campaign in the National Call for Registration for PNC elections.

In June 2011, A Palestinian organization called the Facilitation Office (FO) of the civic registration announced that they have finalized a secure electronic voter registration machine for PNC elections. The registration mechanism was built to provide Palestinians in a variety of different locations and circumstances with the opportunity to register to vote, whilst maintaining the highest international standards of safety and security in the creation of this primary register. The procedures of the registration process are simple: Palestinian civic associations wishing to run a voter registration drive can do so through a secure low-cost process, as part of a popularly-driven, national initiative.

The above office claimed that the procedures applied reflect international best practice and standards, and have been developed with the relevant national and international institutions to ensure equality of principles and practice across the Palestinian communities, mindful of the obstacles and challenges faced by each Months later the central election commission in Palestine announced that e-voting system is not applicable for the case of Palestine, stating that the majority of Palestinian will not trust e-democracy. There is concern though within the Palestinian Authority relating to the skepticism that e-Democracy will not work for Palestinians because a majority of Palestine's constituents do not trust technology.

To address these conflicting opinions a survey to gauge the acceptance level of using technology in participating in democratic processes has been conducted by the authors in 2015. This survey also aimed to establish whether Palestinian people will be happy to use technology to elect their representatives. The survey has targeted Palestinians in Palestine and in different countries and locations across the world aiming to gauge the level of e-trust in digital government services and processes. The key objective was to capture views and measure the different means through which access to the survey was achieved. This last input would demonstrate an ability to utilize and trust a wide range of technologies and thus provide a foundation for the development of trust on e-voting processes [4, 26].

5 Presentation and Analysis of Results

The completed responses have been 320 across the world, with nearly 37% of respondents coming from territories associated with the Palestinian Authority (Gaza, West Bank, East Jerusalem) and nearly 80% of respondents being male. A key finding of the survey had been that over 68% of respondents indicated that they have used internet interfaces to connect with the Palestinian Authority and its governmental services (Figs. 1,2,3,4).

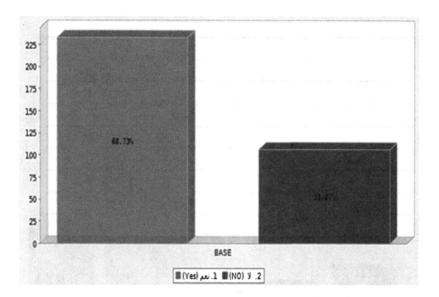

Fig. 1. Internet access of governmental services

In exploring the respondents' willingness to participate in future E-Government/ E-Democracy initiatives, almost 53% of respondents agreed. Further bolstering affirmative responses, over 22% of respondents strongly agreed that they would willingly use the government's online services in the future. Less than 10% expressed a negative response when asked about potential use of the government's online services, while the remaining respondents, less than 15% of the survey group, offered a neutral opinion or no opinion at all.

When asked about the potential of using the E-Voting System in the next election, nearly 2/3 of respondents – just under 66% of the survey group – agreed or strongly agreed. 14.07% of respondents indicated a strong disagreement with the potential use

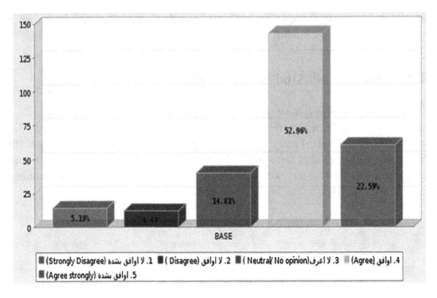

Fig. 2. Willingness in using e-government services in the future

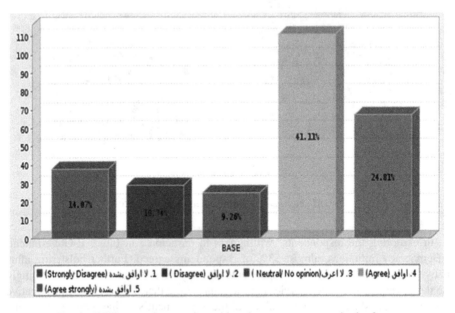

Fig. 3. Willingness in engaging with e-democracy systems in the future

of E-Voting, while 10.74% simply disagreed. 9.26% of respondents indicated a neutral response or did not respond.

What was more encouraging from the outcome of the survey was that nearly 14% of respondents strongly agreed in trusting the outcome of an online election and over

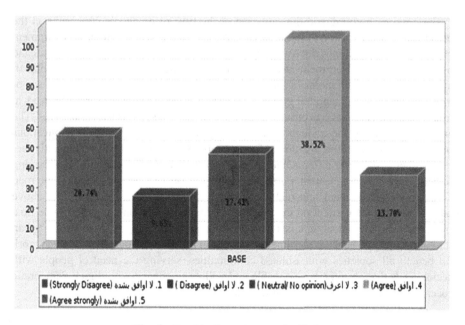

Fig. 4. Trust in the outcome of e-Voting

38% agreeing to it, yielding affirmative a majority of positive responses. That said, a significant minority of the survey group – 20.74% of respondents – strongly disagreed with the statement. Another 9.63% of respondents fell in the "disagree" segment of the survey group. Somewhat surprisingly, 17.41% of respondents offered no opinion or a neutral opinion.

While no survey can provide an exhaustive gauge on public opinion, it appears that a majority of Palestinians may feel comfortable engaging in E-Democracy initiatives as they come online. It would appear that a potential Palestinian state would have a hearty base of support in place upon which future E-Democracy initiatives could flourish and grow. For the parts of constituency in diaspora, the future state's use of a variety of online services and democratic opportunities (general elections, referenda), would afford expatriates opportunities to stay connected and engaged with the homeland. The survey indicates that the Palestinian Authority must work to cultivate trust among its constituents. Expanded delivery of efficient, low cost services would certainly garner the trust of the people. Furthermore, the government's enhanced partnership with technology industries could cultivate additional trust. Calling on the expertise of technology firms to insure that online experiences are safe and private will do wonders for the "trust gap".

There is reasonable evidence to prompt the Palestinian government to start a real initiative to gauge and test out if e-voting can work this might be throw start using technology in small elections such as student unions elections at universities, Unions election, local elections and Palestinian community committees etc. this will provide further evidence about the political will towards enabling people elect their representatives genuinely and regularly.

Furthermore e-voting and the capturing of the trust of its people could present the perfect opportunity for the Palestinian Government to engage in further e-government activities. These could introduce new levels of transparency, efficiency of processes and answer calls for government accountability, allowing for better management of expectations and requirements of such a vastly dispersed peoples [1]. The experience of more organized and integrated countries where smaller populations are dispersed in larger geographical areas has provided enough evidence to support such initiatives. The European initiatives for e-identification and cross-border e-government applications could provide an excellent instrument for developing and supporting e-voting and other cross-border systems for a fragmented population such as the Palestinians [4]. Grasping the trust and cultivating e-trust would be the biggest obstacle to overcome on the road of effective e-government and real e-democracy [10, 27]. Any success in the above could have a resonant effect on the handling of the humanitarian and at the same time governance and identification crisis with the huge influx of refugees in to the European Union that is in full scale at the time of writing. In addition the outcomes of such work will benefit all societies with isolated communities, serving the need of people with special needs that are otherwise capable and willing to engage with digital democratic processes but might be restricted in their movement.

5.1   Can Social Media Enhance the E-Trust Level?

Given the results of the survey above and the review relating to existing theory and practice in the use of social media in digital government processes, there is certainly scope within society in general. Whether this is applicable to Palestinians and other dispersed populations around the globe is yet to be debated and proven. To this effect the authors have embarked into extending their research in capturing the level of trust and sense of security that Palestinians enjoy when using social media. This next level of the research explores the degree to which citizens engage in political debate through the use of social media, how secure they feel and how much they trust social media in exposing their political views, concerns and desires. This part of the work is expected to shed more light into any trust and security concerns that Palestinians might have in using e-government services and e-voting systems. This part of the research is at the time of writing in progress and any early results might be misleading. The authors expect that these results will provide a strong base to extent the findings to other large groups of displaced people and lessons learned from the case of Palestine will benefit refugees around the world, providing their host with solutions as to how to support them in their struggle to engage with their homeland.

6   Conclusions

Electronic Government systems have been embraced by administrations across the world, but have not yet managed to gain the trust and participation by large proportions of the society. Governments are facing a struggle to engage citizens in enhanced democratic processes, but it appears citizens might be unwilling to trade trust and privacy for e-participation. Engaging in the use of commonly shared tools and systems such as social media is seen as the current opportunity to approach more digital citizens, gain their trust and attract them to be involved in crucial e-democracy processes. Linking social media to e-voting could provide a trusted avenue for displaced citizens to be involved in democratic processes in the distant homelands.

References

1. Pimenidis, E., Georgiadis, C.K.: Can e-government applications contribute to performance improvement in public administration? Int. J. Oper. Res. Inf. Syst. 5(1), 48–57 (2014). doi:10.4018/ijoris.2014010104
2. BBC (2016a) http://www.bbc.co.uk/news/world-europe-34131911/. Accessed 02 May 2016
3. Tsagarousianou, R., Tambini, D., Bryan, C.: Cyberdemocracy: Technology, Cities and Civic Networks. Routledge, London (1998)
4. Sideridis, A.B., Protopappas, L., Tsiafoulis, S., Pimenidis, E.: Smart Cross-Border e-Gov Systems and Applications. In: Katsikas, S.K., Sideridis, A.B. (eds.) e-Democracy 2015. CCIS, vol. 570, pp. 151–165. Springer, Cham (2015). doi:10.1007/978-3-319-27164-4_11
5. Mousavi, S.A.A., Pimenidis, E., Jahankhani, H.: Cultivating Trust – An e-Government Development model for addressing the needs of developing countries. Int. J. Electron. Secur. Digit. Forensics (IJESDF) 1(3), 233–248 (2008)
6. Savvas, I., Bassiliades, N., Pimenidis, E., Sideridis, A.B.: Building a logic for a public administration service transformation algorithm. In: Sideridis, A.B., Kardasiadou, Z., Yialouris, C.P., Zorkadis, V. (eds.) E-Democracy 2013. CCIS, vol. 441, pp. 73–79. Springer, Cham (2014). doi:10.1007/978-3-319-11710-2_7
7. Kacem, A., Belkaroui, R., Jemal, D., Ghorbel, H., Faiz, R., Abid, I.H.: Towards collaborative e-government improvement using social media-based citizen's profile investigation. In: Proceedings of ICEGOV 2015–2016, 01–03 March, 2016, Montevideo, Uruguay (2016). http://dx.doi.org/10.1145/2910019.2910029
8. Lacigova, O., Maizite, A., Cave, B.: eParticipation and social media: a symbiotic relationship? Eur. J. ePract. 16, 71–76 (2012). ISSN: 1988-625X
9. Landsbergen, D.: Government as part of the revolution: using social media to achieve public goals. Electron. J. eGov. 8(2), 135–147 (2010)
10. Mousavi, S.A.A., Pimeninidis, E.: Social media applications in e-government: a risk assessment approach. In: Proceedings of the 14th European Conference on eGovernment, ECEG 2014, 12–13 June, Brasov, Romania, pp. 180–188 (2014)
11. Pew Research Center (2016) Presidential candidates' changing relationship with the web. http://www.journalism.org/2016/07/18/presidential-candidates-changing-relationship-with-the-web/. Accessed 31 August 2016
12. Quental, C., Borges Gouveia, L.: Web platform for public e-participation management: a case study. Int. J. Civic Engagem. Soc. Change 1(1), 60–77 (2014)
13. Choi, D.: Supply Chain Governance Mechanisms, Green Supply Chain Management, and Organizational Performance (2012)
14. Galam, S.: Democratic voting in hierarchical structures or how to build a dictatorship. Advs. Complex Syst. 03(01n04), 171–180 (2000)
15. Gritzalis, D. (ed.): Secure Electronic Voting. Kluwer Academic Publishers, USA (2002)
16. Schaupp, C., Carter, L.: E-voting: from apathy to adoption. J. Enter. Inf. Manage. 18(5), 586–601 (2005)

17. PSC (2014). http://www.palestinecampaign.org/information/. Accessed 15 Dec 2014
18. United Nations, PLO (2014). Accessed 11 Nov 2014
19. BBC, Oslo agreement (1993). http://news.bbc.co.uk/1/hi/world/middle_east/7385301.stm. Accessed 10 Jan 2016
20. United Nations, General Assembly Votes Overwhelmingly to Accord Palestine 'Non-Member Observer State' Status in United Nations (2012). http://www.un.org/press/en/2012/ga11317.doc.htm. Accessed 03 Aug 2015
21. Organisation for Economic Co-Operation and Development (OECD), The Case of e-Government in the Palestinian Authority (2011). http://www.google.co.uk/url?sa=t&rct=j&q=&esrc=s&source=web&cd=1&ved=0CCYQFjAA&url=http%3A%2F%2Fwww.oecd.org%2Fmena%2Fgovernance%2F50402812.pdf&ei=pA9mVPXALJPraOuRgegO&usg=AFQjCNGcKbO_f5m4r2jCfZAsqtdzSfiDLw. Accessed 12 Nov 2014
22. Chadwick, D.: E-government will solve the accessibility problem with Palestinian government (2013). http://www.wafa.ps/arabic/index.php?action=detail&id=133955
23. Shat, F.J.F., Mousavi, A., Pimenidis, E.: Electronic government enactment in a small developing country – the palestinian authority's policy and practice. In: Sideridis, A.B., Kardasiadou, Z., Yialouris, C.P., Zorkadis, V. (eds.) E-Democracy 2013. CCIS, vol. 441, pp. 83–92. Springer, Cham (2014). doi:10.1007/978-3-319-11710-2_8
24. Kiayias, A., Zacharias, T., Zhang, B.: On the necessity of auditing for election privacy in e-voting systems. In: Katsikas, S.K., Sideridis, A.B. (eds.) e-Democracy 2015. CCIS, vol. 570, pp. 3–17. Springer, Cham (2015). doi:10.1007/978-3-319-27164-4_1
25. Ntaliani, M., Costopoulou, C., Karetsos, S., Molhanec, M.: Citizen e-Empowerment in Greek and Czech Municipalities. In: Katsikas, S.K., Sideridis, A.B. (eds.) e-Democracy 2015. CCIS, vol. 570, pp. 124–133. Springer, Cham (2015). doi:10.1007/978-3-319-27164-4_9
26. Sideridis, A.B., Pimenidis, E., Protopappas, L., Koukouli, M.: An evaluation of the initiatives and the progress made on e-Government services in the EU, Global Security, Safety and Sustainability & e-Democracy. In: Georgiadis, C.K., Jahankhani, H., Pimenidis, E., Bashroush, R., Al-Nemrat, A. (eds.) ICGS3/e-Democracy 2011. LNICST, vol. 99, pp. 263–270. Springer, Heidelberg (2012)
27. Pimenidis, E., Iliadis, L.S., Georgiadis, C.K.: Can e-government systems bridge the digital divide? In: Proceedings of the 5th European Conference on Information Management and Evaluation (ECIME 2011), Dipartimento di Informatica e Comunicazione, Università dell'Insubria, Como, Italy, 8–9 September 2011, pp. 403–411 (2011)

Systems Security, Safety and Sustainability Cyber Infrastructure Protection

Actor-Network Theory as a Framework to Analyse Technology Acceptance Model's External Variables: The Case of Autonomous Vehicles

Patrice Seuwou[1,2(✉)], Ebad Banissi[1], George Ubakanma[1],
Mhd Saeed Sharif[3], and Ann Healey[2]

[1] Division of Computing and Informatics, School of Engineering,
London South Bank University, London, UK
{seuwoup,banisse,george.ubakanma}@lsbu.ac.uk
[2] Department of Digital Innovation and Creative Enterprise,
GSM London, London, UK
{patrice.seuwou,ann.healey}@gsmlondon.ac.uk
[3] Department of Electronic and Computer Engineering,
Brunel University London, Uxbridge, UK
mhd.sharif@brunel.ac.uk

Abstract. The main factor for growth in a globalised and highly competitive world is to have an innovative and continuous improvement for the new technologies; however, it is difficult to guarantee the success of such factor without considering the human nature of the people. The Unified Theory of Acceptance and Use of Technology (UTAUT2) is a model that has been used for years to help us understand the drivers of acceptance of new information technologies by its users. This paper presents the Actor-Network Theory (ANT) as a framework to analyse external variables influencing technology acceptance. We have identified a new construct and moderating factor enabling the extension of the UTAUT2. The scenario used to conduct our investigation is the Autonomous Vehicle (AV) which is a disruptive technology and may prove to be the next big evolution in personal transportation. The study was conducted using an anonymous survey, over 410 responses so far, and numerous interviews with experts in the field of sociology, psychology and computer science in order to refine the proposed model. Our research findings reveal not only the usefulness of ANT in developing an understanding the human and non-human actants playing a role in consumer's behavioural intention of using AV, but ANT also helps us to argue that culture is a direct determinant of behavioural intention and social class is a very important moderating aspect.

Keywords: Technology acceptance model · Unified theory of acceptance and use of technology · Actor-Network theory · Autonomous vehicles · Security

© Springer International Publishing AG 2016
H. Jahankhani et al. (Eds.): ICGS3 2017, CCIS 630, pp. 305–320, 2016.
DOI: 10.1007/978-3-319-51064-4_24

1 Introduction

The development of information technologies has resulted in an ever-increasing advancement of products which continues to challenge and cater to the attitudes of consumers. Understanding individual acceptance and use of information technology is one of the most mature streams of information systems research [1]. Various theoretical models, primarily developed from theories in psychology and sociology have been devised to predict adoption and use of technology. The case used for our investigation is autonomous vehicles as a disruptive technology examined using the Actor-Network Theory (ANT) as an analytical framework to explore the human and non-human actants influencing the acceptance of self-driving cars. Autonomous vehicles have existed as prototypes and demonstration vehicles since the 1970s. These vehicles can drive themselves without human supervision or input, but for the moment, a fully autonomous vehicle capable of completing an entire journey on public roads without any human input is still some way from being realized [2]. Reliability, safety, cost, appearance, trust, cyber liability, personal freedom, technology dependence, liability, legislation and social acceptance are only a few of the legitimate concerns the public currently have with regards to autonomous vehicles [3, 4]. Certainly the autonomous vehicle is a disruptive technology. Not all technologies predicted by popular media are immediately welcomed into society, and autonomous cars are one such technology. As typical with much advancement, some people will oppose them and the changes that they will bring. There are both human and non-human factors influencing the introduction of autonomous vehicles in the market. Our aim, in this study, is to identify other constructs initially neglected by previous models and theories but that could play a major role on people's behavioural intention to adopt self-driving cars. Since its original publication, UTAUT has served as a baseline model and has been applied to the study of a variety of technologies in both organisational and non-organisational settings. There have been many applications and replications of the entire model or part of the model in various settings that have contributed to fortifying its generalizability. Building on the past extensions to UTAUT, the objective of our work is to use the Actor-network theory as an analytical framework while paying particular attention to the influence of culture and social class on consumers' behavioural intention of using technology.

2 Autonomous Vehicles as a Disruptive Technology

Despite our desire to maintain control over our lives, the bulk of what we do with our lives has been coordinated and adapted by and to the technology that surrounds us [5, 6]. It should come as no surprise that when existing technology evolves or old technology is made obsolete, the phase where new technology enters our lives could be seen as being disruptive. This disruption occurs when the technology, which is introduced effects the social arrangements around which we build our lives [7, 8]. The term "disruptive technology" as coined by Christensen [9] refers to a new technology having lower cost and performance measured by traditional criteria, but having higher ancillary performance. Christensen finds that disruptive technologies may enter and expand emerging market niches, improving with time and ultimately attacking established products in their traditional markets. There are sustaining technologies, which enhance the characteristics of existing products or services and, most of the time, mainstream customers and the market appreciate and adopt these technologies rapidly. Disruptive technologies are radically different and disrupt or challenge the current way of doing things. Products based on such technologies underperform in the current market-place at first, but a few customers value them. However, eventually the innovation becomes so compelling that everyone rapidly abandons their current way of doing things and flocks to what is new.

The transportation business is a \$4 trillion industry globally [10]. This industry is inextricably linked with energy. Certainly, the internal combustion engine automobile will soon be disrupted, an event which will, in turn send disruptive shockwaves through the oil industry. The first wave of disruption of the century old automotive industry is well underway with electric vehicles. The second disruptive wave, the self-driving car, will hit before the first wave is finished crashing. Transportation will never be the same again. Autonomous Vehicles (AVs) will be here much sooner than most people expect and will lead to major changes in transportation, our cities and society as a whole. Most car manufacturers and some technology companies are actively developing and testing AVs. Some preliminary versions of AVs are already commercially available. The new auto technology will bring disruption with massive opportunities. Indeed, near autonomous cars followed by driverless vehicles (smart cars) will transform our commute to work and much more over the next two decades. Electric and hybrid cars are set to become a large part of our fleet, changing the demand for motoring and disrupting our pay-as-you-go revenue base. Most of these vehicles will be powered by electric power. Furthermore, we will expect a much safer and easier commute with fewer fatalities, dramatic accident reductions, and reduced congestion. On the other hand, car-based technologies hold the promise of reducing the billions of pounds we spend on roads by improving how we use them and by saving lives. Public transport will also be challenged as car journeys become cheaper, safer and easier to make and without environmental emissions, lower congestion. Some industries will have to change their business model, reinvent themselves or disappear altogether. When designing infrastructure policies, there is a tendency to assume that the future is simply an extension of the past. AVs are a truly disruptive technology and we cannot forecast the future by simply extrapolating from the past. All of the above issues will change the forecasts for standard infrastructure and major infrastructure projects.

3 Autonomous Vehicles Security and Safety Challenges

With more than 90% of accidents each year caused by driver error, one of the major motivations for developing AVs is the potential impact on vehicle safety. Current technologies utilize sensor arrays (LIDAR is used to a large extent) to create a 3-dimensional model of the space all around the car [56] It is estimated that over 90% of all accidents are due to human error or bad driving behaviour, whether it be reckless driving or driving while intoxicated [57] AV is just an extension of existing technologies such as Vehicle-to-vehicle (V2 V) and Vehicle-to-Infrastructure (V2I) allowing communication between vehicle and road side base stations. One goal of developing AV is to render these types of accidents a thing of the past. In spite of the various benefits of increased vehicle automation, some foreseeable challenges may include liability for damage, resistance of individuals to forfeit control of their cars, software reliability. AVs will have a high level of computer technology on board and may be connected to the internet, other vehicles and possibly their surroundings. As a result cyber security issues need to be carefully considered as car's computer or communication system between cars could potentially be compromised. They will also be ethical issues surrounding the privacy and use of data and testing, certification and licensing. Other challenges will include implementation of a legal framework and establishment of government regulations for self-driving cars, reliance on autonomous drive will produce less experienced drivers when manual control is needed. The loss of driver-related jobs with reduced demand for parking services and for accident related services assuming increased vehicle safety. There is also going to be a reduction in jobs relating to car insurance and traffic police. However, because the transition to driverless cars is likely to be spread over many years, the loss of jobs is likely to be gradual and manageable.

4   Theoretical Background

Throughout the years, there have been several theoretical models, primarily developed from theories in psychology and sociology, employed to explain technology acceptance and use [1, 11, 12]. The Unified Theory of Acceptance and Use of Technology (UTAUT) has distilled the critical factors and contingencies related to the prediction of behavioural intention to use a technology primarily in organisation contexts. UTAUT resulted from the synthesis of existing theories/models of technology use [1]. It was developed on the basis of integrating the dominant constructs of eight prior prevailing models that range from human behaviour, to computer science.

The eight models are: Theory of Reasoned Action [13], Technology Acceptance Model [14], Motivational Model [15], Theory of Planned Behavior [16], Combined TAM and TPB [17, 18], Model of PC Utilisation (MPCU) [19], Innovation Diffusion Theory [20], and Social Cognitive Theory [21]. Since the original publication, UTAUT has served as a baseline model and has been applied to the study of a variety of technologies in both organisational and non-organisational settings [22]. The work in [23] found that overall the UTAUT constructs were a useful starting point in studying scholarly behavioural intention and use of social media as well as various other technologies, but further research is required to better understand the factors influencing human behavioural intention to accept and use technology. The scenario used for our investigation is Autonomous Vehicles (AV) as a disruptive technology. Undeniably, for years, almost all commercial aircraft have had the ability to operate on autopilot. On-board computers can manage most aspects of flying, including even aspects of take-off and landing. This technology displays numerous benefits to the aviation industry and has been accepted by consumers. Today, similar technologies are being introduced in the car manufacturing industry as research shows that traffic accidents are a major source of disability and mortality worldwide. Every year, more than 1.2 million people die and up to 50 million people are injured because of road accidents [24]. In 2005–2007, the DARPA Grand Challenge and Urban Challenge provided researchers with a practical scenario in which to test the latest sensors, computer technologies and artificial intelligence algorithms [3]. Autonomous or highly aware vehicles have the potential to reduce these numbers dramatically and save many lives across the world. Arrival of new technologies always brings new challenges and problems. Normally, there are human and non-human factors influencing the deployment of autonomous vehicles in the market. Therefore, the way the public perceives these self-driving cars will directly affect the way they will be introduced to the market and how quickly they will be seen on the streets. Certainly to accept the concept of vehicles on the roads without a human at the controls, the car users must have faith that the systems are safe. Surely, the public's willingness to accept this technology will determine how car manufacturers develop and market them.

This research attempts to build upon and extend the Unified Theory of Acceptance and Use of Technology (UTAUT2) and to enhance our understanding of the factors that influence people behavioural intention of acceptance and use of technology [12]. A number of studies have identified that people don't like changes as most people are reluctant to alter their habits [25]. Many authors believe that customer acceptance is likely to be the biggest obstacle to autonomous vehicle penetration [2, 26, 27]. At first, many consumers may be reluctant to put their lives in the hands of a robot. Recent studies and surveys have shown a split in opinion as to whether people would like autonomous capability to be available in their vehicles or not. User acceptance is a key ingredient to the successful adoption of autonomous vehicles. Empirical evidence shows that automation has a substantial influence on human behaviour. With automation, the role of the human driver changes substantially. Indeed this is a very important 'human factors' issue and throughout the years, many processes within cars have become automated including cruise control and anti-lock brakes amongst others. However, the transition from humans as drivers to humans as merely passengers in a car that drives itself is a major one. People generally have emotional connections with their vehicles, therefore, are drivers actually willing to give up direct control over their vehicle and under what conditions? If automation of vehicles is not accepted by the users and users refrain from using the technology, the impact of automation on traffic flow efficiency, traffic safety and energy efficiency is mitigated. It is, however, not yet clear to what extent users accept automation and what the determinants of consumer acceptance of automation are [28].

5 Conceptual Model

5.1 Methodology

To gain a better understanding of the current situation, Actor-network theory (ANT), also known as the sociology of translation is the tool adopted in this research for exploring collective sociotechnical processes while analysing the human and non-human actants playing a role in this complex network referred to as assemblage. ANT approach emerged within the sociological research of science and technology, having its roots in French philosophy and semiotics. Since then, ANT has spread into various contexts of sociological inquiry [29, 30, 39]. It is seen as a socio-philosophical approach that seeks to understand complex social circumstances by paying attention to relational factors referred to as associations [31, 32]. This tool will be supplemented by interviews with psychologists, sociologist, computer scientists from various UK universities and a survey as part of the research strategy, drawing on multiple sources of data in order to collect rich evidence and explanations of phenomenon on the issue of what influences individuals to accept or reject autonomous vehicles as a disruptive technology.

5.2   Overview of the Actor Network Theory (ANT)

ANT is a Theory developed in the 1980s from the work of Bruno Latour, Michel Callon and John Law in order to study the relationship between both human and non-human objects within a given scenario. The ANT approach emerged within the sociological research of science and technology, having its roots in French philosophy and semiotics. Actor network theory highlights the nature of relations and theorizes that they can be both semiotic (meaning making) and material. Since then, ANT has spread into various contexts of sociological inquiry [29, 30]. It is seen as a socio-philosophical approach that seeks to understand complex social circumstances by paying attention to relational factors referred to as associations [31, 32]. The [33] argues that the "social is not the glue which holds society together; rather it is what is glued together by many other types of connectors. It is not a specific realm...but only...a very peculiar movement of re-association and reassembling...a trail of associations between heterogeneous elements". [34] Says 'Social scientists have transformed the world in various ways; the point, however, is to interpret it'.

Traditional methods advocate that to examine any given scenario, a framework must first be applied, in order to instruct the observation of the participants, however, Latour and Woolgar's work, at the Salk Institute in California, was conducted in the absence of prior assumptions of scientific methods, approaching their research as if they were anthropologists, observing some unknown phenomena. With the deliberate absence of a hypothesis, focus was centred on the observer's experience as being the only true source for understanding, rather than utilising pre-existing concepts of what should be [35, 41].

This anthropological approach introduced the concept of reflexivity, the idea that both the observer and observed are engaged in comparable activities [36–38, 40]. By the 1980's, due to the work of Michel Callon, Bruno Latour and John Law at the Centre de Sociologie de l'Innovation, the architecture of actor-network theory (ANT) had emerged.

ANT is problematic to define, in that it is more easily understood by application rather than delineation or explanation. This is an attempt to situate it as a starting point for analysis, in order to hurdle the academic predicament that has been established by some of the contrasting approaches to social science.

How legitimate is it, to discuss social classes, and hypothesise certainties about these classes, when inferred from observations based on just a few? Can a sociological account of scientific and technical controversies have any validity, if it is just as susceptible to ideas of ambiguity and uncertainty as the natural sciences? [42].

For the ANT practitioner, it is important to assume nothing, in order to overcome this problem of generality [44]. In the absence of assumptions, understanding is not obscured by prior perspectives. [34] proposed a need to investigate more meticulously what is meant by the notion of the sciences, redefining sociology as a 'tracing of associations' since for the ANT theorist, the starting point is neither society nor the social, as for them, neither are fixed. Thus, the social and natural sciences take on the same roles in an analysis as they are both assumed by the observer to be equally unpredictable [42].

5.3   Actor-Network Theory as an Analytical Framework

ANT enables the delineation of a set of actors (the network) that influence, shape or determine an action [30], which facilitates the identification of relationships within and between actors in the same or different networks. It comprises four main components, the first being the actor or the actant, who is not just seen as a "point object" but rather as an association of various factors, themselves forming an actor-network [45]. An actor or actant may be an individual, a group, an idea, a piece of software, a material object, a plant, natural capital or an animal that acts towards something. It may not inevitably be the source of an action but instead may modify and enhance the state of affairs by making a significant difference [34, 43]. The second component relates to the "links" or relationships that exist between the actors, and may include money transfers, verbal or written communication, publications sent to subscribers, friendships, or resource exchange, including information and overlapping memberships of networks. The third element is the "network", which may be an individual, a group, an idea, a physical object, a plant or an animal. It could also be an interactive assembly of entities, or a group or "series of actions" including a number of potential mediators [43]. The fourth component is the action itself [43], and relates to agency, or taking seriously what the actors (human or non-human) have to say. Figure 1 shows a blending the Technology Acceptance Model (TAM) and the Actor-Network Theory (ANT) to create a combined TAM – ANT model.

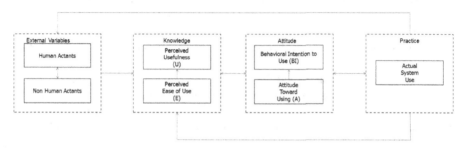

Fig. 1. Combined TAM – ANT model

According to [47], ANT seeks to examine the tools by which relationships emerge, and how the roles of subjects and objects, and intermediaries, human actors (i.e. people, organizations, and groups) and non-humans (the natural environment, software, and computers) are attributed and stabilized. The point of interest is how these and other categories come into existence via the processes involved in constituting a network. The work in [48] claims that these processes of association and reassembling are at the core of Actor-network Theory. ANT supposes that collective action is made up of a series of human and non-human actors, and a translation carried out through a translator or an interpreter will create various relationships between these heterogeneous actors, which then become networked. The process of translation is a concatenation of successive stages, transformations, and redefinitions of the collective project, through which actors (human and non-human) are mobilized in various ways. [33] argue that the network is "a chain of actions consolidated by mediators... [in which] actors and non-humans are associated with the same project".

The main idea behind ANT is that the collective, needs to be distinguished from a collective or the idea of collectivity [47]. This means that it is the relationships and their divergence that are essential, and not the things themselves [47]. Four important points should be noted about this definition: (1) Networks are always being gathered and re-gathered for specific projects; they are constantly in flux. (2) Networks are interim entities; their existence depends essentially on the action of ongoing relationships. (3) ANT, in contrast to other network theories, ascribes power to non-human actors in the network, such as the natural environment, objects, technologies, software, machines, implements and computers. (4) Contrary to mediators, translators are the dynamic element of networks, which effect the changes that lead towards the recognition of specific projects [33]. ANT is based on three methodological principles [46, 49]. The first principle is "agnosticism", which is the requirement of impartiality regarding the actors involved in the network [50]. ANT compels dispassion and holds that all interpretations should be unbiased [42, 43]. The second ANT principle is "generalized symmetry", which offers a counterbalance to the principle of agnosticism as it continues the idea of equivalence between human and non-human actors [51]. Symmetry refers to the idea of networks being formed where human and non-human actors have equally important roles [42]. The third principle, "free association", argues that heterogeneous actors can be linked together through a number of conceptual divisions, such as national/international, cultural/natural, or social/natural [52]. The work in [50] argues that ANT looks at the transformation of heterogeneous networks into aligned networks, which can be composed of individuals, groups, organizations, technologies, animals and more. It examines how the networks emerge, who or what is involved, how the networks are maintained, and how networks of actors compete with other networks. Moreover, ANT investigates the mechanics of power through the networks' construction and maintenance (both human and non-human) (Fig. 2) [50].

The application of this body of theory may thus facilitate an examination of the roles of, and the relationships between, structural actants, digital actants, software actants, hardware actants, cultural actants and human actants which lies at the heart of this study (Figs. 3 and 4).

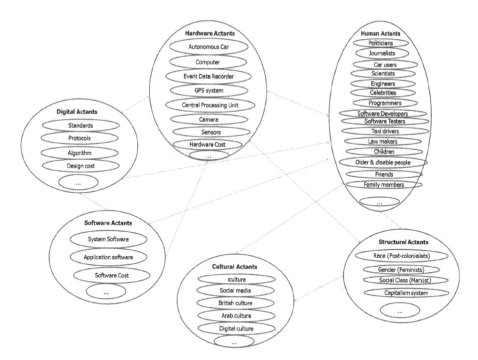

Fig. 2. Connection of actants in an assemblage for autonomous vehicle

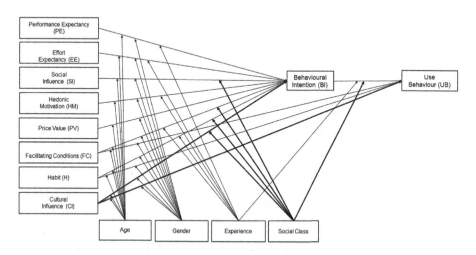

Fig. 3. Proposed research model

Our research framework provides the theoretical basis for explaining how various other important actants have been identified using the Actor-Network Theory which could be used to enhance the existing UTAUT2 Model (Table 1).

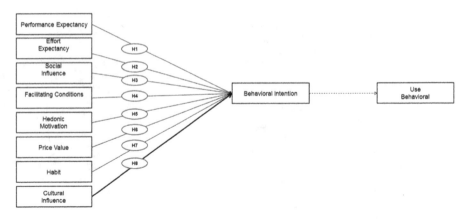

Fig. 4. Consumer acceptance and use of information on technology: extending the unified theory of acceptance and use of technology. Adapted from: [12].

5.4   Proposed Research Model

Table 1. A brief description of the research model constructs

Determinates/constructs	Description
Performance Expectancy (PE)	Performance expectancy is defined as the degree to which an individual believes that using autonomous vehicles will help him or her to attain gains in daily life activities, increase productivity, decrease possibilities of accidents on the road and makes driving more secure. PE also takes into consideration security features of the car; provide some level of satisfaction about trust, and privacy protection. Gender and age is theorised to play a moderating role. The influence of performance expectancy on behavioural intention will be moderated by gender and age, such that the effect will be stronger for men and in particular for younger men
Effort Expectancy (EE)	Effort Expectancy is defined as the degree of ease associated with the use of autonomous vehicles. The ease is associated with learning how to use autonomous vehicles and how clear and understandable the interaction with the technology is. The influence of effort expectancy on behavioural intention will be moderated by gender and age, experience. We suggest that effort expectancy is more salient for women than for men. The gender differences predicted here could be driven by cognitions related to gender roles. Increased age has been shown to be associated with difficulty in processing complex stimuli and allocating attention to information. Thus we propose that effort expectancy will be most salient for women, particularly those who are older and with relatively little experience with autonomous vehicles. The influence of effort expectancy on behavioural intention will be mo derated by gender, age and experience, such that the effect will be stronger for women, particularly younger women and particularly at early stages of experience

(continued)

Table 1. (*continued*)

Determinates/constructs	Description
Social Influence (SI)	Social Influence is defined as the degree to which an individual perceives that important others believe he or she should use the technology. Social influence occurs when one's emotions, opinions, or behaviours are affected by others. Social influence takes many forms and can be seen in conformity, socialisation, peer pressure obedience, persuasion, sales and marketing, and review of information. Furthermore, social influence as a direct determinant of behavioural intend on contains the explicit or implicit notion that the individual's behaviour is influenced by the way in which they b eh eve others will view them as a re suit of having used autonomous vehicles. The impact of social influence on behavioural intention will be moderated by gender, age and experience, such that the effect will be stronger far women, particularly older women, particularly older women in mandatory stages of experience
Hedonic Motivation (HM)	Hedonic Motivation is defined as the fun or pleasure derived from using a technology, and it has been shown to play an important role in. determining technology acceptance and use. Thus the influence of hedonic motivation on behavioural intention will be moderated by gender, age and experience
Price Value (PV)	The cost and pricing structure may have a significant impact on consumers' technology use. In marketing research, the monetary cost price is usually conceptualized together with the quality of products or services to determine the perceived value of products or services. We follow these ideas and define price value as consumers' cognitive tradeoff between the perceived benefits of the applications and the monetary cost for using them [53]. The price value is positive when the benefits of using a technology are perceived to be greater than the monetary cost and such price value has a positive impact on intention. Thus, price value has been added as a predictor of behavioural intention to use autonomous vehicles
Facilitating Conditions (FC)	Facilitating Conditions are defined as the degree to which an individual believes that technical infrastructure exists to support use of the system. This support can be linked to the availability of necessary resources, the knowledge required to use the AVs, and the compatibility of the system with other technologies currently being used. Moreover, the support could also be the existence of a service for assistance with system difficulties or system failure. The influence of facilitating conditions on behavioural intention will be mo derated by age and experience, such that the effect will be stronger for older users, particularly with increasing experience. Thus we propose that facilitating conditions will not have a significant influence on behavioural intention

(*continued*)

Table 1. (*continued*)

Determinates/constructs	Description
Habit (H)	The empirical findings about the role of habit in technology use have delineated different underlying processes by which it influences technology use. Related to the operationalization of habit as prior use, Kim and Malhotra (2005) found that prior use was a strong predictor of future technology use. Habit is the extent that individuals tend to execute behaviours automatically [54], The work in [12] discovered that habit directly and indirectly effects Behavioural Intention to use technology. It was found that increased experience in usage lead to habitual technology use. Given that there are detractors to the operationalization of habit as prior use [16]. some work, such as that of [54] has embraced a survey and perception-based approach to the measurement of habit. Such an operationalization of habit has been shown to have a direct effect on technology use over and above the effect of intention and also to moderate the effect of intention on technology use such that intention is less important with increasing habit [54]
Cultural Influence (CI)	Culture can be defined as what distinguishes the human element in social life from what is simply biologically driven. It refers to all of the beliefs, customs, ideas, behaviours, and traditions of a particular society that are passed through generations. It is also transmitted to people through language as well as through the modeling of behaviour, and it defines which traits and behaviors are considered important, desirable, or undesirable. For example, there is no official law that bans women from driving but deeply held religious beliefs prohibit it, with Saudi clerics arguing that female drivers "undermine social values". Where Autonomous vehicle adoption may be influenced by culture, the influence of culture on behavioural intention will be moderated by gender
Behavioural Intention (BI)	Behavioural intention is defined as an individual's intention to perform a given act which can predict corresponding behaviours when an individual acts voluntarily. Besides that, behavioural intention is the subjective probability of carrying out behaviour and also the cause of certain usage behaviour [55], Thus, intentions show the motivational factors that influence behaviour and are indicators of how hard people are willing to try and the effort they put in to engage in a behaviour. Also, it was found that behavioural intention is to be the main factor of individual mobile services usage and that usage intentions are rational indicators of future system use
Use Behaviour (UB)	Use behaviour is used to measure the actual acceptance and adoption of technologies or the new information systems being investigated

6   Hypothesis Development

H1: Performance Expectancy will be positively related to behavioural intention of using autonomous vehicles

H2: Effort Expectancy will be positively related to behavioural intention of using autonomous vehicles

H3: Social Influence will be positively related to behavioural intention of using autonomous vehicles

H4: Hedonic Motivation will be positively related to behavioural intention of using autonomous vehicles

H5: Price Value will have a significant influence on behavioural intention of using autonomous vehicles

H6: Facilitating conditions will be positively related to behavioural intention of using autonomous vehicles

H7: Habit will be positively related to behavioural intention of using autonomous vehicles

H8: Cultural Influence will have a significant influence on behavioural intention of using autonomous vehicles

H9: Moderating factors such as age, gender, experience and socioeconomic status will have an influence on the determinants of Behavioral Intention

7   Conclusion and Future Work

We advance the view that a more complete understanding of the actors influencing technology acceptance and adoption is necessary. These actants could be both human and non-human. Cultural influence was identified as a new construct and social class was identified as a new moderating factor obtained when combining existing technology acceptance model (TAM) to the unified theory of acceptance and use of technology (UTAUT2) and the Actor-network Theory. Focusing on the context of autonomous vehicles, we derived a set of hypotheses that linked factors related to the sociological, economic and psychological aspects. The proposed UTAUT2 – ANT has wider validity. The model can be applied, with due adjustments, to other contexts where consumers take charge of their decision-making such as for emerging technologies and other disruptive technologies. This study has some limitations that can be addressed by future research. First, we constructed the model based on detailed interviews with academics from various disciplines and surveys of potential users of self-driving cars, and on existing empirical findings and theoretical arguments in the literature across computer science, psychology and sociology. However, we did not empirically test the model. This limitation can be addressed in future research. Second, whilst we derived a set of 9 hypotheses, not all would be equally important in a specific setting. In addition, we may have ignored some moderating and mediating effects related to the considered variables. Future work can focus on both establishing the situation-specific nature of the proposed effects and on deriving more sophisticated hypotheses that incorporate moderating and mediating effects. We hope that this paper provides a foundation for the further exploration and understanding of technology adoption and usage jointly from social, economic, and psychological perspectives.

References

1. Venkatesh, V., Morris, M.G., Davis, G.B., Davis, F.D.: User acceptance of information technology: toward a unified view. MIS Q. **27**(3), 425–478 (2003)
2. ERTRAC. Automated Driving Roadmap: Status 3rd Draft for public consultation (2015)
3. Wei, J., et al.: Towards a viable autonomous driving research platform. In: IV Intelligent Vehicles Symposium (2013)
4. Kuderer, M., Gulati, S., Burgard, W.: Learning driving styles for autonomous vehicles from demonstration. In: IEEE International Conference on Robotics & Automation (ICRA), Seattle (2015)
5. Cowan Schwartz, R.: More Work for Mother: The Ironies of Household Technology from the Open Hearth to the Microwave. Basic Books, New York (1983)
6. Norman, D.: The Design of Everyday Things. Doubleday, New York (1990)
7. Lyytinen, K., Rose, G.: Disruptive information system innovation: the case of internet computing. Inf. Syst. J. **13**, 301–330 (2003)
8. Lyytinen, K., Rose, G.: The disruptive nature of it innovations: the case of internet computing in systems development organizations. MIS Q. **27**(4), 557–595 (2003b)
9. Christensen, C.: The Innovator's Dilemma: When New Technologies Cause Great Firms to Fail. Harvard Business School Press, Cambridge (1997)
10. Seba, T.: Clean Disruption of Energy and Transportation. Milton Keynes (2014)
11. Venkatesh, V., Davis, F.D.: A theoretical extension of the technology acceptance model: four longitudinal field studies. Manage. Sci. **46**(2), 186–204 (2000)
12. Venkatesh, V., Thong, J.Y.L., Xu, X.: Consumer acceptance and use of information technology: extending the unified theory of acceptance and use of technology. MIS Q. **36**(1), 157–178 (2012)
13. Fishbein, M., Ajzen, I.: Belief, Attitude, Intention and Behavior: An Introduction to Theory and Research. Addison-Wesley, Reading (1975)
14. Davis, F.D., Bagozzi, R., Warshaw, P.: User acceptance of computer technology: a comparison of two theoretical models. Manage. Sci. **35**, 982–1003 (1989). doi:10.1287/mnsc.35.8.982
15. Davis, F., Bagozzi, R., Warshaw, P.: Extrinsic and intrinsic motivation to use computers in the workplace. J. Appl. Soc. Psychol. **22**(14), 1111–1132 (1992)
16. Ajzen, I.: Perceived behavioral control, self-efficacy, locus of control, and the theory of planned behavior. J. Appl. Soc. Psychol. **32**, 665–683 (2002)
17. Taylor, S., Todd, P.: Assessing it usage: the role of prior experience. MIS Q. **19**(4), 561–570 (1995a)
18. Taylor, S., Todd, P.: Understanding information technology usage: a test of competing models. Inf. Syst. Res. **6**, 144–176 (1995b)
19. Thompson, R.L., Higgins, C.A., Howell, J.M.: Personal computing: toward a conceptual model of utilization. MIS Q. **15**(1), 125–143 (1991)
20. Moore, G.C., Benbasat, I.: Development of an instrument to measure the perceptions of adopting an information technology innovation. Inf. Syst. Res. **2**(3), 192–222 (1991)

21. Compeau, D.R., Higgins, C.A., Huff, S.: Social cognitive theory and individual reactions to computing technology: a longitudinal study. MIS Q. **23**(2), 145–158 (1999)
22. San Martin, H., Herrero, A.: Influence of the user's psychological factors on the online purchase intention in rural tourism: integrating innovativeness to the UTAUT framework. Tourism Manage. **33**(2), 341–350 (2012). doi:10.1016/j.tourman.2011.04.003
23. Gruzd, A., Staves, K., Wilk, A.: Connected scholars: examining the role of social media in research practices of faculty using the UTAUT model. Comput. Hum. Behav. **28**, 2340–2350 (2012)
24. World Health Organization, World report on road traffic injury prevention, Geneva (2004). http://whqlibdoc.who.int/publications/2004/9241562609.pdf?ua=1. Accessed 26 June 2015
25. Garvin, A.D., Roberto, A.M.: Change through persuasion. Harvard Bus. Rev. **83**, 104–112 (2005)
26. KPMG. Connected and Autonomous Vehicles - The Economic opportunity, s.l., SMMT Driving the motor industry (2015)
27. Stanley, M.: Autonomous Cars: Self-Driving the New Auto Industry Paradigm, s.l., Morgan Stanley Blue paper (2013)
28. Hoogendoorn, R., et al.: Towards safe and efficient driving through vehicle automation: the Dutch automated vehicle initiative (2013)
29. Jóhannesson, G.T.: Tourism translations, actor-network theory and tourism research. Tourist Stud. **5**(2), 133–150 (2005)
30. Rhodes, J.: Using actor-network theory to trace an ICT (telecenter) implementation trajectory in an African women's micro-enterprise development organization. USC Annenberg School for Communication 5(3), pp. 1–20 (2009)
31. Alcadipani, R., Hassard, J.: Actor-network theory, organizations and critique: towards a politics of organizing. Organization **17**(4), 419–435 (2010)
32. Arnaboldi, M., Spiller, N.: Actor-network theory and stakeholder collaboration: the case of cultural districts. Tourism Manage. **32**(3), 641–654 (2011)
33. Cohen, E., Cohen, S.A.: Current sociological theories and issues in tourism. Annals of Tourism Research (2012). http://dx.doi.org/10.1016/j.annals.2012.07.009
34. Latour, B.: Reassembling the Social: An Introduction to Actornetwork-Theory. Clarendon Lectures in Management Studies. Oxford University Press, New York (2005)
35. Latour, B.: The Powers of association. In: Law, J. (ed) Power, action and belief: A new Sociology of Knowledge? Sociological Review Monograph, vol. 32, pp. 264–280. Routledge & Kegan Paul, London (1986)
36. Latour, B.: The prince for machines as well as for machinations. In: Elliott, B. (ed) Technology and Social Process. Edinburgh University Press, Edinburgh, pp. 20–43 (1988b)
37. Latour, B.: Technology is society made durable. In: Law, J. (ed.) A Sociology of Monsters. Essays on Power, Technology and Domination, pp. 103–131. Routledge, London (1991)
38. Latour, B.: We Have Never Been Modern. Harvester Wheatsheaf, Hemel Hempstead (1993)
39. Latour, B.: On actor-network theory—a few clarifications. Soziale Welt-Zeitschrift fur Sozialwissenschaftliche forschung und praxis 47(4), 369 (1996)
40. Latour, B., Woolgar, S.: Laboratory Life, The Social Construction of Scientific Facts, New Edition edn. Princeton University Press, Princeton (1986)
41. Garrety, K.: Actor Network Theory. In: Hasan, H. (ed.) Being Practical with Theory: A Window into Business Research. University of Wollongong, Wollongong (2014)
42. Callon, M.: Some elements of a sociology of translation: domestication of the scallops and the fishermen of St Brieuc bay'. In: Law, J. (ed) Power, Action & Belief: A New Sociology of Knowledge? Routledge & Kegan Paul, London, pp. 196–229 (1986b)

43. Dolwick, J.S.: The social and beyond: introducing actor-network theory. J. Marit. Archaeol. 4(1), 21–49 (2009)
44. Law, J.: Making a mess with method (2003). http://www.lancs.ac.uk/fass/sociology/papers/law-making-a-mess-with-method.pdf
45. Tatnall, A., Burgess, S.: Using actor-network theory to research the implementation of a B-B portal for regional SMEs in Melbourne, Australia. In: 15th Bled Electronic Commerce Conference, Slovenia, 17-19 June (2002)
46. Tatnall, A., Gilding, A.: Actor-network theory and information systems research. In: Proceedings of the 10th Australasian Conference on Information Systems (ACIS), Wellington, Victoria University of Wellington (1999)
47. Van Der Duim, R., Henkens, R.: Wetlands, poverty reduction and sustainable tourism development, opportunities and constraints, Wageningen, the Netherlands, Wetlands International (2007)
48. Paget, E., Dimanche, F., Mounet, J.P.: A tourism innovation case: an actor-network approach. Ann. Tourism Res. 37(3), 828–847 (2010)
49. Ritzer-Encyclopedia (2004). www.sagepub.com/upm-data/5222_Ritzer_Entries_beginning_with_.A_%5B1%5D.pdf. Accessed 2 Nov 2015
50. Rodger, K.J.: Wildlife tourism and the natural sciences: bringing them together. Ph.D. Thesis, School of Environmental Science, Division of Science and Engineering, Murdoch University, Perth, Western Australia (2007)
51. McLean, C., Hassard, J.: Symmetrical absence/symmetrical absurdity: critical notes on the production of actor-network accounts. J. Manage. Stud. 41(3), 493–519 (2004). doi:10.1111/j.1467-6486.2004.00442.x. Publication link:a2df43f6-178d-4c31-88e5-f61c0ebd2d14
52. Burgess, J., Clark, J., Harrison, C.M.: Knowledge in action: an actor network analysis of a wetland agri-environment scheme. Ecol. Econ. 35(1), 119–132 (2000)
53. Dodds, W.B., Monroe, K.B., Grewal, D.: Effect of price, brand and store information on buyers' product evaluations. J. Market. Res. 28(3), 307–319 (1991)
54. Limayem, M., Hirt, S.G., Cheung, C.M.K.: How habit limits the predictive power of intention: the case of information systems continuance. MIS Q. 31(4), 705–737 (2007)
55. Yi, M.Y., Jackson, J.D., Park, J.S., Probst, J.C.: Understanding information technology acceptance by individual professionals: toward an integrative view. Inf. Manage. 43, 350–363 (2006)
56. Connor, M.: Automobile sensors may usher in self-driving cars. Ed. Margery Connor. N.p., 26 May 2011. http://www.edn.com/design/automotive/4368069/Automobile-sensors-may-usher-in-self-driving-cars. Accessed 09 Sep 2016
57. Olarte, O.: Human error accounts for 90% of road accidents. driver risk management solutions (2011). http://www.alertdriving.com/home/fleet-alert-magazine/international/human-error-accounts-90-road-accidents/. Accessed 09 Sep 2016

The Future of Enterprise Security with Regards to Mobile Technology and Applications

F.T. Tagoe[1(✉)] and M.S. Sharif[2,3]

[1] Department of Digital Innovation and Creative Enterprise,
GSM London, London, UK
Tonisha.Tagoe@gsmlondon.ac.uk
[2] School of Architecture, Computing and Engineering,
University of East London, University Way, London, UK
[3] Department of Electronic and Computer Engineering,
Brunel University London, Uxbridge, UK

Abstract. The utilisation of work assigned mobile technology by enterprise staff to chat and upload contents to the social media applications for personal use has become a key issue for a significant number of enterprises. This work aims to understand the trends amongst the users of work assigned phones when unknowingly downloading and using applications which could breach the security of the enterprise. In this paper; we assess current trends amongst employees and organisations' use and trust of hybrid and web based social media applications used on a daily basis to communicate. This information is then evaluated alongside human related cyber security risks presented by such applications to provide instructions and advice on the management of social media application use within organisations in the Healthcare, Education and Energy sectors. The findings may be employed to develop a more robust cyber security strategy which focuses at reducing the user related risks.

Keywords: Social media · Security · Mobile technology

1 Introduction

According to Accenture, from 2012 to 2013 [1] — the number of social network users around the world rose from 1.47 billion to 1.73 billion (about 25% of the world's population), an 18% increase and this is predicted to rise to 2.55 billion in 2017. Aside from this, 77% of Fortune500 companies now have active Twitter® accounts, 70% have Facebook® pages and 69% have YouTube™ accounts. "Social networking, user-generated content and PHP-based applications are prevalent on the web... consider how easily sensitive personal information can be accessed through these channels," said Amichai Shulman, chief technology officer at Imperva [2].

54% of companies had a 100% block on social network use in 2009 but by 2011, this number was reduced to just 31% [3]. With such a fast growing presence online of both individuals and organisations, the benefits of being online and having staff who understand how to use social media effectively is clearly beneficial. The difficulty for

© Springer International Publishing AG 2016
H. Jahankhani et al. (Eds.): ICGS3 2017, CCIS 630, pp. 321–330, 2016.
DOI: 10.1007/978-3-319-51064-4_25

cyber security and information security departments is in designing and building effective management systems that can identify legal and strategic risks. Each company will need to make appropriate considerations regarding their consistent voice to suit their objectives and values [4].

1.1   The Internet - Human Right or Utility?

The United Nations Special Rapporteur on the Promotion and Protection of the Right to Freedom of Opinion and Expression ruled that removing access to the internet is a human rights violation of article 19, paragraph 3, of the International Covenant on Civil and Political Rights [5]. Aside from providing individuals with the security of knowing their rights are protected, this also went a long way towards encouraging people globally to see the internet as a space to speak freely and share their thoughts [6]. For companies, this has increased the ability of customers to provide feedback and praise on dedicated digital platforms as well as social media sites.

More recently, in early June 2016, the Federal Communications Commission (FCC) in the United States voted on the topic and ruled that High speed Internet is a Utility thereby classifying that phones and power and should be available to all Americans [7]. This perspective aligns with President Obama's Net Neutrality agenda. The majority opinion globally is that there is a need to prevent local governments from deciding which companies can compete to provide internet access by deregulating the industry to encourage competition and innovation [8]. Competition is not always healthy, and some companies around the world have been known to attempt to bribe employees of competitors to share private company information. Organisations need to ensure their staff can be contacted when on the move and that they are able to communicate with each other in order to carry out their jobs [9]. This requires the use of technology and mobile technology plays a large part in this [10].

2   Enterprise and Mobile Technology

2.1   Native Social Media Mobile Applications

Native applications are developed to work on specific devices and operating systems and as a result are installed directly to the device. Such applications are readily available on all well-known app stores such as the Apple App Store and Google Play and are required to conform to the security requirements of the Marketplace or App Store they will be downloaded from in order to gain approval [11].

As a result, such applications are unable to function across operating systems and must be developed individually to fulfill security requirements of the App store and the Operating System meaning a larger amount of time and money is involved in the development of such tools. This however does provide increased reliability for developers as the SDK and development tools increase the ease of creation.

The benefit of such applications is that they can be used both offline and online and provide a smoother experience through increased speed of use and ubiquitous access [12]. This is possible through a combination of local storage of information and sychronisation when connected to the cloud. Users are also more attracted to such applications as they provide familiar device-specific functionality such as the cameras and accelerometer increasing User Experience fulfilling user expectations.

The disadvantages of such applications are in the time and resources required to develop multiple applications which are able to function on the wide range of devices available on the market today. Alongside this are the in-creased customer support, maintenance costs and extensive approval processes across the various app stores [13]. Many users are unwilling to download such applications onto their devices as company regulations may discourage such activity. These disadvantages present as barriers for developers who strive for popularity amongst users in order to gain a positive return on investment.

2.2 Web Applications

Web applications unlike Native applications are cloud hosted internet-enabled applications such as which can be accessed through web browsers or web service based native clients installed on the device via the app store [14]. Such apps are written with widely recognized programming language such as HTML, CSS, PHP and JavaScript, providing access to a wider set of devices (Windows, iPhone, Android etc.) and operating systems with the only requirement being access to the internet reducing the development, maintenance and customer support costs to the developer. Such applications also provide ease of access for users through search engines such as Yahoo and Google as well as website integration through device detection processes.

The benefit of the Web application is the removal of the requirement to submit the application for safety and security approval through App Stores and Marketplaces [15]. This means that the applications can be released at will by developers based on their preferences without consideration for security restrictions imposed by any individual Company and users do not need to go to such Marketplaces to access applications developed in this way.

The disadvantages of mobile web applications however lie mainly in the limited access to device features for functionality of elements such as hand gestures and recognition of sensors and cameras [16]. Furthermore, although there is a reduced requirement to develop different versions of the application for marketplaces, there is a need to consider the various web browsers, versions and the relationships that they have with individual devices thereby making it difficult to develop stable applications which function across devices with minimal issues. With the applications not been advertised in marketplaces and app stores, users are less likely to discover whether applications and when they do quality control, safety and more importantly security are not guaranteed.

Although Web Based applications appear to be safer to use, many include the common PHP script (present in over 75% of websites) which can allow extremely sensitive data to be sourced directly from the phone through file inclusion attacks, once the user uploads content, grants permissions at the point of download or is led to believe they are in the application when they may in fact be using a cloned User interface.

2.3   What Are the Main Sources of Risk to Enterprise?

Social media is so widely used in modern day, most people fail to take it seriously and as a result regularly download and install social media applications without looking beyond the default settings [17]. This brings rise to risk as lack of this the configuration of setting provide easy access to those conducting social engineering attack identity fraud and attempting to steal confidential information. The Fig. 1 shows 11 of the top risks as listed by Gartner in relation to social media.

Risk	Description	Security	Type
Malware	Infection of desktops, propagation of malware through staff or corporate profiles on social-media services.	Yes	Technology
Chain of providers	Mashups of applications within a social-media service enable the untraceable movement of data	Yes	Technology
Interface weaknesses	Public applications interfaces are not sufficiently secured, exposing users to cross-site scripting and other exploits	Yes	Technology
Reputation damage	Degradation of personal and corporate reputations through posting inappropriate content	No	Content
Exposure of confidential information	"Loose lips sink ships," breach of IP or other trade secrets, breach of copyright, public posting or downloading of private or sensitive personal information	Yes	Content
Legal exposure	Legal liabilities resulting from posted content and online conversations or failure to meet a regulatory requirement to record and archive particular conversations	Yes	Content
Revenue loss	For organisations in the information business, making content freely available may undercut fee-based information services	Yes	Content
Staff productivity	Workers failing to perform due to the distraction of social-media	No	Behaviour
Hierarchy subversion	Informal social media networks erode authority in formal corporate hierarchy and defined work processes	No	Behaviour
Social engineering	Phishing attacks, misrepresentation of identity and/or authority to obtain information illicitly or to stimulate damaging behaviours by staff	Yes	Behaviour
Identity fraud	Profiles and postings that are erroneously attributed to a staff member or corporate office	Yes	Behaviour

Source: Gartner (January 2010)

Fig. 1. The top 11 risks as listed by Gartner in relation to social media.

Understandably, increasing the level of security on social media account restricts the ability of users being able to be easily found by friends and family and easing his applications to connect with [18]. The issue is about making these accounts more secure without losing functionality, ease-of-use and preventing people from accessing content such as images and Profile pages. This applies to all elements of technology from the mobile handset's preconfigured settings to the individual social media accounts, content and level of access provided to each application. The level of security and user implements is usually based on the level of risk they are willing to take any amount at which they willing to expose themselves online and really a result of deep thought about the security required for or by the company issuing the device (Fig. 2).

What is the number of security incidents detected in the past 12 months?

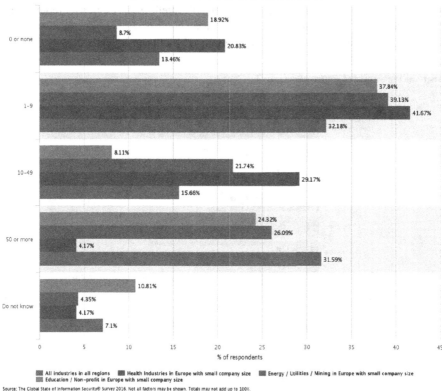

Source: The Global State of Information Security® Survey 2016. Not all factors may be shown. Totals may not add up to 100%.

Fig. 2. The global state of information security survey, PWC, 2016.

A recent study into cyber security threats conducted by PWC asked over 100 companies around the world a range of questions about the state of cyber security within their organisations and future plans to increase security.

These results have been filtered for the purpose of sourcing data specific to the three sectors of focus for this paper (Healthcare, Education and Energy) within Europe. In the table above, 31.5% of companies in the education sector reported 50 or more incidents occurring over the previous 12 months. This number is high however, 26.9% of the energy sector participants reported a similar amount.

Figure 3 shows that current and former employees present the greatest source of incidents with 36.8% of the Healthcare respondents reported employees and while 47.62% of the Energy sector companies reported the highest amount of all threats coming from current employees. Also among the highest responses were from the Energy sector respondents with 42.1% naming organised crime as key sources of incidents over the past year. In contrast to this is the low report of incidents caused by hackers with only 4.7% of the energy sector companies reporting incidents resulting from Hackers.

The impact of the incidents stressed in Fig. 4 resulted in consumer, internal and employee records being compromised, theft of intellectual property, reputational damage, loss of consumers and legal exposure. 60% of Energy sector companies reported that employee records were compromised by the incidents.

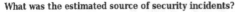

What was the estimated source of security incidents?

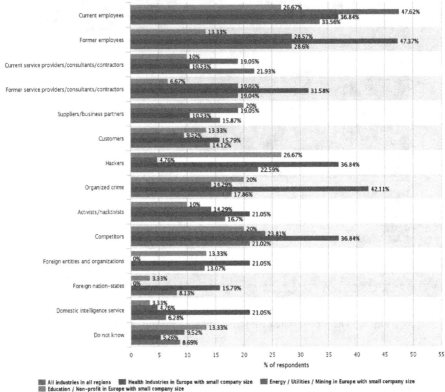

Fig. 3. The global state of information security survey, PWC, 2016.

2.4   The Methodology

The Global State of Information Security Survey in 2016 is a worldwide study by PWC, CIO, and CSO. It was conducted online from the 7th of May 2015 to 12th of June 2015. Readers of CIO and CSO and clients of PWC from around the globe were invited via email to take the survey. The results discussed in this report are based on responses of more than 10,000 CEOs, CFOs, CIOs, CISOs, CSOs, VPs, and directors of IT and security practices from 127 countries. Thirty-seven percent (37%) of respondents are from North America, 30% from Europe, 16% from Asia Pacific, 14% from South America, and 3% from the Middle East and Africa. The margin of error is less than 1%.

How was your organization impacted by the security incidents?

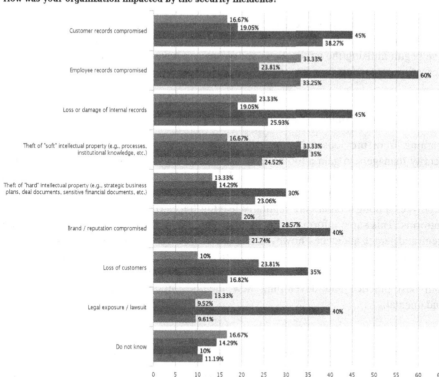

Fig. 4. The global state of information security survey, PWC, 2016.

3 Recommendations for Governance and Use of Social Media Within Enterprise

3.1 Understand the Risks Through Regular Bespoke Risk Assessments

The environment is constantly changing and Hackers are in a position to know more about the device than the manufacturers, distributing companies and staff. Companies have reduced the security restrictions on mobile devices and in some cases remove them in favour of increasing the user experience for staff members.

Two steps verification combined with Single-Sign-On means that once a user is logged into a device which is then stolen or goes missing, not only is there an issue that the data on the device can be accessed; it is possible that someone could access other areas of the company system/database/information using the single sign on feature. Risk assessments and audits should be bespoke to the needs of the specific company and staff requirements.

3.2 Effective Management of Identified Risks

Google play recently changed the rules on how permissions are granted when downloading applications by removing the requirement to grant permissions before users have begun utilising the applications and Whatsapp have recently launched end-to-end encryption protecting user messages from being decrypted.

3.3 Follow and Share Examples of Best Practice

Learning from previous cyber security incidents can play a large role in enabling security managers to gain a foothold on the best strategy to implement as the company however considering that on a daily basis over 5 Petabytes of information such as People's attitudes location images and intentions uploaded to the Internet, it is clear the employees amongst others are regularly leaving traces of information on social media platforms. This same information is regularly used by companies to source insights on client and target audiences however this social intelligence is also available to those who wish to use it to target IT and data infrastructure of the organisation. There is also made a great foundation within the area of risk management, and therefore learning from best practice and developing new methods upon this layout information is fundamental.

3.4 Ensure Engagement from the Organisation's Leadership Team

Many cases of Governments and law enforcement operatives obtaining encryption keys from companies and website owners and so ensuring that the leadership team across all levels of the organisation are actively engaged in the process of regularly assessing the situation. Social media is clearly a requirement in the business world today as the marketing methods and dynamics have grown to involve and require the use of social media marketing tools and applications on a day-to-day basis for both private and corporate use. As a result, the changing landscape of business is further complicated by the addition of social media. It is vital that companies adhere to or develop policies around the encryption and decryption of content on work assigned devices.

3.5 Train the Employees, Including Those Without Work Assigned Technology

Staff who are provided mobile devices are in the most part extremely responsible. It is vital that staff is trained and able to understand security threats and best practise regarding the form of information which can/should be stored on mobile devices. Users frequently visit websites via links which could pose a security risk and as a result put employer's data at risk. Poor password selection can be combatted through the use of 2-step verification in conjunction with single sign on services (SSO) such as Security as Service (SAAS) combinations. However, an employee misplacing an unlocked mobile device and another that conducts a malicious information leak presents the same amount of risk. Disgruntled employees with an in-depth knowledge of technology and mobile security can be a serious source of risk.

4 Conclusion and Future Work

The current trends amongst employees and organisations' use and trust of hybrid and web based social media applications used on a daily basis to communicate have been assessed. This information is then evaluated alongside human related cyber security risks presented by such applications to provide instructions and advice on the management of social media application use within organisations in the healthcare, education and energy sectors. The findings can be employed to develop a more robust cyber security strategy which focuses at reducing the user related risks. The vast amounts of information and possible discussions about the risks to enterprise from social media are not fully discussed. However, this relies heavily on the fact that the full of the risks faced by businesses and the possible impacts are not yet being shared enough across business. The data and findings from the PWC survey clearly shows that a large percent of companies (more than 10%) has said that they either do not know if they have had any cyber incidents in the previous 12 months or that they are not aware of the impacts and/or financial losses incurred as a result.

It is vital that the future of business includes the commitment of all employees to maintaining and preserving security both of themselves as individuals and as of the organisation itself. The education, energy and health sectors have a lot to lose through cybercrime that fracture employee and customer data. As a result, managers and leaders must be forward thinking and work towards developing strategies and infrastructure that prevents and mitigates the most common risks at a minimum level.

The while it is clear that social media as with all elements of the Internet are advancing at a faster pace than most are able to grasp from a security perspective, the rewards of engaging these platforms in ways that allow businesses to engage their audience is safely while will provide untold benefits to all involved. A fundamental factor required for this to take place, is honesty and transparency across industry sectors about incidents which have occurred so that (E lessons can be learned and up-to-date training and information can be distributed as often as necessary.

The work presented in this paper establishes the basis for further research activities and findings in the near future. Our future work will involve gathering effective statistics about the most ten popular apps being downloaded by staff onto mobiles (e.g. tinder) via the technical department of 100 companies. Then we are planning to analyse the ranking of all apps into order from most to least secure apps. Afterwards these apps will be rated accordingly based on different factors such as threats raised, hack attempts etc. Moreover, a technical based solutions and recommendations will be developed to help and support enterprise. This will lead to develop a global system that provides updated training materials and alerts about the recent breaches to all work based phones. This system will be able to provide advice on the need for increased training and governance for all the employees involved in such work.

References

1. Accenture Comprehensive Approach Managing Social Media Risk Compliance
2. Research shows dangers of user-generated content, ComputerWeekly. http://www.computer weekly.com/news/2240150785/Research-shows-dangers-of-user-generated-content. Accessed 28 July 2016
3. Shullic, R.: Risk Assessment of Social Media. The SANS Institute (2012)
4. Jayaram, D., Manrai, A.K., Manrai, L.A.: Effective use of marketing technology in Eastern Europe: web analytics, social media, customer analytics, digital campaigns and mobile applications. Uso Eficaz Tecnol. Mark. En Eur. Este Analíticas Web Medios Soc. Analítica Clientes Campañas Digit. Apl. Móviles 20(39), 118–132 (2015)
5. U.N. Report Declares Internet Access a Human Right | WIRED. https://www.wired.com/2011/06/internet-a-human-right/. Accessed 28 July 2016
6. Preibusch, S.: Privacy behaviors after snowden. Commun. ACM 58(5), 48 (2015)
7. Kang, C.: Court Backs Rules Treating Internet as Utility, Not Luxury. The New York Times, 14 June 2016 (2016)
8. No, the Internet Is Not a Utility, Conservative Review. https://www.conservativereview.com/commentary/2016/06/no-the-internet-is-not-a-utility. Accessed 28 July 2016
9. Jenab, K., Moslehpour, S.: Cyber Security Management: A Review. Bus. Manag. Dyn. 5 (11), 16–39 (2016)
10. Gardner, L.: "Welcome to the Web World. J. Aust. N. Z. Inst. Insur Fin. 38(3), 1–6 (2015)
11. Charland, A., Leroux, B.: Mobile Application Development: Web vs. Native. Commun. ACM 54(5), 49–53 (2011)
12. Dikhit, R.S.: Using android for the enterprise. Open Source You 4(5), 49 (2016)
13. HTML5 vs Native Whats a Mobile Developer to Do 648997. eWeek (2012)
14. de M. Barroca Filho, I., Aquino Júnior, G.S.: Development of mobile applications from existing web-based enterprise systems. Int. J. Web Inf. Syst. 11(2), 162 (2015)
15. The enterprise guide to developing secure mobile apps. Comput. Wkly., 1–19, June 2016
16. Brewer, D.: Native apps vs. web apps. N. H. Bus. Rev. 33(22), 30 (2011)
17. Gatlin, A.: Social media privacy settings get few likes from millennials show high level of distrust but survey finds gen yers still need to improve their cybersecurity awareness. Investor's Business Daily (2015)
18. Cyber security: strategies: comment: social media is revolutionary, but it can damage your business. The Guardian, London, England (2013)

Chemical, Biological, Radiological and Nuclear (CBRN) Protective Clothing – A Review

Maria José Magalhães[1,2], Sérgio Tenreiro de Magalhães[2,3,4(✉)],
Kenneth Revett[5], and Hamid Jahankhani[6]

[1] 2C2T – University of Minho, Guimarães, Portugal
mariajmrm@gmail.com
[2] Faculdade de Filosofia e Ciências Sociais da Universidade Católica Portuguesa,
Braga, Portugal
mjmagalhaes@braga.ucp.pt, stmagalhaes@braga.ucp.pt
[3] ALGORITMI Research Center, University of Minho, Guimarães, Portugal
psmagalhaes@dsi.uminho.pt
[4] Department of Computer Science, University of Beira Interior,
Covilhã, Braga, Portugal
stmagalhaes@di.ubi.pt
[5] Anastamose International, Boston, MA, USA
Ken.revett@gmail.com
[6] GSM London, London, UK
hamid.jahankhani@gsmlondon.ac.uk

Abstract. The attacks with CBRN (Chemical, biological, radiological and nuclear) agents are more and more a concern for the security of the world, especially since some terrorist groups have access to CBRN weapons. This work reviews the developments on CBRN protective clothing and concludes that this is a field of growing interest from researchers all over the world. The research focus on several aspects: military boots, protection clothes, forecasting models of protection and comfort characteristics, the importance of improving the comfort and physiological stress, development of membranes and construction models, etc. The developments that arise in this work are spread over several areas, demonstrating that multidisciplinary knowledge is an important factor for a more efficient and effective progress on CBRN clothing.

Keywords: Protective textiles · Protective clothing · CBRN · Technical textiles

1 Introduction

On conflict situations, safety and security officers are submitted to a large variety of aggressions, like thermal and pressure variations, violent impacts (from bullets or fragments) and toxic substances, from chemical, biological or physical origin. Technical textiles used in the construction of the military uniforms and devices have played an important role in defending the military against these hazards.

In addition to the risks of the use of chemical, biological, radiological and nuclear agents (CBRN) in a war scenario it exists the risk of the use of CBRN devices by terrorists, like the use of sarin, a chemical agent, on 20 March 1995 in the Tokyo

© Springer International Publishing AG 2016
H. Jahankhani et al. (Eds.): ICGS3 2017, CCIS 630, pp. 331–341, 2016.
DOI: 10.1007/978-3-319-51064-4_26

subway. This was the first large-scale attack with a toxic chemical agent from a terrorist group. At that point most thought that de CBRN devices were restricted to the domain of military forces. On this attack 5,100 persons were affected by the sarin, 12 of them were casualties, 40 were heavily affected and more than 900 were moderately affected while others were slightly injured. About 300 members of the rescue team were also affected, being one of the causes the non-usage of properly protective devices for respiratory protection (masks), but also for the dermal protection (suits). Another CBRN terrorism attack happened in the United States of America in October 2001 when letters containing anthrax powder, a biological agent, were sent to several persons related to mass media and State Administration authorities in various States [1]. After those attacks, it was clear that terrorists could acquire the necessary information and equipment to promote a CBRN attack. If, for one hand, the CBRN military attacks are "controlled" by political conventions between countries, the CBRN terrorism attacks are out of control. Therefore, it becomes increasingly important to prepare the defense for the attacks with CBRN agents.

The impact of a chemical, biological, radiological or nuclear attack depends largely on the availability and quality of protective clothes. After the attacks referred above, a large number of websites appeared selling protective suits and masks all over the world. Common people could buy a simple mask to anthrax, but could also buy other filters to a large variety of other chemical and biological agents. It is necessary to prepare a possible CBRN attack not only by developing new defense products but also by making the existing technologies widely available.

1.1   CBRN

On the CBRN denomination, the C agents are chemical agents that can cause damage by chemical reactions when in contact with the body; B agents are microorganisms or toxins produced by living organisms with the objective to cause diseases or death of living organisms; R agents are radiological agents that can cause damage on human bodies resulting from the high-energy radiation that the systems are submitted to; and N agents are nuclear agents that result from an explosion of a nuclear weapon or a power source with a much higher magnitude than R agents [2].

The hazard of a biological agent depends on: their impact on public health; the potential of the biological agent to be delivered to a large number of people; the reaction from people to the risks of the agent and the preparedness of the health institutions to the situation. According to this factors, the United States Centers for Disease Control and Prevention have categorized bioterrorism agents into three categories [3]:

– *"Category A: These high-priority agents include organisms or toxins that pose the highest risk to the public and national security because:*
They can be easily spread or transmitted from person to person
They result in high death rates and have the potential for major public health impact
They might cause public panic and social disruption
They require special action for public health preparedness.

– Category B: These agents are the second highest priority because:
They are moderately easy to spread
They result in moderate illness rates and low death rates
They require specific enhancements of CDC's laboratory capacity and enhanced disease monitoring.
– Category C: These third highest priority agents include emerging pathogens that could be engineered for mass spread in the future because:
They are easily available
They are easily produced and spread
They have potential for high morbidity and mortality rates and major health impact."

Some of the biological agents that can be used on biological terrorism are: *Variola major* (Category A), *Bacillus anthracis* (Category A), *Alphaviruses* (Category B) and *Yellow fever* (Category C) [4].

1.2 Protective Clothing/Technical Textiles

The impact of each CBRN agent depends on being prepared for the specificity of the agent in cause. The protective clothing (suit, gloves, footwear, respirator or other advices) are developed for a very particular situation and a very specific agent [4].

It's a fact that the protection is the main goal of the protection clothing construction, but the comfort and flexibility of the suits are also very important factors for the success of a military operation. The selection of the most adequate materials and constructs to the protection clothing is very important to the success of the final product [4].

The definition of technical textile adopted by the authoritative Textile and Definitions, published by the Textile Institute is "textile materials and products manufactured primarily for their technical and performance properties rather than their aesthetic or decorative characteristics. A non-exhaustive list of end-uses includes aerospace, industrial, military, safety, transport textiles and geotextiles". From this definition we can conclude that all textiles materials used in protective equipment can be considered technical textiles [5]. At the same time that new CRBN weapons are developed, new protective textiles and new treatments are developed to construct protective clothing. In this work a literature review is made to analyze the development of protective textiles against CBRN agents using the scientific databases Scopus and ISI Web of Science, as discussed in the next section (method).

2 Method

For the literature review several queries were made during the months of June and July 2016, of publications indexed in SCOPUS and/or in the ISI Web of Science.

On SCOPUS various keywords and various operators were used. All *"subject areas"* were considered and on *"document type" "Article", "Conference paper" and "Book Chapter"* were considered.

The different combination of keywords was made in different phases which will be described and justified below:

1. Phase I - First the authors combined the keywords *"textile"* AND *"CBRN"* in the fields *"abstracts, keywords and titles"* and the result included 8 documents.
2. Phase II – After obtained only 8 documents in Phase I, it was considered that the keyword *"CBRN"* might not appear in the field *"abstracts, keywords and titles"* but the subject be treated in the rest of the document. The decision was made to create a new query maintaining the keyword *"textile"* in the field *"abstracts, keywords and titles"* AND the keyword *"CBRN"* in the field *"All fields"*. The final result included 16 documents.
3. Phase III – A new query was made with the keyword *"CBRN"* in the field *"abstracts, keywords and titles"* AND the keyword *"textile"* in the field *"All fields"*. The final result included 20 documents.

Finally, it was used a tool from the SCOPUS platform that makes a logical disjunction between the lists of documents obtained on the three Phases (I, II and III) of the queries. The final result included 28 documents indicating that there were 16 documents repeated.

The next step of the work consisted in reading the abstracts of all the 28 final docu-ments, or the total document when it was needed, to exclude the ones which were out of the scope of this work. After analyzing all 28 documents, 15 remained as the final documents.

On the ISI Web of Science queries, the keywords *"textile"* and *"CBRN"* were used in the field Topic but only three documents were found, one was out of the scope and the other two were already included in the ones obtained on the SCOPUS queries.

3   Analysis of the Documents Obtained from the Queries

3.1   Documents by Year

The documents found were published between 2006 and 2014. The number of publications was higher in 2011 and 2012 with 4 publications (Fig. 1).

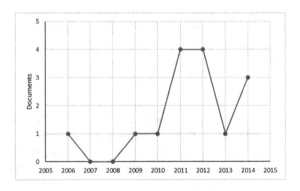

Fig. 1. Number of documents published by year

3.2 Type of Documents

About the type of documents found 60% were articles, 26.7% book chapters and 13.3% Conference Papers (Fig. 2).

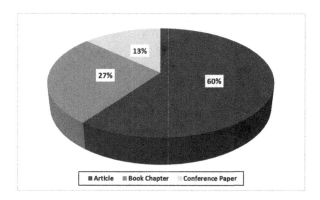

Fig. 2. Percentage of each type of publication

3.3 Subject Areas

Some of the documents are classified on various subject areas. After analyzing which were the documents that had Material Science as scientific domain, which represented 46.7% of the documents, the remaining 8 documents were analyzed and the results are in Table 1.

Table 1. Subject area from the documents on analysis

Subject area	Documents	Percentage (%)
Materials science	7	46,7
Engineering	3	20,0
Chemical engineering	3	20,0
Health professions	1	6,7
Medicine	1	6,7

From the remaining 53.3% of the documents most are considered from the Engineering domain (20%) and from the Chemical Engineering domain (20%).

3.4 Documents by Country

The identification of the country associated at each document depends on the country of the authors, that's why the total of countries is more than the total of documents.

The largest number of documents are from the United States (5), followed by Netherlands (4) and United Kingdom with 3 documents (Table 2).

Table 2. Number of documents associated to countries

Country	Documents
United States	5
Netherlands	4
United Kingdom	3
France	2
Italy	1
Norway	1
Sri Lanka	1
Turkey	1

4   Results from the Analyses of the Documents

The goals of designers and researchers of CBRN protective clothing is to defend the user from the risk agent efficiently, during the most time possible, and at the same time, permitting the movements and agility needed, principally when we are talking about military agents in a conflict scenario.

One of the devices used by military are the boots, that causes physiological stress and skin damage. Némoz compared a normal combat boot with a CBRN overboot on top (FBUT) and a CBRN combat boot constituted of a layer of filter Saratoga laminated with a respirable non-fabric Cambrelle (FBOT). The introduction of the new layers in the combat boot reduces, when compared to the usual combat boots, significantly the thermal strain and its weight (1 kg). Therefore, the new boots maintained the security with greater comfort [6]. The preference for using leather on footwear manufacture is related to its characteristics of ruggedness, flexibility, and low weight. Although, the high porosity of this material brings limitations, when compared finished-leather boots with traditional rubber boots, on the applications on CBRN boots because of the repellency of chemical agents [7]. Bradham concluded that both type of boots has the same number of toxic agents in which they have a better performance, but the ones with leather were more comfortable once they are more flexible and lighter [8].

In [9] the only information found was that in the fourth international textile conference at the Royal College of Physicians in London, "Cath Rogan director of Smart Garment People Ltd, reviewed developments in chemical, biological, radiological, and nuclear (CBRN) protective clothing from insurgent forces".

At a first glance to be thicker and to have a lower air permeability seems to be the answer to a better defensive technical textile. Although, those types of fabrics don't let the water vapor pass and results in high levels of thermal burden. Generally, the construction of protective clothes to CBRN attacks have a filter layer that, at the same time, prevents the entry and stores the toxic agent. In the exterior it has an oil repellent shell. This combination of textiles is permeable to air and water vapor preventing the entry of water but allowing the exit of perspiration for better comfort [4]. The permeability of the membranes used on Individual Protective Equipment is an important characteristic of the materials.

The protective clothing can be divided in air permeable or air impermeable. The air permeable are used widely for military organizations. In the case of air impermeable systems, a membrane or a polymeric film is used as a filter that prevents the specific toxic chemical to penetrate. Some examples are: fluoropolymer coatings, fibrous filtration media and activated carbon. The barriers used can be breathable or non-breathable materials. Non-breathable materials have been widely used in protective garments as Tychem® (DuPont), Barricade™ (DuPont), 4H™ (Safety 4 Company), CPF3™ (Kappler Company), Responder™ (Kappler Company), and Silver Shield™ (Siebe North Company). Although, breathable membranes permit that water vapor escape to the exterior making the clothes more comfortable and helping to maintain the physiological stability. The breathable membrane is between two layers of textile that permits the passage of water vapor but don't let the toxic chemical penetrate. Example of nonporous membranes used on breathable systems are polyester, polyeteher amide or polyurethanes [10]. Böhringer discloses a nonporous membrane based on extrusion with polyamide and 5–30% of polyether amide. Another type of breathable membranes are the elastic ones. Elastic breathable membranes permit that the stretch of the membrane keep the contact to the skin helping the water vapor permeability, reduce the air movements around the user that can cause the entrance of contaminant air through critical seams like the seals [10, 11]. The use of nanoparticles in the composition of the barrier material has been discussed too. The systems referred until now are passive systems in which the performance depends from the environment. Although, there are some systems that react to the changes on the surrounding environment: adaptive or responsive membranes [10].

The possibility of using semipermeable membranes has as objective to incorporate the protection directly into the uniform instead of the usually overgarment reducing the thermal burden, the weight and getting more flexibility of movements without affecting the protection [4].

The influence of porosity and the vapor resistance of the protective clothes (including CBRN clothes) on the heat stress to the users was studied by Havenith. The studies show that an increase on air permeability has more effect on the decrease of heat stress then the reduction of the material thickness contributing for an optimization of protective clothes. Comparing materials with similar thickness, the authors verified a strong correlation of microclimate ventilation inside the clothes due to wind or movement with air permeability. That was verified by the lower skin temperature and heart rate for clothes, which presented a higher air permeability [12].

The importance of comfort during a battle using CBRD-protective clothing is a widespread subject. Brasser develop a model to determine the point where it's possible to get an equilibrium between protection and comfort. The degree of physiological burden depends of the skin, temperature, moisture and the movement of the air inside the protective clothing. On this study the focus was on finding the optimum equilibrium for ventilation and protection. The conclusions were that in the presence of a higher air resistance of the clothing the protection was better but the physiological burden was higher with a higher temperature and relative humidity. On the other end, each mission has specific needs, which means that the model will indicate the level of protection for a certain level of physiological burden depending on the conditions chosen by the decision maker of the mission [13].

Grandcolas developed a photocatalytic textile with self-decontaminating properties. Using a multilayer building method with high aspect ratio WO_3-modified titanate nanotubes, that functionalized the textile substrate, the system permits a photocatalytic degradation of organophosphorous and organosulfide chemical weapon agents under solar light illumination. The time for self-decontamination of the neurotoxic agent simulating DMMP (dimethylmethylphosphonate), with the complete removal of the toxicity of the agent was under 7 min, and for yperite it was within 20 min [14].

The development of nanoscience and nanotechnology had contributed to the new forms of detection, monitoring and abatement of CBRN agents. One example are the nanosystems (chemicals structures between 1 and 100 nm) with catalytic properties on the prevention or minimization of the effects of C, B and not so extensively of N agents. One example is the use of nanofibers of zinc titanate fibers (ZnO-TiO_2), that can be included in textiles and clothes, that can decompose paraoxon (a nerve agent simulant) and 2-chloroethyl ethyl sulphide (CEES, a mustard agent stimulant) in acetone by itself at room temperature. A new class of electrospun nanofibrous polymers based on a dimethylacrylamide-methacrylate copolymer backbone presents properties of chemical and biological decontamination [15].

Delkumburewatte developed a system to maintain the temperature inside the protector suits under extreme conditions. The system is composed of a cooling system consisting of peltier units and mini refrigerant channels that are incorporated in a technical textile - a knitted spacer structure [16]. The system works like this:

– The sweat from the body is absorbed and retained by the technical textile;
– The heat of the body is absorbed by the cold parts of the peltier units;
– The heat absorbed are transferred to the refrigerant and it is converted to gas by the absorption of evaporative heat.

The mini refrigerant channels are connected to a high pressure liquid refrigerant cylinder and to a gas receiver via polymer tubes [16].

One of the ways to prevent the passage of hazardous gases is to combine a layer of activated carbon between two layer of textile. The protection factor (PF) of the material depends on the characteristics of the activated carbon layer, the hazardous gas and the velocity of the polluted airstream. In his research Ambesi studied the relation between the filter geometry, the properties of the hazardous gas, the airstream velocity and the PF. The model obtained can be used to find the best compromise between PF and the pressure drop coefficient of the activated carbon (K_W). For a specific PF to get the lowest K_W the layers have to have high porosity and small particles diameter [17].

Still on the system of protective clothing with activated carbon and textiles, Ambesi proved that computational models may be used to optimize the results for three-layers CBRN material according to the values of permeability of the inner and outer textile layers and the values of the porosity and particle size of the carbon facilitating the decisions about the design of protective clothing adapting the level of protection and thermal strain to the requisites [18].

On what concerns to biological protective finishes, the antimicrobial finishes of protective textiles to biological agents can act by three different mechanisms [19]:

- The release of the antimicrobial agent is controlled by its partition coefficient, surface absorption, vapor pressure and water solubility;
- The regeneration principle in which the antimicrobial agent could be continually regenerated by bleaching agents or by the exposure to UV radiation;
- The barrier or blocking properties that can be an inert physical barrier, application of a coating impenetrable by the agent or reacting against the agent.

Some examples of antimicrobial finishes are *chitosan, silver, quaternary ammonium salts* and *N-halamines*. Recently, there are indications about the potential of natural enzymes that can be used as biological protective finishes on textiles. The lysozyme, an enzyme that exists in human milk, tears, semen, mucous and saliva, is effective against the bacterium that causes anthrax. The antibodies from llamas are effective against different types of botulinum neurotoxins. There is also ongoing research on the use of Elafin against agents such as *B. anthracis* and *Y. pestis* [19].

On chemical protective finishes, the three processes involved on the action of chemical agents on the protection textile finishes are: permeation, penetration and sorption. It also involves, one or more, of three basic mechanisms: barriers to permeation of liquids; repellence and sorption of liquids and liquid penetration through porous materials. There is another type of finishing: the reactive coating. In this case when the agent contacts the coating layer, a chemical reaction occurs that neutralizes the agent. The use of Paraoxanase 1 (PON1), an enzyme that exists in the liver, to neutralize nerve agents like sarin is being study, as well as the potentially of being used as coatings to chemical protective finishes [19, 20].

5   Conclusions

From this work one can conclude that in addition to the concern for the protection of safety, security and defense agents in relation to CBRN agents, the comfort related to physiological stress is also a strong concern among researchers. There is a concern with the improvement of the materials used in protective boots in order to obtain a better air permeability, as well as reduce the weight of the boots to allow a greater comfort in its use. There are also results that show a strong correlation of microclimate ventilation inside the clothes due to wind or movement with air permeability, confirming the importance of permeability of the materials used in clothing with the comfort, so important for users of these suits. One work features a self-controlled temperature system within the suits to use in extreme working conditions. Regarding the use of activated carbon, forecasting models arise for protection and permeability and thermal strain characteristics based on the activated carbon layer. The application of biological and chemical treatments on protective materials are also a topic widely studied as well as the use of nanofibers.

The developments that arise in this work are spread over several areas demonstrating that multidisciplinary knowledge is an important factor for a more efficient and effective progress on CBRN clothing.

Acknowledgments. This work has been supported by COMPETE: POCI-01-0145-FEDER-007043 and FCT – Fundação para a Ciência e Tecnologia within the Project Scope: UID/CEC/00319/2013.

References

1. Vičar, D., Vičar, R.: The CBRN terrorism: a contribution to defense, analysis of risks. J. Def. Res. Manag. **2**(2), 21–28 (2011)
2. Dickson, E.F.G.: Personal Protective Equipment for Chemical, Biological, and Radiological Hazards: Design, Evaluation, and Selection. Wiley, Hoboken (2012)
3. Centers for Disease Control and Prevention: Bioterrorism Overview (2007). http://emergency.cdc.gov/bioterrorism/overview.asp. Accessed 20 Aug 2016
4. Ormond, R.B., Barker, R.L.: Chemical, biological, radiological and nuclear (CBRN) protective clothing. In: Protective Clothing: Managing Thermal Stress, pp. 112–145. Elsevier Inc. (2014)
5. Scott, R.A. (ed.): Textiles for Protection. Elsevier, Amsterdam (2005)
6. Némoz, G.: Efficient CBRN protective clothing. TUT Text. Usages Tech. **59**, 26–30 (2006)
7. Thompson, D.B., Barker, R.L., Deaton, A.S., Montero, G.A., Bradham, A.E., Beck, K.R., Liston, G.C.: Chemical resistant leather materials for CBRN boots. In: American Association of Textile Chemists and Colorists International Conference 2010, pp. 407–413 (2010)
8. Bradham, A.E., Beck, K.R., Barker, R.L., Montero, G.A., Deaton, A.S.: Analytical techniques for measuring toxic industrial chemicals in CBRN boot materials. AATCC Rev. **11**(6) (2011)
9. Holme, I.: Smart and nano fabric innovations. Int. Dyer **194**(4), 33–34 (2009)
10. Brewer, S.A.: Recent advances in breathable barrier membranes for individual protective equipment. Recent Pat. Mater. Sci. **4**(1), 1–14 (2011)
11. Böhringer, B.R., Van de Ven, H.J.M., Spijkers, J.C.W.: U.S. Patent No. 6,706,413. U.S. Patent and Trademark Office, Washington, DC (2004)
12. Havenith, G., den Hartog, E., Martini, S.: Heat stress in chemical protective clothing: porosity and vapour resistance. Ergonomics **54**(5), 497–507 (2011)
13. Brasser, P., Sobera, M.: Modelling the comfort and protection qualities of chemical, biological, radiological and nuclear (CBRN) protective clothing. In: Advances in Military Textiles and Personal Equipment, pp. 238–259. Elsevier Inc., UK (2012)
14. Grandcolas, M., Sinault, L., Mosset, F., Louvet, A., Keller, N., Keller, V.: Self-decontaminating layer-by-layer functionalized textiles based on WO 3-modified titanate nanotubes. Application to the solar photocatalytic removal of chemical warfare agents. Appl. Catal. A: Gen. **391**(1), 455–467 (2011)
15. Guidotti, M., Rossodivita, A., Ranghieri, M.C.: Nano-structured solids and heterogeneous catalysts: powerful tools for the reduction of CBRN threats. In: Vaseashta, A., Braman, E., Susmann, P. (eds.) Technological Innovations in Sensing and Detection of Chemical, Biological, Radiological, Nuclear Threats and Ecological Terrorism, pp. 89–97. Springer, Dordrecht (2012)
16. Delkumburewatte, G.B., Dias, T.: Wearable cooling system to manage heat in protective clothing. J. Text. Inst. **103**(5), 483–489 (2012)
17. Ambesi, D., Bouma, R., den Hartog, E., Kleijn, C.R.: Predicting the chemical protection factor of CBRN protective garments. J. Occup. Environ. Hyg. **10**(5), 270–276 (2013)

18. Ambesi, D., Kleijn, C.R., Hartog, E.A., Bouma, R.H., Brasser, P.: Forced convection mass deposition and heat transfer onto a cylinder sheathed by protective garments. AIChE J. **60** (1), 353–361 (2014)
19. Turaga, U., Singh, V., Ramkumar, S.: Biological and chemical protective finishes for textiles. In: Functional Finishes for Textiles, pp. 555–578 (2015)
20. Turaga, U., Kendall, R., Singh, V., Lalagiri, M.: Advances in materials for chemical, biological, radiological and nuclear (CBRN) protective clothing. Adv. Mil. Text. Pers. Equip. 260 (2012)

Performance Analysis for Traffics in Mobile Ad Hoc Network

Firas Hazzaa and Sufian Yousef[(✉)]

Department of Engineering and Built Environment,
Anglia Ruskin University, Chelmsford, UK
firas.hazzaa@pgr.anglia.ac.uk,
sufian.yousef@anglia.ac.uk

Abstract. Mobile ad-hoc network (MANET) is a set of mobile nodes that communicate with radio links. MANET network infrastructure is not defined and there is no centralized administration for controlling the other activities. Classification of traffic types in MANET is initial and would lead to comprehension of quality metrics for each kind of this traffic. In this work we simulate many types of traffic like FTP, Voice, and video conference and we got many results that will help us to decide which security methods could be used without affecting QoS. These simulation scenarios are conducted and testing data is analyzed to test delay in each scenario, the results show significant differences among these scenarios, so we should be more careful when to implement security methods on Voice and multimedia in MANET.

Keywords: MANET · Ad hoc · Traffic in MANET

1 Introduction

A wireless ad hoc network (WANET) is a decentralized type of wireless network. The network is ad hoc because it does not rely on a pre-existing infrastructure, such as routers in wired networks or access points in managed (infrastructure) wireless networks. The importance of this network is valuable because it makes the service available anytime anywhere [10]. It is an infrastructure-less network, so it is cost-effective, easily deploys and could create immediately. For these reasons, it is used in many applications such as mobile ad hoc network (MANET) which is a continuously self-configuring, infrastructure-less, network of mobile devices connected without wires. And Vehicular ad hoc networks (VANETs) are used for communication between vehicles and roadside equipment. In addition, Internet-based mobile ad hoc networks (iMANETs) that link mobile nodes and fixed Internet-gateway nodes. Also, it used in military and rescue operations.

Ad-hoc network systems communicate directly with each other in the absence of router. In Ad hoc networks, the node does not start out with the known topologies of its own network; instead of, they have to discover it [1]. The main idea is that a new mobile node may proclaim its attendance and should pay attention to announcements broadcast by its neighbors.

© Springer International Publishing AG 2016
H. Jahankhani et al. (Eds.): ICGS3 2017, CCIS 630, pp. 342–350, 2016.
DOI: 10.1007/978-3-319-51064-4_27

In this paper, the traffic classification will be explained in the next section. After that, we will discuss the simulation setup and parameters and then will show the results. Finally, we will discuss more in conclusion.

2 Traffic Classification

Traffic classification is very important for any researcher in network area because it would help them to understand the characteristics of each type of traffic, this will help to know the requirement of each type in term of QoS [2]. As we know, there are many differences between real time traffic and other traffic. In real time traffic, there is a huge requirement for Quality of Service metrics such as Voice and Video Conference, while it is less important in another kind such as FTP. As we mentioned in the first paragraph, understanding the characteristics of each type of traffic will help to know the requirement of each type in term of QoS. For example, when we need to encrypt the data, we should consider the QoS metrics because each type of traffic has some specific requirement, like the delay in real time traffic. In this work we simulate many types of traffic like FTP, Voice and video conference and we got many results that will help us to decide which security methods could be used without effecting QoS.

3 Simulation Setup and Parameters

The OPNET 18.5 modeler and the wireless suite are used in our simulation. 50 nodes are involved for the creation of topology on 1 km × 1 km space. Different traffic is chosen: FTP, Voice and Video Conference. The effect of different traffic is tested. Figure 1 show the network topology which designed with many components such as Application Definitions that used to create the applications in the network. Also the profile configuration is used to describe the activity applications used by users through a period of time.

Table 1. Simulation Parameters on OPNET Modeller

Number of simulations	10	Simulation Area	1000*1000 sq.m.
Simulation Duration	60 min	Data Rate	11 Mbps
Num. of Nodes	50	Transmission Power	0.001 w
WLAN Physical Characteristic	802.11	Buffer Size	32 KB
Frequency Band	2.4	Routing Protocol	AODV
Packet Size	512	Traffic	FTP, Voice, Video Conference
Fragmentation Threshold	1024	Simulation	50000 events
Simulation Seeds Num.	182	Values per statistic	100

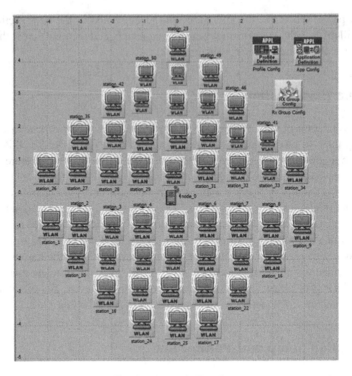

Fig. 1. Network Topology

The simulation parameters for the above network are illustrated in Table 1, as we can see, the number of simulation which have done are: 10 and the duration 60 min.

4   Simulation Results and Analysis

Three scenarios are carried out, in each scenario we passed one type of traffic FTP or Voice or Video conference. In this section we consider two set of parameters: QoS metrics and AODV parameters vs. Traffic type.

4.1   QoS Metrics Versus the Traffic Type

Here we consider the delay, network load, throughput and retransmission attempt. In this section we are going to show the obtaining result as in following figures:

Figure 2 illustrate the result of Delay (sec) in the designed network for three scenarios, in each scenario we passed one type of traffic: FTP or Voice or Video conference. As we can see there are many differences in the result among the traffic

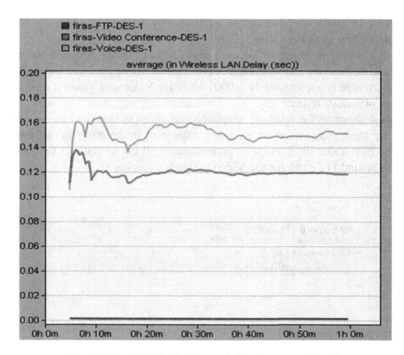

Fig. 2. The Delay in the Network for three type of traffic

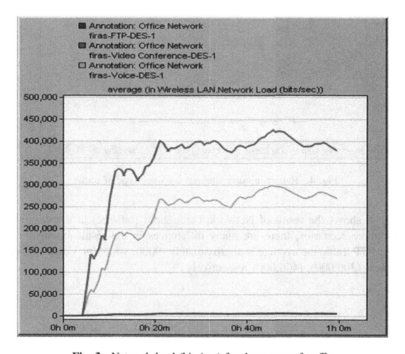

Fig. 3. Network load (bits/sec) for three type of traffic

types. For FTP traffic the average is approximately (0.0014 s) while for Voice it reaches near (0.16 s) and for Video is (0.13 s).

Figure 3 shows the result of Network load (bits/sec) in the designed network for three scenarios, there are many differences in the result among the traffic types. For FTP traffic the average is approximately (6000) while for Voice and Video it reaches near (300,000), (450,000) respectively.

Figure 4 illustrate the result of retransmission attempts (packets) in the designed network for three scenarios, there are many differences in the result among the traffic types. For FTP traffic the average is approximately (0.10) in contract for Voice the average is around (1.2) and for the Video is roughly reaches (1.2).

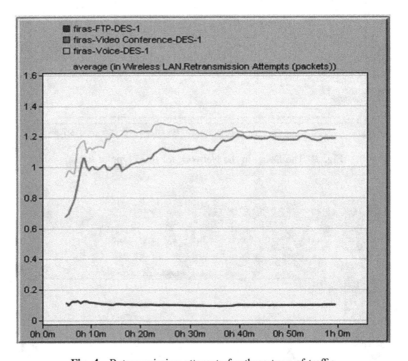

Fig. 4. Retransmission attempts for three type of traffic

Figure 5 shows the result of Network Throughput (bits/sec) in the designed network for three scenarios, there are many differences in the result among the traffic types. For FTP traffic the average is approximately (9000) while for Voice and Video it reaches near (300,000), (400,000) respectively.

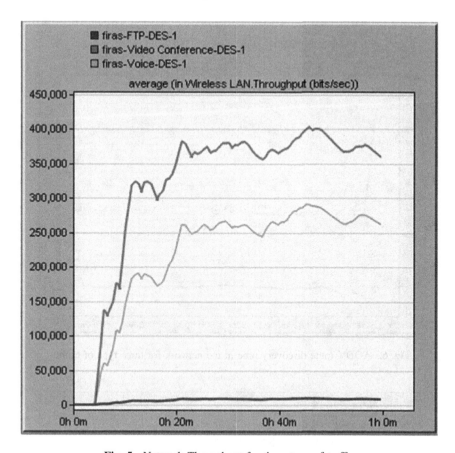

Fig. 5. Network Throughput for three type of traffic

4.2   Statistical Analysis for AODV Routing Protocol

Figure 6 shows the result of AODV route discovery time in the designed network for three scenarios, in each scenario we passed one type of traffic FTP or Voice or Video conference. As we can see, there are many differences in the result among the traffic types. For FTP traffic the average time is approximately (0.50) while for Voice and Video it reaches near (1.2), (2.0) respectively.

Figure 7 illustrate the result of AODV routing traffic received (pkts/sec) in the designed network for three scenarios, there are many differences in the result among the traffic types. For FTP traffic the average is approximately (14) in contract for Voice and Video which are exactly the same and roughly reach (80).

Figure 8 illustrate the result of AODV routing traffic sent (pkts/sec) in the designed network for three scenarios, there are many differences in the result among the traffic types. For FTP traffic the average is approximately (5) and for Voice it hit the peak on (35) also for video is near (35).

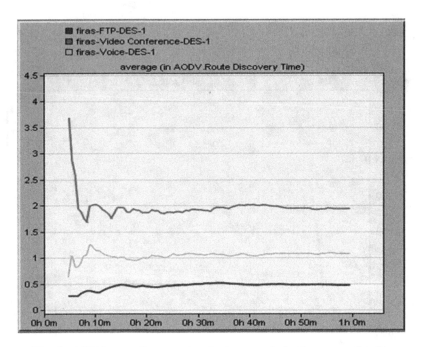

Fig. 6. AODV route discovery time in the network for three type of traffic

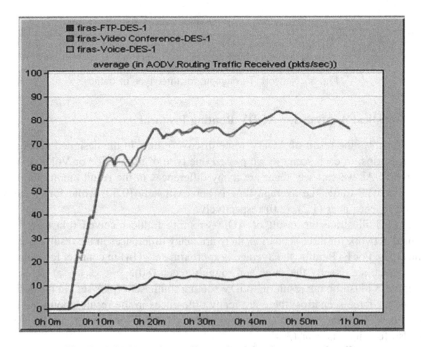

Fig. 7. AODV routing traffic received for three type of traffic

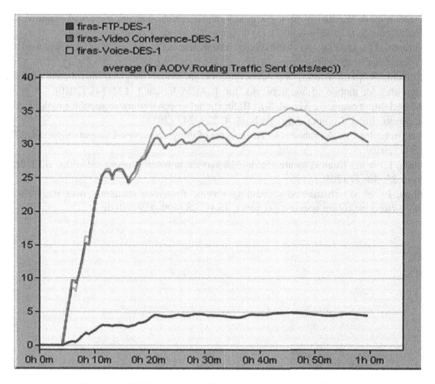

Fig. 8. AODV routing traffic sent for three type of traffic

5 Conclusion

The evaluation effort of this paper aims to highlight the differences and the impact of traffic type on MANET. The importance of the knowledge of characteristics of each type is useful because it will help us to understand the QoS metrics for each type of traffic and then we can decide which security algorithm is suitable for each type to keep QoS in an acceptable range.

This paper investigates many QoS metrics and it gave us a result which let us now to choose which Encryption method which suit for VoIP and Multimedia traffic, especially these traffic are real time traffic and they need high QoS like delay and throughput.

References

1. Singh, R., Shiwani, S.: Analysis of application level traffics and routing protocols in mobile Ad Hoc network. **3** (2014)
2. Zhou, L., Chao, H.-C.: Multimedia traffic security architecture for the internet of things. IEEE Netw. **25**, 35–40 (2011). Print ISSN: 0890-8044
3. Kundur, D., et al.: Security and privacy for distributed multimedia sensor networks. Proc. IEEE **96**, 112–130 (2008)

4. Eskicioglu, A.M.: Recent progress in key management, authentication, and watermarking. Multimedia Syst. **9**, 239–248 (2013)
5. Susanto, H., Muhaya, F.: Multimedia information security architecture framework. In: Proceedings of the FutureTech (2010)
6. Hussein, A.R.H., Yousef, S., Arabeyyat, O.: A novel weighted distributed clustering algorithm for mobile ad hoc networks. Int. J. ACM Jordan **1**, 134–143 (2010)
7. Ahmed, M., Yousef, S., Aboud, S.J.: Bidirectional search routing protocol for mobile ad hoc networks. Int. J. Comput. Eng. Technol. **4**, 229–243 (2013)
8. Atzori, L., Iera, A., Morabito, G.: The internet of things: a survey. Comput. Netw. **54**, 2787–2805 (2010)
9. Zhou, L., et al.: Context-aware multimedia service in heterogeneous networks. IEEE Intell. Syst. **25**, 40–47 (2010)
10. Zhou, L., et al.: Distributed scheduling scheme for video streaming over multi-channel multi-radio multi-hop wireless networks. JSAC **28**, 409–419 (2010)

Global Triumph or Exploitation of Security and Privacy Concerns in E-Learning Systems

Asim Majeed[1(✉)], Said Baadel[2,3], and Anwar Ul Haq[4]

[1] Birmingham City University and QA Higher Education, Birmingham, UK
asim.majeed@bcu.ac.uk
[2] Canadian University Dubai, Dubai, UAE
s.baadel@gmail.com
[3] University of Huddersfield, Huddersfield, UK
[4] QA Higher Education, London, UK
anwar.haq@qa.com

Abstract. This paper identifies the causes of privacy concerns which emerged when an educational institution launched an automated proctoring technology to examine E-Learners. In the modern era of information, privacy is an integral concern due to its fluid, dynamic and complex nature. In certain situations where it is very difficult to understand the privacy concerns, privacy is often misunderstood by the interactive systems designers. The qualitative data in this research was collected using content analysis approach from 120 online bloggers and useful insights were found; those that pertained to the privacy concerns for E-Learners. The findings revealed both practical and theoretical implications for both the institutions offering online courses and organization designing tools for proctoring.

Keywords: E-learning · Exploitation · Online education · Privacy · Security

1 Introduction

The recent advancements in information technology have made privacy a critical factor of online learning environments. Modern universities and higher educational establishments have tended to adopt Open Learning Environments (OLEs) to deliver their contents and courses through the internet [3]. These resources are freely available to everyone who wants to study. Multimedia tools are used to deliver these courses and most of the web browsers are designed to support their execution [6]. The development of OLE's is not limited to learning and teaching resources, pictures, documents, and audio video learning and discussion forums but also enriched with online quizzes and simulations. The availability of these resources to students depends on course to course, institution to institution and moreover on learners intended outcomes [22]. The diversity in OLE's application has made it quite open for anyone to get register with it and may use the resources for malicious purposes [23].

Different open systems have managed student's details in different ways; for example, an honor code is developed by Coursera to set out an agreement between the OLE's providers and students when participating in their courses. This has embarked

H. Jahankhani et al. (Eds.): ICGS3 2017, CCIS 630, pp. 351–363, 2016.
DOI: 10.1007/978-3-319-51064-4_28

on modern organizations to evolving the need of new technologies that dealt with rapidly changing interactions of the learner with technology through more authentic ways and to maintain the system integrity [23]. A new automated remote proctoring technology was implemented in one of the universities in the United States that would detect and report the suspicious behaviors to the concerned management as a basic premise [27]. For example, if a student taking an online exam browsed the web or used a mobile phone to find an answer, then tutors would be informed instantly through Proctortrack, a tool that continuously monitors the learner's movements. Users of this system raised privacy concerns once Proctortrack was deployed. The general themes of these concerns were the complexity of use in addition to the form and nature of privacy understanding [11]. An online petition was filed on the grounds of privacy concerns by 900 students demanding to stop the usage of this proctoring tool. Even though the use of open learning environments is not new, the embedding of the proctor tracking technology for detecting movements is the first of its kind technology in the world in this regard. Thus, the developments of these systems require more knowledge about learners privacy concerns [15]. Useful insights are provided here while looking at the dynamic and compelled nature of privacy concerns of OLE learners. The rest of the paper is organized as follows: Sect. 2 presents an overview and background of the privacy concerns. Sections 3 and 4 presents methodology used including the analysis of our findings. Finally Sect. 5 will briefly provide conclusion of our work.

2 Privacy

2.1 An Overview

The association of remote access in e-learning has advocated privacy concepts applications which include user's participation and availability of teaching material from diverse platforms [8]. The system and procedures of e-learning are affected by implementing modifications that certainly lead to the reliability, security and privacy concerns [13]. The European and national data privacy legislation enlists that the online resource providers should adequately and appropriately look into the security and privacy concerns, and devise conceptual policies to minimize the risks [18]. Modern information age has clustered privacy as a vital issue for organizations as well as online course providers [6]. The complex nature of e-learning has proved to be difficult to define and to apply concrete solutions to maintain privacy [5].

Research conducted by different e-learning providers indicates that privacy concerns are associated with various factors of user's studying routines, platform access points and access of materials [1]. Therefore, prime focus on maintaining the privacy and security issues in e-learning should be to protect the individual's personalized facts. Any absence of privacy related paradigms would lead to privacy, procedures, security, and reliability problems [19]. Security and privacy among global interconnections through e-learning platforms could be increased dramatically by infusing encryption tools within the data privacy policies [28]. The central theme of setting security and privacy policies is to prevent vector attack incidents and restoring the system after a successful attack. Not only should there be more than one layer in the system that contributes towards maintaining the privacy and security concerns, but also include tools, procedures, and rules on every hierarchical layer that contributes and enforces it [12]. The concept of privacy-preserving keeps high solitude when dealing with a person's personal information and system credentials [23]. E-learning environment has a primary principal to secure the individual's information ensuring successful global interconnections communication through unique encryption resources. Exploration of privacy demands and e-learning solitude can make e-learning criteria's a standard for online education providers [18].

3 Privacy and Security: Overlapping

An online user's personal information is an integral when they access the contents of various courses online [7]. The form and nature of a user's online information could be easily identifiable and accessed due to its persistent nature. Modern age central concern is the privacy of personal data due to its fluid, complex and dynamic nature; consequently making it difficult to define privacy [26]. Many interactive systems designers tend to ignore and misunderstand some of the potential privacy issues and concerns. Higher education institutions are becoming more reliant on online courses due to their nature of novel technical revolution and in consideration of a natural evolution of technology [25]. Online courses paradigm does have the potential to reduce the costs and increase the economic efficiencies through optimization. The online courses provide an infrastructure of a computing model accepted globally with a significant collaboration and enhanced agility [16]. This collaboration leads to security issues and the privacy and security solutions designed as an afterthought could potentially lead to a huge failure when leveraging this revolutionizing tech driven global learning paradigm.

4 Data Security and Open Online Courses

The association of online learning with accidental or malicious misuse causes security concerns requiring protection [4]. This concept of security and privacy leads us to three prime pillars namely; availability, integrity and confidentiality. The protection of sensitive information is generally referred to as confidentiality especially when an unauthorized person tries to access it. Online learning is empowered by a large number of users hence requiring authenticating registered user's privileges to safeguard authorized access [2]. Strong delimitation and login systems should be caged to access online courses. Safeguarding of encryption and authentication are fused within the system to protect personal information. One of the critical issues of security in online data integrity is limiting unauthorized accidental changes and protecting the data from misuse [21]. Absence of proper system alterations checks will require data security mechanism that assures data is in its original, complete and correct form and that it has not been destroyed or modified maliciously or accidently [17].

Online learning environments maintain their integrity through access control. The correct service is readily available through "Availability" connoting the authorized access of online learning system by authorized users only [24]. Authorized access assures the availability of resources to the authorized person in a timely, readily and reliable manner. Data processing capabilities could damage the Availability through the loss of data or by the denial of service [8]. A large number of variant security risks may induce in online learning when applying information communication technology which includes vandalism of public information services, critical data exposure and loss of availability and confidentiality [12]. Some of the security issues in online learning environments are usually attributed and linked to the user's lack of education, improper behaviors and poor knowledge of security measures. These days, online learning environments are adopting the mechanisms of security protection to minimize the security concerns through installing anti-virus software and firewalls [21].

The prime theme of proliferating these security ties is to protect their resources from unauthorized access and improper use [1]. Continuous advent of technology and content is integrated within the online systems in order to make online learning secure. Although the modern user is well informed about security and privacy concerns as these concerns continue to grow, there are still different security issues such as loss of confidentiality, insiders and outsiders manipulation of information that have recently grown tremendously [28]. The element of trust is essentially important to online learning and plays an integral role to retain the users. Security and privacy breach would lead student's perceptions to dramatic fall, if concerns over the reliability of e-learning systems are not addressed [13]. It is very difficult to nominate and identify those factors that contribute in causing the security issues within e-learning platforms. This has led to the development of counter-measures to mitigate the risks involved in privacy and security methodologies [7].

Higher education institutions, as well as most prestigious universities, are integrating and offering more online courses embedded with media tools, audio and video features in the platform [16]. The measures of digital privacy and data security raise concerns with the growth of e-learning and prevent unauthorized access of computers [3]. Data security is a meticulous priority for modern organizations and especially for higher education institutions that are running e-learning courses. Open learning environments (OLE) are new paradigms that are embraced by e-learning technology developments. Higher education institutions are transformed to e-platform and massively using the OLE's for teaching purposes [19]. The embedment of OLE's within the higher education business model has been the central pillar of debate over the past few years, especially when linked to assess its impact on privacy and security issues [24]. OLE's are designed and developed while keeping in view the mass access to these platforms through the web [15]. These populations of diversified students have demanded the development of e-platforms that satisfy student's concerns while accessing course materials such as the implementation of privacy policies to keep the user's personal information private and secure [5].

The economic utility and evolutionary development are behind the OLE's transformation as an essential theme constituting the cause of computing technologies advancements in a distributed manner [5, 16]. The important semantic of OLE's is to improve the economic efficiencies through reducing cost and embedding optimization [23].

One of the significant features of OLE's is to enhance collaboration and agility through globally accepted infrastructure and computing model. However, the confusion arises when comparing OLE's with existing models in regards to privacy, security and adoption techniques [26]. Failure and avoidance of appropriate security and privacy solutions in OLE's could make the revolutionary advancements a huge failure.

5   Methodology

Some of the concerns of privacy leakages have been investigated in this research with the adoption of case study based approach [9]. A tracking tool called Proctortrack was launched for students which lead to many privacy and security concerns while providing online proctoring services. This proctoring tool was designed to monitor the student's behavior and find out if the user is a legitimate student. A webcam was fitted within the Proctortrack services capturing facial features of students for the verification purposes and being sensitive to their movements which may lead to any misconduct or cheating (Fig. 1).

Fig. 1. Case study based approach (Garber, 2012)

The advantage of using a case study based approach is that it gives an analysis of a person, institution, policy, event or group of people [9]. The case study based approach is feasible for a research with its ability of in-depth examination of people behavior and illuminates those decisions taken by the participants [10]. The other reason of using case study approach is due to being an empirical and explanatory method and the researcher has no control over the events [11]. The participant observation, physical artifacts, direct observation, interviews, documentation and archival records are used as evidence along with their weaknesses and strengths [9]. The research methodology can also be utilized to depict solutions for an existing problem [11]. This approach also helps to add more insight data to the existing literature especially when insufficient literature has been conducted on certain areas.

Traditional media sources have been used by higher education institutions with the adoption of virtual learning models. Web technology advancement have increased computing capabilities transforming the idea of traditional to massive open online course; MOOC. The methodology approach takes central importance to protecting privacy and avoiding the misuse of data. The equilibrium between other stakeholders and knowledge is provided through maintaining and establishing a trust relationship with the people who are studying. The educational resources are freely provided by MOOCs but needs to have invasion of privacy requirements enthused through informed consent.

The views and comments of 130 online bloggers were collected through web blogs and forums regarding the use of Proctortrack for a particular case. We used the content analysis approach in this research to analyze the qualitative data [11]. The content analysis was initially used for quantitative data but from over a decade, it has also been utilized for qualitative data [10]. A key advantage of content analysis is diversification ability that can be used to analyze the behaviors and patterns where data is evident and can be linked to these [9]. On the other side, it could also be used as a latent content analysis interpreting the data that involves very small evidence of showing the relationship with participant's behaviors [14]. The analysis of the current research is based on latent contents which focus on observing not only the users behavior but also the causality of such behavior [11].

Both the inductive or deductive approaches could be used for content analysis as deductive approach moves from general theme to specific whereas inductive moves another way round [10]. In cases where enough knowledge is not available about a certain behavior or phenomenon, the inductive approach is used for analysis. Otherwise deductive approach is used when the analysis is conducted on the existing material [14].

The inductive approach is used in this study to oversee the emotional state and specific behaviors of learners. A model presented by Elo and Kynga [9] iterates the process of content analysis in three stages; preparation phase, organizing phase and reporting phase. A theme or a word would be required in the preparation phase to start the analysis. The themes emerging from sentences would lead to the organizing phase and in the last phase the conceptual and abstract theme would be analyzed (Fig. 2).

The inductive approach is used in this study to oversee the emotional state and specific behaviors of learners. A model presented by Elo and Kynga [9] iterates the process of content analysis in three stages; preparation phase, organizing phase and reporting phase. A theme or a word would be required in the preparation phase to start the analysis. The themes emerging from sentences would lead to the organizing phase and in the last phase the conceptual and abstract theme would be analyzed.

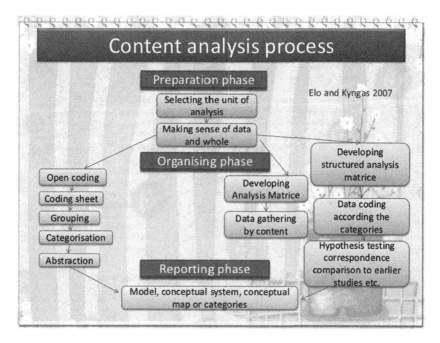

Fig. 2. Inductive content analysis (adapted from Elo & Kynga, 2007)

6 Findings and Data Analysis

Key-Words-In-Context (KWIC) is used in the preparation phase of the content analysis to depict main areas of privacy and security concerns. The word "concern" has been searched through the respondent feedbacks and following sample results have been coined up.

The central theme of this discussion is to find the concerns of learners when new facial recognition and verification technology was introduced in the university. The given data does not confer directly that the privacy has been an issue for students and when they were asked about their understanding about privacy, everyone answered differently.

Certain behaviours and phenomenon are analysed through latent thematic analysis approach which have tried to probe various meanings of privacy concerns (Figs. 3 and 4).

This facial recognition feature of this tool collecting images for online verification tool has raised concerns about privacy issues primarily among the learners. The potential for misuse of this technology caused anxiety in the users and it was compounded by the fact that their biometric data coupled with their private spaces could be compromised. The perceived invasion of privacy was linked with the sense of insecurity and injustice when using such system, for example students felt that they are being tracked and they perceived that if they made a mistake or if someone else made a mistake whilst using this proctotrack system, they may not have a chance to justify their actions and hence be flagged as cheaters.

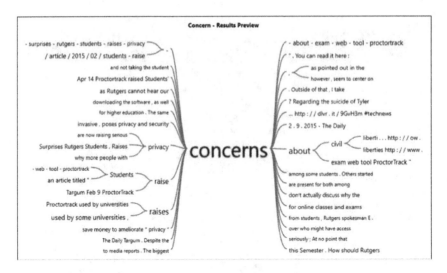

Fig. 3. Sample themes generated ("concerns")

Fig. 4. Sample themes generated ("security")

Our findings suggested that privacy is a fundamental right of everyone regardless of whether their learning environment is offline or online. The protection of personal information including images is central in the modern world where learners could be anointed if they are in an environment where their every move is monitored. The United States Federal Trade Commission has enlisted in the Fair Information Practice principles (FIPPs) that the fundamental principal of publishing any personal information requires the consent of all stakeholders. The institution that launched the Proctortrack tool for verification purposes was based in United States.

The learners were never informed about this so their anxiety and annoyance was justified. The consumers should have been made aware of this feature when launching any verification related tool. It is also paramount for the companies to inform the users on how their data would be collected and for what purposes it would be used and for how long this information will be stored (Fig. 5).

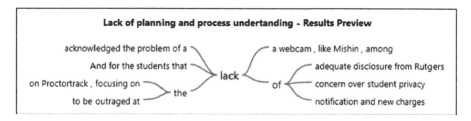

Fig. 5. Sample themes generated

This particular case study was a classic example where users were neglected and no mention of their private data was made aware to them on how it will be utilized. The credibility and acceptability of this tool have practical implications not only for the organization that introduced the tool but also the university. The petition against the launch of Proctortrack has an immense capacity of tarnishing the reputation of both organizations. The integration of this innovative tool used for verification purposes has turned out to be a shambolic act not only for the institution but also for the company who programmed this tool since the design and functionality of Proctortrack completely ignored the online learning environments and privacy concerns. The online courses offered by MOOC's are massive and are highly admired by the colleges and higher educational institutions. One major concern of such a massive implementation is the maintenance of academic integrity and originality of student work. This requires the establishment of a process which could authenticate them. The automatic ID validation in online courses is consistently increasing as more and more institutions are moving onto the online courses and at the same time various organizations (e.g.; Udacity and Coursera) have started collaborating with them to offer tools.

Students appearing for the exams through the traditional way do not needed any further security layer whereas those taking online courses require authentication to verify their student IDs. Many organizations offering MOOC are showing interest in maintaining the integrity of online learning through leveraging new proctoring tools.

Privacy concerns of learners must be examined before the launch of any proctoring tool and institutions that apply these tools should be given ample time to minimize the anxiety and privacy concerns of the learners. Many institutions utilizing these tools claim they lacked appropriate understanding of the Proctor tool, its integration, configuration and awareness.

According to Patel et al. [20] there is an interesting realization that the information security is related to the security of information which is directly related to the asset, in comparison to cyber security which related to the protection of cyberspace itself and entities which function within cyberspace and the assets which are approached via cyberspace. This differentiation could be coupled with the ISO/IEC 27005:2011 frame that provides the context (Context establishment; Risk assessment; Risk treatment; Risk acceptance; Risk communication; Risk monitoring and review) for clear direction for the practitioners when designing and deploying tools such as Proctortrack. Our study highlights the importance the need of coupling security and privacy measures, systematic understanding of information security and privacy contextualization and enabling measures for the awareness of all stake holders (Fig. 6).

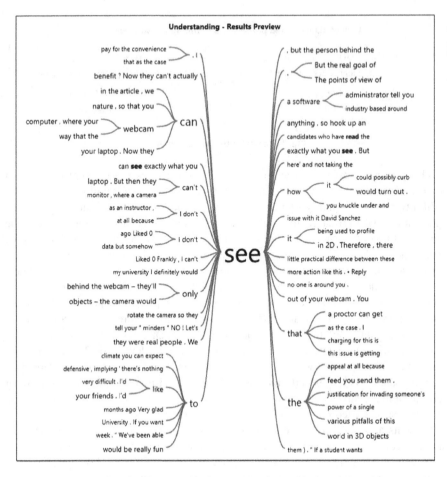

Fig. 6. Coding sample showing the data analysis process

Theme	Users un-satisfaction with prospective and evident privacy and security threats and perceive lack of risk analysis	
Category	Anxiety over hardware and software cost and lack of awareness of risks such security and privacy invasion	
Sub-category	Anxiety on Security and Privacy Threats	Anxiety over hardware/software costs and lack of awareness for product features and risks
Codes	"I am outraged that a great university like Rutgers would decide to implement such software. Proctortrack is invasive and threatens fundamental rights of privacy. Being watched makes one	"Not everyone who attends college and opts for online courses has the access to webcams" "How it was implemented was unprofessional"

(continued)

(continued)

uncomfortable - especially in such a threatening screen as Proctortrack presents. There are so many rules & no way to keep track of them all. There is one in particular that says you can't look away from the computer screen while taking the test! These procedures are so stringent and outrageous that an in-class proctored exam would be easier and a better choice too"

"This is absolutely creepy, and it probably means you also can't get up to get some water or go to the bathroom which is cruel and unusual"

"The problem? First, the whole thing is a ridiculous waste of money. From top to bottom, none of it really makes sense – it's incredibly invasive: it tracks your eye motion through your webcam, it scans your knuckles as some weird form of identification, it uses facial recognition to make sure that you're not someone else – and above all, it can be bypassed rather easily. I'm not saying I have a better solution to make sure that students don't cheat on online exams – but this solution is intrusive, and the "Big Brother"-ness of it is so crazy it sounds like it must be a joke (like knuckle scanning, for instance)"

"Making Proctortrack MANDATORY software for all online course students is infuriating. It's unnatural that students are faced with the prospect of compromising their privacy in order to earn a grade"

"I feel Proctortrack is an invasive mechanism. While the ultimate goal is to lessen and ultimately eliminate cheating, Proctortrack is invasive, poses privacy and security concerns, as pointed out in the petition, and it wasn't announced until AFTER the period of which I would be able to ADD/DROP classes. Plus, I had already paid the $100 online course support fee, which WAS clearly stated prior to my registration."

"I've taken online courses and have numerous friends that have gone to Rutgers; this should not be mandated at all. If the college wants to use this software fine, but offer in person options...what if you didn't have a personal computer? Not a fan of this"

"Due to costs of the actual online course, adding this Proctortrack software at the cost of $32 is also unjust, while we, as students, are already paying tuition. This is not fair to any student who is already on financial debts"

"It is not only an invasion of privacy, but an invasion of privacy we have to pay for. We already pay tons of money in tuition; pay extra course fees for online courses, now we have to pay to make their job easier for them"

"With Rutgers systems being hacked recently with quite ease, it would seem extremely foolish to have students give up their privacy. What if ProctorTrack too gets hacked?"

7 Conclusion

The current study investigated the privacy concerns as well as the factors causing anxiety. The integration of online verification tool within the e-learning system through conceptual formation could be used by academics, designers, planners and decision presented in this research paper. Although the use of Proctortrack tool on its own is a good idea and may solve many problems, proper contextualization for the product launch and risk management should be done a priori. This case study also shows the need for a robust framework for the awareness of all stakeholders where novel technology is used in untested scenarios. An in-depth understanding of users privacy concerns has been discussed and shown in this study and not doing so, would damage the institution's reputation and unsatisfied users. The privacy concerns in delivering online courses are not triggered just because of the webcam use but using webcam at the private place could lead to the data security breach and raise anxiety over privacy.

References

1. Dharmawansa, A.D., Nakahira, K.T., Fukumura, Y.: Detecting eye blinking of a real-world student and introducing to the virtual e-learning environment. Procedia Comput. Sci. **22**, 717–726 (2013)
2. Alw, N., Fan, I.S.: E-learning and information security management. Int. J. Digital Soc. **1**(2) (2010)
3. Besiki, S., Gasser, L., Twidale, M.B., Smith, L.C.: A framework for information quality assessment. J. Am. Soc. Inform. Sci. Technol. **58**(12), 1720–1733 (2007)
4. Buyukozkan, G., Ruan, D., Feyzioglu, O.: Evaluating e-learning web site quality in a fuzzy environment. Int. J. Intell. Syst. **22**(5), 567–586 (2007)
5. Chen, Y., He, W.: Security risks and protection in online learning: a survey. Int. Rev. Res. Open Distance Learn. (2013). http://www.irrodl.org/index.php/irrodl/article/view/1632/2712
6. Craciunas, S., Elsek, I.: The standard model of an e-learning platform, chap. 2, Bucharest, Romania (2009)
7. Diaz, V., Golas, J., Gautsch, S.: Privacy Considerations in Cloud-Based Teaching and Learning Environments. EDUCAUSE (2010)
8. Dobre, I.: Critical study of the present e-learning systems, chap. 2, Academia Romana, Romania (2010)
9. Elo, S., Kynga, H.: The qualitative content analysis process. J. Adv. Nurs. **62**, 107–115 (2007)
10. Franzosi, R.: Content analysis: objective, systematic, and quantitative description of content. In: SAGE Benchmarks in Social Research Methods: Content Analysis, pp. 2–43 (2008)
11. Graneheim, U.H., Lundman, B.: Qualitative content analysis in nursing research: concepts, procedures and measures to achieve trustworthiness. Nurse Educ. Today **24**, 105–112 (2004)
12. Garber, L.: The challenges of securing the virtualized environment. Computer, 17–23 (2012). [5] Social Media and Data
13. Johnson, H.: Dialogue and the construction of knowledge in e-learning: exploring students' perceptions of their learning while using blackboard's asynchronous discussion board. Eur. J. Open, Distance E-Learn. ISSN 1027-5207 (2007)

14. Kondracki, N.L., Wellman, N.S., Amundson, D.R.: Content analysis: review of methods and their applications in nutrition education. J. Nutr. Educ. Behav. **34**(4), 224–230 (2002)
15. Kultan, J.: Issledovanije ispoľzovanija LMS Moodle v processe obučenija, pp. 295–300. Izdateľstvo Juniversum, Kazaň (2011)
16. Manadhata, P.K., Wing, J.M.: An attack surface metric. IEEE Trans. Softw. Eng. **37**(3), 371–386 (2011)
17. Meyer, J.P., Zhu, S.: Fair and equitable measurement of student learning in MOOCs: an introduction to item response theory, scale linking, and score equating. Res. Pract. Assess. **8** (1), 26–39 (2013)
18. Moneo, J.M., Caballe, S., Prieot, J.: Security in learning management systems. eLearning Papers (2012). Catalonia, Spain
19. Neville, K., Heavin, C.: Using social media to support the learning needs of future IS security professionals. Electron. J. E-Learn. **11**(1), 29–38 (2013)
20. Patel, A., Taghavi, M., Júnior, J.C., Latih, R., Zin, A.M.: Safety measures for social computing in wiki learning environment. Int. J. Inf. Secur. Priv. (IJISP) **6**(2), 1–15 (2012)
21. Pendegraft, N., Rounds, M., Stone, R.W.: Factors influencing college students' use of computer security. Int. J. Inf. Secur. Priv. (IJISP) **4**(3), 51–60 (2010)
22. Sasikumar, M.: E-learning: opportunity and challenges (2013). http://www.cdacmumbai.in/design/corporate_site/override/pdf-doc/elearning.pdf
23. Song, K., Lee, S.M., Nam, S.C.: Combined biometrics for e-learning security. ISA 2-13 ASTL **21**, 247–251 (2013)
24. Srivastava, A., Sinha, S.: Information security through e-learning using VTE. Int. J. Electron. Comput. Sci. Eng. **2**(18), 528–531 (2013)
25. Zuev, V.I.: E-learning security models. Manag. Inf. Syst. **7**(2), 024–028 (2012)
26. Wang, F., Ge, B., Zhang, L., Chen, Y., Xin, Y., Li, X.: A system framework of security management in enterprise systems. Syst. Res. Behav. Sci. **30**, 287–299 (2013)
27. Chen, Y., He, W.: Security risks and protection in online learning: a survey. Int. Rev. Res. Open Distance Learn. **14**(5), 108–127 (2013)
28. Zuev, V.: E-learning security models. Management **7**(2), 24–28 (2012)

Efficient Energy and Processes Time Algorithm for Offloading Using Cloud Computing

Rakan Aldmour, Sufian Yousef[(⊠)], Faris Albaadani,
and Mohammad Yaghi

Faculty of Science and Technology, Anglia Ruskin University, Chelmsford, UK
rakan.aldmour@pgr.anglia.ac.uk,
sufian.yousef@anglia.ac.uk

Abstract. The best way to execute big files in better performance and short times while the available resources on the core server is the new technique called offloading in cloud computing. However, the offloading technique is not the right place to execute, so it is much better to execute files on the node in some cases. In this issue there is a trade-off, while the power limitation in the local node, so in this paper an innovative algorithm is proposed based on the file size. So in this issue the file size is measured and after that the decision is taken for the execution file, if is it locally on the node, or offloading by sending the file to the core cloud. The most important issue is to preserve time while the performing file. However, the second and important issue especially for the small nodes, is to preserve the energy limitation for big files, because of the power consumption is very high. The cost of the power consumption, execution time, and file size for the core cloud, and local node is calculated to denote an input to the execution decision.

Keywords: Cloud computing · Mobile cloud computing · Execution time · Power consumption · Offloading

1 Introduction

At the early years of the 1970s, the offloading system was used at its early stages. It was first used among servers to find an optimum load of balancing. Offloading has many ways to describe it for instance Bowen et al., has defined offloading as the method that can improve the proficiency, quality, or even the performance of some calculations task by assigning the servers with an enormous powerful computation to deal with heavyweight data rather than the local servers [1]. Memory, energy consumption, processing, storage, as well as the executing time are the examples of the computation factor where more than one of these factors can be used at the same time. The communication between local and remote machines is the medium required in order for the offloading to be executed. Hence that's why the communications is an essential key for the offloading tasks. However these communications require local processing and this would result in too much energy consumption. Network interface together with the processor are the biggest power consumption thus offloading need to be aware of the total consumptions and communications. Offloading has many motivation to and

© Springer International Publishing AG 2016
H. Jahankhani et al. (Eds.): ICGS3 2017, CCIS 630, pp. 364–370, 2016.
DOI: 10.1007/978-3-319-51064-4_29

advantage that make it an essential to be used as Karthik et al., has proposed [2]. To begin with, offloading minimizes the required time of processing and works towards rising the responding time for the application. As approved for this, Wolski et al., has proposed an offloading decision algorithm based on the bandwidth with an objective to support the offloading with a code in order to select the optimum wireless medium [3]. In addition, recent studies has shown superior result when using a powerful server rather than restricted power servers, hence offloading can rise up the performance of an application. Moreover, offloading was initially used to balance the load between the used servers. Finally, on the word of Stephen et al., offloading can be used as a technique to preserve the energy consumptions and minimize the latency which can be observed clearly from the smartphones devices [4].

2   Background

Karthil and Yung have considered most of the application used from a mobile device for instance voice recording and games as high energy consumption. For this they have proposed the clouding techniques to avoid such consumption [5]. Furthermore, Amiya et al., have also proposed a new system to save the energy consumption for the smartphones. This system aims to have an assessment of the energy cost for the offloading tasks. They have used five different brands of mobile phones as a way to validate their system, where they were able to show some result on how accurate their system can estimate the needed energy for offloading tasks [6].

JADE is a new system developed by Qian and Andresen [7]. This system works on improving the smartphone applications performance as well as reducing the energy consumption. They have been able to prove that their system was capable to decrease the energy consumption to approximately 39%. The JADE system was designed to be able to handle the offloading tasks within the Android device themselves and also between Android and non-Android devices. JADE is a multi-level offloading which means that JADE is capable of offering an optimal method to transmit the workloads to the optimal server based on the performance and the energy consumption.

Smartphones energy weight comparison for upload and download a large file such as a video from and to a different multimedia cloud computing was proposed by Altamimi et al. [8]. WIFI and 3G network interface together with FTP and HTTP internet protocols was used in this system. This system works to estimate the energy weight for the similar file used on the mobile device. Result has shown that MCC preserve the energy of the smartphone devise between '30% to 70%', also offers various different functionalities for smartphone devices.

Majid and Kshirasagar, have proposed a decision to engine the capability of handling experiments to decide on the cost of different parameters involved in the Android devices system as well as the Amazon EC2 and S3 clouds. For instance, to transform a video type, the decision engine tasks has the ability to decides on perform this task on a local mobile device or alternatively offload to the cloud [9].

ANEKA interface is a new mechanism on the mobile client library which was proposed by Rajkumar, and Tiago. They used the application performance time and the mobile battery life as two different mobile applications to validate their proposed mechanism. This mechanism works to minimize the process which can involves in sending and serializing the messages, desterilizing and gathering the messages' responses for the communication that occurs in a mobile devise to cloud [10].

Most Common application such as multimedia are a big power consumption as well as delay for the network, thus a new cloudlet-based application was proposed by Yasar et al. [12] to overcome these challenges. Result using this proposed application on·the smartphones has shown a significant redundancy in power consumption and communication latency [11].

CUCKOO is a module used in Android application that has the capability of taking a decision whether to execute part of the task locally or offload it to the cloud. CUCKOO module was developed by Henri et al., and was a perfect fit with an innovation tool to perform locally or remotely. Wireless medium, memory, and device type are some examples of the local resources of the smartphones which have a huge impact on executing the offloading decision.

Mobile devices and cloudlet provider need an intermediate layer to help in taking decision in where to offload the data either to the cloudlet or the clone. Therefore a new decision-making algorithm in the intermediate layer was proposed by Magurawalage et al. [13]. This is algorithm has taking the power consumption into consideration to enhance the MCC performance, as well as other tasks to be considered such as responding time and data caching procedure to cloudlets.

Shiraz et al. [14] have carried out some analysis for computational frameworks with regards to the MCC (Mobile Cloud Computing) offloading. This research has investigated on the recent studies of the latest computational offloading mechanisms considering the limited resource-intensive. This research has conclude that data sent for offloading with 13241.1 KB can consume approximately 31.6% extra energy, and 39% extra time.

3 Proposed Algorithm

The new media contains all different types such as video, sound, text, and pictures. To perform this kind of media in a high performance, it requires a powerful resource for instance cloud computing. However, smartphones have a limited functions. Mobile battery limitation is one of the biggest concern for the smartphones improvement. To overcome this issue, the new offloading technique is one of the best and proper ways for the power consumption for smartphones devices and battery life limitation. This novel method supports smartphones to execute the intensive tasks by forwarding them from the mobile to the CC. Our new innovative system helps smartphone users to offload to CC taking into account the file size for instance, the file size will be calculated in advance. The created new paradigm includes on a decision engine to check the possibility of the offloading, as well as to preserve smartphones energy. The New paradigm checks possibility the smartphones could save energy by sending the tasks to cloud computing. The core work for this technique is based on the file size, and the way of working, basically it is to check two of the most important parameters. Firstly, it assess the time which is needed to perform the tasks on the mobile and on the CC. Secondly, it assess the power consumption while execution the tasks, on the mobile or on the CC. The following step is related to the decision engine to determine is it worth to offload or not. After the appropriate decision has been taken by the decision engine, the tasks start execution on the smartphones, otherwise the task take place on the cloud by offloading. In this case, the queuing and the latency on the server will be supplied by decision engine then send acknowledgment to clients which contains on the power consumption, time needed, and queuing. In our proposed paradigm, it is significant to check the time required as well as the power consumption for different types of tasks. As the power consumption varies among interface networks such as 3G, 4G and WLAN, it is very important to know the weight of upload and download files through cloud computing while using various kinds of network interface. The smartphones access the cloud via Internet and mobile applications that are connected to the cloud. The network interfaces has a specific feature for each type. So each one consumes a level of power and support different throughput. The proposed paradigm, study network interface and find out the greatest way to preserve energy and fast execution. The mobile devices contain software and hardware. The Software is part consists for the applications and the operating systems. The hardware is part consists of RAM, CPU, HDD, and WNI. The power is spent in smartphones by hardware parts, which are being run using the operating system that based on the applications requirements. As a result, the consuming of power based on the application kind, because every service delivered needs a specific hardware.

4 Experiments and Results

To check the power consumption and the execution time on the node and remotely, in our experiment we have used the Java programming language and Android Studio. The table below presents the results for various file size: (Table 1).

Table 1. Power consumption and execution time for the mobile and cloud

File size	Local node		Offloading	
	Execution time (min)	Power consumption	Execution time (min)	Power consumption
1 MB	1.94	.7%	4.16	.8%
2 MB	2.79	1.1%	4.07	.1%
5 MB	6.69	2.3%	5.83	1.3%
7 MB	9.87	4.8%	6.33	1.9%
9 MB	14.05	6.01%	7.2	2.5%

The first test of the algorithm in Fig. 1 has studied the relation between the execution time and file size as locally or remotely. The results illustrates that the more of the file size is, the more the performing time will be. The experiments check the file size among 1 MB to 9 MB. As we noticed from the results that the rising in the file size consumes the power as well as increase the time process for the node, contrary on the cloud less power consumption and less time process. This is the evidence of

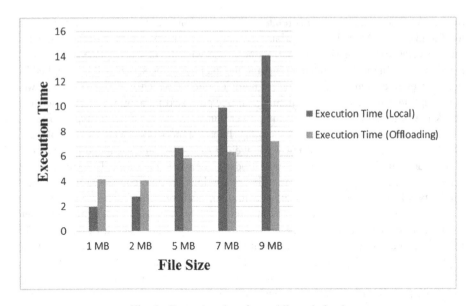

Fig. 1. Execution time for mobile and cloud

hypothesis, for instance at file size 7 MB the power consumption for the node is more than double compare to cloud.

In Fig. 2 the execution time at file size 1 MB in the node is more than tripled compared to cloud which is 2% while on the node is almost 8%. So it is very paramount to employ this algorithm to help in taking the suitable decision to preserve the power and time.

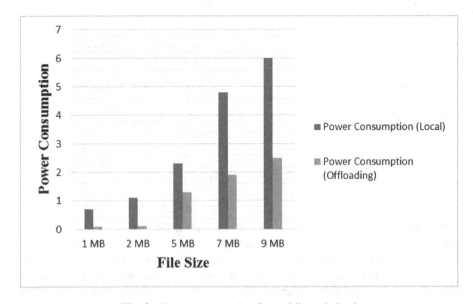

Fig. 2. Power consumption for mobile and cloud

5 Conclusion

The proposed algorithm to check the power consumption, the performing time, and the file size has been created and tested. The experiments for a various file size and the comparison between local node and cloud server was performed. After each experiment it is clear to perform on locally on mobile or on remotely cloud computing by offloading technique. The results show that there is a big sharp in the consuming the power and the performing time especially in the big files, so it is obvious to execute the files on the cloud server core by offloading instead execution on the mobile, for instance at file size 9 MB the execution time is doubled in the node at file size is 1 MB. In this issue there is a big decrease regarding to power consumption. For future research topic, it is recommended there are some of parameters should involves such as utilization and queuing.

References

1. Zhou, B., Dastjerdi, A.V., Calheiros, R.N., Srirama, S.N., Buyya, R.: A context sensitive offloading scheme for mobile cloud computing service. In: 2015 IEEE 8th International Conference on Cloud Computing (CLOUD), pp. 869–876. IEEE, June 2015
2. Kumar, K., Liu, J., Lu, Y.-H., Bhargava, B.: A survey of computation offloading for mobile systems. Mob. Netw. Appl. 18(1), 129–140 (2013). 31, 33
3. Wolski, R., Gurun, S., Krintz, C., Nurmi, D.: Using bandwidth data to make computation offloading decisions. In: 2008 IEEE International Symposium on Parallel and Distributed Processing, IPDPS 2008, pp. 1–8. IEEE, April 2008
4. Gao, B., He, L., Liu, L., Li, K., Jarvis, S.A.: From mobiles to clouds: developing energy-aware offloading strategies for workflows. In: Proceedings of the 2012 ACM/IEEE 13th International Conference on Grid Computing, pp. 139–146. IEEE Computer Society, September 2012
5. Kumar, K., Lu, Y.H.: Cloud computing for mobile users: can offloading computation save energy? Computer 4, 51–56 (2010)
6. Altamimi, M., Abdrabou, A., Naik, K., Nayak, A.: Energy cost models of smartphones for task offloading to the cloud. IEEE Trans. Emerg. Topics Comput. 3(3), 384–398 (2015)
7. Qian, H., Andresen, D.: Reducing mobile device energy consumption with computation offloading. In: 2015 16th IEEE/ACIS International Conference on Software Engineering, Artificial Intelligence, Networking and Parallel/Distributed Computing (SNPD), pp. 1–8. IEEE, June 2015
8. Altamimi, M., Palit, R., Naik, K., Nayak, A.: Energy-as-a-service (EaaS): on the efficacy of multimedia cloud computing to save smartphone energy. In: 2012 IEEE 5th International Conference on Cloud Computing (CLOUD), pp. 764–771. IEEE, June 2012
9. Altamimi, M., Naik, K.: A practical task offloading decision engine for mobile devices to use energy-as-a-service (EaaS). In: 2014 IEEE World Congress on Services (SERVICES), pp. 452–453. IEEE, June 2014
10. Justino, T., Buyya, R.: Outsourcing resource-intensive tasks from mobile apps to clouds: Android and Aneka integration. In: 2014 IEEE International Conference on Cloud Computing in Emerging Markets (CCEM), pp. 1–8. IEEE, October 2014

11. Jararweh, Y., Ababneh, F., Khreishah, A., Dosari, F.: Scalable cloudlet-based mobile computing model. Procedia Comput. Sci. **34**, 434–441 (2014)
12. Kemp, R., Palmer, N., Kielmann, T., Bal, H.: Cuckoo: a computation offloading framework for smartphones. In: Gris, M., Yang, G. (eds.) MobiCASE 2010. LNICST, vol. 76, pp. 59–79. Springer, Heidelberg (2012)
13. Magurawalage, C.M.S., Yang, K., Hu, L., Zhang, J.: Energy-efficient and network-aware offloading algorithm for mobile cloud computing. Comput. Netw. **74**, 22–33 (2014)
14. Shiraz, M., Sookhak, M., Gani, A., Shah, S.A.A.: A study on the critical analysis of computational offloading frameworks for mobile cloud computing. J. Netw. Comput. Appl. **47**, 47–60 (2015)
15. Shiraz, M., Gani, A., Shamim, A., Khan, S., Ahmad, R.W.: Energy efficient computational offloading framework for mobile cloud computing. J. Grid Comput. **13**(1), 1–18 (2015)

A Novel Anonymity Quantification and Preservation Model for UnderNet Relay Networks

Gregory Epiphaniou$^{(\boxtimes)}$, Tim French, Haider Al-Khateeb, Ali Dehghantanha, and Hamid Jahankhani

School of Computer Science and Technology, University of Bedfordshire, Luton, UK
{gregory.epiphaniou,tim.french,haider.Al-Khateeb}@beds.ac.uk,
A.Dehghantanha@Salford.ac.uk, hamid.jahankhani@northumbria.ac.uk
http://www.beds.ac.uk

Abstract. With the wide spread of Internet applications in both the surface net (Internet) and Darknet, the necessity to safeguard privacy and anonymity has become more prominent than ever. In an attempt to assure untraceability and undetectability between entities, as part of the communication process, traditional confidentiality mechanisms have proved insufficient to address attacks against those principles. In addition, different international laws and cross-continental cybercrimes become immune from being affected by a global public policy on how data traffic should be treated. In this article, a holistic view of anonymity preservation approaches and techniques is given with emphasis on the partial articulation of a novel anonymity preservation model based on infrastructure elements, circuit attributes and adversarial engagement rates on clustered and unindexed portions of the cyberspace.

Keywords: DarkNet · Anonymity · Cyberspace · ToR · Engagement rate

1 Introduction

Anonymous networks employ the concept of virtual circuits to establish a connection between hosts with strong cryptographic primitives to assure confidentiality whilst also, enabling entities to protect their identity and preserve privacy without exposing information to an adversary. This plethora of virtual connections over multiple hops can offer the privacy required between the communication parties making identification and traceability a difficult task to be achieved with some tradeoffs especially, between anonymity and performance, especially, in dynamic P2P networks [21,24]. Most of the virtual tunnels and their length are usually dictated by the type of application used to establish the communication. For instance, ToR [7] network can establish up to three tunnels whereas other implementations such as Crowds [25] and MorhMix may vary in terms of the circuits enabled as well as the probability of detecting active neighboor peers

© Springer International Publishing AG 2016
H. Jahankhani et al. (Eds.): ICGS3 2017, CCIS 630, pp. 371–384, 2016.
DOI: 10.1007/978-3-319-51064-4_30

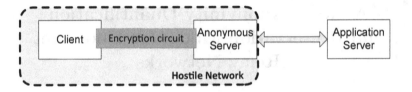

Fig. 1. A single-hop anonymity model

and servers. The effectiveness of these networks in terms of anonymity preservation, often varies based on the number of simultaneous users accessing the network, routing/relaying strategies and adversaries' skills to control nodes or paths. Figure 1 presents the interaction between different entities and anonymous networks in the cyberspace. A key distinction is made between *high-latency* and *low-latency* anonymous networks in a mixnet scenario where public key cryptography is used to assure confidentiality. The concept of "mixing" attaches itself to the process of randomly diffusing dummy messages mixed with legitimate ones for a given pool between intermediate forwarders.

Anonymity in cyberspace has always been a domain of conflicting interests as regards freedom of speech, but at the same time gives enough power to adversaries to masquerade their illegal activities. Certain services in the hidden web such as dynamic content, unlinked pages, private web, limited access content and scripted pages offer a higher degree of anonymity preservation, much wider access to information which can be potentially invaluable information to companies, organisations and governments, but also to organised cybercrime [2]. There is a considerable increase on the hactivist phenomenon with a rise of attacks made by hactivists at an alarming frequent rate against large organisations worldwide using the Deep Web as an attack vector. The exponential use of social media and networks has become an excellent "recruitment" agent for cybercriminals to impose devastating attacks against privacy with an impressive number of participants willingly offering their time and resources for this purpose.

1.1 Anonymity Disclosure

Active traffic analysis is often employed by adversaries to inject traffic into legitimate communication channels in an attempt to enumerate and analyse underlined traffic by initiating rogue routers. These common and easy to deploy attacks may seriously undermine anonymity in anonymous communications and proactive network defense techniques are often used against them. Attacks in this category usually involve metadata for a given network connection such as timing information and source and destination of messages to degrade anonymity. A typical defense scenario includes anonymous servers sending probe ("heartbeat") messages into the network informing peers about the current status of the network [6] or imposing tarpits between the intermediate hops. If anomalies are detected then the sender is informed and either seizes the communication or else deceptive network defense is used in an attempt to improve the anonymity of valid messages. Different implementations include but are not limited to delay traffic routes, block traffic completely, insert time-stamps and integrity checks on messages or subscribe peers to dedicated router services using a digital currency (bitcoins) and honeytokens.

A very common approach is to distinguish different types of traffic in a given network based on the protocol used for the actual communication known as deep packet inspection (DPI). ToR network can protect against traffic analysis and behavior online pattern identification/matching by distributing traffic sourced from a single peer to the destination as if it is coming from multiple sources. An example of a protocol used to preserve anonymity in the cyber space is the ToR Hidden services protocol (see Fig. 2). A hidden service in the ToR network is anything that can be accessed through the network (web site or a service) without disclosure of logical addressing or geo-location information for all the entities in a session. Using the most strict definition, even peers participating in a session are not aware of each others location or identity.

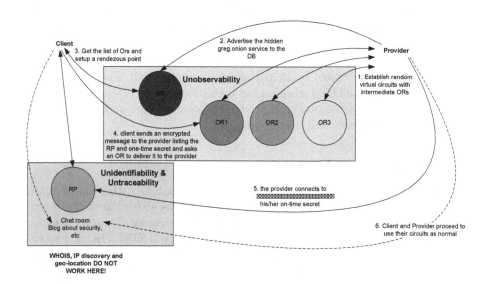

Fig. 2. ToR hidden services protocol

An artificial insertion of rate traffic in a circuit within an anonymous relay network and monitoring delay variations at the intermediate proxies, might yield useful information to an adversary about the possibility of a relay being an actual part of the circuit itself [27]. Different variations of this attack include congesting an intermediate relay to the point of saturation by amplifying adversary's traffic through the establishment of long paths through the sample network [9] and increase traffic flaws to observe changes in the forwarding capabilities of relays [3]. A different approach is presented in [13], where observations of round-trip delays in a given circuit using malicious code inserted by an adversary, might leak information about the geographical location of the client. The common characteristics of these attacks is that they are highly intrusive as certain traffic must be inserted in the relay network. A stealthier attack using throughput fingerprinting is introduced in [23]. The authors argue that streams multiplexed into the same circuit and destined for at least two servers at the same time, can yield invaluable information to an attacker. The attack can lead to information leakage by simply correlating the observed throughput between a pair of circuits for a given path formation.

The success of failure of these attacks are typically influenced by the type of the anonymous network (wired, wireless, hybrid), the means of access into the network and the protocols used during the message exchange. Traditional security attributes for each entity within these networks, proper threat management and modelling and clear justification of the system design are core elements towards a mutually shared interest between legitimate users and adversaries, which is the need to preserve their anonymity. For example, particularly in ToR the threat model only accounts for adversaries who can passively or actively monitor traffic patterns for a fraction of the nodes within the sample network. The ToR threat model does not provide strong protection from an adversary that controls most of the nodes/paths in the actual communication path [27]. The system is based on circuit anonymisation following TCP streams only, with certain nodes (usually three) participating within each circuit. Packet anonymisation rather than path anonymisation has been proposed in [17] but with several limitations in terms of the overhead produced (packets generated) and random paths between the source and destination.

1.2   A Fragile Cyber Ecosystem

Open source intelligence gathering tools are also used to gather information using open methodologies to publicly share observations about the methods and tools used to impose surveillance and censorship in cyberspace. Typical examples include the Open Observation for Network Interference (OONI), Herdict monitoring Project and OpenNet Initiative. It is clear that hidden networks are used by both criminals and legitimate users driven by distinctively different motives. It is unfair to characterise this portion of the cyber space as a pool of illegal activities hidden beneath the coat of anonymity or pseudo-anonymity these networks can offer. There is clear evidence to suggest an increasing use of these networks by users disinclined to expose their physical location for legitimate reasons, activists and protests avoiding Internet censorship introduced by governments in different geographical locations, governments for covert operations and journalists. Cyber criminals cannot be excluded from this hidden space[1] with their own distinct ecosystem clearly manifested as a core entity of this space. The cyberspace ecosystem is a complex immersion of the Cyber-Physical-Natural (CPN) world with UnderNet (Hidden Web) just a small fraction of it. Certain elements related

---

[1] Hidden space, hidden Web, or UnderNet refers to the portion of the cyberspace which is not indexed by traditional search engines in the surface Net (Internet).

Table 1. Attack classification against anonymous networks

Attack type	Effects
Brute force attacks	Identify trends within the network
Timing attacks	Investigate traffic variation
Intersection attacks	Intersecting sets of online peers
Denial of service attacks	Resource starvation
Tagging attacks	Modify packets in the network path
Partitioning attacks	Segregate nodes and create fragmented networks
Predecessor attacks	Define geographical proximity of nodes
Harvesting attacks	Profile users and establish references to other peers
Identification through traffic analysis	Identify communication protocols
Sybil attacks	Fake identities and trust violation
Buddy exhaustion attacks	Targeted circuit establishment
Cryptographic attacks	Attacking cryptosystems used
Floodfill attacks	Attackers acting as floodfill routers
Other network database attacks	Craft bad, slow or no network responses
Attacks on centralized resources	Attacks on externally-reachable resources
Development attacks	Attacks on software design
Implementation attacks	Bugs leading in vulnerabilities being exploited

to technology, operation, experience and the their interaction with information marketplace, interconnection networks (telecomms, autonomous systems) and computing utilities (pervasive systems, information appliances), constitute our modern cyberspace (See Table 1) [14]. It is therefore safe to assume, that attacks in one part of this ecosystem unavoidably affect more that one area related to the CPN architecture rendering security and sustainability extremely complex processes to achieve. The same applies to anonymity preservation during broadcasting between different elements of this ecosystem with potential systemic failures of privacy to its cyber citizens.

Several aspects of anonymous communication networks related to flexibility and load balancing make these platforms an attractive means for anonymous and or pseudo-anonymous communications. However it is a common belief that the actual scale of such a communication network can play a crucial role in terms of the anonymity level preserved as part of its core operation(s). There is also a distinct trade off between the anonymity preservation properties of such networks and the size and number of participants in the actual communication process with elements such as trust and reputation adding further complexity to an attempt to quantify anonymity levels. Anonymity has to be approached as a dynamically changing ontology within the context of a session, with different levels clearly defined by the ability/inability to defend against specific attack vectors. Several anonymous networks achieve diverse levels of anonymity against modern attacks (active of passive) with converged networks (VoD, VoIP, MMOGs, BYOD) exponentially increasing the attack surface an adversary can utilise.

2   Background

With the wide spread of Internet applications in both the surface (Internet) and hidden web (dark net or underNet), the necessity to safeguard privacy and anonymity have become more prominent than ever. In an attempt to assure untraceability and undetectability between entities, as part of the communication process, confidentiality mechanisms have proved insufficient to address attacks against those principles. In addition, different international laws and cross-continental cyber crimes are still immune from being affected by a global public policy on allowed/prohibited data flows. The complexity and de-centralisation management provided by anonymous networks can lead to information leakage that can be potentially catastrophic at the hands of an adversary. Assuming that the notion of security in any electronic communication is not absolute, even with minimization of exploitable bugs in a given application, this does not assure that the number of attacks vectors will be reduced but rather change [1,22]. A typical example is clearly manifested in the so-called supply chain attacks with SE and phising attacks some of the most prominent examples. Several implementations of anonymous networks are registered in the literature each with unique characteristics in terms of the protocol and relay strategies used. Namely, ToR [7] Anonymizer [12], Crowds [25], DC-Net [4], WonGoo [20] and Tarzan [10] are illustrative examples of protocols used (or have been used) in wired anonymous networks.

A distinction is also made in the different anonymity models currently employed between single-hop and multi-hop communication. Typical single-hop implementations are VPNs and certain tunnel protocols such as OpenSSH. In the multi-hop scenario cases like ToR network seek to address the single point of failure often faced in the single-hop cases whereby a single compromise somewhere in the communication path will expose all clients' traffic with a trade-off between performance and security between the two models [31]. A cluster of attacks against anonymous networks irrespectively to their communication model are summarised in Table 1. There is a different variation on the stealthiness of these attacks based on their active or passive nature and the way that traffic attributes are collected by adversaries (e.g. packet distribution, time, traffic volume, packet order). The ability of attackers to embed traffic and extract patterns using correlation techniques becomes more complex as it is realised in different layers of the network communication stack from packet and flow levels down to signalling aspects [19,28,32]. For instance, in specific anonymous networks the adversaries can alter the way packets are encapsulated and encryption is applied to gain information about the syncronisation counters distributed across these nodes and impair the encryption/decryption process in a multi-hop environment. Different threat modelling employed in each implementation underpins the probability of anonymity exposure rate based on these actions. Integrity attacks are also manifested especially in cases where integrity verification does not take place while traffic in encrypted between different nodes. ToR network in particular does not verify the integrity of the encrypted cells exchanged between different ORs in the network path. An adversary who can tamper the contents of an encrypted message at the entrance node will cause problems in the decryption process at the exit node due to the lack of intermediate integrity verification within the actual TLS-enabled network [19]. At the application layer different protocols such as bit-torrent tunnelled through ToR can also introduce security implications as it seems to ignore proxy settings and establish direct connections with nodes. This can leak information about location or source IP exposing certain privacy aspects promised by ToR.

2.1 Anonymity Preservation Models

The list of anonymous networks is not limited to the aforementioned protocols but expands to additional ones for wireless and hybrid networks. An exhaustive list of these networks has been discussed by Kelly et al. [16] where a summary of their strengths and limitations is given. In spite of the type of anonymity mechanism used, it is fundamental to have reliable models to measure the level of anonymity of a system in a given scenario. For end users, this can help to assess risk encountered and have a criterion to decide on which solution to use. Further, measuring anonymity helps system architectures to test the effects of new updates prior to implementation. Same authors have measured anonymity using traditional probabilistic methods capturing changes to the anonymity level as a function of adversary-specific criteria and actions. They have introduced anonymity set size and k-anonymity based on three different levels, namely, preserved, degraded and eliminated. These levels are based on an adversary's prior knowledge of sender-receiver pairs with perfect probabilistic anonymity expressed as $Pr_i = min(Pr_i) = \frac{1}{3}, \forall i \in AS$, where AS is defined as the anonymity set. The anonymity set in this context includes the total number of pairs (sender-receiver) whose existence is known to the attacker extracting the agents compromised. Both adversary's prior and posterior knowledge of a given set is captured by $H(X) = -\sum_{i \in X} PR_{(i)} \log_2 Pr_{(i)}$ and the conditional entropy $H(X|C) = -\sum_{i \in X, j \in C} Pr_{(i,j)} \log_2 Pr(i|j)$ respectively. C is the set of intercepted items (compromised agents or messages), $Pr_{(i,j)}$ the joint probability of agent i and intercepted item j and $Pr(i|j)$ is the conditional probability that agent i is identified using information from the intercepted item j.

The combinatorial anonymity degree metric $d(P)$ is introduced in [8]. The metric is used to measure the whole communication to the links established between the sender and receiver in anonymous mixed networks. The probabilities are globalised to the entire network rather than mapping values to each entity in the participating session. These probabilities are fed into a matrix representing the possible link probabilities for the sample network calculated as $\sum_{\pi} \prod_{i=1,n} P(i, \pi(i))$, where π is the prior probability and $Per(P)$ is bounded to the inequality $n!/n^n \leq Per(P) \leq 1$. The authors have argue that the global network anonymity strength as $\sum_{\pi} \prod_{i=1,n} P(i, \pi(i))$. This quantification fails to account for anonymity loss when more than one messages exchanged between peers, a problem clearly identified and addressed in [11].

The type of network transmission that messages between peers are exchanged is also important as recorded in [29]. Multicast transmissions are subject to slightly different arrangements when measuring anonymity as one-to-many relationships between senders and receivers using a k-any incomplete tree structure. In these multicast transmissions a distinction is made between anonymous agents, non-anonymous agents and forwarding nodes (nodes responsible to provide packet forwarding capabilities within the sample network). Authors assign weights to each agent in the tree structure based on the adversary's belief that this is an anonymous agent. The probability of each anonymous agent to be broken is given by $P_{broken} = C/\sum_{i=0,L}\sum_{j=1,k}q_{i,j}$ where $q_{i,j}$, is the value given to each agent, L is the actual tree depth, k is the tree degree and C the number of exploited peers. The probability of identifying a real receiver subject to an attack is calculated by $P^R attack = \sum_{j=1,k}(w_{u-1,[t/k]}/\sum_{u=1,L}\sum_{t=1,k}w_{u,t})/k, u < 1$, where $w_{u,t}$ is the actual weight assigned to the anonymous agent and $w_{u-1[t/k]}$ is the weight of the parent node. The receiver anonymity degree is the probability of an anonymous agent's anonymity is exposed and extracted by $P^R reveal = (1-(1-P_{broken}))^2 + (1-P_{broken})^2 P^R attack$, where anonymity improves when P_{broken} decreases and L, k increase. Additional metrics assigned to the agents such as frequency (τ), delay (δ) and periodical constraints to both sender and receiver pairs, led into the localised real-time anonymity. This metric calculates the maximum probability $P(\beta, S)$ that an attacker assigns to a particular sender sending at least one message within a time interval $[\tau_{min}, \tau_{max}]$ expressed as the upper bound limit $P^\wedge(\beta, S) = \frac{\sum_{i=1}^{\Delta_{min}} max(i-1)\tau_{min}\leq q\leq i-\tau_{min}f(\delta)}{|S|\cdot\sum_{i=1}^{\Delta_{max}} min(i-1)\tau_{max}\leq q\leq i-\tau_{max}f(\ delta)}$ [26].

Work in [30] identifies anonymity boundaries on a zone-based receiver k-anonymity metric. The sender will apply a specific area x with certain radius for each receiver and all the forwarding agents in the sample network deliver the message to a proxy who broadcasts the message to all agents in that particular zone. In this approach the geographical location, node density and radius are crucial metrics to calculate the probability of exact number of nodes preserving receiver k-anonymity expressed as $p = p\{t_d > t_1\} = \int_{t_1}^{\infty} f_{t_d}(t_d)dt_d = e^{-t_1/\bar{t}_d}$, where t_d is the time (sec) a receiver node stays in the anonymity zone (AZ), $f_{t_d}(t_d)$ is the probability density function of the receiver staying in AZ, and $\bar{t}_d$ is the mean time node stays in AZ. Finally, p accounts for the probability the receiver node stays in AZ after t_1. The model also accounts for dynamic changes to the number of nodes in a specific circumference C in meters (m) reflecting a realistic change to the number of participants in a given anonymity zone for a given time instance. The metric generality is low, which means it binds to specific protocol implementations with a clear trade off between mathematical rigor and utility [16].

A more general approach that measures anonymity quantitatively using information theory with entropy related to P2P networks is introduced in [33]. The authors have used a normalised entropy of an anonymous communication system X (denoted as $H^*(X) = maxH(X)$) with the presence of an adversary expressed as $D(X)-h(X) = H*(X)-\sum_{x\in X}^{X}[P(F-X)H(X|F-x)] = H*(X)$. Authors clearly demonstrate the trade-offs between anonymity preservation and system performance, throughput and latency in particular. Also, variable tunnel length is the much preferred option rather than a static length approach (in onion routing) in terms of the anonymity preservation but with additional challenges to control it. There is clear empirical evidence that reliability concerns might also affect anonymity [23]. A clear justification on the expected/normal operation of an anonymous network under specific and pre-defined system-oriented parameters as well as cases of unintended operation conditions are of paramount importance when modelling system anonymity. The security properties of the system should be clearly mapped onto the influence they have to the anonymity of an entity affected by these security policies. Additional mapping should be achieved onto the affects of these properties back to adversary actions once anonymity is exposed.

In a scenario where the anonymity channel is used repeatedly, the implementation of entropy-based metrics would not be sufficient since they do not calculate or give a time indication on how fast attacks against the channel could de-anonymise a targeted message. Given that even a perfect anonymity channel will consequently leak communication patterns to potential adversaries [15], a good discussion in [5] propose that differential privacy (DP) can be the new approach in an attempt to measure the security of a -prefect- anonymous channel. To demonstrate an example, assume that Alice is sending a message to Bob (AB) through a perfect anonymous channel in a given system along other messages (V_o). Alice's message is sent with probability p_{AB} such that $0 \leq p_{AB} < \frac{\epsilon}{1+\epsilon}$, while others send messages to Bob with probability p_{OB} and the observed messages going to Bob (V_B) where $(0 \leq V_B \leq V_o+1)$, [5] shows that: $\Pr[V_B|p_{AB}] \leq e^{\epsilon}\Pr[V_B|p'_{AB}] + \delta$, where $\delta = \frac{\epsilon.e^{2p_{OB}(1+\epsilon)}}{(1+\epsilon)^2 V_o p_{OB}(1-p_{OB})}$. This theorem can be interpreted such that a perfect anonymous channel gives (ϵ, δ)-differential privacy.

3   Strategic Anonymity Preservation

In this work we quantify the anonymity degree in UnderNet relay networks from a different perspective. We derive a strategy upon which anonymity degree is built based on core infrastructure elements, such as the number of servers running RS_i, the total number of exit servers RE_i, total number of guard servers RG_i an i node can utilise and circuit related attributes. We compartmentalise the sample network in smaller areas K within which a given node i may initiate a connection through j number of circuits such as $j \leq j_{max}$, where j_{max} is the maximum number of circuits allowed in a given sample network for that particular node i. We define this as the anonymity set (AS) for that particular compartment K after extracting the total number of compromised agents (active and inactive) C_β. We assume the adversary has no global access to the network such as $C_\beta \leq \frac{1}{2}\mu$, where μ is the total number of nodes $i \in K$ defined as:

$$K = AS = \left(j_{max} * \left(\frac{RS_i * RE_i * RG_i}{\mu}\right)\right) - \sum_{j=1}^{j_{max}} C_\beta).$$

Typical source anonymity is achieved if an adversary cannot distinguish the sender of a message even if the destination server (or node in case of P2P) is known. It is assumed that the adversary's ability (AB) to identify an agent acting as a sender of a receiver within a given compartment K is AB $\propto K^{-1}$. The overall anonymity can be partially degraded if any of the sender-receiver pair is known to the attacker. Our model assumes the existence of an adversary in a sample compartment K with the probability $P(\alpha_t^j)$ of engaging in any a particular illegal activity in a given time t characterised by the network traffic patterns N_p and link characteristics L_c. Both N_p and L_c, can yield invaluable information about the type of attack(s) implemented by an adversary exploiting a virtual circuit between network agents. We define the probability of an attacker α participating in such activities within the period time where circuits are active (t, t_{max}) vary between different network implementations as adversary's engagement $E(\alpha_t^j) = \int_t^{t+1} \frac{dP(\alpha_t^j)}{d\alpha_t^j} d\alpha_t^j$, where the normalisation condition over t_{max} is $\int_t^{t_{max}} \frac{dP(\alpha_t^j)}{\alpha_t^j} d\alpha_t^j = 1$. In ToR network, $t_{max} = 10\,\text{min}$ which is the maximum time a specific circuit j is active between relay routers.

We denote the adversary's engagement rate E_r over a given period of time t, as the number of times k an adversary a successfully establishes a circuit j, over maximum attempts ϕ in a given compartment K. Although simple participation does not constitute manifestation of an attack. However it is safe to assume that as the engagement rate increases, then the probability of an attack also increases with additional information related to N_p and L_c adding to this probability. We assume static participation in a given K at each time although is perfectly feasible to manifest attacks simultaneously from the same attacker to different compartments. The adversary's engagement rate can be therefore expressed as follows:

$$E_r(k) = \frac{\prod_{k \in \phi}\left[\left(\phi! \prod_t^{t_{max}} P^k \left(1 - P(a_i^j)\right)^{\phi-k}\right)^{-\phi!(\phi-k)}\right]}{100}$$

The ability of the attacker to posteriori associate an intercepted circuit $j_c \in j_{max}$ to a pair of sender-receiver in the compartment K can be given by calculating the conditional entropy described as follows:

$$P(K|j_c) = -\sum_{k \in K, j_c \in j_{max}} P\left(E_r(k), j_c\right) \log_2 P\left(E_r(k)|j_c\right)$$

Where $P\left(E_r(k), j_c\right)$ is the joint probability of adversary's engagement rate and compromised circuit j_c, where $P(j_c) \neq 0$ and $P\left(E_r(k)|j_c\right)$ is the conditional probability that a circuit j is compromised (j_c) based on adversary's engagement rate. It is assumed that higher entropy values will result in increased difficulty to de-anonymise a given circuit (pair) between anonymous nodes. We assume that there is a residual risk for an attacker to compromise at least one circuit $j \, \forall j \in j_{max}$ as a function of the participation he/she has in a particular communication system. This will lead to anonymity degradation within a particular anonymity set (AS). To make our model a more realistic representation of the actual sample network, we assume that certain active circuits can be multiplexed over a single TCP stream with variations of the traffic pattern. This is clearly manifested in Tor network within which the circuit setup process often include multiplexing. Manipulating inter-arrival packet delay within the circuit buffers has been recorded as a very successful attempt to expose communication in a sender-receiver pairs and degrade overall communication anonymity [28]. Most of the attacks in this domain are primarily based on the fact that packet timing correlation does not change between anonymised and normal traffic making these attacks quite effective in low-latency anonymous networks.

The overall packet size during a transmission within a given circuit also plays a role in the effectiveness of this type of watermarking attacks in the communication channel. There is a significant evidence to suggest that fixed size packet can increase watermarking detection rates, therefore, expose a sender-receiver pair to an adversary [18]. If the fixed packet size is fully controlled by an attacker, relays cannot repackage the frame at the exit node that effectively destroy the watermark, a typical case in Tor. This type of attack is focused at the exit node as the traffic is not subjected to encryption. To accommodate for these elements we derive L_c as a variable of the network flow for a given pair of sender-receiver F_{sr}, number of active circuits $j \in F_{sr}$, relay bandwidth R_b and packet size P_s. Although fixed packet size can accommodate certain threats we assume in our model that $P_s = MTU$ which can be a mitigation against variable packet length features used in certain watermarking attacks where signal can be embedded into victim's traffic [31].

The number of intermediate relay routers to be selected by the sender, otherwise known as the path length, could present variable L_c values in a given compartment K with a high correlation between the time it takes to place a packet in the TCP output queue and time it takes to push the cell (Tor frames) to that queue (circuit output delay). The times a particular circuit $j \in F_{sr}$ is compromised between successive adversary's tries can be exponentially modelled as $f(E_r(k)) = \alpha e^{-aE_r(k)}, E_r(k) > 0$, where λ is the compromisation rate for a given circuit j assuming at least one adversary α present in each $AS \subseteq K$. The actual control over a certain portion of the Tor network can be manifested through donation of entrance and exit routers. These routers can be virtual instances running on a Cloud Service provider so as to completely masquerade the location and actions of an adversary. The mean and variance are given by:

$$\mu = E(E_r(k)) = \int_0^{t_{max}} \lambda E_r(k) e^{-\lambda E_r(k)} d(E_r(k))$$

$$\sigma^2 = V(E_r(k)) = \int_0^{t_{max}} \left(E_r(k) - \frac{1}{\lambda} \right) \lambda e^{-\lambda E_r(k)} d(E_r(k))$$

Where t_{max} is the maximum time a given circuit is active and may vary for different relay implementations (e.g., 10 min for ToR).

4   Conclusion

Anonymity networks and degradation attacks against them seems to be a "green field" with respect to existing literature and attempts to properly quantify their impact and importance in our modern cyberspace. This article tries to articulate current work in the anonymity preservation models currently employed and draw a road map on the co-evolutionary dynamics between attack defence ability and offense capability using these networks as a vector. A novel quantification model is preliminary presented that takes several attributes under consideration when risk of contaminating a communication circuit is investigated towards a more holistic view of quantifying anonymity or pseudo-anonymity online.

References

1. Burmester, M., Magkos, E., Chrissikopoulos, V.: Modelling security in cyber-physical systems. Crit. Infrastruct. Prot. **5**, 118–126 (2012)
2. Chaabane, A., Manils, P., Kaafar, M.A.: Digging into anonymous traffic: A deep analysis of the tor anonymizing network. In: 2010 4th International Conference on Network and System Security (NSS), pp. 167–174. IEEE (2010)
3. Chakravarty, S., Stavrou, A., Keromytis, A.D.: Traffic analysis against low-latency anonymity networks using available bandwidth estimation. In: Gritzalis, D., Preneel, B., Theoharidou, M. (eds.) ESORICS 2010. LNCS, vol. 6345, pp. 249–267. Springer, Heidelberg (2010). doi:10.1007/978-3-642-15497-3_16
4. Chaum, D.L.: The dining cryptographers problem: unconditional sender and recipient untraceability. J. Cryptol. **1**, 65–75 (1988)
5. Danezis, G.: Measuring anonymity: a few thoughts and a differentially private bound. In: Proceedings of the DIMACS Workshop on Measuring Anonymity (2013)
6. Danezis, G., Sassaman, L.: Heartbeat traffic to counter (n-1) attacks. In: Jajodia, S., Samarati, P., Syverson, P.F. (eds.) Workshop on Privacy in Electronic Society (WPES), pp. 89–93. ACM, Washington (2003)
7. Dingledine, R., Mathewson, N., Syverson, P.: Tor: the second-generation onion router. In: Proceedings of the Thirteen USENIX Security Symposium, 9–13 August 2004, USA, pp. 303–320
8. Edman, M., Sivrikaya, F., Yener, B.: A combinatorial approach to measuring anonymity. In: IEEE Intelligence and Security Informatics, pp. 179–186. IEEE (2007)
9. Evans, N.S., Dingledine, R., Grothoff, C.: A practical congestion attack on Tor using long paths. In: Proceedings of the 18th Conference on USENIX Security Symposium, Montreal, Canada, pp. 33–50. ACM (2009)
10. Freedman, M.J., Morris, R.: Tarzan: a peer-to-peer anonymising network layer. In: 9th ACM Conference on Computer and Communication Security. ACM, Washington (2002)
11. Gierlichs, B., Troncoso, C., Diaz, C., Preneel, B., Verbauwhede, I.: Revisiting a combinatorial approach toward measuring anonymity. In: Proceedings of the 7th ACM Workshop on Privacy in the Electronic Society, pp. 111–116. ACM, Alexandria (2008)
12. Guan, Y., Fu, X., Bettati, R., Zhap, W.: An optimal strategy for anonymous communication protocols. In: 22nd International Conference on Distributed Computing Systems, pp. 257–266. IEEE (2002)

13. Hopper, N., Vasserman, E.Y., Chan-TIN, E.: How much anonymity does network latency leak? ACM Trans. Inf. Syst. Secur. **13**, 1094–9224 (2010)
14. Hsu, D.F., Marinucci, D.: Advances in Cyber Security. Fordham University Press, The Bronx (2013)
15. Kedogan, D., Agrawal, D., Penz, S.: Limits of anonymity in open environments. In: Petitcolas, F.A.P. (ed.) IH 2002. LNCS, vol. 2578, pp. 53–69. Springer, Heidelberg (2003). doi:10.1007/3-540-36415-3_4
16. Kelly, D., Raines, R., Baldwin, R., Grimaila, M., Mullins, B.: Exploring extant and emerging issues in anonymous networks: a taxonomy and survey of protocols and metrics. IEEE Commun. Surv. Tutorials **14**, 579–606 (2012)
17. Landsiedel, O., Pimenidis, L., Wehrle, K., Niedermayer, H., Carle, G.: Dynamic multipath onion routing in anonymous peer-to-peer overlay networks. In: GLOBE-COM, pp. 64–69. IEEE (2007)
18. Ling, Z., Luo, J., Yu, W., Fu, X., Xuan, D., Jia, W.: A new cell counter based attack against Tor. In: Proceedings of the 16th ACM Conference on Computer and Communications Security, pp. 578–589. ACM (2009)
19. Ling, Z., Luo, J., Yu, W., Fu, X., Jia, W., Zhao, W.: Protocol-level attacks against Tor. Comput. Netw. **57**(4), 869–886 (2013). doi:10.1016/j.comnet.2012. 11.005. http://www.sciencedirect.com/science/article/pii/S1389128612003799
20. Lu, T., Fang, B., Sun, Y., Cheng, X.: Wongoo: a peer-to-peer protocol for anonymous communication. J. Parallel Distrib. Process. Tech. Appl. **3**, 1102–1106 (2004)
21. Mislove, A., Oberoi, G., Post, A., Reis, C., Druschel, P., Wallach, D.S.: Ap3: cooperative decentralised anonymous communication. In: ACM Proceedings of the Eleventh ACM SIGOPS European Workshop, 19–22 September 2004, Belgium (2004)
22. Mislove, A., Oberoi, G., Post, A., Reis, C., Druschel, P., Wallach, D.S.: Privacy and cybersecurity: the next 100 years. In: Proceedings of the IEEE 100 (2012)
23. Mittal, P., Khurshid, A., Juen, J., Caesar, M., Borisov, N.: Stealthy traffic analysis of low-latency anonymous communication using throughput finger-printing: Chicago, Illinois, USA. In: Proceedings of the 18th ACM Conference on Computer and Communications Security, pp. 215–226. ACM (2003)
24. Nambiar, A., Wright, M.: Salsa: a structured approach to large scale anonymity. In: Juels, A., Wright, R.N., di Vimercati, S.D.C. (eds.) Proceedings of the Thirteen ACM Conference on Computer and Communication Security: 11 December 2006, pp. 7–26. ACM, Alexandria (2006)
25. Reiter, M.K., Rubin, A.D.: Crowds: anonymity for web transations. ACM Trans. Inf. Secur. **1**, 66–92 (1998)
26. Tóth, G., Hornák, Z.: Measuring anonymity in a non-adaptive, real-time system. In: Martin, D., Serjantov, A. (eds.) PET 2004. LNCS, vol. 3424, pp. 226–241. Springer, Heidelberg (2005). doi:10.1007/11423409_14
27. Urdoch, S.J., Danezis, G.: Low-cost traffic analysis of Tor. In: Proceedings of the 2005 IEEE Symposium on Security and Privacy, pp. 183–195. IEEE (2005)
28. Wang, X., Chen, S., Jajodia, S.: Network flow watermarking attack on low-latency anonymous communication systems. In: 2007 IEEE Symposium on Security and Privacy, SP 2007, pp. 116–130 (2007). doi:10.1109/SP.2007.30
29. Xiao, L., Liu, X., Gu, W., Xuan, D., Liu, Y.: A design of overlay anonymous multicast protocol. In: International Parallel, Distributed Processing Symposium (IPDPS), 20 May 2007. IEEE (2006)
30. Xiaoxin, W., Bertino, E.: Achieving k-anonymity in mobile ad hoc networks. In: 1st IEEE ICNP Workshop on Secure Network Protocols, 6 November 2005, pp. 37–42. IEEE, Massachusetts (2005)

31. Yang, M., Luo, J., Ling, Z., Fu, X., Yu, W.: De-anonymizing and countermeasures in anonymous communication networks. IEEE Commun. Mag. **53**(4), 60–66 (2015). doi:10.1109/MCOM.2015.7081076

32. Yu, W., Fu, X., Graham, S., Xuan, D., Zhao, W.: DSSS-based flow marking technique for invisible traceback. In: 2007 IEEE Symposium on Security and Privacy, SP 2007, pp. 18–32 (2007) doi:10.1109/SP.2007.14

33. Zhang, J., Duan, H., Liu, W., Wu, J.: Anonymity analysis of p2p anonymous communication systems. Comput. Commun. **34**, 358–366 (2011)

A Novel Energy Sleep Mode Based on Standard Deviation 'ESMSD' Algorithm for Adaptive Clustering in MANETs

Faris Al-Baadani, Sufian Yousef$^{(\boxtimes)}$, Rakan Aldmour,
Laith Al-Jabouri, Shashikala Tapaswi, Kiran Kumar Patnaik,
and Michael Cole

Faculty of Science and Technology,
Anglia Ruskin University, Chelmsford, Essex, UK
Faris.Al-baadani@pgr.anglia.ac.uk,
sufian.yousef@anglia.ac.uk

Abstract. Redundant transmissions to the sink is one of the real issue that mobile ad-hoc networking (MANET) is still facing; therefore clustering is one of the most proven technique to avoid such complexity in MANET. Clustering will result in a better utilization of the MANET limited network resources such as energy consumption. Recent studies which have been proposed in the literature have introduced different algorithms for clustering. Unfortunately, these algorithms are resulting in a massive number of message exchanges, which lead to a high usage of the energy residual. In this research, a unique technique for clustering using the standard deviation as our base of choosing the optimum cluster head is proposed. The new ESMSD protocol uses the distance and the connectivity as the main factors which will be involved in choosing the cluster head. This work has been extended to add the sleeping mode to the entire member nodes in the cluster in order to come with a better utilization in terms of the energy consumption. Simulation results have proved that ESMSD new protocol outperforms the AODV protocol in all the parameters used in this study.

Keywords: AODV · SD · ESMSD · MANET · Throughput · Average delay

1 Introduction

Mobile Ad hoc Networks (MANETs) are one of the hottest topics in recent years while pervasive of using smartphones, and this is because of many applications based on it, such as Email, Facebook. MANETs include on wireless mobile nodes developing in a network in ad hoc form. One of the benefits for ad hoc networks is to connect smartphone devices without any network infrastructure. Mobile nodes, basically work as a router sending the information to other nodes in order to keep the connection in the network. When the connection getting failed in the normal network there are some of

This work is part of a UKIERI project with the IIITM (Indian Institute of Information Technology and Management), Gwalior, India.

H. Jahankhani et al. (Eds.): ICGS3 2017, CCIS 630, pp. 385–393, 2016.
DOI: 10.1007/978-3-319-51064-4_31

ways to keep the connectivity, one of them is re- organize it in ad hoc form. The re-organization of the network involves information for different types of network structures for instance cluster based structure. This topology contains a number of cluster-heads where cluster head plays the rule of the routers in the wireless network architecture developed in ad hoc form. Having such a system would results information of many clusters within the network; this network contains many different wireless mobile nodes where they are associated with their individual cluster head. The most important thing in cluster-head is to allocate the available network resources and to keep the dynamic topology of the network to the nodes that belong to every cluster-head. This procedure of clustering is developed in two stages:

(1) Cluster formation; this stage is to select the cluster-heads between node. After the cluster-head is selected, each node belonging to that cluster routs its data to the cluster head. Because nodes are mobile so, there is possibility for the node to move from one cluster to another cluster. The second stage has come to develop mobility issue in the first stage. This was named as (2) Cluster Maintenance. The process for this stage is to incur message exchanges between cluster-heads and nodes. However, the high amount of exchanging messages is waste the nodes energy and this will cause reducing network lifetime. To decrease the computation in the cluster maintenance stage, this issue is very important because that leads to select the ideal cluster-head. In this paper, we propose a weighted cluster-head selection algorithm based on the standing deviation. There are two essential parameters in order to choose the ideal cluster-head; these parameters are distance and connectivity of the nodes.

Rest of the paper is structured as the following: Sect. 2, Discusses the related work to this research. Section 3, is a brief description of the parameters used at the simulation time. Section 4, discuss and analyses the result obtained from this research. Finally Sect. 5 present the conclusion and future work of this research.

2 Related Work

The maximum level Algorithm is recognized as connectivity-based algorithm and it is depends on the nodes level, which is supposed to be the amount of neighbors for a given node. It is compulsory for each node to send its ID to the cluster-head. After the degree will be calculated based on the degree, in this case if the node in high degree it may be communicate with high number of neighbors. Additionally if the node received a highest number of IDs, this leads to choose it as a cluster-head. The obstacle for this algorithm is the mobility node. Because of the mobile nature the network degree changes with time. So the cluster-head choice has to allocate several times. However, that effect on the network resources for instance, energy. Moreover, the number of nodes in a cluster is unlimited (Baker and Ephremides 1981).

On the other hand, another technique called Lowest-Identifier (LID) as well it's a recognizer based clustering algorithm. One of the benefits is to select the node with the lowest ID as a cluster-head. According to the results present the LID system performance is better than Highest-Degree in regarding to throughput. The obstacle of this technique prefers the small degrees, and this will effect on the energy node. At the end this approach failed to allocate the load regularly across the nodes (Lin and Gerla 1997).

DCA and (DMAC) are weight based methods. Regarding to these algorithms, a cost is allocated to each node depends on its abilities to be a cluster-head. If the node has highest weight this helps to choose it as cluster-head. In DCA method it is expected that network topology is fixed while the performing the algorithm. The algorithms execute better than Lowest-Identifier algorithms and Highest-Degree in terms of the amount of messages are affected. Because of node mobility, the appointed weights change with time which results in extreme computation in cluster-head creation stage. However, system parameters such as power control and throughput are not enhanced (Basagni 1999a, b).

WCA is another weight based clustering method in which some of parameters such as transmission power, degree, and mobility. The differences are measured in order to execute clustering and choose the cluster-head. To distribute the load on whole cluster-heads equally, for each number of node thresholds is predefined. A node in the cluster can be either cluster-head or ordinary node. Cluster-head has more responsibility as compared to the ordinary nodes belonging to that cluster. Thus it is required to select the cluster-head optimally while considering its residual energy along with the other parameters such as mobility, transmission power and degree difference. Based on these parameters, each node is assigned a weight and the node with the optimum weight is elected as the cluster head. The cluster head election algorithm terminates once all the nodes become either a cluster head or a member of a cluster head. This algorithm is both mobility and scalability aware (Chatterjee et al. 2002).

Ko, Young-Bae propose Location-Aided Routing (LAR), the benefits of this technique is to limits the searching for a new route to an expected "demand zone". One of the main purposes of the geographic location information is to limit the route order flooding to a smaller zone. The order region is expected depends on the previous destination's location and its mobility form. However, if the mobility information is not precise, that could effect on the request zone may and may enlarge to the entire network (Ko and Vaidya 2000).

3 Research Methodology

The most common open source simulation software NS2 was used in this study to carry out all the simulation experiments. Continuous Bit Rate (CBR) was used in these experiments as the source of traffic. The network filed which has been used in this study was set to 800 * 600 m, in this area 50 Nodes were deployed randomly. Also the start and end point for every node was randomly located. This part of the paper will also cover in details the experimental set up as well as the performance valuation for our new protocol ESMSD. This study has used many different keys as the performance valuation for our experiments such as throughput, delay packet delivery ratio, routing overhead, control overhead, number of packets send and dropped, and energy consumption. Table 1 one shows the simulation parameters which has been used in our study.

Table 1. Simulation parameters

Parameter name	Value
Routing protocols	AODV, ESMSD
Mobility model	Random waypoint
Simulation time	500 s
Number of nodes	50 nodes
Simulation area	800 × 800
Transmission range	250 m
Traffic type	CBR
Packet size	512 bytes
Bandwidth	2 Mbps
Simulator	NS2

4 Results

The figures blow Figs. 1, 2, 3, 4, 5, 6, 7, 8 and 9 are showing different analyses for the AODV and ESMSD to investigate the effects considering various values of the inter arrival time. The two protocol were used in these experiments are the AODV which been represented in blue, and the proposed protocol ESMSD which been represented in green. The inter arrival time has been used to evaluate the two systems under different environments. The inter arrival time consider more packets to be sent when the value decrease. For instance at the value 1 there will be 1 packet sent every second, where in the other hand an inter arrival time with value 0.01 would sent a 100 packets every second. This mean an experiment with low value of inter arrival time make the network busier than others.

As shown from Fig. 1, the values of the throughput is changing in each experiment. ESMSD shows better result compare to the AODV in most of the experiments, ESMSD

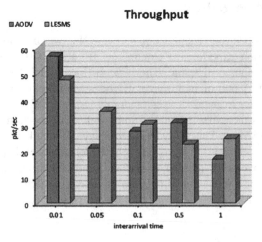

Fig. 1. Throughput (Color figure online)

shows a throughput of 35 packets/second when the inter arrival time is 0.05 where AODV shows only 20 packets/second. Similarly at the inter arrival time of 1 where the difference between ESMSD and AODV was better with around 10 packets/second. Again at the inter arrival time of 0.1 ELSMS shows a slightly higher than AODV with approximately 5 packets/second. AODV has shown better at the inter arrival time of 0.01 and 0.5.

Figure 2 shows the delay data for both AODV and ESMSD. As it can be observed, ESMSD is showing the best result in terms of delay. In all the experiments the ESMSD has lower delay which start from 0.7 s at the inter arrival time of 0.01 which is the

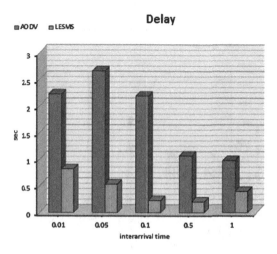

Fig. 2. Delay (Color figure online)

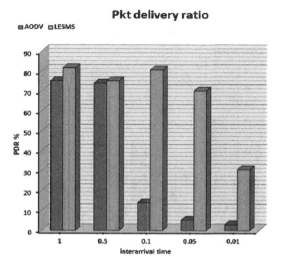

Fig. 3. Packet delivery ratio (Color figure online)

heights delay and reached the lowest delay at the inter arrival time of 0.5. Unlike the AODV which shows a high delay in all cases especially at the inert arrival value of 0.05 where it has reaches its high delay time 2.6 s.

Figure 3 shows the packet delivery ratio for AODV and ESMSD. As observed from the graph ESMSD has always shown much better performance than AODV in all cases. It's clearly noticed that ESMSD have high performance especially when the network is busy hence smaller inter arrival time.

Control Overhead performance is shown in Fig. 4. AODV shows a big lack in the control overhead where the lowest control overhead was around 4000 this was the best performance of the AODV at inter arrival time of 1. The lowest performance for

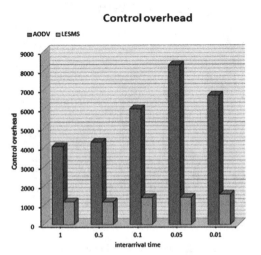

Fig. 4. Control overhead (Color figure online)

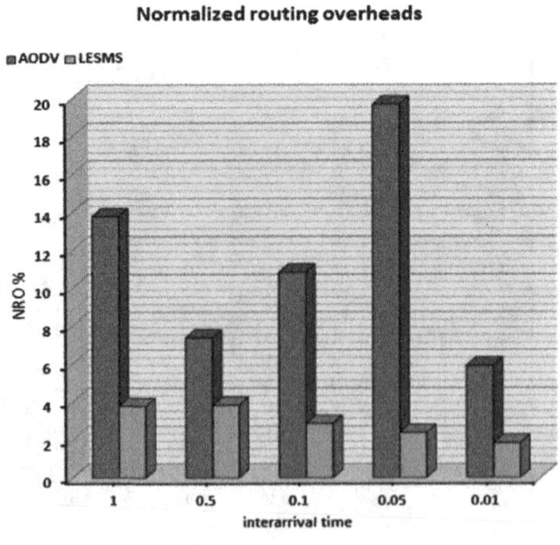

Fig. 5. Routing overhead (Color figure online)

AODV was at inter arrival time of 0.05 where it has overcome the 8000. However, the ESMSD outperforms the AODV at all the inter arrival time values and kept the control overhead between 1000 and 1500 in all cases.

Normalised routing overheads analysis is shown in Fig. 5. AODV is lacking again in the routing overheads where is almost reached %20 at the inter arrival time of 0.05 even when the network is not busy is still show a lower performance in routing overheads. On the other hand ESMSD has performed very well and kept the routing overhead value between 1.5% and 3.5% in all the experiments. ESMSD keep controls over the routing overheads even when the network is fully active as it shows on the graph.

Figures 6 and 7 describe the data obtained for the 'Number of packets sent' and 'Number of packets dropped'. For both of sent and dropped investigates, both protocols

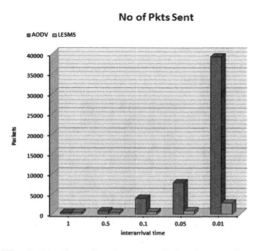

Fig. 6. Number of packets sent (Color figure online)

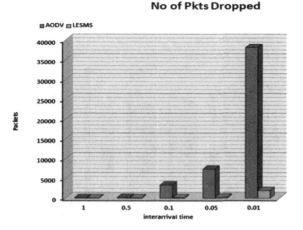

Fig. 7. Number of packets dropped (Color figure online)

AODV and ESMSD are similar in terms of increasing the number of packets I the sent and dropped when the inter arrival value decrease. This is very normal due to the extra number of packets sent in each second. However, ESMSD outperforms the AODV when the network is busier. At the inter arrival time of 0.01 and 0.05 it's clearly shown that ESMSD has the capability of managing the networks where it siganefily decreased the number of sent packets from almost 39000 packets to around 3000 packets at the inter arrival time of 0.01 which shows in Fig. 6. Consequently this will result in reducing the number of packets dropped as shown in Fig. 7.

Finally and most importantly, Figs. 8 and 9 shows the Energy consumption and Energy residual, this is the biggest challenges in MANTs. Figure 8 shows that ESMSD has outperformed the AODV in the energy consumption under all the experiments involved. It's noticed at the inter arrival time of 1, 0.05 and 0.01; ESMSD has

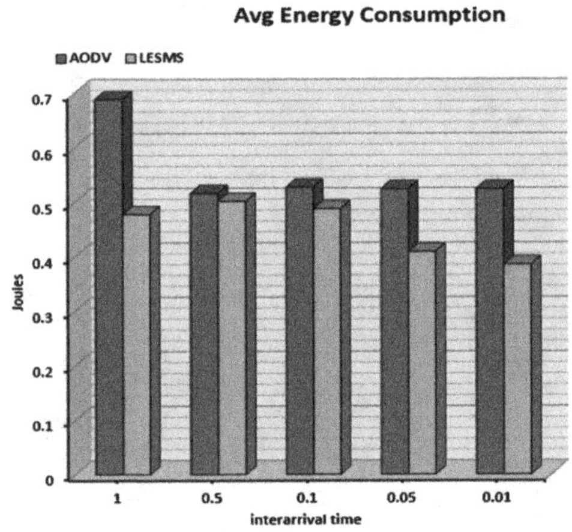

Avg Energy Consumption

Fig. 8. Average energy consumption (Color figure online)

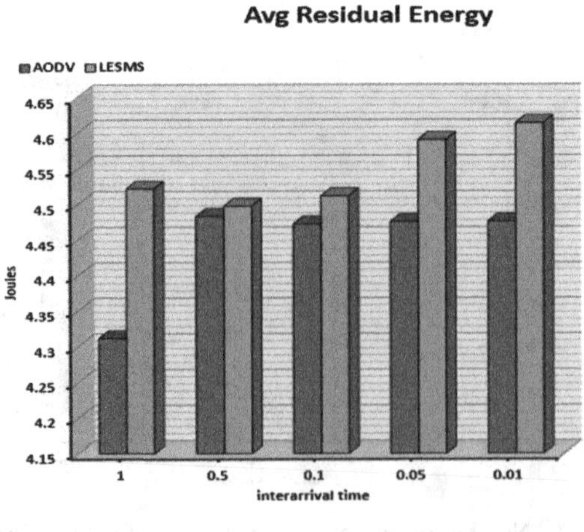

Avg Residual Energy

Fig. 9. Average energy residual (Color figure online)

significantly use less energy than AODV. This means at both busy and not busy network ESMSD can be used where in the normal network for instance at the inter arrival time of 0.5 and 0.1 ESMSD still outperform the AODV but with slightly difference in energy consumptions. Accordingly this will affect the residual energy which has been shown in Fig. 9. Residual energy would be described in a similar way to the Energy consumption analysis where ESMSD undoubtedly outperforms the AODV.

5 Conclusion

In this paper, ESMSD standard deviation sleep protocol is proposed. ESMSD was designed to face the challenges of the redundant transmissions to the sink. ESMSD works towards reducing the number of exchange messages during clustering period. ESMSD was tested under different combination of workload environments in several parameters for instance throughput, delay, control overhead, routing overhead, packet delivery ratio, and power consumption. From the experiment result, ESMSD has proven to outperform the AODV protocol in all the mentioned parameters. This work yet to come in further studies and next contribution will be adding the energy level to be one of the parameters with Distance and connectivity to choose the optimum cluster head.

Acknowledgments. The authors would like to acknowledge the UKIERI.

References

Artail, H., Antoun, R., Fawaz, K.: CRUST: implementation of clustering and routing functions for mobile ad hoc networks using reactive tuple-spaces. Ad Hoc Netw. **7**, 1064–1081 (2009)

Baker, D.J., Ephremides, A.: The architectural organization of a mobile radio network via a distributed algorithm. IEEE Trans. Commun. **29**(11), 1694–1701 (1981)

Chatterjee, M., Das, S.K., Turgut, D.: WCA: a weighted clustering algorithm for mobile ad hoc networks. Cluster Comput. **5**(2), 193–204 (2002)

Ravi, G., Anil, G.: AdHoc networks. Jmacademy IT Manag. **1**, 18–22 (2011)

Shayeb, I.G., Hussein, A.H., Nasoura, A.B.: A survey of clustering schemes for Mobile Ad-Hoc Network (MANET). Am. J. Sci. Ind. Res. **20**, 135–151 (2011)

Ko, Y.-B., Vaidya, N.H.: Location-Aided Routing (LAR) in mobile ad hoc networks. Wirel. Netw. **6**(4), 307–321 (2000)

Lin, C.R., Gerla, M.: Adaptive clustering for mobile wireless networks. IEEE J. Sel. Areas Commun. **15**(7), 1265–1275 (1997)

Basagni, S.: Distributed and mobility-adaptive clustering for multimedia support in multi-hop wireless networks. In: Vehicular Technology Conference, VTC 1999 - Fall. IEEE VTS 50th, Amsterdam, vol. 2, pp. 889–893 (1999a)

Basagni, S.: Distributed clustering for ad hoc networks. In: Fourth International Symposium on Parallel Architectures, Algorithms, and Networks, (I-SPAN 1999) Proceedings, Perth/Fremantle, WA, pp. 310–315 (1999b)

Talapatra, S., Roy, A.: Mobility based cluster head selection algorithm for mobile ad-hoc network. Int. J. Comput. Netw. Inf. Secur. 42–49 (2014)

Facial Recognition Cane for the Visually Impaired

Asim Majeed[1]([⊠]) and Said Baadel[2,3]

[1] Birmingham City University and QA Higher Education, Birmingham, UK
asim.majeed@bcu.ac.uk
[2] Canadian University Dubai, Dubai, UAE
s.baadel@gmail.com
[3] University of Huddersfield, Huddersfield, UK

Abstract. The modern era is accompanied by various traditional mobility aids which help visually impaired to stay independent and enabling them detecting the objects and scanning surroundings. The use of haptic touch, as well as ultrasound, is embedded in today's smart canes which detect obstacles up to 3 m distance, GPS navigation, informs the user through Bluetooth and earpiece, and guide the visually impaired to direct from one location to another. The evolution of this technology has motivated the integration of inexpensive camera technology within the cane for facial recognition purposes. The concept of developing this intelligent smart cane which would detect obstacles from up to 10 m as well as recognises friends and family faces, was envisioned by students at Birmingham City University. The developments in this product and adopted technologies guide a visually impaired user to detect obstacles and to find an alternative route while at the same time try to recognize any family or friends within the vicinity. These have been reflected in this research paper along with the limitations and wider issues which may come up when adopting the high-tech advances.

Keywords: Facial recognition · Visually impared · XploR

1 Introduction

The revolutions in cane development have made visually impaired safe and independent in their day-to-day mobility facilitating detecting the obstacles, drop-offs and head level obstructions over a meter away [4]. This development of high-tech cane has been considered an effective primary device which has enabled the user movement from one point to another [6]. The detection of physical obstacles is matured through vibrating motors, haptic touch, laser sensors and ultrasound. The integration of GPS navigation system facilitates the user more easily to navigate at an extended distance [10]. The bone conduction Bluetooth earpiece is used to feedback the corresponding information to the user. The bone-conduction helps to reduce the aural distraction using vibrations and ultimately helping to communicate the information [10]. The integration of various electronics within the cane has opened a challenge of recognising people but certainly helped users to identify and sense the objects within their surroundings. The concept

© Springer International Publishing AG 2016
H. Jahankhani et al. (Eds.): ICGS3 2017, CCIS 630, pp. 394–405, 2016.
DOI: 10.1007/978-3-319-51064-4_32

envisioned by students at Birmingham City University is now in the development phase whereas electronics engineers have embedded GPS navigation, obstacle detection from 10 m, Bluetooth, and camera for facial recognition within the cane. The initial study of this technology was presented recently in an international conference in Dubai to be published by Springer [29].

The prosaic cane "XploR" with computing capabilities has been long considered to be an effective and affordable mobility aid for visually impaired. The central theme of XploR cane is to scan people within its specified range to recognise the faces if stored in the database. The internal SD card is used to store the database of facial photos of user's friends and family members. The Bluetooth earpiece transmits the GPS's verbal directions guiding the user in directing to that person. The pioneering facial recognition cane "XploR" is undoubtedly an innovative and technological paradigm on the sector and echoed by Biometric Technology Today, IET E&T Magazine, Dailymail UK, Phys.org, LiveScience, CNN, and Wired Magazine in May 2015. This paper will focus on the integration of facial recognition feature in "XploR" to the existing capabilities of the cane. The rest of the paper is organized as follows: Sect. 2 presents an overview and background of the technology. Sects. 3 and 4 present the proposed framework of the "XploR" cane and some of its existing features. After that a discussion on the development of facial recognition follows. Finally Sect. 9 will briefly provide conclusion of our work.

2 Background

The integration of facial recognition feature in XploR is the new addition in the existing canes but detecting obstacles and scanning environments are not novel in the smart technologies. A portable device called NavBelt equipped with sensors was developed and tested in University of Michigan (Advanced Technologies Lab) in 1989 [14]. The devised heavy and complex system presented two operational modes. The view of obstacles up to 120-degree was produced by NavBelt image mode where the image was translated into stereophonic audio cues helping users to determine which way is blocked due to obstacles and which one to follow [19]. The comprehension of audio cues required considerable conscious efforts to transform and transmit the images. The loophole in the NavBelt was that the test subject could only travel 0.3 m/sec and the response time was rather very slow, resulting in hundred hours of training time required for the visually impaired [19].

The second version of "NavBelt" named "GuideCane" was introduced with a sensor head and long handles after six years of its first development [17]. The unpowered but steerable axle based two-wheeled had a mounted sensor head. The GuideCane was presented with a new feature of up steps and down steps as separate solutions [17]. Another device for visually impaired named "MiniGuide" was introduced in 2001 which could detect objects up to 8 m away using ultrasonic echolocation. This device used a strong haptic touch of vibrations when an obstacle got closer to the cane carrier [9]. This concept brought two major organisations, AmbuTech from Canada and Royal Institute of Blind People (RNIB) from the UK to apply the same concept and developed a pair of sunglasses called "iGlasses" [12]. The iGlasses were able to detect wire fence from 5 feet away as well as a large tree from 10 feet [12]. A laser profilometer called Teletact was embedded within the white cane which measured the obstacle's distance of up to 15 m from where the user is paused. The information was transmitted through the headset to the user notifying 32 different musical notes. These musical notes corresponded to different intervals of distances along with the vibrating interface. The complimentary accessories were not much appreciated by the users as they found them as a burden to carry all the time [24, 27].

The Indian Institute of Technology Delhi (IITD) designed and created a SmartCane in 2014 helping visually impaired to avoid obstacles and hazards not only on the ground but also in the air [7]. The prototype of this cane was based on the pre-existing model of White Cane detecting obstacles up to 3-meter using ultrasound rays. This technology was embedded with various vibrations sets directing the user to go right or left [21]. Other technologies such as Viio and UltraCane have embedded the same haptic touch and navigation technology consisting two devices, Viirect and Viitect [3]. These technologies used voice-interactive Global positioning systems through which a user can input voice and receive audio feedback instructing the direction to take.

Bluetooth is used to connect Viitect and Viirect with each other and as soon as that happens the feedback can be felt through the actuated vibrations converting the audio input to the system [1, 7]. The Guide Dogs charity, Microsoft and Future Cities Catapult unlocked the research project in 2014 explaining the development of headset which would scan and give all the information about the surroundings to the cane carrier [21]. This information would be transmitted to the user when paired the device with the smartphone via Bluetooth. The headset would offer the audio guidance as soon as the user programs his route in Microsoft's Bing maps [8]. The contextual information is delivered via the audio technology developed by Microsoft [5]. The navigation, orientation and message transmission is delivered through vibrations in the headset transmitting the message through the cheek bone and jaw [20]. This concept was further tailored by Apple and Andriod, they developed the apps Android (Powered) and Apple (iDevices) to help in navigating the user [28]. The Eyes-Free Project introduced WalkyTalky and users using these apps could get an instant update on their surroundings [24]. The information included addresses of the near locations, walking directions and the current location.

The blind or visually impaired could instantly recognize the objects through LookTel Recognizer App [18]. The objects range from CD's, grocery store, soda cans and identity cards to packaged goods. The object recognition is made possible in this app through cloud-based approach [15]. The processed results are transmitted back to the user after images are received in the micro-cloud. The devised approach in this model seemed simple and used the strong points of both cloud-based systems (system resources, processing memory, memory, etc.) and apps (touch screen, simple navigation, etc.). This model generated the results of 4–15 fps if used with a 3G network and with a proximity delay of 100–300 ms on a round-trip.

Researchers at the University of Southern California designed and developed a Guide Vest in 2011. The Guide Vest was embedded with a binocular camera mounted in the helmet taking pictures and sending wirelessly to a computer installed with Simultaneous Localization and Mapping (SLAM) software [13]. This software helps to identify obstacle and find the safe paths through building maps. The user receives the route information through the guide vest which comprises of four micro motors embedded into waist and shoulders [16, 26]. The purpose of this advancement was to drift away from the helmet and the use of a micro camera associated with the glasses. The team of researchers developed a white cane at the Hebrew University of Jerusalem in 2014. A camera along with a computer was embedded into this device. The acoustic interface was used to recommend the user of some avoidable paths when obstacles detected. The online background estimation using image streaming is used to extract obstacles and then it renders occupancy grid map [26]. This grid map then transmitted to a neural network and using the machine learning algorithms, the right recommended way is dictated to the user [11].

3   Proposed Framework: "XPLOR" Cane

The formation of "XploR" requires a model based proposal which would have sounds, information assistance, GPS navigation and Obstacle detection along with the facial recognition features. Figure 1 below represents the proposed framework of "XploR" cane which comprises of various interfaces ("Assistance Interface for Navigation",

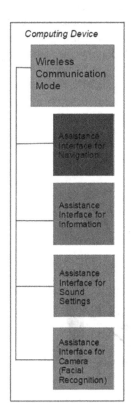
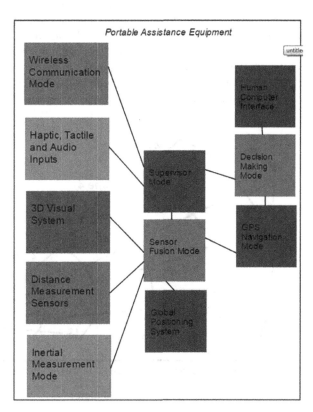

Fig. 1. Block diagram of the proposed system [29].

"Assistance Interface for Information", "Assistance Interface for Sound Settings", "Assistance Interface for Camera") for user usability.

All interfaces are co-coordinating with each other through the Wireless Communication Mode [5]. This mode is comprised of four sub-systems managing individual functionalities. The Assistance Interface for Navigation would store the current and destination locations and help a user in mobility. The Assistance Interface for Information would alert the user if there was any obstacle on the way and what alternative options were available for routing.

The Sound Setting Interface would help in increasing or decreasing the sounds. The Assistance Interface for Camera is used to capture the images of friends and family members even those standing in a crowd and matching them against a stored database. It will alert the user if any matches were found along with directing him to the person.

4   Formation of Zones: Obstacle Detection

The obstacle detection has been a challenge for "XploR" especially when 10-meter zone was benchmarked for this cane. The Nottingham Obstacle Detector is used to sense the objects having a capability of dividing the zone into 5 sub-zones. The parameter set for each zone was 2 m and through a Mowat motor, various vibrating alerts are enthused. Figure 2 represents the angular coverage of the 10-meter zone with 2 ms each sub-zone. A different haptic touch would be felt by the user when the obstacle enters in a respective sub-zone. This technology would have higher vibrating alert when the obstacle is sensed within a 0–2 m range.

The sensor continuously emits the sound waves and as soon as these hit any object, they are reflected back to the source with the location and distance of the obstacle.

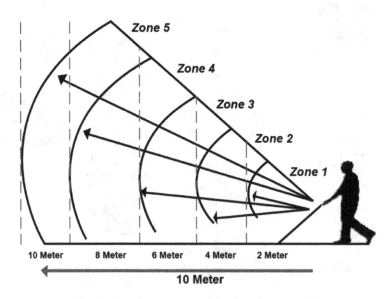

Fig. 2. Angular coverage of the detection zone [20]

The functionality of "XploR" cane is based on Bluetooth Antenna, Bluetooth headset, HD Camera, Power Supply (via Rechargeable Battery), ON/OFF Button, Mowat.

Sensor (Vibrating Motor), Hardware Rest Button, Micro SD Slot (SD/MMC), HDMI Port, 4 GB DDR3 SDRAM, EEPROM, Nottingham Obstacle Detector (NOD), GPIO Extension (1, 2, 3 and 4), Recovery Button, Hardware Rest Button and 32 GB NAND Flash.

5 Facial Recognition: "XPLOR" Development

The aforementioned technologies are undoubtedly marveling, but in order to help blinds and visually impaired through facial recognition of family and friends is certainly a new benchmark of revolution [5]. The previous models of canes have never considered the facial recognition challenge. The conceptual model of "XploR" is classed as "smartphone technology" considering this product as inexpensive. The camera embedded within the "XploR" cane captures much of the environment using the 270-degree lens. A database of family and friends pictures and names has been designed and drawn into the MicroSD card fitted in the cane. Along with the database, developers could use API's introduced by Intel® RealSense™ SDK for face recognition and pose detection. The data will be captured by the camera using an image size of 48 × 48 pixels with 30 frames per second and start comparing the captured images with those in the embedded database.

The software used for facial recognition is an open source algorithm of computer vision. As soon as it detects a face, it would start scanning the database for any matches [20]. If the picture matches with any of those listed in the database, the distance and location would be calculated by the software between the cane user and the other person with a recognized face. This information would be transmitted to the user through an earpiece with Bluetooth bone-conduction. This technology would reduce the aural distraction and use vibrations to communicate the information [17]. The usability and security needs of the cane users were determined via market research and its development is ensured to be reasonably affordable to everyone in the world. The purpose of developing this advanced technology was to help the blind and visually impaired to not carrying heavy devices but rather a lightweight cane with all the revolutionary features and also ensuring the security and privacy concerns of those whose pictures would be taken by the camera. To remove the data breach barrier, the "XploR" cane technology does not store all the pictures take and discards them as soon as it finishes scanning the stored database.

5.1 The Phenomenon of Facial Recognition in "XploR"

Human beings have considered the concept of face recognition to be not an easy process even under controlled situations of blurred, angular movements, and variant motions [11]. When applying similar concepts to machines, it seems quite complicated as well especially when the object is in outdoor lighting and poor staging. The automatic recognition of faces requires an enormous amount of calculative paradigms and angles, so to engage better exposure of subjects. Various researches have been conducted by various research scholars and found that only 2.47% of the set faces could be identified by humans even when handed the actual images before their participation in the identification purposes [23]. The technology evolution for face recognition is consistently growing but the mystery of complete recognition remains unsolved even with the aid of the best monocular sensor based cameras being used due to their features such as accuracy, range and cost effectiveness [10]. The social network technology is increasingly combined with inexpensive camera technologies due to the raised needs and demands of detecting friends and family members automatically.

Since the concept of facial recognition is not that novel, there are various mathematical tools and algorithms that have evolved with time covering the automatic face detection of human faces in arbitrary scenes [18]. The literature on facial recognition is quite vast and has attracted variant researchers, neural networks and pattern recognition engineers along with computer graphics designers [22]. The research conducted to date on facial recognition demand that face detection process to be efficient and feedback to the user must be closer to real time. The development of "XploR" prototype is by no means an easy feat and required cross departmental collaboration. The internal functionality of "XploR" can be described in the following steps.

6   A Database of Pictures

The "XploR" cane requires having a database which stored the images of friends and family members. The photos of various people stored in the cane database must include different features, poses, and angles.

Needless to say, the process of face extraction is an offline process but requires a huge amount of computer vision techniques, intensive inside computing operations dealing with the distinctive face features and then recognizing them. There are many forms of image processing techniques based on grey-level intensity, the direction of the face, magnitude, distance, area, length and color combinations. Different facial recognition techniques require different features (frontal face, Jawline, etc.) in order to identify the face but in "XploR", only the left eye, right eye, mouth and nose positions are looked at. The software used in "XploR" is Open Source Computer Vision (Fig. 3).

Library2 (OpenCV) which is not only high-powered open source software but also very precise in generating accurate information.

The pictures taken by the camera are in the form of bitmap images in grey scale. Each grey pixel represents a specific number with regards to the intensity, variation, and preciseness of the facial feature. An infrared sensor is used to detect the grey scale image. This phase is multi-functional and performs high-tech processing on the taken image such as de-blurring and equalization tasks to enhance the quality of the image before it is saved to the cane database. The intensity distribution of the graphical representation of the image consequently improves the image contrast. The exploration of an efficient face descriptor appearance is the key issue in the face recognition process. Previous researches on face recognition are classified in two categories; template matching (holistic), and feature-based. There are other facial recognition methods and techniques such as template-based feature extraction, Gabor wavelet transform, and appearance-based techniques that console their results based on face

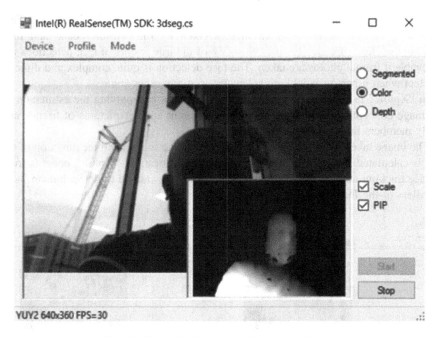

Fig. 3. Example of a grey scale intensity image

expression, colour contrasts, illumination and colour noise. The compositions of faces on the basis of such features have always been a great challenge along with designing and educating the artificial intelligent algorithm to detect the faces in real time.

7 Complexed Sematic: Face Recognition

The face detection is the central theme of "XploR" and in order to mature this functionality, various classifiers such as vector-matching, Bayesian systems, and network-based methods are applied for machine learning. The sub-regions of an image could be easily found by applying these methods as they locate instances of the face image which can distinguish one object from another. These classifiers require many negative and positive images in order to learn features extraction for face detection. In a model proposed by Yardley et al. [28], Haar cascade classifier is used in "XploR" to detect an object effectively. The cascade functionality of this model gets trained through a lot of negative and positive images within the supervised machine learning approach. This classifier is tree-based and the algorithm is being consistent applied on several small classifiers on the object until its existence is either accepted or rejected by the databases.

The local appearance of objects can be encoded by the Haar model functions easily without even entering into the mathematical foundations. The last decade has seen tremendous growth in open source face detection software. OpenCV introduced several different classifiers not only for frontal face detection but also for the poses, whole body detection, mouth detection, nose detection, eye detection and side views. While performing various experiments on images taken by the "XploR" cane and then applying the Haar cascade classifier, 90–95% of the true results of face detections are achievable if frontal photos are taken. The face detection is quite complex and difficult to detect when a person is looking sideways or at any other angle.

In "XploR" face detection we have minimized this by applying the estimation of 3D image concept along with the storing of different angular pictures of friends and family members in the database.

The image taken from the camera shows pose of the subject and the direction of the pose is calculated by determining the eyes and nose location. "XploR" benefits from the face tracking auto focus function which enables the camera to detect human faces regardless of the face angle [23] (Figs. 4 and 5).

Fig. 4. Poses and face recognition

Fig. 5. Laser surface scan

8 Recognition Process

The first task of "XploR" cane is to detect whether it's a facial object and then proceed to scan across the existing database of pictures of friends and family members. There are variant methods of face recognition in literature such as Local Binary Patterns Histograms (LBPH), Fisherfaces and Eigenfaces. All these three methods detect and identify the faces through some training sets of known faces. Our experiments find the Fisherfaces method to be more accurate and quite competent due to its robustness and accuracy in producing results when finding changes in illumination at a large scale.

The camera on the cane detects and captures a face that is sent via 4G to a server in the cloud which then completes feature extraction and face recognition and then returning the results to the cane. The wear-ability requirement for the new cane is also a critical issue in our design of the prototype. For instance, most of the electronic canes described above require significant training for their use. Usability of the facial recognition feature is very high. Furthermore, algorithms used in this regard are to be extensively validated in order to make the system robust, efficient and accurate to reduce risks and errors.

9 Conclusion and Future Work

The "XploR" cane review of design and development are the state-of-the-art in this domain and future prospects with the use of this technology. The tandem aim of achieving the real-time results is based on the selection of software and hardware. There are many organizations (e.g. Google and GaussianFace's face recognition algorithms) working towards the facial recognition technology and the momentum this revolution has adopted stands a fairly good chance that in the not-so-far future the anonymity for visually impaired would be a dead notion. The two sides of the coin are again controversial as the possibilities of these inventions go far and beyond, i.e., cameras that can be used to locate individuals in a crowd, to track their movements, to identify specific customers, or to monitor their activities and habits. Indeed, the legal aspects of facial recognition technology and the global adoption of the appropriate enforcement mechanisms are still very much an open question. The "XploR" cane utilizes cutting edge technologies and sensors and is optimized for real world scenarios and usage. The cane adopts cutting edge technology to guide a visually impaired user to detect obstacles and to find an alternative route while at the same time try to recognize any family or friends within the vicinity.

Our future work will continue to address the privacy and security issues by extending the functionality of such systems with the use of social media data or tracking data and patterns stored in the cloud and by leveraging the friend's utility in the social media platform such as Facebook. Another avenue to explore is the development of machine to machine exchange of data e.g. usage of this product to communicate to a driverless car in a scenario where a blind or visually impaired person could be waiting at a spot and a signal is sent to the car and the car autonomously drives to the subject where the person is waiting to be picked up and driven home.

References

1. Wagner, A., Wright, J., Ganesh, A., Zhou, Y., Ma, Y.: Toward a practical face recognition system: robust pose and illumination via sparse representation. In: CVPR (2009)
2. Acquisti, A., Gross, R.: Predicting social security numbers from public data. Proc. Natl. Acad. Sci. 106(27), 10975–10980 (2009)
3. Tkacik, G., et al.: Natural images from the birthplace of the human eye. PLoS ONE 6, e20409 (2011)
4. Jegou, H., Douze, M., Schmid, C.: Hamming embedding and weak geometric consistency for large scale image search. In: Forsyth, D., Torr, P., Zisserman, A. (eds.) ECCV 2008. LNCS, vol. 5302, pp. 304–317. Springer, Heidelberg (2008). doi:10.1007/978-3-540-88682-2_24
5. Jia, H., Martinez, A.: Face recognition with occlusions in the training and testing sets. In: FGR (2008)
6. Jia, H., Martinez, A.: Support vector machines in face recognition with occlusions. In: CVPR (2009)
7. Hartzog, W., Selinger, E.: I see you: the databases that facial recognition apps need to survive. The Atlantic (2014)
8. Kim, J., Choi, J., Yi, J., Turk, M.: Effective representation using ICA for face recognition robust to local distortion and partial occlusion. PAMI 27(12), 1977–1981 (2005)
9. Wright, J., Ma, Y.: Dense error correction via ℓ^1- minimization. Preprint (2008)
10. Wright, J., Yang, A., Ganesh, A., Sastry, S., Ma, Y.: Robust face recognition via sparse representation. PAMI 31, 210–227 (2009)
11. Jernigan, C., Mistree, B.: Gaydar: Facebook friendships expose sexual orientation. First Monday 14(10) (2009)
12. Bowyer, W.K., Chang, K., Flynn, P.: A survey of approaches and challenges in 3D and multi-modal 3D + 2D face recognition. Comput. Vis. Image Underst. 101, 1–15 (2006)
13. Zhang, L., Samaras, D.: Face recognition from a single training image under arbitrary unknown lighting using spherical harmonics. IEEE Trans. Pattern Anal. Mach. Intell. (TPAMI). 28, 351–363 (2006)
14. Zhang, L., Shan, S., Chen, X., Gao, W.: Histogram of Gabor phase patterns (HGPP): a novel object representation approach for face recognition. IEEE Trans. Image Process. 16(1), 57–68 (2007)
15. Arandjelović, O., Cipolla, R.: A pose-wise linear illumination manifold model for face recognition using video. Comput. Vis. Image Underst. (CVIU) 113, 113–125 (2009)
16. Arandjelović, O.: Recognition from appearance subspaces across image sets of variable scale. In: Proceedings of the IAPR British Machine Vision Conference (BMVC) (2010)
17. Ohm, P.: Broken promises of privacy: responding to the surprising failure of anonymization. UCLA Law Rev. 57, 1701 (2010)
18. Phillips, P.J., Newton, E.: Meta-analysis of face recognition algorithms. In: Proceedings of the Fifth International Conference on Automatic Face and Gesture Recognition, p. 235 (2002)
19. Braje, W.J.: Illumination encoding in face recognition: effect of position shift. J. Vis. 3, 161–170 (2003)
20. Phillips, P.J., O'Toole, A.J.: Comparison of human and computer performance across face recognition experiments. Image Vis. Comput. 32(1), 74–85 (2014)
21. Yan, S., Xu, D., Yang, Q., Zhang, L., Tang, X., Zhang, X.J.: Multilinear discriminant analysis for face recognition. IEEE Trans. Image Process. 16(1), 212–220 (2007)
22. Starr, M.: Facial recognition app matches strangers to online profiles, CNET (2014)

23. Tsukayama, H.: Facebook facial recognition policy draws attention from German privacy regulator, Washington Post (2013)
24. Wilmer, J.B., Germine, L., Chabris, C.F., Chatterjee, G., Williams, M., Loken, E.: Human face recognition ability is specific and highly heritable. Proc. Natl. Acad. Sci. **107**(11), 5238–5241 (2010)
25. Wilson, R.R., Blades, M., Pascalis, O.: What do children look at in an adult face with which they are personally familiar? Br. J. Dev. Psychol. **25**, 375–382 (2007)

Author Index

Printed in the United States
By Bookmasters